VIETNAM
A NATURAL
HISTORY

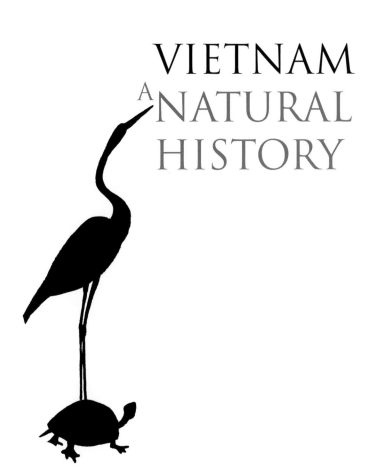

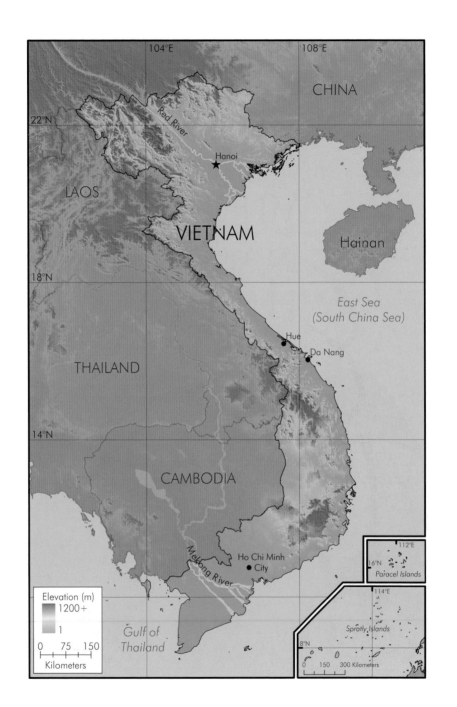

VIETNAM
A NATURAL HISTORY

Eleanor Jane Sterling

Martha Maud Hurley

Le Duc Minh

WITH ILLUSTRATIONS BY JOYCE A. POWZYK

Yale University Press New Haven and London

Published with assistance from the Mary Cady Tew Memorial Fund.

Designed by Sonia Shannon
Set in Minion type by Tseng Information Systems, Inc.
Printed in Italy by EuroGrafica SpA.

Library of Congress Cataloging-in-Publication Data
Sterling, Eleanor J.
Vietnam : a natural history / Eleanor Jane Sterling, Martha Maud
Hurley, Le Duc Minh ; with illustrations by Joyce A. Powzyk.
p.   cm.
Includes bibliographical references (p.   ) and index.
ISBN-13: 978-0-300-10608-4 (clothbound : alk. paper)
ISBN-10: 0-300-10608-4 (clothbound : alk. paper)
1. Natural history—Vietnam. I. Hurley, Martha Maud, 1966–
II. Le, Minh Duc, 1973– III. Title.
QH184.6.S74 2006
508.597—dc22   2005029254

A catalogue record for this book is available from the British Library.

10 9 8 7 6 5 4 3 2 1

The current destruction of our forests will lead to
serious effects on climate, productivity and life.
The forest is gold. If we know how to conserve and
manage it well, it will be very valuable.

Phá rừng nhiều như vậy sẽ ảnh hưởng đến khí
hậu, ảnh hưởng đến sản xuất, đời sống rất nhiều
. . . Rừng là vàng nếu mình biết bảo vệ,
xây dựng thì rừng rất quˇ
–Ho Chi Minh 1963

CONTENTS

PREFACE

The name *Vietnam* once evoked images of soldiers sweating in tropical jungles, villagers dressed in handsome textiles and conical hats, emerald-green rice paddies dotted with water buffalo, and perhaps colonial hill stations framed against jagged mountains. Those more familiar with the country's contemporary demeanor supplant these mostly rural and historic snapshots with impressions of the crowded city streets and newly built roads of a bustling economy.

Tucked away behind such manifestations of human activity is Vietnam's living environment: its plants and animals, waterways and deltas, hills and mountains, habitats and ecosystems. Vietnam's biodiversity—the variety of life in all its forms—is the focus of this book. Vietnam's wildlands are rich in species, and many of them are found nowhere else in the world. Research continues to uncover new plant and animal species, increasing Vietnam's profile in global conservation.

Vietnam: A Natural History originated from research and conservation efforts undertaken by staff from the Center for Biodiversity and Conservation at the American Museum of Natural History (<http://cbc.vietnam.amnh.org>). In 1995, the Socialist Republic of Vietnam's Ministry of Agriculture and Rural Development decided to increase the country's network of protected forested lands. Since 1997, the Center has worked alongside international research teams and Vietnamese scientists to advise the government on where to locate new reserves, addressing both biodiversity conservation priorities and local people's relationship to the land and resources.

As we were undertaking this research, we found no written sources providing comprehensive overviews of the country's natural history for researchers, conservation managers, or the merely curious. Important information is scattered throughout published books and papers (many from the early twentieth century), poorly distributed reports, and unpublished manuscripts and lists, as well as in the heads of dedicated scientists. The available literature, written in many languages, including Vietnamese, French, Chinese, Russian, and English, poses a challenge for even the most gifted polyglot.

In this book, we draw from these scattered resources to describe Vietnam's current species diversity and distribution, exploring its evolutionary roots in Southeast Asia's geological, climatic, and historical complexity. We broaden the more traditional scope of natural history narratives by addressing threats to the country's living resources. As in all nations, human activities imperil Vietnam's biodiversity and any detailed examination of it merits a consideration of threats and challenges to conservation.

In chapter 1, we provide an overview of Vietnam's natural and cultural environment and introduce the main themes covered in the rest of the book. Chapter 2 describes human history in Vietnam and the relationship between Vietnam's peoples and their environment. Chapter 3 explores the evolutionary roots of Vietnam's diversity in the region's dynamic physical environment. Chapter 4 presents an overview of the country's flora and living environments, and Chapter 5 deals with the country's faunal groups. Chapters 6, 7, and 8 depict the biodiversity of northern (Bac Bo), central (Trung Bo), and southern (Nam Bo) Vietnam, respectively. This geographical organization highlights the substantial biological and cultural differences between the areas. Each geographical chapter covers regional topography, climate, ethnic diversity, and characteristic habitats, plants, and animals, as well as recommendations for viewing wildlife. Chapter 9 considers historical and continuing threats to Vietnam's biodiversity, and Chapter 10 reviews ongoing efforts to counter them.

Throughout the book, Vietnam's plants and animals are presented largely through watercolor illustrations. Many of the species depicted have rarely been seen or collected for museums or herbaria, much less photographed in the wild. The illustrator, Dr. Joyce A. Powzyk, relied on original species descriptions, historical plates, museum specimens, field guides, the occasional photograph, and repeated expert opinions to render the plants and animals as accurately as possible.

Joyce Powzyk's experiences reflect an important thread that surfaces through the book: Vietnam's biological diversity remains incompletely documented. Despite explorations dating back to the mid-nineteenth century, research on Vietnam's flora and fauna fell to a minimum during the First Indochinese War, which began soon after World War II and lasted until 1954, and the Second Indochinese War (also known as the Vietnam War and referred to here as the Vietnam-American War), lasting from 1955 to 1975. Starting in the early 1990s, new scientific information again began to flow from Vietnam, at times initiating a reexamination of previous conclusions. The natural history presented here reflects the state of knowledge as of publication and remains far from a finished portrait.

Last, a word of caution to those hoping to see the wealth of wildlife described in this book when they visit Vietnam. Portions of Vietnam are stunningly beautiful, yet no forest in Vietnam can be considered pristine, and few natural forests remain even relatively intact. People have lived in Vietnam for millennia, and even the most isolated areas are less than a few days' walk from the nearest human settlement. The remaining natural areas are, in effect, fragmented islands in a sea of human habitation. They are often located in politically sensitive zones along the nation's borders where access is restricted and the threat of unexploded ordnance remains. As a result, the likelihood of glimpsing a Saola (*Pseudoryx nghetinhensis*) or even the much more common forest-dwelling Red Muntjac (*Muntiacus muntjak*) is slim. Yet Vietnam remains a fascinating place—biologically, geologically, and culturally—and has much to share with visitors of its beauty, history, and diversity, both past and present.

CONVENTIONS ON LANGUAGE, NAMES, AND DATES

Questions about the use of proper names for both places and people arose frequently when we were writing this book. We have tried to use familiar and standardized names while avoiding those with unduly negative connotations or contexts.

Names can be ill defined or misleading. Western geographers appear to have created the term *Indochina* in the late 1700s or early 1800s. Although defined by the *Oxford English Dictionary* as the region between India and China, *Indochina* more commonly refers collectively to the countries of Vietnam, Lao People's Democratic Republic (Laos), and Cambodia, as it does in this book. (The larger area encompassing Myanmar, Thailand, and Peninsular Malaysia we refer to as mainland Southeast Asia.) The term *Indochina* implies that Vietnam was a cultural and political void before the influence of India and China. This was not the case: archaeological work clearly shows that sophisticated indigenous trade networks existed before Indian and Chinese trade influenced the region.

Some names may be offensive to the Vietnamese, dating from times of occupation. The most widely used name for Vietnam's major mountain chain, the Annamites, comes from the term *An Nam*, derived from *Ngannan* in Chinese. It translates as "southern subdued" or "pacified south" and arose during Chinese occupation of Vietnam's lands in the early seventh century. We have substituted Vietnamese names where possible. The French commonly used the terms *Tonkin, Annam,* and *Cochinchina* to denote northern, central, and southern Vietnam; ornithologists still use these designations. The Vietnamese terms are Bac Bo, Truong Bo, and Nam Bo, respectively.

Proper names, for both places and people, differ between contemporary Vietnamese and English. Vietnamese retains a characteristic of its roots in the Chinese language: the tendency to break down a word into individual symbols (analogous to characters) that represent the components of its meaning. Thus, Vietnam is written as Viet Nam, Hanoi as Ha Noi, and Danang as Da Nang. In this book, we follow Vietnamese conventions for place-names except Vietnam and Hanoi, whose long usage in the West has displaced native spellings. The rest, however, appear as they do on Vietnamese maps and gazetteers. For Vietnamese place-names, with the exception of Fan Xi Pan (Phan Si Pan), we followed the *Vietnam National Atlas* (Dang Hung Vo, 1996). In the case of proper names, the Vietnamese use an inverse of most Western conventions, placing family name first, given name last, and an additional, often familial, name in the middle. All Vietnamese names are written out fully in the national style.

The name *Vietnam* itself has been in use for less than two centuries.

In the early nineteenth century, Emperor Gia Long attempted to name the country "Nam Viet" and requested approval from the Chinese emperor. The emperor responded that Nam Viet was too similar to "Nam Viet Dong," an ancient Chinese kingdom, and to avoid confusion (and possible territorial disputes), he recommended reversing the name to Viet Nam, meaning "people of the south."

For historical dates, we use the convention "of the common era" (C.E.) and "before the common era" (B.C.E.), which are equivalent to "in the year of the Lord" (*anno Domini;* A.D.) and "before Christ" (B.C.), respectively.

CONVENTIONS ON TAXONOMY

The species is the fundamental unit of classification in the living world. The question of exactly what constitutes a species — the species problem — remains among the most contentious in biology, thoroughly resistant to consensus. Despite this, most biologists concur about two attributes of species. First, they agree that species are real units defined by measurable differences in characteristics such as color, dimension, and behavior. That is, species are not artificial entities generated by the very human desire to classify the world around us. Second, they agree that species are one or more closely related evolutionary lineages whose genetic exchange with other lineages is limited. Although this disagreement may seem academic, differences in species definitions reflect the complex set of evolutionary processes from which all life's diversity originates.

In naming species, scientists still depend largely on binomial nomenclature, first developed by the eighteenth-century Swedish botanist Carolus Linnaeus. In this system a combination of two words, the genus and the species (for instance, *Panthera tigris*), uniquely identify each species (in this case, the Tiger). By convention both words are italicized, and when a sequence of species in the same genus is written out, the generic name is abbreviated in all except the first usage. The genus is the next level above species in a taxonomic hierarchy that groups organisms into increasingly inclusive sets. Species sharing a set of traits are grouped into a genus, genera into a family, families into an order, orders into a class, classes into a phylum (or division for plants), and finally phyla/divisions into a kingdom. The goal at each level of classification is to include all descendants of a single evolutionary lineage within the grouping.

An additional category exists below the species level: the subspecies, sometimes referred to as geographic races. As with species, the definition of the subspecies varies. Most generally it is one or more populations occupying subsets of a species's range and varying in a detectable manner from other populations of the species. That is, the populations are different—but not enough to be considered a full species. Many biologists who study evolutionary relationships ignore subspecies classifications as being too flexible and inconstant to be informative. However, they are very useful in mapping biodiversity and identifying key populations for conservation efforts. They may often represent previously unrecognized species.

The taxonomic classification of an organism at any hierarchical level is not fixed and unchanging. New discoveries and ongoing research on evolutionary relationships using morphological, behavioral, and (increasingly) genetic techniques can precipitate reclassifications and name changes. To ensure clarity in this volume, where possible we chose a standard set of references for both common and scientific names. Mammalian scientific names are after Corbet and Hill (1992), with the exception of the primates (Brandon-Jones et al., 2004). Mammalian common names are after Duckworth and Pine (2003). Avian scientific names follow Inskipp et al. (1996); common names follow Robson et al. (2000). Amphibian taxonomy follows Frost (2002); reptilian taxonomy follows Uetz et al. (2004). Plants, fishes, and invertebrates lack comprehensive taxonomic reviews for the region. In these cases we relied on the advice of experts and a variety of published works. We referred to relevant, peer-reviewed publications for revisions of taxonomic groups and the taxonomy and common names of species described after the publication date of the standard reference.

CONVENTIONS ON CONSERVATION STATUS

The global conservation status of species is another regularly changing classification, and here we rely on the World Conservation Union (IUCN) assessments of global extinction risk, known as the IUCN Red List. Groups of specialists evaluate each species, using information on population sizes and rates of decline and the degree of habitat fragmentation within their distributional range to place them into three threat categories depending on the risk of extinction in the wild: Critically Endangered (extremely high risk), Threatened (very high risk), and Vulnerable (high risk). Specialists can also categorize a species as Near Threatened if it is likely to qualify for a threat category in the near future and Data Deficient if information on population status or distribution is inadequate to reach a conclusion. The final categories—Extinct and Extinct in the Wild—are self-explanatory. At the national level, Vietnam has joined other countries in publishing its country-based conservation assessments in the form of Red Data Books for plants and for animals.

The primary tool for controlling international trade in wild plants and animals is the Convention on International Trade in Endangered Species of Wild Flora and Fauna (CITES). First adopted in 1975, this agreement requires that signatory nations authorize the international trade of species identified as at risk by a system of import and export permits. Species considered by CITES to be threatened by trade are listed in appendixes according to the degree of protection needed. Species listed in appendix 1 are threatened with extinction, and commercial international trade is generally prohibited; those in appendix 2 are not necessarily currently threatened with extinction but risk becoming so if trade is not controlled. Vietnam became a signatory of the convention in 1993.

ACKNOWLEDGMENTS

This book would not have been possible without the assistance of a great number of individuals both at the American Museum of Natural History and beyond.

We thank our editors, Jean Thomson Black and Laura Jones Dooley, and their colleagues at Yale University Press, including Chris Coffin, Laura Davulis, Molly Egland, Sonia Shannon, Jessie Hunnicutt, and Maureen Noonan, for their patience, expertise, and support.

Invaluable research assistance or other contributions were provided by many people, including Walter Bachman, Raoul Bain, Josh Berman, Kyle Beucke, Georgina Cullman, Kevin Frey, Kevin Koy, Jimin Lee, Finn Longinotto, Darrin Lunde, Ho-Ling Poon, Jack Regalado, Kimberly Roosenburg, Daniel Ross, Cal Snyder, Tania Sosa, Sacha Spector, Ally Migani Wall, and the staff of the library at the American Museum of Natural History.

Illustrating Vietnam's diversity was extremely challenging, and we relied on the help of many people. Joyce Powzyk wrestled with limited guiding resources to produce watercolors that are both scientifically accurate and have a vitality rarely communicated on the printed page. Kevin Koy produced the maps and figures with invaluable skill, detail, and clarity. Photographs were generously provided by Jeb Barzen, Eleanor Briggs, Kevin Frey, Kevin Koy, Phan Ke Loc, Cal Snyder, Rob Timmins, and Tran Triet.

Many people carefully read through drafts of the manuscript, giving us insights into Vietnam's plants, animals, and people as well as our writing: Sally Anderson, Raoul Bain, Josh Berman, Fiona Brady, Will Duckworth, Sibyl Golden, George Harlow, Ian Harrison, Laurel Kendall, Melina Laverty, Darrin Lunde, Phan Ke Loc, Ana Luz Porzecanski, Jack Regalado, Phil Rundel, Jennifer Stenzel, Rob Timmins, and several anonymous reviewers.

Kevin Frey in particular burned the midnight oil reading many drafts over the past four years.

Last, we thank our friends, family, and our collaborators in Vietnam, including Le Xuan Canh, Le Dien Duc, Nguyen Tien Hiep, Phan Ke Loc, Khuat Dang Long, and other colleagues too numerous to mention.

Portions of this volume were produced with funding from the National Science Foundation Grant No. DEB 9870232 and from the John D. and Catherine T. MacArthur Foundation.

VIETNAM
A NATURAL
HISTORY

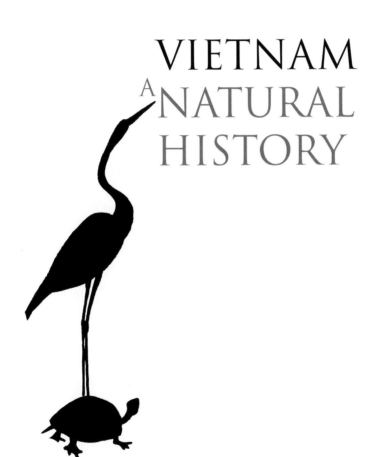

ONE

An Introduction to Vietnam

Vietnam, officially known as the Socialist Republic of Vietnam, holds within its boundaries a great variety of the world's richest and grandest natural places, including vast deltas, fantastically eroded limestone towers, high-elevation cloud forests, red sand-dune coastal forests, and savanna-like grassland and forest mosaics. Yet Vietnam remains relatively unstudied when compared with other regions of high biodiversity. Since the mid-twentieth century, war and political turmoil have made research difficult and many parts of the country inaccessible. Despite these challenges, Vietnam's biodiversity draws scientists for several reasons: the country harbors a globally significant diversity of species; scientists have described an unexpectedly large number of new species since 1992; and a high proportion of its species are endemic — found only in Vietnam (and adjacent regions, in some cases) and nowhere else.

Vietnam is also home to substantial cultural diversity. Researchers currently recognize fifty-four ethnic groups in Vietnam. (In this volume, we follow accepted ethnic divisions, with the caveat that experts recognize these groupings to be flawed.) The Viet (or Kinh) is the most numerous of the groups, constituting over 85 percent of the population. After the Viet, ethnic groups range in size from around a million people (the Tay, Thai, Muong, Hoa, and Khmer) to just a few hundred (the O'du and Ro'mam) (fig. 1; see appendix 1). Linguists divide Vietnam's ethnic groups into eight language groups within five language families, spanning all the existing Southeast Asian languages south of China's Yangtze River (table 1). Widely distributed across the country, the ethnic groups exhibit an intermingling of customs, including tattooing, teeth blackening, betel-nut chewing, ani-

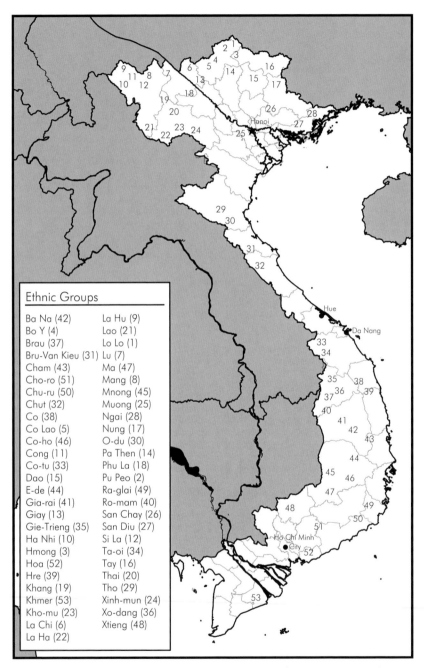

Ethnic Groups

Ba Na (42)	La Hu (9)
Bo Y (4)	Lao (21)
Brau (37)	Lo Lo (1)
Bru-Van Kieu (31)	Lu (7)
Cham (43)	Ma (47)
Cho-ro (51)	Mang (8)
Chu-ru (50)	Mnong (45)
Chut (32)	Muong (25)
Co (38)	Ngai (28)
Co Lao (5)	Nung (17)
Co-ho (46)	O-du (30)
Cong (11)	Pa Then (14)
Co-tu (33)	Phu La (18)
Dao (15)	Pu Peo (2)
E-de (44)	Ra-glai (49)
Gia-rai (41)	Ro-mam (40)
Giay (13)	San Chay (26)
Gie-Trieng (35)	San Diu (27)
Ha Nhi (10)	Si La (12)
Hmong (3)	Ta-oi (34)
Hoa (52)	Tay (16)
Hre (39)	Thai (20)
Khang (19)	Tho (29)
Khmer (53)	Xinh-mun (24)
Kho-mu (23)	Xo-dang (36)
La Chi (6)	Xtieng (48)
La Ha (22)	

Figure 1. Map of the ethnic groups within Vietnam; information on population size, geographic location, and language groups can be found in appendix 1 (After Dang Nghiem Van, Chu Thai Son, and Luu Hung 2000)

Table 1. The major language families
and subgroups of Vietnam's ethnic
groups

Language family	Subgroup
Austro-Asiatic	Viet-Muong
	Mon-Khmer
Thai and Co Lao	
Hmung-Dao	
Austronesian	Malayo-Polynesian
Sino-Tibetan	Han
	Tibeto-Burman

mism, totemism, and various rituals and festivals that reflect extensive cultural interchange between the Vietnamese groups and those in other parts of Southeast Asia.

TOPOGRAPHY

Topography plays a vital role in the distribution of Vietnam's wildlife and vegetation and in the interaction between humans and their environment. With a mainland area of 127,240 square miles (330,591 km²), Vietnam is less than two-thirds the size of Thailand, slightly smaller than Germany, and about three-quarters of the size of California. Its curved, hourglass shape widens to flat deltas in the north and south connected via a narrow central region that at one point tapers to just 30 miles (50 km) in width. Vietnam's northern border abuts China's Yunnan and Guangxi Provinces just below the Tropic of Cancer (23° 30′N), and its southern tip meets the Gulf of Thailand. Laos and Cambodia bound the country to the west, and the East Sea (also known as the South China Sea) lies to the east (fig. 2).

Descriptions of Vietnam often emphasize the hilly and mountainous nature of three quarters of the country, though much of the land lies at moderate elevations. One fourth of the country sits below an elevation of 65 feet (20 m), primarily the two delta regions and the narrow coastal plains fringing the East Sea in Vietnam's central region, while another fourth lies

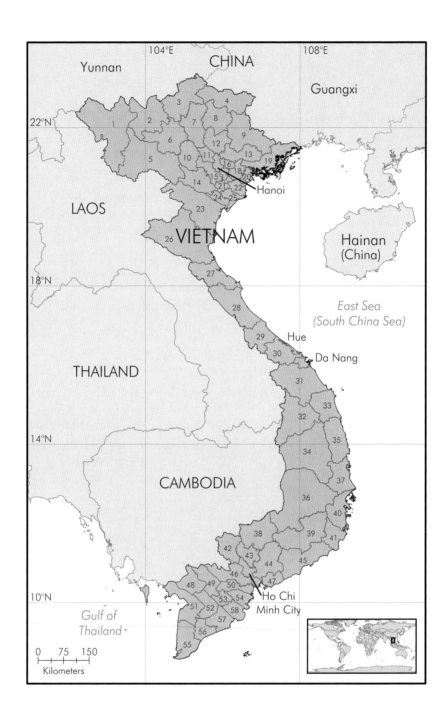

above 2,050 feet (625 m). The remaining half of Vietnam's land thus lies in hills and lower slopes.

Vietnam's mountainous areas lie in the country's northern and central regions. West of the Red River, the Hoang Lien Son Range represents the southeasternmost extension of the Himalayas. It runs northwest to southeast, paralleling the river's course. Vietnam's highest peak, Fan Xi Pan, is found here, rising to 10,312 feet (3,143 m) above sea level. Several smaller ranges lie in northeastern Vietnam, including the Viet Bac and Bac Son uplands (fig. 3) and large areas of limestone are exposed here. Central Vietnam's highland areas are part of the Truong Son (also called the Annamite) Range, which stretches for 750 miles (1,200 km) from around 20° N, along Vietnam's western border with Laos, ending south of the Da Lat Plateau in south-central Vietnam.

Vietnam's two major delta regions, the Red River Delta in the north and the Mekong Delta in the south, are perhaps its best-known topographic features. Both lie on average only a few yards (meters) above sea level and are heavily populated and largely agricultural. The two deltas differ greatly in their hydrology, in the timing and extent of flooding, and in their floral and faunal communities. Such divergence arises from climatic and geological differences between the two regions and from the nature of the rivers that flow into them. Vietnam's mainland is edged by a substantial area of shallow, submerged continental shelf (part of the Sunda Shelf) and thousands of islands pepper the coastline from north to south. The disputed

Figure 2. Administrative boundaries of Vietnam. In alphabetical order: An Giang (48); Ba Ria-Vung Tau (47); Bac Giang (13); Bac Kan (8); Bac Lieu (56); Bac Ninh (16); Ben Tre (54); Binh Dinh(35); Binh Duong (43); Binh Phuoc (38); Binh Thuan (45); Ca Mau (55); Can Tho (52); Cao Bang (4); Dac Lac (36); Dong Nai (44); Dong Thap (49); Gia Lai (34); Ha Giang (3); Ha Nam (21); Ha Tay (15); Ha Tinh (27); Hai Duong (18); Hai Phong City (20); Hoa Binh (14); Hung Yen (17); Khanh Hoa (40); Kien Giang (51); Kon Tum (32); Lai Chau (1); Lam Dong (39); Lang Son (9); Lao Cai (2); Long An (46); Nam Dinh (25); Nghe An (26); Ninh Binh (24); Ninh Thuan (41); Phu Tho (10); Phu Yen (37); Quang Binh (28); Quang Nam (31); Quang Ngai (33); Quang Ninh (19); Quang Tri (29); Soc Trang (57); Son La (5); Tay Ninh (42); Thai Binh (22); Thai Nguyen (12); Thanh Hoa (23); Thua Thien-Hue (30); Tien Giang (50); Tra Vinh (58); Tuyen Quang (7); Vinh Long (53); Vinh Phuc (11); Yen Bai (6)

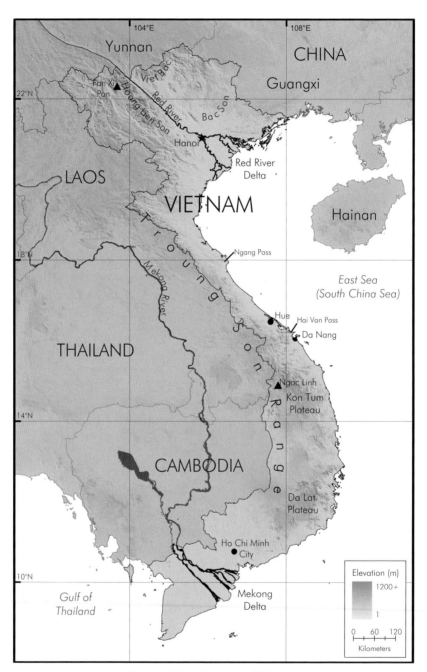

Figure 3. Major features of Vietnam

Paracel (Hoang Sa) and Spratly (Truong Sa) Islands, which China, Taiwan, Malaysia, and the Philippines also claim, lie in the East Sea midway between Vietnam and the Philippines (see frontispiece). These uninhabited islands, mostly coral outcroppings, may sit atop substantial oil reserves.

CLIMATE

Because of Vietnam's shape, topography, and location along mainland Asia's southeastern edge, the country experiences many climatic regimes. Southeast Asia's climate is closely associated with monsoons, major wind systems that reverse direction seasonally. The dynamic monsoon circulation patterns produce two main seasons, a dry, cool winter and a warm, wet summer, that are interrupted by short transitional periods.

The winter monsoon season begins in mid-November and lasts until the end of March. During this time, monsoon winds arise from cold high-pressure zones over the eastern Asian continent and flow southward toward hot, low-pressure zones over Australia (fig. 4a). These polar air currents arcing across Siberia and China bring chilly conditions to northern Vietnam. April and May are transitional months and are followed by the summer monsoon season, which lasts through September. In summer, monsoon winds from high-pressure areas in the southwest bring moist air from the Indian Ocean and the Gulf of Thailand toward China's interior (fig. 4b). This causes heavy rains to fall in Vietnam, particularly in mountainous areas. October and November mark the end of the rainy season and the transition to another winter. Vietnam's broad variation in the timing and amount of rain falling in different parts of Vietnam is due largely to these circulation patterns (fig. 5).

Vietnam's topography affects temperature, humidity, and rainfall regimes at different scales. Locally, as elevation increases, temperature decreases, and water is deposited in the form of fog, mist, rain, and dew, creating the cooler and wetter conditions experienced on hilltops and higher mountain slopes. At a regional level, hills and mountains influence climate through the rain shadow effect. Rain shadows occur when warm, moisture-bearing clouds ascend the windward side of mountains such as the eastern slopes of the Truong Son. As the rising air cools, it releases its moisture as

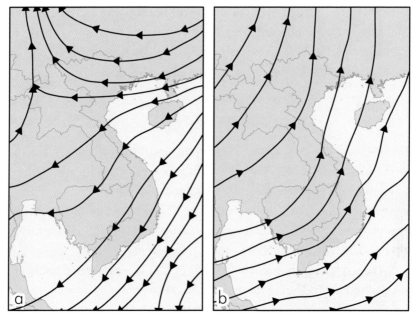

Figure 4. Patterns of atmospheric flow across mainland Southeast Asia during the East Asian–Australasian monsoons. Lines represent mean 1000hPa streamlines (1982–1994) during January (a) and July (b); arrows indicate direction of flow. (After An 2000)

precipitation. As the now drier air descends the leeward side, it compresses and warms, having a drying effect on the opposite slopes and lowlands.

Climate plays a substantial role in determining the plant and animal communities in an area. Both extended dry seasons and particularly cold winters stress plants and animals and set climatic boundaries for species unable to survive under these conditions. In northern Vietnam, from the Chinese border south to 18° N (around the Ngang Pass), both temperature and rainfall are noticeably seasonal. Cold, humid winters with occasional light rains last from November to April, and frost is not unusual in high mountain regions. Depending on the location, dry periods can vary from zero to six months. Summers are hot, muggy, and rainy and last from May to October. The hottest months in the north are June, July, and August, when humidity reaches 80 to 100 percent. Further south (to 16° N), temperatures are less seasonal, and the timing of the wet season varies, particularly be-

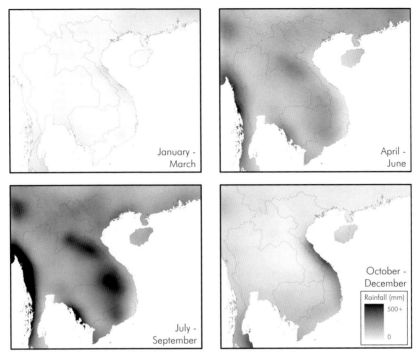

Figure 5. Average rainfall per quarter (Hijman, Cameron, and Parra 2004)

tween coastal and inland areas. Winters are cool, with rains extending from summer through autumn and into winter and a dry season of zero to three months. Around the coastal city of Hue the cold season lasts from November to March, with regular weeklong drizzles.

Inland regions south to the Mekong Delta experience smaller seasonal fluctuations in temperature than areas to the north, with summer rains and a dry season of zero to five months. On the high plateaus of the central region, temperatures are lower and conditions wetter, with dry seasons lasting for only three months. Coastal areas experience a rainy season in the autumn and winter (September to January) followed by a dry period of up to seven months. Farther south in the Mekong Delta, temperatures are quite warm and stable year-round. Rains fall in the summer from May to October, with the heaviest rains occurring in July and August. The dry season varies from two to six months. The hottest period is from March to May, with high humidity in the latter month.

Climate also affects marine areas, with cold streams flowing along the coast from northeast to southwest and warm currents flowing from the southwest to the northeast. South of the Hai Van Pass (c. 16° N), waters remain above 68°F (20°C) year-round. In contrast, the northern water temperatures during the winter can drop to 55°F (13°C).

VIETNAM'S BIODIVERSITY

Vietnam lies north of a well-known area of biotic transition—sometimes known as Wallacea—that bridges the different plant and animal communities found in Asia and Australia. Within Vietnam, transitions occur across both elevation and latitude. For instance, east of the Red River, the tropical plants and animals of northeastern Vietnam's limestone ranges are similar to the biota of southern China. To the river's west, the Hoang Lien Son Range resembles the subtropical southeastern foothills of the Himalayas; in spring, an explosion of pink, yellow, and white rhododendron (genus *Rhododendron*) flowers decorates its upper slopes. By contrast, southern Vietnamese vegetation shares its dry deciduous forests and peat swamp communities with the lowland tropics of Southeast Asia's mainland and island archipelago. Central Vietnam's Truong Son Range is a transitional region between these subtropical and tropical communities, and it harbors many endemic species.

NEW SPECIES

Among the many benefits of peace has been increased access to the nation's borders and other secured areas previously of limited access to scientists. In part because of their political sensitivity, these areas contain much of Vietnam's remaining forests. Political stability has been accompanied by an increasing openness to foreign researchers, and collaborative multinational research teams play key roles in documenting Vietnam's biodiversity (box 1).

As a consequence, since the last decade of the twentieth century, scientists have made extraordinary new scientific discoveries in Vietnam. Their finds include species previously unrecorded by science as well as a surprising number of known ones that had long gone unrecorded (see appendixes

BOX 1

History of Biodiversity Research

Biodiversity research in Vietnam can be divided into three phases, reflecting major events in the country's history: (1) before 1954; (2) from 1954 to 1975; and (3) from 1976 to the present. Before 1954 most biodiversity research was carried out by non-Vietnamese scientists, among them Cecil Boden-Kloss, Herbert Stevens, Jean Delacour, members of the Kelley-Roosevelts Expedition, J. Lewis Bonhote, Oldfield Thomas, and René Bourret. Their collected specimens are held largely in museums in Paris, Chicago, New York, and London.

In 1954, when northern Vietnam attained independence from France, Vietnamese scientists began to conduct biodiversity research. Until 1960, most biodiversity research was carried out by small groups of scientists on a modest scale, and the results were used for teaching at universities and other institutions. During the 1960s, the Vietnamese government took the first official steps toward nature conservation by promulgating decrees for protection of some forests and several rare and valuable species, such as the Asian Elephant (*Elephas maximus*) and Tiger (*Panthera tigris*). Local authorities also issued protective regulations, and the first national park in northern Vietnam, Cuc Phuong, was decreed in 1962. In the same year, biological research was first organized on a large scale with the participation of scientific institutions, including the faculty of biology of Hanoi University, the Institute of Forestry Planning, the Institute of Agriculture, and the State Scientific-Technical Committee. Biological research was carried out widely in northern Vietnam, and many zoological and botanical specimens were collected and housed in Vietnamese museums and gardens. One of the first Vietnamese scientists to carry out substantial research on Vietnamese fauna was Dao Van Tien, who published more than seventy scientific books and articles over twenty years. Vietnamese scientists inspired by him include Thai Van Chung, Vo Quy, Duong Huu Thoi, Mai Dinh Yen, Le Hien Hao, Nguyen Thanh, Dang Huy Huynh, Vu Dinh Tuan, Do Ngoc Quang, and Cao Van Sung.

The end of the Vietnam-American War in 1975 marked the beginning of the third period of biodiversity research in Vietnam. From 1976 to 1980, the Vietnamese government initiated a program to study and assess biodiversity and biological resources in central Vietnam's Tay Nguyen Plateau (composed of the Kon Tum, Play Ku, and Dac Lac Plateaus), focusing on socioeconomic development. During the 1980s, concerted efforts were made to ground conservation on a more solid scientific basis. A national program was created to research issues of conservation and the sustainable use of resources. Early in the decade, research on biodiversity and biological resources was concentrated on important ecosystems such as mangroves and other forest habitats, and scientists improved the understanding and classification of vegetation cover. Since 1987, a group of scientific research institutions has participated in the general protection and monitoring of ecosystems throughout the country. Starting in 1991, marine science and resource use have been the focus of Vietnam's two oceanographic institutes, located in Hai Phong and Nha Trang, and Marine Protected Area projects are beginning to emerge at the local level. Beginning in the early 1990s, Vietnamese scientists made great strides in understanding the country's biodiversity. Working collaboratively with international experts and organizations, they will further their understanding of the diversity of life and its underlying processes and will create sound conservation plans.

Le Xuan Canh, Institute of Ecology and
Biological Resources, Hanoi

3 and 4). One of the earliest and most exciting discoveries was the identification of, not only a new species, but an entirely new genus of large hoofed mammal, the Saola (*Pseudoryx nghetinhensis;* box 2). The discovery of this antelope-like wild ox in Vietnam and neighboring Laos in 1992 drew global attention because it was the world's largest land-dwelling animal discovered since 1937, when scientists described the Kouprey (*Bos sauveli*), another Indochinese hoofed mammal. As with the Saola, many mammals described since 1992 are surprisingly large-bodied, such as three new deer species, the Silver-backed Chevrotain (*Tragulus versicolor*), Large-antlered Muntjac (*Muntiacus vuquangensis*), and Annamite Muntjac (*M. truongsonensis*), and a monkey, the Gray-shanked Douc (*Pygathrix nemaeus cinerea*), classified by some as a full species (*P. cinerea*).

Also new to science are the Annamite Mouse-eared Bat (*Myotis annamiticus*), Cao Van Sung's Mountain Shrew (*Chodsigoa caovansunga*), and the fascinating Annamite Striped Rabbit (*Nesolagus timminsi*), whose closest known evolutionary relative is restricted to the Indonesian island of Sumatra. Three new bird species, all babblers, have been discovered on central Vietnam's Kon Tum Plateau since 1999: the Black-crowned Barwing (*Actinodura sodangorum*), Golden-winged Laughingthrush (*Garrulax ngoclinhensis*), and Chestnut-eared Laughingthrush (*G. konkakinhensis*). Other taxa newly described between 1992 and 2004 include three turtles, fifteen lizards, four snakes, thirty-one frogs, and more than forty-five fish. Less well studied organisms are just as rich in new discoveries: between 2000 and 2002, scientists described more than 500 invertebrates, and specialists estimate that the country harbors thousands of species not yet known to science. New botanical discoveries include more than 200 vascular plants, including an unusual conifer, the Golden Vietnamese Cypress (*Xanthocyparis vietnamensis*).

These discoveries are accompanied by rediscoveries of species feared extinct. In 1988, a local hunter shot an adult female Lesser One-horned Rhinoceros (*Rhinoceros sondaicus annamiticus*) in Lam Dong Province, some 80 miles (130 km) northeast of Ho Chi Minh City. The Lesser One-horned Rhinoceros is the rarest rhinoceros; the only known population outside Vietnam consists of fifty to sixty animals of a different subspecies (*R. s. sondaicus*) living in southwestern Java. Researchers subsequently con-

BOX 2

An Unexpected Discovery

Vietnamese and foreign biologists discovered hunting trophies of an unidentified large mammal hanging from the rafters in local houses during a field survey of central Vietnam's Vu Quang Nature Reserve in 1992. Research over the next few years led to the collection of twenty partial specimens, including three complete skins and two skulls, and several photos taken by remotely operated cameras. Examination of this evidence led scientists to describe a new species, the Saola (*Pseudoryx nghetinhensis*). The Saola's generic name refers to the slightly curved, backward-sweeping horns, resembling those of the oryxes (genus *Oryx*), a small group of arid-adapted antelopes of Africa and Arabia to which the Saola is only distantly related (fig. 6). The specific name refers to its earliest known distribution, in the Vietnamese province formerly named Nghe Tinh. Local communities have long known this animal, which they call Saola (*Sao* = spindle and *la* = post) because its long horns resembled the two parallel tapered posts used on local spinning wheels.

Weighing 190–220 pounds (85–100 kg), the Saola is thickset, with a rich brown coat that darkens toward the extremities and white marks on the face, rump, and ankles. Unusually large glands below the eyes and nose nestle under a muscular skin flap that the Saola can raise and lower. These glands secrete a pungent, viscous substance that the Saola may use for communication. Genetic analyses indicate that it is a primitive member of the cattle subfamily (Bovinae), although its physical appearance and some skull characteristics resemble those of serows and goats (Caprinae).

The Saola is found only in the foothills of the Truong Son

Figure 6. Saola (*Pseudoryx nghetinhensis*)

Range, where it occupies one of the smallest ranges of any large mammal in the world. Its distribution within the known range appears to be irregular, fragmented into small patches. Although population sizes are unknown, scientists estimate the population to number in the hundreds.

Despite intense interest in the species, scientists have never seen a wild Saola in its natural setting. Most information on Saola ecology and behavior comes from hunters and from scientists' limited experience with captive individuals. Saola seem to favor small, steep streams in wet evergreen forest. Social units are small, probably from one to three animals, likely family groups. Threats to Saola include hunting, inadvertent snaring, and forest loss. Initial captive breeding efforts have failed as all animals died during capture or in captivity.

firmed a population of five to eight individuals along the Dong Nai River in Cat Tien National Park. Three additional mammals rediscovered in Indochina had not been recorded since their original collection and description: Heude's Pig (*Sus bucculentus;* described from Vietnam in 1891, rediscovered in Laos in 1997), Roosevelts' Muntjac (*Muntiacus rooseveltorum;* described 1929, rediscovered 1999, both in Laos), and the Tonkin Snub-nosed Monkey (*Rhinopithecus avunculus;* described 1912, rediscovered 1992, both in Vietnam). Two birds endemic to Vietnam have also been resighted: Edwards's Pheasant (*Lophura edwardsi*) and the Gray-crowned Crocias (*Crocias langbianis*). The Sooty Babbler (*Stachyris herbeti*) was recorded in Vietnam in 1995, the first sighting since the initial description from Laos in 1920.

Every species discovered (or rediscovered) is a concrete contribution to the record of Vietnam's biodiversity. Lists of new or rediscovered species are only one way to characterize a country's biodiversity, however. They do not identify species of particular interest, such as endemics or threatened organisms, and they are notably poor estimators when comparing biodiversity between regions. To better describe Vietnam's current flora and fauna, scientists employ two additional measurements of biodiversity: species richness and endemism.

SPECIES RICHNESS

The term *species richness* refers to the number of species recorded from a given area or geographic region, such as a sample plot, nature reserve, country, or continent. Comparing these numbers between countries is complicated by differences in country sizes and the completeness of surveys. Taking area into account, Vietnam is a nation of high species richness. At the turn of the twenty-first century, it ranked in the top twenty-five countries in the world in the number of plant, bird, and mammal species per unit area.

Species richness values always underestimate the number of species present, since it is nearly impossible to collect and identify every organism in any sizable area. This tendency for underestimation is particularly true for countries like Vietnam, where surveys are rapidly adding organisms to known species lists. In addition to its invertebrates and fungi, Vietnam's plants are the most affected by incomplete records. Botanists estimate that 13,000 vascular plant species live in Vietnam, yet fewer than 10,000 have been recorded so far. The current surge in research has also caused rapid shifts in diversity estimates. Between 1999 and 2004, the number of amphibians (Order Anura: frogs and toads; Order Caudata: salamanders and newts; and Order Gymnophiona: caecilians) known from Vietnam rose from 100 to 157, a 57 percent increase in species richness.

Vietnam contains high levels of diversity in groups whose richness peaks in Asia. Southeast Asia is well known for its diversity of babblers, an assemblage of more than 200 songbirds currently placed in the Family Timaliidae. Vietnam's avifauna includes almost two-thirds of mainland Southeast Asia's babbler species in two major groups: 67 percent (26 of 39) of the laughingthrushes (Subfamily Garrulacinae) and 64 percent (76 of 119) of the babbler subgroup (Timaliini). Freshwater turtle and tortoise diversity also centers on the Asian continent, where eighty-nine native species are listed to date. Vietnam is home to twenty-nine of them, ranking in Asia's top five countries for known richness after the larger nations of China, India, Myanmar, and Indonesia. It is also a center of species richness for cycads (families Cycadaceae, Stangeriaceae, and Zamiaceae), the oldest living lineage of seed-bearing plants and a group of great conservation concern. Vietnam has twenty-four species, more than any other country in Asia (including China with twenty-one). This represents 38 percent of Asia's cycad species and 8 percent of the world's.

Because species richness estimates give equal weight to all species — rare and common, endemic and widespread — they record only an organism's presence in the area of interest. When describing a country's biodiversity, scientists are also interested in its unique aspects.

ENDEMISM

A large number of Vietnam's species are endemic. Some are endemic to the country, while others are limited to small areas stretching into adjacent countries. The term *restricted-range species* is often a better fit for those organisms with small range sizes that overlap political boundaries, since it emphasizes the size of the range and not the range's location with respect to national borders.

Endemism is not distributed evenly across Vietnam's taxonomic groups, and some stand out for their high proportion of endemic species (see appendix 2). Most of Vietnam's twenty-seven primates (nineteen species and eight subspecies) have restricted ranges. Over a quarter (seven) are endemic to the country, including two taxa endemic to islands and four leaf monkeys representing three separate genera (*Trachypithecus, Pygathrix,* and *Rhinopithecus*). An additional seven are restricted to small areas of Vietnam and adjacent Laos and Cambodia and two to northern Indochina and across the Chinese border into southern Yunnan and Guangxi Provinces. Among Vietnam's babblers, five are found only in Vietnam, and an additional seven have ranges that lie across Vietnam's border with Laos and, for a few, Cambodia. High rates of endemism in vascular plants are found in cycads, where more than half (thirteen of twenty-four) are true Vietnamese endemics, and orchids, where 19 percent of this family's species are restricted to Vietnam and an additional 16 percent are found only in Indochina.

Endemism is not distributed evenly across Vietnam's landscape. The archipelagos of Con Dao off the southeastern coast and Ha Long Bay (including Cat Ba Island) in the north are home to unique mammals, reptiles, fish, and a number of plants, including cycads and palms. This is not unusual: the isolation of island populations from their mainland counterparts often favors the evolution of unique forms. Stressful ecological conditions may also foster locally adapted endemic species. Vietnam's eroded limestone hills, with little available water and poor, thin soils, are areas of high plant endemism, particularly among orchids with lithophytic (growing on rocks) and epiphytic (growing on other plants) lifestyles. Endemic mollusks, reptiles, cave-dwelling fish, and the François's Leaf Monkey (*Trachypithecus francoisi*) group are also concentrated on these formations. Limestone outcroppings isolated by intervening lowlands often harbor different species assemblages on each island of suitable habitat.

Other areas of high endemism in Vietnam do not seem especially isolated or associated with sharp differences in ecology, geology, or climate.

The Truong Son Range is one such area. The muntjacs and other larger mammals recently found in its hills are all restricted-range species, as are the three recently described montane babblers. Red-, Gray-, and Black-shanked Doucs (genus *Pygathrix*) are also largely confined to its evergreen and semi-evergreen forests. These new records coincide with older evidence of the Truong Son's concentrated endemism, including Edwards's Pheasant (1896), Black-hooded Laughingthrush (*Garrulax milleti;* 1919), Annam Flying Frog (*Rhacophorus annamensis;* 1924), and Krempf's Pine (*Pinus krempfii;* 1921). The Truong Son is a long mountain range of moderate elevation covered primarily with evergreen forests, presenting neither stressful nor unique conditions. It is also not particularly isolated from other, similar hills and habitats, particularly for such highly mobile species as birds. Its current elevated endemism may reflect past barriers of climate, habitat, and geology that are no longer visible. Research on frogs and orchids suggests that northern Vietnam and adjacent southern China may be another area of elevated endemism.

The high number of endemic species in Vietnam is exciting. It can also be misleading about the true distribution of diversity, especially for the recently discovered species and those in poorly known groups. With continued surveys, some endemic species known from only one or two locations will turn out to be more widespread and common. Surveys of northeastern Vietnam's mountains have shown that frog communities west of the Red River, which scientists once considered unique to this region, share a number of species with communities to the east.

Biologists have drawn on a number of research techniques, including innovative field survey methods, remote sensing (see box 18), and molecular genetic analysis, to explore and map Vietnam's biodiversity. Emerging techniques such as camera trapping are important research tools in field surveys of large, elusive species (such as Saola and Tiger, *Panthera tigris*), particularly in remote areas. Researchers place cameras equipped with motion detectors in a study area; when an animal passes, it triggers the detector and the camera takes a picture (fig. 7). The technique is particularly effective for capturing information on nocturnal, low-density, and/or shy species. Scientists use camera-trap images to record the presence of a species and, when individuals can be individually identified, to gather in-

Figure 7. Vietnamese scientists setting camera traps on Mount Ngoc Linh in Quang Nam Province (Photograph by Kevin Frey and Eleanor J. Sterling)

formation on species abundance and the movement of individuals. In the late 1990s, researchers from Hanoi's Institute of Ecology and Biological Resources (IEBR) used camera traps to rediscover the Hairy-nosed Otter (*Lutra sumatrana*), a creature thought extinct in Vietnam (see box 14).

VIETNAM IN THE PRESENT

Heightened biological interest in Vietnam coincides with increasing pressure on the country's natural resources, brought on by a large and growing human population of about 80 million and an opening market economy. Vietnam has undergone a period of economic and political transition in recent decades, and this development has important implications for the country's biodiversity. In 1986, the government of Vietnam embraced Doi Moi (literally "Renovation"), a gradual, calculated move from state-run operations toward individual responsibility in agriculture and greater encouragement of commerce. Small-scale entrepreneurship began to increase in the late 1980s, and the government cautiously sought foreign investments. The expanding market economy has drastically changed day-to-day life in Vietnam, bringing new levels of prosperity and previously unheard-of consumption. It has also widened the chasm between rich and poor and has the potential to severely affect ethnic minority communities in rural areas.

Economic development has accelerated demands for Vietnam's natural resources. Logging, fuelwood demand, forest fires, armed conflicts, shifting cultivation practices, large-scale agricultural conversion for cash crops, and one of the highest human population densities in Southeast Asia have left the nation significantly deforested. For technical, political, and semantic reasons, accurate measures of forest cover are extremely tentative. Estimates of land with some degree of forest (including mangroves) range from 17.4 to 27.5 percent of Vietnam's area; only a small subset of this area can be considered in healthy condition. The government has tried to overcome problems stemming from high population density, particularly near the Red River and the Mekong Deltas. Unfortunately, this has often meant moving people to the less populated and environmentally less degraded highland regions of central Vietnam, accelerating habitat destruction there. Vietnam's remaining natural forests are now largely restricted to isolated mountain regions that are poorly studied but potentially high in species richness and endemism. Local and international markets in plant and animal species, continuing habitat fragmentation, invasion of non-native species, and pollution threaten what remains of the nation's biodiversity.

Vietnam thus finds itself at a decisive moment in the exploration and conservation of the country's biodiversity. In 1995, the government decided to address problems of overexploitation and habitat loss by increasing significantly the size of its system of national parks and reserves. It chose to increase the amount of forested area in parks and reserves from 3.2 million acres (1.3 million ha, or 4 percent of the land area) to 5 million acres (2 million ha, or 6 percent) and to remove degraded areas of little conservation value from the system. Similar efforts are unfolding in other biomes, such as the marine realm.

The challenge in the early twenty-first century is to find ways to protect what remains of Vietnam's precious biodiversity while meeting the needs of its growing human population.

TWO

Humans and the Environment

Complex interactions between people and their environment have stretched over millennia in Vietnam. Tracing their course and ramifications over such a long time frame is not easy. Scholars are still revealing the prehistory of Southeast Asia, so knowledge of the initial relations of humans with the natural world resembles a tattered ancient volume with blurred ink or missing pages.

The earliest histories derive from archaeological evidence and from oral traditions, such as the telling of myths and legends. Later written down and embellished, these myths and legends are often the only sources of information about prehistoric times. In the historical era, the Chinese and European scholars and explorers who were the main recorders of Vietnamese life were fascinated by rulers, courts, and temples and generally overlooked the activities and concerns of the main populace. Chinese records speak from the conqueror's perspective, frequently downplaying pre-Chinese history and indigenous customs. Accounts by European scholars are likewise distorted, since they often could not conceive of attributing advanced art and cultural forms to the indigenous peoples. In some instances they even concocted convoluted histories that described Southeast Asian bronze art forms as originating in Europe. Small wonder that when Vietnamese scholars took over constructing their history they strove to push back dates for the first Vietnamese peoples, states, and cultures, sometimes to extremes. One thing is clear, however: parts of Vietnam (notably the Red River Delta) are among the oldest continuously modified environments in the world.

EARLY HISTORY

Vietnam's history begins in the north. The first traces of modern humans in Vietnam, found in what is now Thanh Hoa Province, may date from 30,000 years ago. Scientists dispute that date, however, because of differences in dating methods and interpretation of the results. Undisputed evidence establishes that humans were living in caves and rock shelters in the limestone hills lining the Red River Delta somewhere between 18,000 and 9,000 years ago. Although the origins of these people remain unclear, anthropologists believe that some of them were Austronesians, descendants of island peoples from Southeast Asia and the Pacific. Tools, utensils, hearths, shells, bones, and red-ocher paintings found in caves in northern Vietnam imply established cultural centers. During this time, people generally fashioned tools from stone rather than animal bones or horn. Hunting and food gathering were the primary activities; there is no evidence of agriculture or domesticated animals, with the possible exception of dogs. People hunted hoofed animals, including wild cattle (genus *Bos*) and rhinoceros (probably the Lesser One-horned Rhinoceros, *Rhinoceros sondaicus*), Asian Elephant (*Elephas maximus*), bears (genus *Ursus*), and primates (Order Primates), and collected fish and shellfish.

Around 10,000 to 8,000 years before the common era (B.C.E.), fishing communities developed along the coast in what is now Nghe An Province, as evidenced by mounds (called middens) of discarded mollusk shells 16 to 20 feet (5 to 6 m) high and thousands of square feet (hundreds of square meters) in area. These middens also contained hoofed animal and dog bones. Stone tools in coastal areas, as well as shells in caves quite far inland, indicate early trade between regions. Unfortunately, little else is known about these cultures; the postglacial rise in sea levels and related sedimentation submerged many coastal sites, erasing all evidence of human occupation.

The domestication of plants and the advent of agriculture had a profound and lasting effect on the world's peoples and environments. The first evidence for rice cultivation in Asia comes from the region encompassing southern China, northeastern Thailand, and northern Vietnam. People appear to have first domesticated and regularly cultivated Asian rice in the Yangtze Delta around 6,400 B.C.E., and communities to the south, in present-day Vietnam, were cultivating rice by 3,000 to 2,000 years B.C.E.

In the late Neolithic, about 2,000 years B.C.E., people from what is now southern China flowed into Southeast Asia, mixing with indigenous inhabitants and their cultures. At this time, much of the Red River Delta was still inundated by an inland sea that had covered the land for thousands of years and was starting to recede. In the foothills surrounding the delta and in the highlands further south, a distinct culture began to emerge. People in these regions began to cultivate rice in upland and lowland areas, adapting their techniques to the distinctive soils at different elevations.

How these farmers prepared the land for rice crops is unknown. Substantial differences between contemporary lowland and upland rice cultivation techniques may illuminate early modifications of their environment by the first peoples of Vietnam. Today, lowland farmers clear existing vegetation and transform an area from wetlands, grassland, or lowland forest to paddies. Thick soil embankments retain water in the paddies. Paddy agriculture is labor-intensive, requiring a high degree of social organization and cooperation for transplanting seedlings, controlling pests, regulating the water supply, and harvesting. Strong family ties often provide the basis of such agricultural cooperation.

In upland areas, farmers grow dry rice, depending on rain for irrigation. Using a technique often called swidden or shifting cultivation, farmers clear land for planting and harvest crops for a few years until the soil nutrients are exhausted. They then leave the land fallow, allowing time for the soil to recuperate and again be capable of supporting crops. There are hundreds, perhaps thousands, of different kinds of swidden systems, depending on such factors as how long an area remains under cultivation, how long it is left fallow, how degraded the soil becomes, what crops are planted, how large the cultivated area is, and who in the community is entitled to plant and harvest a swidden field. Different swidden systems have varying effects on natural environments and on forest regeneration processes.

Remnants from agricultural sites can also shed light on early human-environment interactions in Vietnam. Archaeological evidence dating from the beginning of rice cultivation suggests that people inhabiting open-air dwellings in central Vietnam's Gia Lai and Dak Lak Provinces manufactured axes, knives, polishers, stone hoes, and pottery in a style considerably different from elsewhere in Vietnam. No further information exists on them or their agricultural methods, however. Further south, in the Dong Nai River basin just north of present-day Ho Chi Minh City, there is clear evidence of rice cultivation dating to the Neolithic at almost fifty sites. The Dong Nai culture practiced dry rice cultivation and may have given rise to the Oc Eo culture in the Mekong River Delta in the first century of this era.

As agriculture and domestication of animals took precedence over hunting and gathering, people became increasingly sedentary and the requirements of daily life began to have broader impacts on the local environment. To meet agricultural needs, people throughout Vietnam started to fell trees and clear expanses of land. They hunted wildlife with blowpipes and began to domesticate livestock. As pottery making flourished, it had growing implications for the surrounding environment. Although early pottery was probably fired lightly, as glazes and other finishes became thicker and more sophisticated, kiln temperatures needed to be hotter, necessitating more fuelwood.

Two important and distinctive cultures, the Dong Son and Sa Huynh, flourished in Vietnam between 1,000 B.C.E. and the beginning of the common era. The Dong Son culture, named after the site in Thanh Hoa Province where remarkable bronze drums were found, flourished about 3,000 years B.C.E. Archaeologists find Dong Son artifacts in many places in Southeast Asia and China, suggesting extensive trade networks, but the most spectacular are from Vietnam, particularly the Red, Ma, and Ca River valleys. Decorations on the drums illuminate perceptions and uses of the environment during this time. Illustrations depict the sun, herds of deer, aquatic birds, and men robed in garments decorated with feathers of aquatic birds. Many other artifacts provide evidence of the continued development of rice cultivation, including bronze plowshares, scythe and sickle blades, and depictions of people planting or pounding rice.

At the end of the first millennium B.C.E., another spectacular civilization, the Sa Huynh culture, developed in the region between the Ngang

Pass, on the border of what are now Ha Tinh and Quang Binh Provinces and the basin of the Dong Nai River. The primary economies in this culture were rice and grain crops, grown on hills and flatlands, and sea fishing. Forest animals may also have been important, however; jade earrings dating from 2,000 years ago, attributed to the Sa Huynh culture, depict what may be Saola (*Pseudoryx nghetinhensis*) heads. Although the species was new to science in 1992, the local Vietnamese have known about it for millennia. Scientists still debate the relationship between the Sa Huynh and the kingdom called Champa that formed in the coastal plains of Vietnam in the first century C.E.

DEVELOPMENT OF THE STATE

Vietnamese historians place the emergence of the first embryonic state of Vietnam some 2,000 years B.C.E. in Bac Ninh Province north of Hanoi. According to legend, Lord Lac Long Quan, descendant of a dragon god, married a fairy, Au Co, and the two had 100 sons. When the two later parted, fifty sons followed their mother into the mountains while all but one remaining son followed their father to the plains and coastal regions to the south. Some anthropologists interpret this legend to signify the marriage of a seafaring civilization with continental peoples or the marriage of highland and lowland peoples to form the Vietnamese nation. The legend goes on to say that the remaining son became the founder of the Hung kings of the Van Lang Kingdom. Although the Dragon God and Fairy Queen remain as myths, archaeological evidence supports the existence of the Van Lang Kingdom, appearing around 700 B.C.E. in northern Vietnam. According to legend, eighteen Hung kings subsequently ruled the land, organizing people in a feudal system with the assistance of civilian and military officials. This kingdom also now serves as a symbolic and perhaps idealized representation of good governance.

According to legend, the last of the Hung kings had a beautiful daughter, My Nuong. Two suitors wooed her: Son Tinh (Mountain Genie) and Thuy Tinh (Water Genie). The king pledged his daughter to whoever arrived first with the requisite wedding gifts. Son Tinh triumphed and carried the daughter to the mountains. An angry Thuy Tinh lashed the mountains with floods, but Son Tinh and his bride simply moved farther up the mountain and Thuy Tinh had to withdraw. The annual floods that can devastate the north's low-lying delta are said to stem from this epic battle. The legend reflects the constant struggle to control water in the Red River Delta, which most certainly contributed to the development of centralized communities. Water management was most effective when individuals banded together.

In the third century B.C.E., the Lac Viet group in Van Lang Kingdom merged with the Au Viet group (ancestors of the upland minority groups in northern Vietnam) to create the Au Lac Kingdom, whose capital was in Co Loa (now a district of Hanoi) and whose people were guided by a Golden Turtle spirit. Archaeological studies have uncovered a moat and ramparts encircling a city that spanned 1,500 acres (600 ha).

Simultaneously, the Han people from the Yellow River Basin were unifying China and spreading southward, increasingly threatening the northern proto-Vietnamese. The Chinese saw Vietnam as a source of such goods as pearls, aromatic woods for incense, elephant tusks, rhinoceros horn, tortoiseshell (*Eretmochelys imbricata*), coral, and feathers from parrots and parakeets (Family Psittacidae), kingfishers (Families Acedinidae and Halcyonidae), and pheasants (Family Phasianidae) for decoration. The Au Lac kings managed to maintain their freedom until Chao To, an invader from southern China, conquered them in the late third century B.C.E. and united northern Vietnam and southern China into one political unit, which he called Nam Viet, meaning the Kingdom of the Southern People. This political unit was in turn conquered by the Han Chinese emperor in 111 B.C.E. Historical records subsequently show Vietnamese tributes to the Chinese imperial court of elephant ivory, mother-of-pearl, coral, sandalwood (genus *Santalum*), and live Asian Elephants and rhinoceroses.

For the next 600 years, the Chinese emperors continued to treat Vietnam both as a launching point for expansion into Southeast Asia and as a colony for exploitation, placing further pressure on Vietnam's natural resources. Although periodic Vietnamese revolts against China were unsuccessful, they kindled a national consciousness. During the ninth century, rebellions multiplied, and the proto-Vietnamese state gained independence in the tenth century, when China was weakened by the disorder of a crumbling Tang Dynasty. Throughout this period of struggle against China's occupation, the northern Vietnamese were simultaneously absorbing Chinese cultural, political, and religious practices.

Despite their preoccupation with ousting the Chinese, the northern Vietnamese continued to develop innovative agricultural techniques and crops, accompanied by changes in land use. Archaeological evidence and written records indicate that rice farming intensified in the first century C.E., with the use of fertilizers increasing production to two crops per year. This intensification was most likely associated with a rising northern Vietnamese population. Chinese records estimate this to be 1 million people in the first century C.E. Farmers diversified their crops to include sweet potato, sugarcane, and mulberry. They also gathered additional resources from the wild, including silkworms (silk-producing larvae in the Order Lepidoptera), Betel or Areca Nuts (*Areca catechu*), bamboo (giant grasses in the Tribe Bambuseae), and rattan (Subfamily Calamoideae). This diversification and intensification of agriculture substantially altered the landscape. Hydraulic works such as dikes and canals sprang up across the countryside to irrigate the crops.

Water management has played a central role in Asian civilizations for millennia. Propelled by religious and socioeconomic motives, Southeast Asian monarchs oversaw the fabrication of tremendous irrigation networks, water tanks, sluices, and dams. The spectacular Angkor complex in northwestern Cambodia is but one example of a political entity built on irrigation networks. As political units emerged in what is now northern Vietnam, so water schemes developed. In the Red River Delta, the primary environmental threat the population faced was uncontrollable floodwaters and people built rudimentary dikes there in the first century C.E. Yet it was not until a thousand years later that major hydraulic works emerged to limit the daunting severity of floods and droughts and ensure water for dry-season crops.

Despite a lesser threat from unmanageable floods than in northern Vietnam, the Mekong Delta's inhabitants' struggle to gain access to suitable quantities of fresh water has similarly dominated their interactions with the environment. Details about the early peopling of the Mekong Delta pre-date recorded history or lie shrouded in lost ancient monographs. Chinese dynastic records note, however, that people of the Fu Nan (Kingdom of the Mountain) political unit lived in the western Mekong Delta from the first through the seventh centuries C.E. They settled in Oc Eo, where the rich alluvial soils could support rice crops to feed sailors who could wait months for favorable winds to carry them around the southern tip of Vietnam. These maritime people employed sophisticated agricultural hydraulic techniques, building canals for transport as well as for draining wetlands and irrigating crops. The canals linked the Gulf of Thailand and the East Sea, shortening the route from India to China. Locally, villagers devised innovative water-management devices and social schemes regulating access to water throughout the year according to such criteria as gender and social status.

The cosmopolitan Fu Nan people thrived in this region for several centuries, trading widely and acquiring Roman and Persian medallions and coins, Greco-Roman jewelry, Indian seals, and Chinese mirrors. Chinese records document Indian influences in the Fu Nan culture, particularly in the writing system. The Fu Nan regional hegemony declined in the fourth century as Chinese and Indian merchants opted for new ports emerging in Indonesia that were able to supply spices unavailable through the Fu Nan, such as pepper, cloves, nutmeg, and mace. The Fu Nan culture dissipated around 550, engulfed by Khmer people moving south from Cambodia. Although their culture disappeared, the Fu Nan left a lasting imprint on the delta with their well-developed canal system.

Around the second or third century, Chinese accounts document a third major political unit to develop in Vietnam, the Champa state (though this name for the state does not appear until the seventh century). The Cham people, of Indonesian origin but profoundly influenced by Hindu civilizations of South and Southeast Asia, settled in the narrow coastal plain between what are now Quang Binh and Quang Nam Provinces. Their economy rested on agriculture, ocean fishing, and trade. They delivered salt and metal products to ethnic minorities living in the Truong Son Range in return for such forest resources as cinnamon bark, pepper, elephant ivory, rhinoceros horn, and timber. The Chams in turn traded the forest resources for silk and other exotic goods from foreign sites. Wet rice cultivation developed swiftly in the region, and the Chams developed a revolutionary early ripening rice strain.

Conflicts developed between the Chams and the northern Vietnamese in the third century and continued until the mid-thirteenth century, at which point the animosity between the two groups briefly faded in response to the shared threat from Kublai Khan and his Mongol troops. Only by joining forces were the Chams and the northern Vietnamese able to repel the Mongol invasion; hostilities resumed shortly thereafter. The northern Vietnamese ultimately defeated the Chams in 1471. The Cham Kingdom continued to lose territory to both the northern Vietnamese in the north and the Khmer in the south, and its aristocracy dissolved in the early nineteenth century.

Several royal dynasties (most significantly the Ly in the eleventh and twelfth centuries, the Tran in the thirteenth and fourteenth centuries, and the Le from the fifteenth to eighteenth centuries) continued to unite and organize the northern regions both politically and economically. The chiefly agrarian society evolved through several stages. Until the 1400s, the king owned all the land, distributing key fiefdoms to dignitaries of the court and Buddhist monasteries. Within the fiefdoms, peasants tilled the land for the aristocracy. Over time, particularly during the fifteenth century, village communes with landowning peasants increased in number. High population growth rates in relation to available land soon created conflict between peasants and the rulers. Civil war eventually broke out in the north, driven by growing tensions between human population growth and the inability of the land to produce sufficient food.

Toward the end of the sixteenth century, this civil war and the concomitant agrarian crisis caused individuals and families in the Viet ethnic group to migrate south, first to central Vietnam, then to southern Vietnam. In central Vietnam, the migrants encountered traders in locations such as Hoi An, just south of Da Nang along the central coast. Hoi An merchants specialized in trading swiftlet nests (Germain's Swiflet, *Collocalia germani*) starting in the seventeenth century (see box 22 and fig. 69). At first, nearby villagers gathered nests opportunistically. Later the government forced villagers to collect them systematically and pay taxes on this resource to the state. The swiftlet nest trade flourished throughout the next few centuries, becoming one of the port's key export products. Other commodities, all derived from natural resources, included rhinoceros horn, sea turtle shells (Family Cheloniidae), elephant tusks, and spices.

Early in the nineteenth century, Vietnam's final dynasty, the Nguyen Dynasty, was founded in Hue. It oversaw the building of extensive canals for communication and transport, and the Mekong Delta became its rice basket. During this precolonial period, although small streams and tributaries were corralled, no one had devised a way to harness the great Asian rivers, and the Mekong was no exception. Along the river's length, communities developed different relationships with the Mekong, governed by the annual cycles of flooding and retreat. Those in the lowlands organized their lives around the regular floods, whereas people upstream adapted to water being available mostly along the banks of the river. The Mekong River in its entirety remained a mystery, each community maintaining its own perceptions and adaptations. This situation lasted until colonial powers began to focus on Vietnam and especially on the Mekong region.

THE COLONIAL PERIOD

The 1800s were a time of political intrigue in the region. Siam (as Thailand was known until 1939) and Vietnam battled for control of Cambodia and Laos, and western European powers developed an interest in the Mekong River. Access to markets in China was a prize for European colonialists, and at first the river seemed to present a commercial freeway to thousands of producers and consumers. French naturalist and photographer Henri Mouhot brought European attention to the Mekong River when in 1860 he documented the ruins at Angkor in Cambodia. He died the following year of an illness contracted on his way upstream. Six years later, concurrent with David Livingstone's search for the source of the Nile, the similarly ill-fated French-led Mekong River Expedition set off to investigate upland waters. The explorers, lulled at first by the easily navigable, slow-moving lower waterways, forged upstream only to encounter the rapids, waterfalls, and related obstacles of the middle and eventually upper reaches of the river. Several other explorers attempted to find the Mekong's source to no avail, until one was reported in 1894. (The exact location of the source of the Mekong remains controversial to this day. Exploration in the 1990s located several sources further from the mouth than the location marked in 1894, though now the controversy concerns differences in feet [m] between potential sources rather than in miles [km].)

The Mekong Delta underwent intense modification and conversion to agriculture in the mid- to late 1800s. With the arrival of French colonialists there in the 1860s, settlement rates and concomitant environmental degradation increased considerably. The French oversaw the dredging of old and new canals, fragmenting the delta's natural areas into spiderwebs of canal networks—more than 1,475 miles (2,375 km) in total—in order to connect the central provinces and districts. Vietnamese settlers migrated via the canals, colonizing ever deeper into the delta. Canals and resulting activities modified the landscape, draining surface waters and altering natural flood patterns. Dredging and draining transformed thousands of acres of wetlands into rice fields capable of producing several harvests a year. These irrigation works allowed the area of land under rice cultivation to quadruple between 1880 and 1930. Yet individual villagers' consumption of rice decreased during this same period. The landowners were rich individuals, Vietnamese collaborating with the French or French speculators. Landless Vietnamese tenants planted and harvested the crops for rents of up to 60 percent of the yield. The new class of Vietnamese landlords sold the harvest in Saigon (now Ho Chi Minh City) for export. Mounting rice export figures reflected both a larger area under cultivation and increased exploitation of peasant laborers.

As French interest in the region and its resources increased during the nineteenth century, the Vietnamese were focused on internal conflicts between the aristocracy and peasants. In part because the Nguyen Dynasty was occupied with quelling Vietnamese rebellion against its own authority, France was able to gain control of the country. The French first annexed the southern region as a colony in the 1860s. Over the next several years, they moved to create protectorates in central and northern Vietnam. Having

BOX 3
Rubber Barons

The South American Rubber Tree (*Hevea brasiliensis*) came to Vietnam from Brazil via Britain's Kew Gardens, Sri Lanka, and Singapore. Spurred by the expansion of the automobile industry because of Henry Ford's mass production techniques, demand for rubber multiplied in the early 1900s. In response, French companies invested millions of francs and converted hundreds of thousands of acres (ha) of land into rubber plantations across French colonies in mainland Southeast Asia. By producing rubber as well as rice for export, Vietnam emerged as a prime producer of natural resources for France.

established control over Vietnam's more accessible lowlands, the French looked toward the mountains for further expansion and colonization. The lowland Viet ethnic majority group had long traded with highland peoples but otherwise avoided Vietnam's montane areas. This avoidance resulted in part from fear of diseases, fierce animals, and evil spirits believed to haunt the mountainous areas and in part from their belief that minority groups in the upland areas were a source of societal destabilization. These upland groups differed substantially from the lowland people in their culture, economics, politics, spiritual beliefs, and relationship with the environment. In contrast to the permanent settled agriculture of the lowlands, highlanders subsisted on swidden agriculture, hunting, fishing, and occasional trade with coastal merchants. The frontier that divided upland from lowland people was fluid, shifting frequently in response to periodic clashes.

During the early twentieth century, the French opened up the highlands to development, building roads into the formerly isolated areas. They hoped to profit from the natural resources in the mountains (boxes 3 and 4), and they viewed these areas as strategic locations, installing outposts and

BOX 4

Coffee Clashes

Coffee was discovered in Ethiopia before the tenth century, when a goatherd noticed his charges displaying exuberant behavior after dining on a hard red berry. In the 1700s, the Dutch started new plantations in Java; before long, the island became the world's largest coffee-producing area. The French first planted coffee on the highlands north of Ho Chi Minh City (then Saigon) in the early twentieth century. They grew Arabica, a high-quality variety preferred to the coarser Robusta but harder to grow because it is extremely susceptible to disease and prefers slopes above 3,000 feet (1,000 m). Following independence from France, smallholder minority populations invested in coffee in the 1960s. Wartime prices brought substantial profits to the smallholders, but Vietnam's land was not well suited for growing Arabica coffee, and fewer than 20,000 acres (8,000 ha) were under harvest in 1975 when the government nationalized its markets. Postwar rebuilding and resettlement programs concentrated on agriculture, and particularly on coffee, though its cultivation remained relatively modest. Export was to the Eastern markets, which dominated Vietnam's economy from 1976 to 1986. After the government allowed individual smallholders to begin to operate again in the mid-1980s, the Vietnamese planted the less-refined Robusta coffee, and yields increased.

Global coffee prices reached a ten-year high in 1994, and Vietnam was among the world's top ten producers. The government set its sights on capturing fifth place in the world market by the year 2000. By planting more than a million acres (400,000 ha) of coffee between 1990 and 2000, Vietnam surpassed this goal and overtook Colombia as the second largest

exporter, trailing only Brazil. At first this seemed to be a brilliant move, especially when frost damage to the Brazilian crop
in 1997 sent the price of coffee soaring and Vietnamese farmers
prospered. Their success was short-lived, however. In 1999, coffee prices fell to their lowest level in a century. Vietnam was
blamed for the fall, accused of flooding the market and upset-
ting the delicate balance between supply and demand.

The growing market for cheap, low-grade Robusta coffees
spurred Vietnam's rapid rise in the global coffee market at the
expense of forests and other land uses. Multinational conglom-
erate coffee roasters developed new steam-cleaning technologies to eliminate the harsh Robusta flavor. They also began to
market flavored coffees, such as hazelnut, French vanilla, and
Irish coffee, which masked the inferior Robusta taste. (Some
Vietnamese restaurants sell specialty coffee in which the Robusta flavor is masked by drenching the freshly roasted beans
in butter and fish sauce or passing the beans through the digestive system of civets [Family Viverridae] or lorises [Family
Lorisidae] and then mixing the coffee with generous quantities
of sugar and condensed milk.)

other military facilities there. The French also came to see the mountains as
sites for rest and recreation complexes. Between 1893 and 1933, the French
developed seven hill stations in northern and central Vietnam: Bach Ma,
Ba Na, Ba Vi, Tam Dao, Da Lat, and Sa Pa. These hill stations provided seasonal refuges for beleaguered expatriates fatigued by tropical temperatures,
diseases, and other difficulties to which they were not accustomed.

By far the jewel in the crown was Da Lat. The inveterate explorer and
natural historian Dr. Alexandre Yersin first brought the Da Lat region to
the attention of the French. The Swiss-born Yersin lived in Nha Trang and
had studied with Louis Pasteur. He is best remembered for identifying the

bacillus *Yersinia pestis*, the cause of bubonic plague, and developing a serum to combat the disease. Yersin was a strong proponent for the establishment of hill stations as health resorts and recreation centers. The hill stations served this function for many years. Today they are popular tourist sites for local and foreign visitors. Yet the growth and development of these stations has placed considerable pressure on the natural resources and habitats they once celebrated. The hill station at Da Lat was created as a retreat partly because of the spectacular coniferous forests gracing its hillsides. Today, despite restrictions on cutting, its forests are disappearing due to fuel and lumber harvesting and other development

Toward the end of the 1800s, the French began to develop infrastructure that benefited biodiversity. They established research institutes, such as the Geological and Geographic Services and a forestry school, to understand Vietnam's natural resources. The French undertook in-depth surveys of forested areas, documenting forest loss and degradation. They also created a forestry service and hired forest guards to protect the environment in selected areas. These institutions lasted until the French left following Vietnam's successful bid for independence in 1954.

INDEPENDENCE AND REUNIFICATION

A national independence movement arose in Vietnam in the early twentieth century and gained strength after World War I. Successive efforts to oust the French culminated in the First Indochinese War, which began in the late 1940s between the French and a national front for independence called the Viet Minh that was driven primarily by the Communists. Ho Chi Minh, the founder of the Viet Minh, was one of the most influential leaders of the twentieth century and furthermore influenced national land-use management with his policies once he became president of North Vietnam. Following official division of the country in half at the Geneva conference in 1954, the governments of both North (Democratic Republic of Vietnam) and South (Republic of Vietnam) Vietnam established significant relocation programs to develop the highland areas, substantially affecting the natural upland systems.

BOX 5

Weather Warfare

In 1966 the U.S. military launched an experimental program, code-named Popeye, aimed at altering the weather in northwestern Vietnam and eastern Laos. Aircraft flying over these regions dropped cartridges of silver iodide and lead iodide aerosol to seed cloud formations, thereby stimulating rain showers.

This technology had been used before in the United States and elsewhere to combat drought, but in Vietnam the objective was to intensify and lengthen the rainy summer monsoon season and disrupt the movement of North Vietnamese troops and matériel south along the Ho Chi Minh Trail by swelling streams, flooding roads, and rendering crucial mountain gaps impassable. American military personnel knew that any changes in Vietnam's weather patterns could also have substantial impacts on the civilian population, and a secret debate roiled within the Johnson administration regarding this precedent-setting strategy.

Because scientific understanding of both weather and weather modification was limited and documentation was not a priority, it is impossible to assess accurately the results of the operation. North Vietnam experienced severe flooding in 1971, the year that the program reached its zenith. But Vietnam had experienced equally significant flooding in prewar years.

The long duration of the program and the high volume of seeding units dropped raise questions about the extent of Popeye's environmental impacts. Although some data show that silver iodide may slow growth in aquatic life, including some algae, invertebrates, and fish, most evidence suggests that the small amounts of chemicals used as seeding material do not have significant detrimental effects on human health or ecosystems and are trivial compared to releases from mining, industrial, and photo-processing activities. Cloud-seeding might have affected species abundances and distributions, depending on whether the various species benefit or are harmed by excessive rainfall. And it could lead to erosion in hilly terrains.

Public disclosure of the weather modification operation surfaced in the media in 1971 and 1972 and led to a probe in hearings before the U.S. Senate Subcommittee on Oceans and International Environment of the Committee on Foreign Relations. Subsequent international negotiations culminated in the signing of an international agreement in 1977 that prohibits the hostile use of environmental modification techniques. It is generally accepted that this treaty would outlaw the Popeye program today.

Walt Bachman, Center for Biodiversity and Conservation, American Museum of Natural History, New York

The most debated questions of human impact on Vietnamese lands in the later twentieth century undoubtedly concern the effects of the Vietnam-American War. In an attempt to avoid committing large numbers of ground forces, the U.S. government employed sophisticated, remotely delivered munitions. The goals were to limit enemy freedom of movement by destroying forest cover and to ruin local crops and diminish local food sources. Americans employed large-scale, long-lasting, anti-environmental actions as a military strategy, introducing the term *ecocide* to the common lexicon. The diversity of methods used to scour the landscape was as remarkable as the methods were effective and included high-explosive munitions, defoliants, napalm, mechanized land clearance, wetland drainage, and other techniques (box 5).

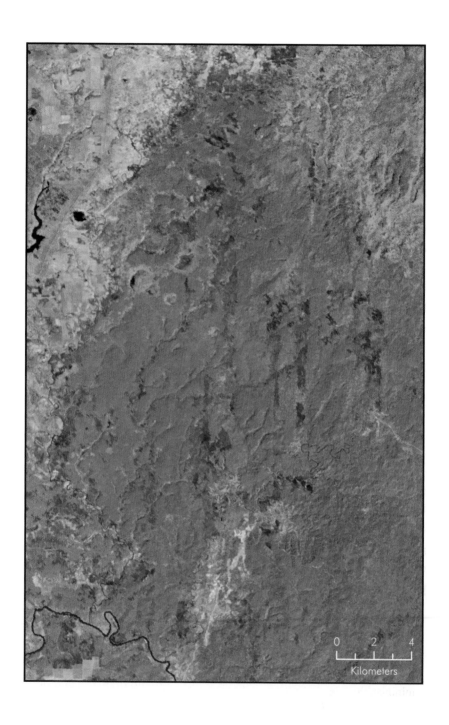

Perhaps the best-known and least understood military tactic used during the war was the spread of herbicides between 1961 and 1971. In an era before widespread environmental awareness in the United States (although Rachel Carson's *Silent Spring*, published in 1962, had started to call attention to pollutants), few people thought about the long-term implications of these chemicals both for humans and for the environment. The U.S. military and the Republic of Vietnam sprayed more than 20 million gallons (72 million liters) of chemicals known as Agents Orange, White, Blue, Green, Pink, and Purple after the color of their containers to defoliate forests, clear growth along borders of military sites, and eliminate enemy crops. Agent Orange (comprising about two-thirds of the total volume of defoliants sprayed), as well as Agents Purple and Pink, contained dioxin, a by-product of the herbicide manufacturing process that is highly toxic to humans. Agent Blue, predominantly used for crop destruction, consisted mainly of an organic arsenic compound. During the war, these chemicals reduced leaf cover and helped American and Republic of Vietnam soldiers locate North Vietnamese fighters, likely reducing their casualties.

Scientists are still struggling to understand the long-term impacts of these defoliants on the environment as well as on military personnel and civilians on both sides of the conflict. Spray was concentrated along strategic watercourses, thus heavily affecting both riverside vegetation and wetlands. Intact and diverse natural areas, such as U Minh in the Mekong Delta, provided excellent refuges for soldiers fighting for North Vietnam, drawing fire to these ecologically important habitats. Reliable quantitative data on the area of forest affected are difficult to find, in part because there are few good estimates of the forest extent before 1960. In terms of environmental effects, defoliation regularly led to soil compaction and degradation, which prevented the regeneration of vegetation. Repeated or extensive applica-

Figure 8. Landsat TM 1989 satellite image of a region 45 miles (72 km) north of Ho Chi Minh City; orange represents forested areas, blue human-dominated ones. Parallel straight blue-green lines represent vegetation scars from chemical defoliants sprayed during the Vietnam-American War. Forest regrowth is minimal; the stripes are disappearing owing to loss of intervening vegetation. (Image from the U.S. Geological Survey)

tion of defoliants sometimes eradicated all vegetation. Weedy, tenacious species such as Alang-alang (also known as Cogon or American Grass; *Imperata cylindrica*) often invaded cleared areas, outcompeting other plants and preventing normal regeneration. In many areas, these weeds continue to dominate the landscape decades after the defoliants were sprayed (fig. 8).

Scientists have found that dioxins still surface in freshwater animals decades after the war. The likely cause is the presence of dioxins in the sediment at the bottom of small aquaculture ponds. Ducks and fish stir up and ingest the sediment, incorporating the dioxins into their fat. Nothing is known about the immediate or long-term effects of these chemicals on domestic, much less wild fauna. The litany of medical problems affecting humans and evidence for deformities in laboratory animal fetuses exposed to dioxins leaves open the possibility that they could affect wild animals. In addition to direct effects on individuals, the defoliants undoubtedly and perhaps permanently modified species distribution patterns through habitat degradation and loss, particularly in wetland systems.

Attempts to eradicate forests directly were not the only military activities to affect Vietnam's environment. During the war, the U.S. military dropped 14 million tons of bombs or cluster-bomb units onto northern and southern Vietnam, Laos, and Cambodia, leaving an estimated 10 to 15 million large bomb craters and extensive unexploded ordnance. Little is known about the effects of these bombs, or of napalm, land mines, and other wartime technology, on Vietnam's biological communities. In addition, the war, as is often the case, facilitated encounters between people with guns and wildlife. Military diaries and records provide anecdotal evidence for hunting of wild animals, including Tigers (*Panthera tigris*) and Lesser One-horned Rhinoceros for trophies by Americans as well as many other animals for subsistence by Vietnamese soldiers. The United States also produced detailed field guides to southern Vietnam's mammals and reptiles for field medical personnel during the war. These publications remain important sources of natural history information.

The Vietnam-American War and other regional twentieth-century conflicts may also have conserved some of the country's biodiversity. Strategic military zones along border regions with Laos and Cambodia, and the Demilitarized Zone (DMZ), which separates what was North and South Vietnam, harbor some of the most intact forested regions remaining, in part because the government restricts access to these regions and in part because some of these areas, such as the DMZ, are still so heavily mined that it is unsafe to live or walk there.

THREE

Biogeography of Vietnam

Our knowledge of Vietnam's wildlife and vegetation is incomplete, but when we examine what we do know of the country's plants and animals, intriguing patterns emerge. The field of biogeography—the study of the current and historic geographic distribution of plants and animals—can help us discern these patterns and reflect on their causes. Biogeographers look to the ecology of a species and degree of evolutionary relatedness among species as a key to understanding distribution patterns. When studying the current distribution of a species (or set of species) they consider the distributions of closest living relatives and information on when the species diverged into separate forms. When they find congruence (or lack thereof) in patterns across species, they look for common explanations, relying, for instance, on a strong understanding of how long-term geological and climatic history can influence species distributions and the genesis of new species.

The most perceptible—and simplest—pattern in the distribution of species in Vietnam extends from the subtropical north to tropical south. The country's northern plants and animals include a subset of the taxa found in the Himalayas and southern China as well as their close evolutionary relatives. Examples include a group of high-elevation pheasants (Phasianidae) whose ranges extend across the Himalayan foothills and Vietnam's endemic Tonkin Snub-nosed Monkey (*Rhinopithecus avunculus*), related to Chinese primates in the same genus that are able to live in snowbound forests at 3,900 feet (1,200 m) and above. Both groups occupy subtropical and temperate forests dominated by rhododendrons (genus

Rhododendron), birches (genus *Betula*), walnuts (genus *Juglans*), and other cold-tolerant plants.

Moving south, gradual changes in climate and topography result in the slow replacement of this typically northern diversity with plants and animals favoring warmer and less seasonal conditions. Southern Vietnam's communities have strong evolutionary links to tropical ones found on the Malay Peninsula and on Southeast Asia's island archipelagos. Many of these distinctly southern species live in inundated wetlands or coastal areas, including mangrove forests. Examples include the Hairy-nosed Otter (*Lutra sumatrana*), Milky Stork (*Mycteria cinerea*), Blood Python (*Python curtus*), and Black Marsh Turtle (*Siebenrockiella crassicollis*). A parallel transition occurs along elevational gradients in Vietnam. The dominant species change from tropical to subtropical at around 3,300 feet (1,000 m), though the transition is lower in the north. This change in the composition of species is most easily observed in the frog, small mammal, and floral communities. None of these boundaries are hard and fast. Rather, the contributions from different biogeographic areas vary with local conditions, creating a complex and unique admixture of plants and animals across Vietnam.

Within this countrywide pattern, however, some north-to-south species gradients occur across too small a scale to be comfortably explained by latitudinal variation alone. For instance, in central Vietnam there are similar patterns of species replacement in two distantly related primate groups: the White- and Yellow-cheeked Crested Gibbons (Family Hylobatidae) and the doucs (Family Cercopithecidae). Each consists of a cluster of three taxa, all endemic to central Indochina, that replace each other from north to south along the Truong Son Range (fig. 9). In each, the northern and central representatives are related more closely to each other than they are to their southernmost counterparts. A broad shift from subtropical to tropical biota cannot explain their distributions, so researchers have been exploring other possible explanations. Similar patterns have also been observed in other groups. A genetic analysis conducted in 2004 identified a comparable pattern of north-to-south replacement in the species complex of the Indochinese Box Turtle (*Cuora galbinifrons, C. bourreti,* and *C. pic-*

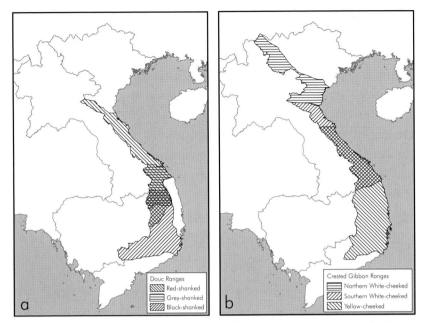

Figure 9. Distribution of (a) Red-shanked (*Pygathrix nemaeus nemaeus*), Grey-shanked (*P. n. cinerea*), and Black-shanked (*P. nigripes*) Doucs and (b) Northern (*Nomascus [Hylobates] leucogenys leucogenys*) and Southern (*N. [H.] l. siki*) White-cheeked Crested Gibbons and Yellow-cheeked Crested Gibbons (*N. [H.] gabriellae*) within Vietnam. Ranges are approximate and depicted as continuous areas, which they likely were originally. (After Geissmann et al. 2000 and Nadler et al. 2003)

turata), a group recorded from southern China, Laos, and northern and Central Vietnam.

Not all of Vietnam's species occupy ranges that overlap with or abut close evolutionary relatives. Large distances separate some species from their relations, a distribution pattern referred to as disjunct. This is the case with the Golden Vietnamese Cypress (*Xanthocyparis vietnamensis*) and western North America's Nootka Cypress (*Chamaecyparis nootkatensis*); these two related taxa are separated by the width of the Pacific Ocean. Large areas of inhospitable habitat may also separate populations of the same species. The Crested Argus (*Rheinardia ocellata*), a stunning pheasant restricted to broad-leaved evergreen forests, occupies two distinct upland regions separated by extensive lowlands: the Truong Son Range and Peninsular Malaysia.

A unique, often complex history underlies the evolution and distribution of each species. Current topographic and climatic conditions are major components determining recent patterns as are past events, including the movement of continents over geological time (plate tectonics), climate change, and the fluctuation of sea levels. The physical and climatic descriptions of Vietnam in chapter 1 are of contemporary conditions — Vietnam has not always appeared as it does today and it has not always experienced current climatic patterns. When did the mountain ranges form? How long has Vietnam experienced a seasonal monsoon climate? How did these physical and climatic factors determine Vietnam's biodiversity?

GEOLOGICAL HISTORY OF SOUTHEAST ASIA

Geologically, Southeast Asia is a collage of continental fragments of varying sizes located at the confluence of three continental plates: Eurasia, Indo-Australia, and the Philippine Sea (fig. 10). The earth's outer layer (the crust) is composed of rigid plates that move across its surface. The underlying mantle, a solid yet flexible layer of highly heated metals and minerals, propels movement of the plates. Gravitational forces also influence their travels as the leading edge of one plate slides beneath another in a region known as a subduction zone. Zones where plates diverge, converge, or slide past one another have high rates of earthquakes, volcanic activity, and mountain building. These movements can create fractures in the plates where rocks slide past each other along faults. All possible interactions between plates occur in Southeast Asia, areas of which exhibit the highest rates of plate convergence and separation on the globe.

Because of past and ongoing plate movements, Southeast Asia is among the Earth's most intriguing geological regions. Vietnam's geological history is complex, beginning hundreds of millions of years ago when the earth's surface looked vastly different. Geologists have pieced together a number of clues — including data on the Earth's magnetic field, rock ages, and fossilized plants and animals — to determine that Vietnam and surrounding

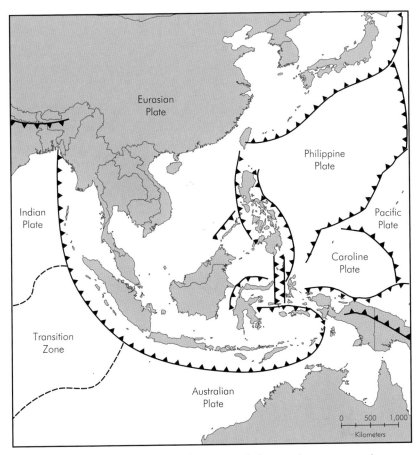

Figure 10. Current position of continental plates and suture zones in
East and Southeast Asia; arrows designate direction of movement
(After National Geographic Society, U.S. 1999)

areas of Southeast Asia once lay along the northern margin of a large, now
extinct supercontinent. Called Gondwanaland, this supercontinent (which
also included South America, Africa, Australia, India, and Antarctica) was
located at low latitudes in the southern hemisphere during the Paleozoic
Era (540–250 million years ago; fig. 11a).

Starting around 350 million years ago, slivers of Gondwanaland, each
composed of fragments called terranes, separated one after the other and
slowly migrated northward across the large Paleo-Tethys Ocean. As each

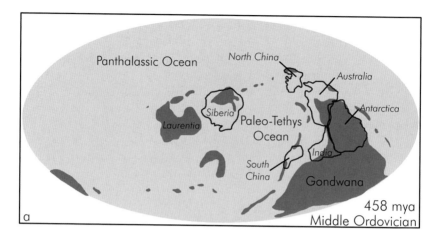

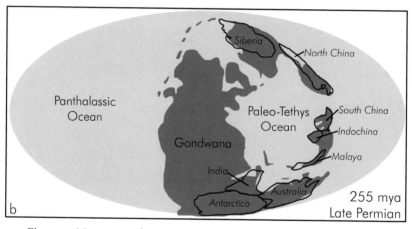

Figure 11. Movement of continental plates through geological time (a–d)
(After Scotese 2001)

sliver splintered off, an ocean basin filled the gap between it and the parent supercontinent (fig. 11b). Over time, the terranes coalesced again but in different geometries and at higher latitudes. All that remains of the former ocean basins (which became trapped between fusing terranes) are suture zones, fault lines in present-day East and Southeast Asia. Many of Vietnam's mountain ranges were created during these fusion events. The Truong Son Range was likely uplifted in the early Triassic (estimated at 250–230 million years ago). The uplift was caused in part by the simultaneous collision of

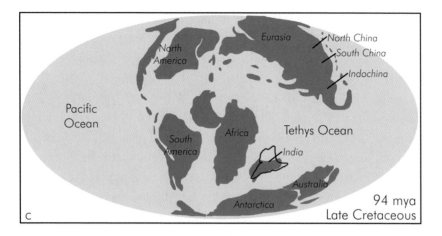

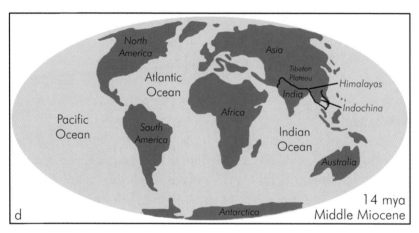

two terranes with the core of what is now Indochina. One terrane now comprises Thailand, Burma, west Malaysia, and Sumatra and the other South China and northern Vietnam.

Around 150 million years ago, the rest of Gondwanaland slowly started to break up, with India and Australia later beginning to drift north (fig. 11c). India moved more quickly, colliding with Eurasia approximately 50 million years ago. Three major plate movements around this time — the collision of India and Eurasia, the collision of Australia with islands to its north, and the clockwise rotation of the Philippine Sea plate — significantly modified Indochina's orientation and topography. The combined effect of India pushing on the northwest corner of mainland Southeast Asia and the Philippine plate pulling toward the east caused a torquing of the peninsula into its now-familiar S-shape.

India's collision with Eurasia was one of the most profound tectonic events of the past 100 million years. Its impact rippled throughout Southeast Asia and the surrounding continents and seas, with widespread consequences for geology, climate, and species distributions. The first moments of contact were relatively gentle, as evidenced by the slow replacement of deep-water organisms with shallower forms in the seaway between the two plates and by the lack of upheaval in the contiguous terrains. The extinction of this seaway led to increased aridity in the interior of Eurasia, initiating the Asian monsoon circulation system. Continued northward movement of India forced the oceanic crust lying along the southern margin of Eurasia underneath the converging Indian plate, giving rise to the Himalayan Mountain Range (fig. 11d). One of the most spectacular remnants of the India-Eurasia collision, this range extends from northern Pakistan to northwestern Vietnam.

Another effect, the uplift of Central Asia's Tibetan Plateau, which took place from 50 to 5 million years ago, shifted wind and rainfall patterns in East and Southeast Asia, making them more strongly seasonal. This also reinforced the cyclical monsoon climate, which intensified some 10 to 8 million years ago. The impact redirected the flow of Asia's major rivers, whose current courses were born in the wake of the Himalayan genesis. As mountains were built, they created new sources of sediment, which settled offshore at river outflows. These offshore deposits tracked shifts in the rivers' courses in response to the changing topography over time and show that the Mekong River changed its course several times due to faulting and the evolving climate. Two million years ago, sections of the Mekong ran in four separate river basins (fig. 12). Over time, the upper Mekong and the Yangtze River crisscrossed and separated, as did the Yangtze and the Red River. Around 1.5 million years ago, the Mekong appears to have flowed straight across central Cambodia through the Tonle Sap basin, emptying into the Gulf of Thailand near Kampot. Not until 5,000 years ago did faulting divert

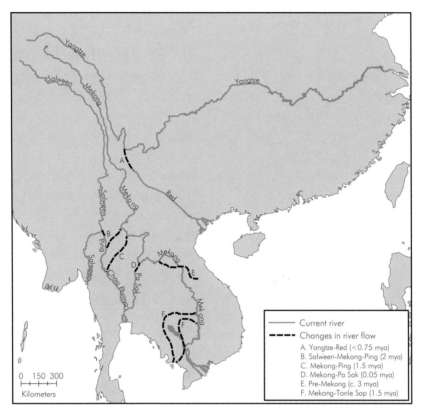

Figure 12. Shifting courses of East and Southeast Asian rivers over the
past 2 million years (After Attwood and Johnston 2001)

the upper Mekong from Thailand's Pa Sak to its present course and the Mekong emerge as Indochina's principal river. To the north, the upper Yangtze
River likely followed the current course of the Red River, emptying into the
East Sea. Around 75,000 years ago or later, an easterly draining river extended westward and captured the Yangtze, turning its course toward the
East Sea. This left the Red River a truncated and independent river continuing to flow along the lower course it had followed for 5 million years.

CLIMATE AND SEA LEVEL CHANGES

Sea levels have risen and fallen throughout the earth's history. The shallow marine basins surrounding Southeast Asia's mainland and islands have been repeatedly exposed and submerged, profoundly influencing the region's flora and fauna. During the Tertiary (65–2.6 million years ago), the Earth's climate gradually cooled while oscillations in climatic conditions and sea level strengthened over time. At 35 million years ago, the Antarctic continental ice cap was established and mountain glaciers likely started forming from the middle Miocene (14 million years ago) onward. With the appearance of the Arctic ice sheet approximately 2.4 million years ago, the dynamic, large-scale global glaciations of the Quaternary (2.6–0.01 million years ago) began; these have become increasingly dramatic over time.

Conditions fluctuated between cooler, drier periods associated with glacial events and warmer, wetter ones during interglacials. During glaciations, water formed into ice at both poles, sea levels dropped, and the area of exposed land increased. Larger areas of emergent land in Southeast Asia led to decreasing evaporation and lower moisture content of monsoon winds, resulting in drier conditions. As temperatures dropped and conditions became less humid, montane forest species previously restricted to higher elevations descended to lower levels, where they displaced lowland evergreen forest vegetation. Lowland forests growing in more seasonal areas were replaced by open savannah and grassland vegetation. Conversely, during interglacial periods, the climate became warmer, wetter, and less seasonal, and surviving wet evergreen forest species expanded to higher elevations and latitudes. Generally, the greatest expansion of these ever-wet tropical forests and mangrove formations occurred during the highest sea levels, when the climate was at its warmest.

During periods of lower sea level, the Sunda Shelf, a shallow seabed that connects mainland Southeast Asia and Sumatra, Java, Borneo, and other Southeast Asian islands, emerged to form a land bridge connecting the continent and the archipelago (fig. 13). Conditions about 18,000 years ago, the most recent maximum extent of the glaciers, appear to be among the most extreme of the past several million years. Precipitation in Asia fell

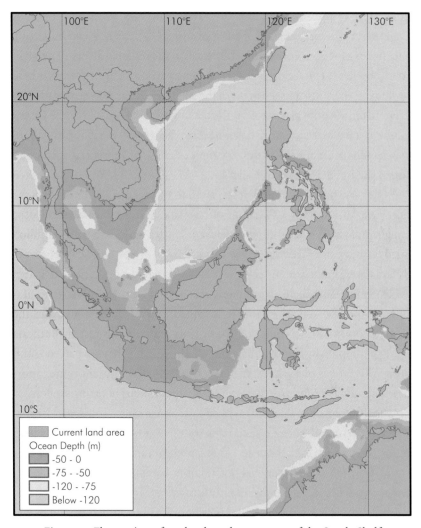

Figure 13. Fluctuation of sea levels and emergence of the Sunda Shelf
(From Voris 2000; © Field Museum)

to 30 to 50 percent of current levels, and mean temperatures were 7°F–13°F
(4°C–7°C) cooler. Sea levels fluctuated widely and at times were as much as
400 feet (120 m) lower than today. This exposed most of the Sunda Shelf,
which became covered with a mixture of wet evergreen forests, drier forests and woodlands, and grasslands, crisscrossed with river networks. The

emergence of the Sunda Shelf is central to Southeast Asia's biogeography; it allowed the interchange of plants and animals between the mainland and the islands and exerted a strong influence on the region's diversity patterns. At 13,000 years ago, sea levels were closer to 250 feet (75 m) below present levels, and the still-exposed areas of the shelf were covered with swamp forests and large freshwater lakes. At the termination of the Pleistocene around 11,000 years ago, seas had risen another 80 feet (25 m) and the Sunda Shelf was largely submerged, cutting off the exchange of terrestrial species between the mainland and the islands.

Over the past 40 million years, similar and recurring climatic oscillations, expansion and contraction of habitats, and emergence and loss of land bridges have had profound effects on species richness and distribution. Such changes can foster speciation (the genesis of new species), as genetic differences accumulate in newly separated, isolated populations that then evolve independently from one another. They can also lead to extinctions of populations and species unable to migrate or adapt as their environments change. During drier, cooler periods plants and animals restricted to formerly widespread warmer and wetter conditions may have survived within refugia — vestiges of wet evergreen forest isolated amid drier or more montane habitats. Similar sanctuaries also existed in marine environments.

The outcomes of such changes can differ across related species, as the eclectic mixture of lineages that make up Vietnam's conifer diversity illustrates. Some, such as the northern hemisphere's Taiwania (*Taiwania cryptomerioides*), retreated to pockets of suitable habitat as the climate cooled and dried; this species persists in only four isolated populations worldwide, one of which is in Vietnam's Lao Cai Province. Others, notably members of the southern hemisphere's tropical conifers, the podocarps (Family Podocarpacea), migrated northward and colonized Vietnam's montane areas. Also present are ancient relict species, such as the endemic Krempf's Pine (*Pinus krempfii*), and more recently evolved, widespread Southeast Asian ones, such as the Benguet Pine (*P. kesiya*).

ORIGINS OF SPECIES

Achieving a good understanding of the biogeography of species found in Vietnam entails looking more broadly at how species arise and how they move, or disperse, across the globe. Species found in Vietnam have two possible origins: either they dispersed from another area into the region or they evolved in place. Species apparently absent from Vietnam may never have been there, may be there and not yet found, or may have once been there but their populations are now extinct.

Organisms have many ways of dispersing into new areas. They can move by air, land, or water; produce seeds carried by the wind or other organisms; and travel on species as parasites or as more benign hitchhikers. Continental plates facilitate movements of organisms by acting as rafts that introduce novel species when their landmasses collide or pass close by. This is particularly true for sedentary organisms, such as plants, or groups unable to survive exposure to seawater, such as amphibians. Hardier species can drift across the seaways dividing islands and continents on floating vegetation. Dispersal can also occur over land bridges exposed during periods of lower sea level. These movements between areas can cause the extinction of resident species if the new organisms outcompete, prey on, or otherwise negatively affect resident species. Dispersal is sometimes the first step in the formation of new species. Organisms dispersing between two previously separated areas are occasionally the seeds from which new populations arise and radiate as the species adapt to new climates, habitats, and ecological communities.

Divisions of species' ranges can also underlie speciation events. The fragmentation of a species into isolated populations arises when climatic barriers or geographic barriers such as mountains, rivers, deserts, and seaways divide a species's range. This phenomenon of physical separation is known as vicariance. As the now-divided populations evolve independently, they accumulate genetic differences that may be expressed physically, physiologically, behaviorally, and chemically. If, over time, the separated populations diverge into significantly different forms, they will constitute new, closely related species. Fragmentation can also occur when continental plates break up, each carrying separate populations of a common ancestor. The diversity and distribution of the ratites—a group of flightless birds that includes Australia's Emu (*Dromaius novaehollandiae*), South America's rheas (Family Rheidae), and New Zealand's extinct Bush Moa (*Anomalopteryx didiformis*)—appears to have resulted from the breakup of Gondwanaland, home to their common ancestor.

Dispersal and vicariance, as well as historical events such as volcanic eruptions, work together to produce distribution patterns that may appear similar even though reached through different paths. Fragmented populations may represent relics of a formerly widespread species that, because of climatic or ecological changes or competition with newly evolved or invading species, now occupy small portions of their previous geographic range. Magnolias (Family Magnoliaceae) are one of the oldest of the flowering plant families, and for 70 million years they were distributed continuously in a wide belt around the northern hemisphere. In the past 2 million years, their range has been reduced to fragments covering a strip of the Americas from northeast to northern South America, East Asia, and Southeast Asia, including Vietnam. This rapid fragmentation and range reduction was likely caused by intensifying cycles of glaciation.

Disjunct distributions of evolutionary relatives can also come about through separation followed by speciation. The distribution of agamid lizards (a group of arboreal Old World lizards in the Family Agamidae) across the Pacific region appears to be primarily the result of vicariance events. The Chinese Water Dragon (*Physignathus cocincinus*) found in mainland Southeast Asia and southern China is the sister taxon (the closest living relative) to a group of fourteen agamid lizards occurring in Australia and New Guinea. These close relatives share a common ancestor that once lived in Gondwanaland. The lineage became separated hundreds of millions of years ago when the Southeast Asian plate split from the supercontinent's northern margin, from which the Australia–New Guinea plate would later separate. Subsequent divergence and passive movement to new locations on the globe via continental movement resulted in the current distribution and richness of this group.

Because the richness and distribution of organisms are contingent on historical events, investigating the definitive causes of current patterns can be extremely challenging, and the results are often difficult to test. The disciplines involved in these investigations include geology, paleontology, genetics, and palynology (the study of living and fossil plant pollen), in addition to evolution, ecology, and systematics. Caution should be taken when accepting current distributions as representative of a species's natural geographic range. Habitat loss, degradation, and exploitation can all blur patterns and hence their interpretation. At this point, far too little is known about most species in Vietnam and the neighboring countries to provide comprehensive biogeographical analyses. As research uncovers additional evidence on distributions, speciation, plate tectonics, and climate change, these patterns will become better defined. With these caveats in mind, it is interesting and informative to examine how geological and climatic history may have shaped Southeast Asia's flora and fauna.

BIOGEOGRAPHY OF SOUTHEAST ASIA

Incorporating the processes of speciation, dispersal, and vicariance into the region's physical history brings the biogeography of Southeast Asia into better focus. Returning to the beginning of the Tertiary, 65 million years ago, India's collision with Eurasia had two important consequences for the biodiversity of the newly joined continents. First, it fostered the mixing of formerly isolated groups as Gondwanan plants and animals from India colonized Eurasia and, to some extent, vice versa. Evidence from fossils, current distributions, and recent genetic analyses suggest that India may have served as a giant, slow-moving ferry bringing novel species to the Eurasian continent. These include both groups that started on the raft from Gondwanaland as well as African species that India is thought to have picked up when it passed close to Africa and Madagascar during its northward drift. Groups introduced in this manner are diverse and include most of Southeast Asia's soil-feeding termites, freshwater snails in the Family Potamiopsidae, a family of underground-dwelling, limbless, and often blind amphibians called caecilians (Ichthyophiidae), three lineages of frogs (Family Ranidae), and a large number of plants. Some of these, notably the three frog groups (Rhacophorinae, Raninae, Dicroglossinae) and the flowering tropical dipterocarp trees (Dipterocarpaceae), diversified greatly across Southeast Asia and are currently at their peaks of species richness in this part of the world. The docking of India also had negative effects on Eurasian biodiversity. Dispersing Indian plant species are thought to have caused the extinction of Eurasian plant taxa that had evolved 65 to 50 million years ago. Curiously, scientists have found few plant species to date that successfully dispersed in the opposite direction, from Eurasia into India.

The second major consequence of the India-Eurasia collision was the subsequent rise of the Himalayas and the Tibetan Plateau. This growing geographic barrier separated formerly contiguous Asian and Southeast Asian flora and fauna, as reflected in the distribution of a number of Southeast Asia's reptiles and amphibians. Glass lizards (Family Anguidae) illustrate how vicariant events—in combination with dispersal—can result in complex distributions of biodiversity. Glass lizards originated in North America and dispersed to Eurasia before the opening of the Atlantic Ocean. They then radiated throughout Africa and Asia. Between 25 and 10 million years ago, the uplift of the Tibetan Plateau isolated new species in East Asia from their West Asian relatives. Simultaneously, a lineage from East Asia dispersed back to North America, this time via the Bering land bridge. As a result, Vietnam's three species of glass lizards count different North American species as close relatives and distant ancestors (fig. 14). The distribution of Asian softshell turtles in the Family Trionychidae also seems determined in part by the plateau's rise. The Euphrates Softshell Turtle (*Rafetus euphraticus*) inhabits the Tigris and Euphrates drainages in southern Turkey, Syria, Iraq, and Iran; its closest relative, the Shanghai Softshell Turtle (*R. swinhoei*), is known from northern Vietnam and southern China. This pattern is likely due to separation of their common ancestral population by the rising Himalayas.

Climate change can also fragment populations by resulting in shifts in habitats and dispersal opportunities. For two Vietnamese species currently restricted to the Truong Son Range—the newly discovered Annamite Striped Rabbit (*Nesolagus timminsi*) and Heude's Pig (*Sus bucculentus*), re-

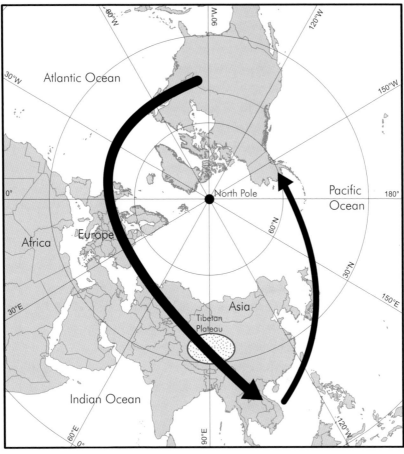

Figure 14. The dispersal of glass lizards (Family Anguidae) from North
America to Eurasia (thick black arrow) was followed by uplift of the Tibetan
Plateau, isolating the Southeast Asian populations. Dispersal of Southeast Asian
populations back to North America (thin black arrow) resulted in the North
American fauna including both close relatives and distant ancestors of
Vietnam's glass lizards. (Macey et al. 1999)

discovered after more than 100 years—their closest relatives are found on
islands 1,500 miles (2,500 km) to the south and east. The Sumatran Striped
Rabbit occupies montane forests at 1,800 feet (600 m) and above, primarily
in Sumatra's Barisan Mountains, while its mainland relative is found in wet
evergreen forest at lower altitudes. Genetic data suggest that these species

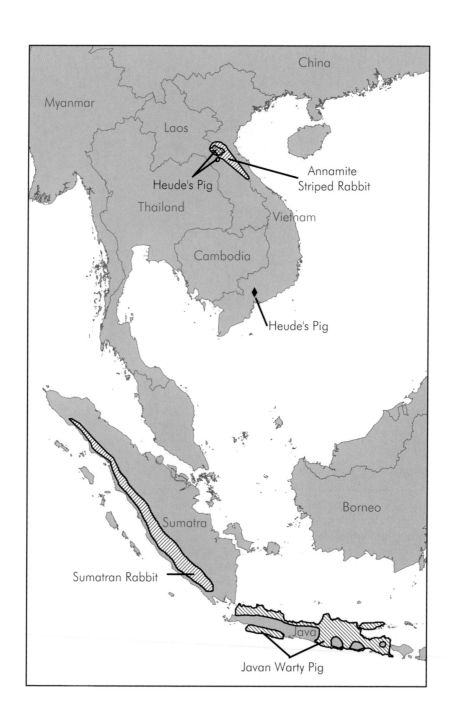

have been diverging for approximately 8 million years. Presumably they represent relict populations of a formerly widespread species once connected by the emergent Sunda Shelf and isolated by cycles of climatic and habitat change (fig. 15; box 6). Examples of disjunct distributions similarly occur in several vertebrate and invertebrate marine groups where the Sunda Shelf region seems to serve as a dividing line between Indian and Pacific taxa and lineages.

Island communities off mainland Southeast Asia reflect dispersal and vicariance events initiated by climate change. The Con Dao Archipelago, located in the East Sea off Vietnam's southwest coast, is home to diverse species endemic to its islands, including an impressive array of endemic plants. Subspecies of three southern Vietnamese mammals are also present: the Con Son Long-tailed Macaque (*Macaca fascicularis condorensis*), Con Dao Black Giant Squirrel (*Ratufa bicolor condorensis*), and Con Dao Variable Squirrel (*Callosciurus finlaysonii germaini*). These taxa likely diverged from mainland relatives when isolated by fluctuations in sea level and changes in the intervening habitat quality.

Not all island endemics represent forms that evolved in situ from stranded mainland species, however. Four of Vietnam's endemic island geckos, the Vietnamese Leopard Gecko (*Goniurosaurus lichtenfelderi*), Boulenger's Scaly-legged Gecko (*Cnemaspis boulengeri*), Con Dao Bow-fingered Gecko (*Cyrtodactylus condorensis*), and another species of gecko (*Gonydactylus paradoxus*), live only on islands off the country's coasts. These likely represent relict populations of species previously present on the mainland but now extinct there due to the loss of their forested habitats.

Climate change also influenced the distributions of species restricted

Figure 15. Distributions of two species endemic to the Truong Son Range, the Annamite Striped Rabbit (*Nesolagus timminsi*) and Heude's Pig (*Sus bucculentus*), and their closest living relatives, the Sumatran Striped Rabbit (*N. netscheri*) and the Javan Warty Pig (*S. verrucosus*), respectively. Heude's Pig locations shown in southern Vietnam are the origin of the two specimens upon which the initial description was based; it is unclear if these were collection localities or points of purchase. (After Flux 1990; Dang N. Cahn et al. 2001; Groves 1981; Groves and Schaller 2000; Oliver 1993)

BOX 6
Heude's Pig and the Annamite Striped Rabbit

In 1892 Pierre Jean Heude, a French Jesuit missionary and keen amateur naturalist, described a new wild boar based on two skulls sent to him from southern Vietnam by a friend. He designated it a new species, *Sus bucculentus*. The lithographs accompanying his description portray a skull quite similar to that of the Javan Warty Pig (*S. verrucosus*), a resemblance Heude and subsequent taxonomists all noted. At some point the skulls that Heude based his description on disappeared, and when no additional remains surfaced, Heude's Pig entered a taxonomic purgatory—believed at best to be elusive, at worst erroneous.

Two events in the 1990s have gone some way toward clarifying this pig's status. In January 1995, researchers exploring the northern Truong Son along the Laos-Vietnam border obtained the skull of a juvenile male pig reported by indigenous hunters as being from a species other than the common Eurasian Wild Boar (*S. scrofa*). And in July 1996, the skull bearing Heude's handwriting on which the initial description had been based was unearthed in the basement of China's Beijing Institute of Zoology, where it had resided in an unmarked crate along with many other of Heude's specimens. Comparisons with the new skull from Laos showed them to be identical (except for age) and confirmed the presence of Heude's Pig in Indochina.

The journey of the Annamite Striped Rabbit (*Nesolagus timminsi*) to scientific legitimacy is less thorny and of more recent origin (fig. 16). In early 1996, Western scientists saw unusual rabbits in the food market of Ban Lak, a rural Laotian town in the northern Truong Son near Vietnam's Ha Tinh Province. The rabbit's most curious characteristic was its striped fur, a trait shared by only one other hare: the rarely seen Sumatran Striped Rabbit (*N. netscheri*). This species, next to which the Laotian rabbits appear almost indistinguishable, was described in 1880 as having "a system of coloration as beautiful as it is uncommon among the hare-tribe" (Schlegel 1880, 61). Despite this close similarity, genetic analyses detect greater divergence between these sister species than any other rabbits or hares sharing a genus. Their strikingly similar appearances, including short ears and legs and an almost nonexistent tail, may be attributable to their persistence in a shared habitat of wet, evergreen forests.

The physical appearance of Heude's Pig is not known. If it resembles the Javan Warty Pig externally, it should have a long snout with projecting lower tusks and pairs of enlarged warts on its face and a reddish to yellowish coat with a mane extending along the back. It would also be among the most sexually dimorphic of wild boars; Javan males weigh 240 pounds (108 kg), almost twice as much as the females at a little less than 100 pounds (44 kg). Heude's Pig's range is also in doubt. The first skull recovered was marked "Bienhoa," a French colonial center next to what was then Saigon, and in 1898 Heude described the pigs as originating "sur les bords du Donnai" (from the banks of the Donnai [River]) in southern Vietnam (Heude 1898, 116). Yet Heude did not acquire the skulls himself, and these locations may only be the places where they first came into his friend's hands. The Annamite Striped Rabbit's range is better known but still expanding; it is now confirmed from Vietnam's Nghe Anh, Ha Tinh, and Quang Binh Provinces.

Figure 16. Annamite Striped Rabbit (*Nesolagus timminsi*)

to Vietnam's mainland, mostly in mountainous areas. Current surveys report that a subset of northern Vietnam's montane frog species also live
in the highlands of central Vietnam's Kon Tum Plateau—montane habitats separated by hundreds of miles (km). This pattern might reflect the
fragmentation of once broader ranges these frogs occupied when montane
habitats extended to lower elevations during cooler, drier glacial periods.
During intervening warmer eras, the species became isolated when these
habitats crept back upslope. Such cycles of habitat change may also have led
to varying degrees of divergence in a few widespread frog lineages. Scientists are finding that some commonly recognized single frog species are
actually groups of outwardly similar yet distinct species, as is the case with
species complexes of the Green Cascade Frog (*Rana livida*), Blyth's Wart
Frog (*Limnonectes blythii*), Kuhl's Wart Frog (*L. kuhlii*), and Thai Asian
Toad (*Leptolalax pelodytoides*). Referred to as cryptic or hidden species,
they may represent evolutionary lineages that diverged as montane forest
distribution shifted.

A GROUP STUDY: PRIMATES

Among vertebrate groups, Vietnam's primates are remarkable for the number of endemic species. Six, or roughly one-fourth of the primate taxa known from Vietnam, are found only here: the Con Son Long-tailed Macaque, Delacour's Leaf Monkey (*Trachypithecus delacouri*), Cat Ba Leaf Monkey (*T. poliocephalus poliocephalus*), Gray-shanked Douc, Tonkin Snub-nosed Monkey, and the Eastern Black Crested Gibbon [*Hylobates (Nomascus)* sp. cf. *nasutus* population]. Nine others are endemic to Indochina and a small region of southern China.

During most of the Tertiary, the interchange of fauna and flora between Eurasia, North America, and Africa was relatively unrestricted though episodic. Around 16 million years ago, low sea levels allowed the initial migration of primates from Africa to Eurasia across an Afro-Arabian corridor. A second major migration took place about 4 million years later, at another period of lowered sea level, and a final one occurred roughly 1.5 million years ago. Subsequently, Asia's environments and habitats became more varied, and any immigration corridors were narrow and short-lived. This constriction of dispersal fostered speciation—and resulting high levels of endemism—among Asia's primates.

Before 4 million years ago, ape taxa such as gibbons, orangutans (genus *Pongo*), and a now-extinct giant ape genus, *Gigantopithecus,* were widespread in Asia's humid evergreen forest environments. By contrast, monkeys appear to have had relatively more local distributions and lower species richness when compared to apes. (Conclusions from this evidence must be drawn carefully, because the early fossil record of monkeys is extremely scanty, especially when compared to that of the apes.) However, the geographic ranges of all of Asia's apes began contracting some 3 to 4 million years ago. This contraction intensified around 1.5 to 2 million years ago, mainly because the boundary between the region's tropical and subtropical zones, which was the northern limit of ape distributions, made a profound shift southward. Unable to adapt to the increasingly seasonal environments that accompanied this shift, ape species richness declined. First the enormous ape *Gigantopithecus* and then the orangutan went extinct in mainland

Southeast Asia. By the late Pleistocene (several hundred thousand years ago), the gibbon—the only family of primates believed to have evolved in Asia—became the only ape to persist in continental Southeast Asia.

Monkeys began to flourish at the beginning of the Quaternary (2.6 million years ago). The group underwent a major expansion, with increased species richness and the evolution of a number of endemic species such as Indochina's diverse group of François's Leaf Monkeys (*Trachypithecus françoisi*). Monkeys thrived during this period in part because of their versatile diets and ability to occupy a range of habitats, including temperate, subtropical, and tropical forests and grasslands. This flexibility allowed them to withstand the increasingly seasonal conditions that appear to have had such strong negative effects on ape species richness.

Yet monkeys were not completely immune to massive climatic changes. There was a general trend among all primates toward an increasingly southern distribution, with one exception. The snub-nosed monkey group was initially distributed across southern China and northern Vietnam, and they remained there while subtropical conditions prevailed. As climatic conditions deteriorated further for primates during the Pleistocene (1.8–0.01 million years ago), surviving snub-nosed monkey populations became confined to montane refuges in these areas. The snub-nosed monkey species able to survive the most severe climates of this epoch were those adapted to colder conditions. Some populations in China exhibit characteristics that indicate populations at the end of the Pleistocene dwindled to very small sizes, creating a population bottleneck. Three species now occupy different montane habitats in China's Yunnan Province and are among the few primates able to survive in temperate environments. The fourth species in the genus, the Tonkin Snub-nosed Monkey, is the last remnant of the ancestral group that continues to live in a more tropical environment.

Thus the primates in Vietnam, as with other groups, are a mélange of older and newer taxa. Some, such as gibbons, are descendants of relatively archaic forms (dating to 23 million years ago or earlier) that persisted through long-term geological and climatic changes. Newer groups, such as leaf monkeys, represent taxa that have diversified in the past 2 million years.

As the primates illustrate, the biogeography of the entire region represents the outcome of interactions between geology, climate, speciation, dispersal, vicariance, and history, including a degree of chance. The elevated physical and evolutionary complexity of Southeast Asia makes it challenging to tease apart possible mechanisms of distribution and diversity for each taxon and area of interest, yet information on species distribution and endemism patterns is critical to setting conservation priorities. Along with continued research into the region's geology, climate, ecology, and evolutionary history, advances in climate modeling and species distribution modeling will surely help elucidate these puzzles.

FOUR

Vietnam's Living Environments

A region's biogeography, the product of its geological, climatic, and evolutionary history, is often best recorded in the distribution, diversity, and evolutionary affinities of its flora. Plants are relatively ancient for fair-sized living creatures; the origin of seed-bearing plants (including cycads, conifers, and flowering plants) dates back more than 350 million years. With the evolution of seeds, plants became less dependent on moisture for reproduction, but seed dispersal is generally limited and geographical ranges migrate slowly. Combined with their frequent longevity, these traits make seed plants an excellent group for examining an area's long-term history. The presence on northern Vietnam's Mount Fan Xi Pan of a flora of ancient character with strong affinities to that of southern China provides evidence that earlier in time a similar and more tropical climate extended across the region. More detailed climate reconstructions can be made using ancient pollen grains shed 300,000 years ago or more and embedded in sedimentary layers.

Plants are also excellent indicators of current conditions. Their geographic ranges reflect a number of nonliving factors, including temperature, rainfall patterns, elevation, hydrology, and underlying soil characteristics. Vegetative communities associated with subsets of these conditions share attributes of structure, composition of their flora, and seasonality. Plant communities form the backbone of habitats and ecosystems. Because green plants are uniquely (excluding algae) capable of transforming the sun's light into organic compounds, they are the primary source of energy and productivity in most land communities and some aquatic ones. Green plants compose the bulk of living habitats (including food and shelter) for terrestrial animals. In turn, animals shape plant communities through pollination, seed dispersal, and patterns of consumption.

It is extremely difficult to discuss a country's natural history without a common system for identifying and classifying its plant communities. This is particularly true in Vietnam, given its wide range of physical conditions. Vegetation classification systems attempt to divide vegetative communities into categories based on species composition; structural aspects, including complexity, forest height, and tree density; and a few abiotic variables, such as rainfall and elevation (box 7). Ideally, each category would be defined by a unique collection of such descriptors, and the vegetation types could be mapped with clearly defined boundaries. In practice, the classification and mapping of vegetative communities is far messier since most flow into one another across transitional areas, either along a gradient or as a mosaic of interspersed types. The complexity of Vietnam's monsoon-dominated climatic patterns and its topography and extensive coastline increase the difficulty of classifying and subsequently mapping these boundaries.

Vegetation also varies with latitude at a continental scale, corresponding to major climactic zones. The tropical or equatorial zone stretches around the Earth as a wide belt centered on the equator and extending 15° to 25° to the north and south. Here temperatures are high and stable throughout the year, though rainfall may be seasonal. Regions 30° to 60° north and south of the equator lie in the temperate zone, experiencing climates with wide seasonal temperature fluctuations and rainfall that is either seasonal or spread more evenly across the year. In between, at 20° to 35° north and south, lies the subtropical zone. In Southeast Asia, subtropical climatic zones experience wider seasonal temperature fluctuation than the tropics, though summers remain quite warm and the winters are relatively mild. Rainfall is strongly influenced by the monsoons, creating seasonally dry winters.

Vietnam's climate is primarily tropical, grading into subtropical in the north of the country, especially at higher elevations. Broad climatic patterns strongly influence plant evolution and distribution. Affinity to or association with a climatic zone is often included in descriptions, such as the tropical families of the dipterocarps (Dipterocarpaceae) and sumacs (Anarcardiaceae) and the temperate families of the heaths (Ericaceae) and beeches

BOX 7
Classifying Vegetation

To differentiate among vegetation classes or communities, botanists consider a number of criteria:

- canopy closure, which determines the extent of light penetration to lower layers of vegetation and the forest floor;
- the number of stories or levels in the forest;
- leafing patterns: plants can be classified as deciduous, dropping their leaves annually, or evergreen, maintaining their leaves throughout the year;
- total annual rainfall or the length of the dry season;
- annual temperature extremes: this value is usually correlated with elevation;
- dominant species, genera, or families of plants (floral composition); and
- disturbance history: habitats can be classified as primary vegetation, which has experienced little or no disturbance; as secondary vegetation, which has experienced medium to high levels of disturbance and is now regrowing; or as agricultural formations such as plantations and rice paddies.

Other criteria, such as the type of soil or rock underlying the vegetation or the depth, periodicity of flooding or inundation, and salt content of standing water, may also be useful for classifying communities.

(Fagaceae). Description is not destiny, however, and because topography and local weather patterns vary, species and vegetative communities can be found outside these geographic and climatic limits. This is particularly true of temperate species, which can be found at high elevations in subtropical regions, a situation that occurs along the Hoang Lien Son Range in northwestern Vietnam.

Vietnam's natural terrestrial vegetation falls into four main categories. Two are forests distinguished by elevation: lowland forests, which in turn are subdivided into evergreen, semi-evergreen, and deciduous forms; and montane forests, which are evergreen and occur in mountainous areas. The term *evergreen* can be confusing to the reader unfamiliar with tropical forests. Any plant that retains its leaves for an extended period (through winter seasons or over several years) and whose individual leaves may drop during any season is called an evergreen. In colder, temperate regions, evergreens are generally conifers like pines and firs bearing cones and needle-like leaves. In contrast, in tropical and subtropical environments, evergreens are more often broad-leaved flowering plants. Deciduous trees across all climatic zones are generally broad-leaved trees that drop all of their leaves during one season.

Evergreen forests are found in consistently wet and humid conditions, whereas deciduous forests occur in regions with long (more than five months) dry seasons. The transition from lowland to montane forests occurs at 3,600–3,900 feet (1,100–1,200 m) in south-central Vietnam and moves down to 2,300–3,000 feet (700–900 m) in northern areas of the country; forests in this turnover zone are referred to as submontane. Scrub, grasslands, and wetlands make up the remaining major vegetation categories and are usually restricted to low-lying areas. Evergreen forests, scrub, grasslands, and wetlands are considered zonal communities, responsive to broad patterns of climate change in their evolution and distribution. Azonal vegetative communities also exist, where both structure and composition are affected primarily by unusual soils, nutrients, and water regimes, as is the case with mangrove forests.

Studies of Vietnam's floral richness, diversity, and structure began in the early twentieth century, with much of the published work carried out by French, Russian, and Vietnamese botanists. Along with identifications and classifications, researchers, forestry workers, and conservation managers were interested in mapping distributions of these formations on a national scale. Such work initially combined aerial photographic surveys with field sampling and some educated guessing. With the placement of remote sensors on satellites as well as airplanes and other airborne platforms, the data available for interpretation have increased, though uncertainty remains. Broad determinations between forest, wetlands, and grasslands are relatively straightforward, and more thorough, seasonal analyses can usually differentiate between evergreen and deciduous forest types. The distributions of zonal plant communities whose ranges are determined by large-scale climatic and geological conditions can also be modeled with some success. Yet using remotely sensed data to interpret species composition in Vietnam's highly diverse forests remains nearly impossible.

Vietnam's flora is rich for a country of its size. More than 10,000 native vascular plant species are known, and scientists estimate that more than 13,000 exist. Some groups are particularly rich in both species and number of endemic taxa, including the orchids (box 8), cycads (box 9), and conifers (box 10). Described below are the major vegetative formations found in Vietnam and some of the dominant plant groups associated with them. Azonal plant communities restricted to a single region, such as the peat swamp forests of southern Vietnam, are described where they occur.

LOWLAND EVERGREEN FORESTS

Lowland evergreen forests are the type most frequently associated with the term *tropical rain forest*. Multistoried, with trees up to 100–160 feet (30–50 m) in height, vines strung across limbs and around trunks, and epiphytes clinging to branches and trunks for support, their canopies are closed and their understory is darkened. They grow in wet regions of the world where annual rainfall exceeds 80 inches (2,000 mm) and the dry season lasts one to three months. In Vietnam, lowland evergreen forests occur where annual monsoons and local topography generate high rainfall and regular fogs and mists.

The richness of Vietnam's lowland evergreen forests is similar at the generic level but lower at the species level when compared with those occurring to the south in Indonesia and Malaysia, the stronghold of Old World tropical lowland forests. Vietnam's evergreen forests are found up to 2,300 feet (700 m) from the coasts northeast of Hanoi south to Lam Dong Province in the southern Truong Son Range. Floristically they are characterized by a number of large, ecologically important evergreen dipterocarps, species belonging to the dominant Old World tropical tree family Dipterocarpaceae. These generally disappear from forests at 2,000–3,000 feet (600–900 m), with a few species reaching 3,900 feet (1,200 m) or slightly higher in southern Vietnam. North of Hanoi, lowland forest communities may resemble intergradations between the evergreen forests characteristic of the Truong Son Range and the subtropical broad-leaved evergreen forests of southern China. Lowland evergreen forests are some of the most threatened forests in the world because their accessibility places them under the greatest pressure from exploitation, agriculture, and development. This is particularly true in Vietnam. Alternate names for this forest type include wet, moist, or humid lowland evergreen forest, broad-leaved lowland evergreen forest, lowland rain forest, and lowland evergreen rain forest.

SEMI-EVERGREEN FOREST

Semi-evergreen forests are unique to mainland Southeast Asia, where they are restricted to suitable conditions up to 2,300 feet (700 m) in Indochina and northern and central Thailand. Characterized by a mixture of evergreen and deciduous trees, they grow in areas with moderate yet highly seasonal rainfall of 50–80 inches (1,200–2,000 mm) per year and a dry season of four to five months. Due to their continuous distribution across a large portion of the mainland, semi-evergreen forests have evolved a number of widespread endemic species, few of which are restricted to a single country. Compared with evergreen forests, the multilayered canopies of semi-evergreen forests have fewer species and are often more open and lower, at 100–130 feet (30–40 m). Buttressed trees, bamboos, and palms are all present and vines are abundant. Although semi-evergreen forests have a significant proportion of deciduous trees, evergreen species usually (but not always) dominate in the upper canopy.

Frequently intermingled as a mosaic with more drought-tolerant de-

BOX 8

Orchid Extravaganza

Vietnam is home to a great richness of orchids, many of them unique to the country (figs. 17–19). Leonid Averyanov of the Komarov Botanical Institute, Saint Petersburg, has spent more than twenty years studying Vietnam's orchids and, with Vietnamese and foreign colleagues, has documented 897 orchid species in 152 genera. Scientists estimate that the number of orchid species in Vietnam may exceed 1,100. New botanical explorations in mountainous regions, particularly along the country's western and northern borders, are expected to yield important additions to the orchid flora. Sadly, the destruction of forest habitats and the overharvesting of orchids for commercial exploitation make them one of the most threatened plant groups in Vietnam. The most endangered are spread across more than twenty-five genera, many of them widely collected as ornamental plants for sale in the domestic market and for export.

The slipper orchid genus (*Paphiopedilum*) deserves special attention for conservation. The greatest concentration of the world's slipper orchids is found in south China's Yunnan and Guangxi Provinces and in northern Vietnam. Twenty-two species and natural hybrids have been credibly reported from Vietnam. Although all wild slipper orchids in Vietnam are thought to be globally threatened, only three species, *P. appletonianum, P. delenatii,* and *P. hirsutissimum,* have been included in the 1996 Red Data Book of Vietnam.

Jack Regalado, Missouri Botanical Garden, Saint Louis

Figure 17. A species of slipper orchid (*Paphiopedilum micranthum*)
from northern Vietnam

ciduous dipterocarp forests, semi-evergreen forests favor regions with deep, wet soils. They are often found as riverine or gallery forests lining rivers and streams in areas with long dry seasons. Along with their greater sensitivity to drought, they also recover more poorly from fires than do deciduous dipterocarp forests. Frequent fires often convert semi-evergreen forests to this drier forest type. Within Vietnam, semi-evergreen forests are found from Quang Ninh Province in the north to Tay Ninh Province in the south; the

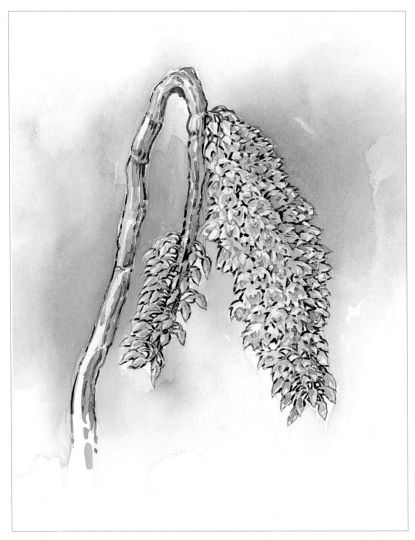

Figure 18. A species of lily-of-the-valley orchid (*Dendrobium secundum*)
from central and southern Vietnam

most extensive formations were probably once found in Kon Tum, Dak Lak,
Ninh Thuan, Binh Thuan, and Gia Lai Provinces. Semi-evergreen forests
experiencing relatively short dry seasons on the Truong Son Range's eastern slopes contrast with drier formations on the western slopes in Laos and
Cambodia. Alternate names for this forest type include semi-deciduous for-

Figure 19. A species of Medusa's head orchid (*Bulbophyllum farreri*)
from southern Vietnam

est, dry evergreen forest, seasonal evergreen forest, tropical semi-evergreen
forest, and monsoon forest.

DECIDUOUS DIPTEROCARP FOREST

Though deciduous dipterocarp forests represent only a small part of Vietnam's land cover, they dominate the rest of mainland Southeast Asia's forests. The name reflects the high proportion of deciduous plants and the

ecological dominance of dipterocarps in these communities. Dipterocarps are a well-studied, highly diverse, and almost exclusively evergreen tropical tree family distributed across South and Southeast Asia, with two species continuing into central Africa. Within Southeast Asia they are the most ecologically and economically important group of the lowland forests. Out of roughly 550 identified species, forty-eight are found in Indochina, forty-two of them in Vietnam. The trees range in height from 30 feet to more than 120 feet (10–37 m), and they frequently exhibit large buttresses at their bases, allowing even tall trees to grow in thin soils. The trunks are smooth and unbranched, supporting a cauliflower-shaped crown that rises to the canopy and is frequently emergent above it.

On Southeast Asia's islands, dipterocarps flower synchronously at irregular intervals, with many species simultaneously producing large masses of showy flowers across tens of thousands of miles (kilometers). This phenomenon, known as mast seeding, produces enormous numbers of large, heavy, two-winged fruits that spiral down to the forest floor, landing close to the parent tree. Mast fruiting events are thought to reduce the loss of seeds to predators by saturating them with excessive supplies at irregular intervals. When dipterocarps do mast they provide food for many lowland forest animals, including Bearded Pigs (*Sus barbatus*) and Orangutans (genus *Pongo*), both of which are known to migrate on the island of Borneo to locate these masting trees. Dipterocarps are also a major source of tropical hardwoods, valued for their strong yet light, straight, and knot-free timber. All Asian species produce oily, aromatic resins that are harvested; in Cambodia the technique entails cutting holes at the tree's base and periodically burning the area to stimulate resin flow.

Only six dipterocarp species are known to be deciduous; all are found in Vietnam, where they dominate the country's dry deciduous forests. Areas supporting these formations are warm, with temperatures rarely below 68°F (20°C), and are not only drier (less than 60 inches, or 1,500 mm, rainfall annually) but experience longer dry seasons (four to five months) than semievergreen forests. In addition to shedding their leaves annually, deciduous dipterocarp trees differ from their evergreen relatives in their shorter stature and broader, thicker leaves. They are also accustomed to frequent fires, with thick, corklike bark and the ability to resprout from rootstock, traits shared by other plants in this fire-adapted community. The combination of drought stress and fires produce moderately diverse, low, open forests with understories dominated by shrubs, grasses, or bamboos beneath a 16-to-26-foot (5–8 m) closed or semi-closed canopy. Dry deciduous forests grow well on thin, sandy, or rocky soil. They also blend with dry lowland pine woodlands dominated by the sun-loving Tenasserim Pine (*Pinus latteri*).

Within Vietnam, these forest communities are most frequently found in Kon Tum, Gia Lai. and Dak Lak Provinces; they once extended from Dong Nai Province in the south as far north as Nghe An Province. Alternate names are dry dipterocarp forest, dry or deciduous dipterocarp woodland, *idaing* in Myanmar, and *forêt claire à dipterocarpacées* in French botanical literature for the region.

SAVANNA WOODLAND

With heavy human pressures, especially repeated fires, both semi-evergreen forests and the fire-adapted deciduous dipterocarp forest become degraded and transformed into open savanna woodland. These communities retain the most fire-resistant species from the forests interspersed amid a mix of grasses and shrubs. Drier forests on rocky and shallow soils and those experiencing annual rainfalls of less than 40 inches (1,000 mm) with a long dry season (four to six months) are particularly vulnerable.

MONTANE FORESTS

Montane forests are found across the uplands of northern Vietnam, extending southward along the Truong Son Range and terminating in south-central Vietnam's Da Lat Plateau. These regions are distinguished from adjacent lowlands by higher rainfall, shorter dry seasons, and cooler temperatures. Annual rainfall along the Truong Son ranges from 80 to almost 140 inches (2,000–3,500 mm) with a short dry season; northern Vietnam's mountains experience a more seasonal, drier climate of 60–100 inches (1,500–2,500 mm) per year. Mean temperature of the coldest month in both areas falls below 59°F (15°C), and it occasionally frosts in the high montane forests of northwestern Vietnam's Hoang Lien Son Range.

BOX 9

Cycads and Dinosaurs

Cycads, a grouping of three plant families (Cycadaceae, Stangeriaceae, and Zamiaceae) whose members usually have swollen bases and a crown of superficially palmlike leaves, flourished alongside the dinosaurs. They were so numerous in Mesozoic times (230–65 million years ago) that the era is often referred to as the Age of Cycads and Dinosaurs. Cycads are nonflowering plants; they produce seeds in massive cones consisting of numerous overlapping, seed-bearing leaves. In the genus *Cycas,* the cluster of seed-bearing leaves superficially resembles a large blossom. In fact, some botanists have suggested that ancient cycadlike plants may have given rise to the flowering plants that dominate the modern landscape. What remains of a once-dominant group of plants includes more than 300 species classified into eleven genera and three families. Although cycads once represented a dominant and very successful plant line, many of today's relict populations are threatened with extinction.

Cycads are found throughout Vietnam in habitats that include northern montane forests, bare limestone ridges, and open, thorny coastal scrub. A record number of twenty-four species of cycads in Vietnam makes it the richest known country in the Asian region. The two principal threats to cycads in Vietnam are habitat loss and selective removal of plants from the wild. Cycads are popular potted plants in Vietnam, adorning houses, pagodas, temples, gardens, and parks. Many cycads are exhaustively removed from the wild for sale in domestic markets or for export to other Asian regions, including China, Taiwan, and the Republic of Korea. Because of cycads' slow growth and reproduction, however, such large harvests from wild populations are not sustainable. There is, however, a growing interest in cycad conservation within Vietnam under the leadership of Dr. Nguyen Tien Hiep at the Institute of Ecology and Biological Resources in Hanoi. The IUCN classifies fifteen of Vietnam's species as globally threatened and the remaining nine as Near Threatened.

Jack Regalado, Missouri Botanical Garden, Saint Louis

Vietnam's montane forests begin at elevations of 2,300–3,900 feet (700–1,200 m), depending on latitude and local conditions. All are evergreen, and the dominant tree species may be broad-leaved, conifers, or a mixture; reasons for the dominance (or nondominance) of a given type are not well understood. All differ from lowland evergreen forests in being generally shorter, with more twisted and branched growth forms and fewer lianas. A dense and diverse covering of orchids, ferns, and other epiphytes drape branches and trunks, especially in the upper canopy. At elevations up to 4,900–5,900 feet (1,500–1,800 m) a dense canopy rises to 65–115 feet (20–35 m) though individual trees (especially conifers) may grow to heights of 150 feet (45 m) or more, emerging above the canopy layer. In formations where the canopy is undisturbed, the understory is dark and relatively sparse, dominated by herbs. The abrupt transition to montane forest is marked by the sudden dominance of temperate broad-leaved families, including the beeches, laurels (Lauraceae), teas (Theaceae), and walnuts (Juglandaceae). Species-level endemism is high in Vietnam's montane evergreen forests, particularly along the Truong Son Range and among the epiphytic orchids.

Vietnam's montane forests stand out in Asia for their high richness of conifer species. This assemblage of thirty-three species includes Vietnam's six endemic species, all known from montane forests, and a subset of around eight southern Chinese conifers that penetrate into the uplands of northern and central Vietnam. The richest and most interesting conifer communities are found in wet, humid upland forests; drier montane areas are dominated by a few species of widespread pines, including the Benguet Pine (*Pinus kesiya*) and Evelyn's Keteleeria (*Keteleeria evelyniana*).

Five conifer families are present in Vietnam, including the Podocarpaceae, a poorly known tropical group largely restricted to Australia, New Zealand, and Southeast Asia, represented by six species found across Indochina. Although generally not abundant trees, they can be a dominant component of Vietnam's montane forests and an important canopy element, reaching heights of 130 feet (40 m) or more. Stands of the podocarps *Dacrydium elatum, Dacrycarpus imbricatus,* and *Podocarpus neriifolius* are found mixed with broad-leaved species and other large conifers, including the highly valued cypress Fokienia (*Fokienia hodginsii*) and the China Fir (*Cunninghamia lanceolata*). In the southern Truong Son Range, two endemic pines restricted mostly to the Da Lat Plateau, Krempf's Pine (*Pinus krempfii;* box 10) and the Da Lat Pine (*P. dalatensis*), are found in these forests, the latter reaching 130 feet (40 m) in height and 3 feet (1 m) in diameter. A few of Vietnam's conifers, such as the cypress Taiwania (*Taiwania cryptomerioides*) in the Hoang Lien Son Range, represent isolated relics of formerly more widespread species.

Fokienia is one of Indochina's largest and most economically important conifers. It ranges across southeastern China, northern and central Laos, and Vietnam, where it grows above 3,000 feet (900 m). A light-loving species, under conditions of high humidity, short dry seasons, and rich soils it reaches heights of 130–160 feet (40–50 m) and a diameter of 6.5 feet (2 m), and can potentially live 400 to 600 years. Fokienia often develops an elaborate root system, with new roots weaving under and over existing roots to form a dense mat above and below ground. It is exploited for its aromatic timber, which can fetch nearly $400 per cubic yard ($300/m³) near harvest areas such as Sa Pa and more than double that in Hanoi. A light, straight, fine-grained, and durable wood, it is sometimes marketed as Siam wood and used mostly for construction and furniture making. The root wood and treetops are distilled to produce an essential oil used in perfume and some traditional medicines. High demand for these products makes it often one of the first tree species to be selectively removed from forests. The IUCN classifies it as Near Threatened across its range.

Additional changes in forest structure and composition occur at 4,600–

BOX 10

The Enigmatic Pine of Central Vietnam Highlands

In the uplands of the Da Lat Plateau's Khanh Hoa and Lam Dong Provinces, principally around the Bi Doup Massif, grows an enigmatic pine that has puzzled botanists since its description in 1921 by the French botanist Henri Lecomte. Krempf's Pine (*Pinus krempfii*) is most unusual for the flat, leaflike shape of its needles. It is an enormous tree, reaching dimensions of 115–180 feet (35–55 m) in height and 6.5 feet (2 m) in diameter. It emerges above the upper canopy in humid, broad-leaved evergreen forests growing on steep slopes at elevations of 3,950–6,550 feet (1,200–2,000 m). Rather than having a pyramidal shape, this forest giant has a broad crown with many large branches, seemingly more like an oak than a pine. The leaves, unlike any other pine needles, are curving, flattened blades, 1–2.5 inches (3–6 cm) long and 0.1 inch (2–4 mm) wide on adult trees but much larger on juveniles. Mature seed cones are 1.5–2.5 inches (3.5–6 cm) long, egg-shaped, and orange-brown. Cones are produced from April to May and the seeds mature from July to September.

The taxonomic position of Krempf's Pine has been problematic ever since its discovery because of a highly unusual combination of characters. Its broad needles resemble those of the yews (genus *Taxus*), but studies of the cones have placed it in a group of pines (genus *Pinus*). Together with characteristics of the wood, this enigmatic combination has driven some scientists to place Krempf's Pine in its own genus, *Ducampopinus*. Others, however, have recognized it only as a member of the pine family with little affinity to other pine species. Recent genetic analyses may have resolved this controversy, clearly placing Krempf's Pine within the pine genus. The IUCN lists

Krempf's Pine as Vulnerable. It can be seen in the wild only within its exceedingly limited range. Few plants are cultivated in botanical gardens and arboretums outside Vietnam.

Jack Regalado, Missouri Botanical Garden, Saint Louis

6,600 feet (1,400–2,000 m). At these elevations moisture in the form of fog, clouds, heavy dew, and rain is almost constant along ridges and mountain peaks. These are ideal conditions for montane cloud forests. Trees in these distinctive communities are mostly conifers or members of the heath family (Ericaceae), including rhododendrons (genus *Rhododendron*). Rhododendrons are a widespread taxon of more than 100 genera and 4,000 species that includes the blueberry (*Vaccinium*) group along with many ornamental species. The genus *Rhododendron* itself encompasses more than 800 species and ranges from the Himalayas through Southeast Asia. Rhododendron species come in all shapes and sizes, from 4-inch (10 cm) groundcover to trees 36 feet (12 m) tall, and most are evergreen. The flowers are showy, tubular to funnel-shaped, and colored white, yellow, pink, scarlet, purple, or blue.

Stunted, twisted, and often quite old, trees in this formation stand 30 feet (10 m) or less and are often completely covered with lichens, mosses, and epiphytic orchids. The underlying soils are frequently thin, acidic, and rich in organic matters that decompose slowly under such conditions. Above 6,600 feet (2,000 m) along northwestern Vietnam's Hoang Lien Son Range are high montane forests dominated by Himalayan Hemlock (*Tsuga dumosa*) and Delavy's Fir (*Abies delavayi fansipanensis*).

VEGETATION OVER LIMESTONE

Vegetation communities growing over limestone are markedly different in structure and species composition from other forest formations. Limestone, sedimentary rock composed of ancient corals and other marine organisms,

Figure 20. Vietnamese Golden Cypress (*Xanthocyarpis vietnamensis*);
facing page shows details of immature needle leaves (top) and mature
scale leaves with cones (bottom)

is found in Vietnam's north, in patches along the northern and central Truong Son, and in tiny outcroppings in the western Mekong Delta. Uplifted
by tectonic movements and subsequently eroded by weathering, much of
this now-exposed rock has been sculpted into striking karst formations at
times reaching 330–650 feet (100–200 m) in height with razor-sharp peaks

topping sheer slopes of 60–90 degrees. Limestone vegetative formations can be found in the lowlands and uplands, and include evergreen and deciduous components.

Limestone formations harbor a larger number of species per unit area compared with other vegetative communities. Many of these are endemic, some known from only a single hill. There are also often substantial differences between the plant communities growing on adjacent hills. Limestone communities hold such high species richness because of their peculiar, varied, and frequently stressful physical conditions. Limestone hills may be covered with sediments deposited by wind and water, but far more often the soil is derived from the underlying limestone itself. The latter soils are thin, alkaline, and poor in nutrients, with the exception of calcium and magnesium levels high enough to prevent some plants from acquiring other minerals and nutrients. Rainwater drains swiftly from karst surfaces, creating harsh, dry conditions. Where rain is caught in poorly drained pockets, peat can form from undecomposed organic materials, creating small patches of acidic soils on these generally alkaline outcroppings. Shade in the lower stories is variable and incomplete. These factors combine to create highly varied microhabitats where soils range from poor to rich, thin to thick, and dry to wet, and the light regime runs from dark to quite bright. This variety allows limestone areas to support a broad spectrum of plants adapted to different conditions.

Among the unusual and endemic species found on Vietnam's karsts is the Golden Vietnamese Cypress (*Xanthocyparis vietnamensis*). Described from limestone ridges in the Bat Dai Son Mountains of Ha Giang Province in 2002, it is the first new conifer described since Australia's Wollemia Pine (*Wollemia nobilis*) eight years previously. This tree, which grows 50–65 feet (15–20 m) tall, is one of the few cypresses to bear both immature (needle) and mature (scale) leaves on the same branch (see fig. 20). Its closest known relative is the Nootka Cypress (*Chamaecyparis nootkatensis*) of western North America. The disjunct distribution of these two closely related species reflects ancient links between East Asia and North America similar to links reflected in the close evolutionary relationship between China's Dawn Redwood (*Metasequoia glyptostroboides*) and North America's Coast (*Sequoia sempervirens*) and Giant (*Sequoiadendron giganteum*) Sequoias. The Golden Vietnamese Cypress is endangered owing to its natural rarity, small range, and exploitation by local people who value its strong, fragrant wood.

Vegetation over limestone passes through clear transitions of structure and composition with increasing altitude, much as Vietnam's other forests do. On the foothills and lower slopes the forest is closed-canopy and evergreen. Higher up the forest becomes shorter in stature, 50–65 feet (15–20 m), and more open, and trees are frequently gnarled and twisted, bearing small crowns. Here the composition is semi-evergreen, with deciduous and semi-deciduous broad-leaved trees and a rich variety of often-dominant conifers, individuals of which can reach 100 feet (30 m). The open environment allows more light to penetrate through the canopy, promoting a high number and diversity of terrestrial, epiphytic, and lithophytic plants. Most plants growing on limestone are adapted to the low water supply and nutrient levels and the high concentrations of calcium and magnesium. Roots insinuate themselves deep into cracks in the limestone to reach below-ground water sources, and most plants are sclerophytic, bearing small, thick leaves to reduce water loss. Leaves are more costly to produce in these environments, so many plants produce toxic secondary compounds to discourage leaf-eaters, and some supplement their productivity with photosynthetic bark or stems. An alternate name for this forest type is karstic vegetation.

MANGROVE FORESTS

Mangrove communities span the interface between marine and terrestrial environments, growing at the mouths of rivers, in tidal swamps, and along coastlines where they are regularly inundated by salty or brackish water. The collective noun *mangrove* does not designate a taxonomic group of plants but instead indicates one united by shared ecology. Mangroves are a diverse assemblage adapted to growth in saline environments and drawing species from families containing nonmangrove members as well. The largest and most conspicuous group is termed true mangroves, large plants capable of forming extensive saltwater stands dominated by one species. Specific adaptations include aerial roots poking above the water surface to absorb air and mechanisms to either exclude or excrete salt. Mangroves also bear small living seedlings, making them the only truly viviparous plant. The seeds germinate while on the plant, forming a propagule that drops into the water and bobs away to settle, put down roots, and grow. Although they are salt-tolerant, mangroves depend on a regular influx of freshwater and therefore grow best in areas where rainfall exceeds 40 inches (1,000 mm) annually and dry seasons are short.

The species composition and structure of mangrove communities vary with temperature, rainfall, and ocean currents. In general, mangrove species richness is higher and the trees grow taller and larger in warmer climates. Mangroves can reach 35–70 feet (10–20 m) in height and grow to cover large areas. Northern Vietnam's natural mangrove forests are not as diverse as those in the south, and include only a subset of the twenty-nine native true mangrove species found in and around the Mekong Delta. Differences in sea temperature between northern Vietnam, where the annual average is 70°F (21°C), and the south of the country, where it is 81°F (27°C), partly explain the more diverse and extensive formations found along the Mekong Delta and Ca Mau Peninsula. Oceanic and coastal currents also play a role. Southern Vietnam receives propagules dispersing from Malaysian and Indonesian mangrove forests to the south and southwest. Currents flowing northward along Vietnam's coast also bear mangrove propagules with them but turn northeast near south-central Vietnam's Cam Ranh Bay, carrying them instead toward Hainan Island. The north's lower winter temperatures prevent the establishment of some common, temperature-sensitive southern species, a few of whose propagules are eventually carried northward but arrive during the winter months. Mangrove communities are rare along central Vietnam's exposed coastal regions.

In comparison with terrestrial forest formations, mangroves are poor in species, and it is their critical role in coastal ecology, not their inherent diversity, that makes them a focus of conservation efforts. Mangroves are the primary source of energy and nutrients in these environments: they stabilize shorelines, minimizing wave damage; trap sediments that can damage offshore coral reefs; serve as nurseries and feeding grounds for fish; and provide habitat for birds, crabs, and snails. Mangrove forests are threatened by conversion to agriculture and aquaculture (largely shrimp farming) as well as by development for recreation; large stretches were also destroyed during the Vietnam-American War. Current reforestation efforts using single species replace some functions of the ecosystem but fail to re-create mangroves' natural richness.

FRESHWATER SWAMP FOREST

Freshwater swamp forests develop in places where the soil is permanently waterlogged. This can occur along deltas as well as in inland areas that undergo seasonal influxes of freshwater, are poorly drained, or both. Most areas satisfying these conditions are found in southern Vietnam, with the exception of a few small montane thickets on the Da Lat Plateau. Swamp forests are evergreen and support distinctive plant communities well adapted to the wet soil conditions. They can be quite tall, with some elements reaching 70 feet (30m) in height, structurally complex, and multistoried. Forests with continuous flooding or waterlogging (true swamp forests) differ from those with four to six drier months per year. Outside the Mekong Delta, freshwater swamp forests are localized; examples can be found in the Blao region of Lam Dong Province and near Ban Me Thuot in Dac Lak Province.

In the Mekong Delta, Cajeput (*Melaleuca cajuputi*) trees dominate the swamp forests. A member of the myrtle family (Myrtaceae), Cajeput is also referred to as Paperbark. These trees can grow to 50–65 feet (15–20 m) in height, have slender trunks, and continually shed their outer bark in thin, brown sheets. Inland paperbark forests are also called rear mangrove communities; they can intergrade with the more coastal mangrove forests across a transition zone from freshwater to brackish and finally saline environments. Paperbark forest was once the dominant natural vegetation of this region; it has been largely lost to agriculture, fisheries, cutting, and fires.

SEASONALLY INUNDATED SAVANNAS AND GRASSLANDS

In seasonally inundated areas, soils are saturated for at least six months of the year and covered with a diversity of grasses (Poaceae) and sedges (Cyperaceae), broken occasionally by scattered trees (usually Cajeput). On higher ground they can support mosaics of grasslands and forests. Once more extensive, these formations have been converted to agriculture or their hydrology has been altered by dikes and canals. Remaining patches of seasonally inundated grasslands can be found in the U Minh region, the Plain of Reeds, and the Ha Tien Plain, all in the Mekong Delta.

OTHER FRESHWATER HABITATS

A variety of other freshwater habitats can be found in Vietnam, including rivers, lakes, small streams, and caves. Large rivers generally have higher temperatures and high nutrient loads, as well as muddy bottoms, and they face regular floods. For these reasons they are quite productive but not necessarily rich in species, since many species may be able to travel from one basin to another via intervening flooded regions. The upper reaches of rivers or streams host generally small fish and often have low species richness. Limited dispersal between the drainages results in communities with a higher proportion of endemic species.

SECONDARY VEGETATION AND PLANTATIONS

The long history of human impact on Vietnam's environment has left a substantial part of the country covered in secondary vegetation, including degraded forests of all types (the trees often overgrown with vines), bamboo-dominated thickets, scrublands, and grasslands. Weedy species (both native and exotic) dominate plant communities within these secondary habitats, often crowding out naturally occurring ones. Plantations, because they are heavily disturbed monocultures of single species, provide little or no habitat for most of Vietnam's fauna.

MARINE HABITATS

In a country with more than 2,000 miles (3,000 km) of coastline dotted with estuaries, lagoons, marshes, dunes, and beaches, more than 3,000 islands, and an extensive and shallow continental shelf, there is room for much diversity. Vietnam's coastal and marine ecosystems include forested coastal dunes, beaches, intertidal mudflats, sea-grass beds, and coral reefs, all of which harbor important components of Vietnam's biodiversity. Sea-grass habitats, transition zones between coastal mangrove forests and shallow coral reefs, are found along the coast of Khanh Hoa Province and around Con Dao and Phu Quoc Islands in the south. These harbor a minimum of fourteen sea-grass species (including the genera *Halophila, Enhalus,* and

Thalassia), providing forage and shelter for sea turtles (Superfamily Chelonioidea) and sea horses (Subfamily Syngnathidae). Shallow waters and sandy beaches are home to a species of Asian horseshoe crab (*Tachypleus tridentatus*) and provide nesting areas for Hawksbills (*Eretmochelys imbricata*).

Although not visually compelling, intertidal mudflats are an important component of Vietnam's coastal ecosystems. Distributed along the Red River and Mekong Deltas and the Cau Mau Peninsula, mudflats are crucial habitat for many, largely migratory shorebird species. Southern Vietnam's coastal flats and estuaries support several globally threatened species, such as the Chinese Egret (*Egretta eulophotes*) and Spot-billed Pelican (*Pelecanus philippensis*), both listed as Vulnerable by the IUCN, and globally significant numbers of the Near Threatened Asian Dowitcher (*Limnodromus semipalmatus*). The Red River Delta's mudflats include Xuan Thuy Nature Reserve, an important staging and wintering area for migratory birds moving along the East Asian–Australasian Flyway. More than 30,000 shorebirds passed through the reserve in 1996, including Nordmann's Greenshank (*Tringa guttifer*), Saunders's Gull (*Larus saundersi*), and Black-faced Spoonbill (*Platalea minor*), all classified as globally threatened. The 19,000-acre (7,690 ha) reserve was Vietnam's first Ramsar site, an international designation given to rare and unique wetlands important for conserving global biodiversity.

Coral reefs are critical habitat for marine organisms, providing the food and shelter to support these complex communities; the reefs at Con Dao provide habitat for more than 200 species of reef fish. All four of the world's coral reef types grow in Vietnam: fringing, barrier, and platform reefs and atolls. Fringing reefs are shallower and lie closer to shore, occurring in areas where water conditions do not allow coral skeletons to build up. Barrier reefs are more massive accumulations of limestone, whereas atolls usually contain a central lagoon. Platform reefs can be very large and are found in the open ocean. Reef development depends on marine conditions, and there are many examples of the different types intergrading. The reefs of northern Vietnam are all fringing reefs, whereas in the south there are fringing, barrier, and platform reefs.

FIVE

The Fauna of Vietnam

Vietnam's diversity of animals reflects the richness of its vegetation. A wide variety of habitats provides many opportunities for organisms to diversify because it allows them to become differentiated from others by where they live and what they eat. And the more complex environments, such as the multi-storied broad-leaved evergreen forests of the Truong Son Range, provide a greater variety of niches for species to exploit successfully. Not all environments are equally rich in all faunal groups, however, since general characteristics such as sensitivity to temperature (dipterocarp trees, Family Dipterocarpaceae), reliance on aquatic environments for breeding (amphibians, Class Amphibia), and toleration of aridity (some lizards, Suborder Sauria), can limit (or expand) the habitats appropriate for different groups. Once successfully invaded, harsh environments, such as northeastern Vietnam's exposed limestone ridges, often support fewer competitors than milder habitats.

Each new study brings the vertebrate and invertebrate species and communities that inhabit Vietnam into better focus. The limited nature of early surveys, which generally focused on birds and mammals, along with the rush of research starting in the 1990s, means our current knowledge of Vietnam's species richness and distributions is still incomplete. The values for species richness and endemism given here will necessarily change as new species are discovered both in the wild and in museum and herbarium collections and as the ranges of known species are clarified. Caveats are especially relevant to those taxa considered endemic to the country, and this number will likely change as work progresses both in Vietnam and the lesser-surveyed forests and grasslands of neighboring Laos and Cambodia.

Last, research (primarily genetic) into understanding evolutionary connections between species, genera, families, and other higher taxonomic levels will affect some of these relationships as well.

MAMMALS

Mammals are the second best known vertebrate group in Vietnam, following birds. Many species, especially smaller-bodied ones, are nocturnal, either arboreal (living in trees) or fossorial (living underground), and dependent on camouflage and behavior to elude predators. These traits and, until recently, limited interest in surveying for smaller mammals, account for stark differences in knowledge between different mammalian orders.

In spite of wide variation in size, appearance, and behavior, all mammals are linked by shared traits. The most characteristic trait is a universal ability of female mammals to nurse young with milk, buffering infants from the challenges of fluctuating environments and accelerating their growth and development. Another prominent trait they generally share is specialized dentition where the teeth (incisors, canines, premolars, and molars) have developed to fulfill different functions. Reliance on milk may have facilitated the evolution of specialized teeth by freeing them and the jaw from selective pressures to collect and process food immediately after birth. Both traits have contributed to the evolutionary diversification of the group.

More than 270 mammalian species have been recorded in Vietnam to date. These include seven newly described mammals, most of them large species in the deer and primate groups (see appendix 3). Although other new mammals will likely be uncovered in Vietnam, most additions to the country's list have and will continue to come from first sightings of species known from elsewhere. This is especially true for less well known groups such as insectivores (Order Insectivora), bats (Order Chiroptera), and rodents (Order Rodentia). In addition to the recently described Annamite Mouse-eared Bat (*Myotis annamiticus*), eighteen bat species new to the country were recorded between 1997 and 2004. This raises the number of bat species in Vietnam to slightly under 100, or roughly one-third of the mammal species list.

After bats, the most species-rich mammalian orders in Vietnam are the rodents (sixty-four species), carnivores (Order Carnivora; forty species), primates (Order Primates; nineteen species), and the even-toed ungulates, including pigs, deer, and cattle (Order Artiodactyla; eighteen species). Their prominence in Vietnam mirrors the high species richness of these groups across the globe. Less species-rich yet distinctive are two largely tropical Old World orders, pangolins (Order Pholidota; two species) and treeshrews (Order Scandentia; two species). Endemism is unevenly distributed across the mammals, with the vast majority of restricted-range taxa concentrated in the primates (seventeen), followed distantly by the artiodactyls (six) (see appendix 2).

Among the country's most prominent mammalian communities is a group of large herbivores and associated predators that roam the lowland semi-evergreen and deciduous dipterocarp forests in central and south-central Vietnam, including the Asian Elephant (*Elephas maximus*); Lesser One-horned Rhinoceros (*Rhinoceros sondaicus annamiticus*); two wild cattle species, the Gaur (*Bos gaurus*) and Banteng (*B. javanicus*); Eld's Deer (*Cervus eldii*); Sambar (*C. unicolor*); and Southern Serow (*Naemorhedus sumatraensis*). Found alongside these large mammals is a suite of carnivores, including the Tiger (*Panthera tigris*), Leopard (*P. pardus*), Clouded Leopard (*Pardofelis nebulosa*), Golden Jackal (*Canis aureus*), and their pack-hunting relatives, Dhole (*Cuon alpinus*). These mammal populations are now much reduced due to hunting. Three species native to this habitat in Vietnam, the Kouprey (*B. sauveli*), Wild Water Buffalo (*Bubalus arnee*), and Indochinese subspecies of Hog Deer (*Axis porcinus annamiticus*), are most likely extinct.

PANGOLINS (ORDER PHOLIDOTA)

Asia's and Africa's seven species of pangolins share many characteristics with South America's anteaters. Both groups have strong claws, are toothless, and feed exclusively on ants and termites, a resource they exploit using their exceptionally long and sticky tongues. The two pangolin species found in Vietnam inhabit nonoverlapping geographic ranges: the Chinese Pangolin (*M. pentadactyla*) is restricted to the country's north and the Sunda Pangolin (*M. javanica*) to its center and south. The pangolin's most striking external characteristics are the overlapping scales that cover the entire body except the belly and insides of the limbs. Shaped like artichoke leaves, these brown scales are formed from keratin, the structural protein that is also the major component of mammalian horns, hoofs, nails, hair, and wool. In addition to their scales, pangolins are easily recognized by their pointed muzzles, elongated bodies, and long, tapered, prehensile tails capable of grasping branches and limbs. Both Chinese and Sunda Pangolins are 31–35 inches (80–90 cm) long from snout to tail tip, with the males larger than the females. When threatened, pangolins face their attacker with erect scales. If this deterrence fails, they curl up into a tight ball, effectively shielding all vulnerable parts.

Internally, the pangolin's most striking characteristics are extensive adaptations for its highly specialized diet of ants and termites. After locating their prey by scent, Vietnam's pangolins burrow into anthills and termite mounds with sturdy claws and extract their food with strong, probing tongues. Extending up to 10 inches (25 cm) in length and anchored at the pelvis with muscular roots, the tongue is covered with viscous saliva produced by an enlarged salivary gland located in the chest. Pangolins lack chewing muscles as well as teeth, depending instead on the grinding action of tiny pebbles in a thick-walled and muscular stomach to process their prey, much like a chicken's gizzard grinds grain.

Vietnam's pangolins are terrestrial, living in deep burrows and foraging mostly on the ground, though they can easily climb trees. They are thought to bear one (rarely two) offspring cared for exclusively by the mother. Born underground with soft scales, the young emerge after two to four weeks, the mother carrying them about with her on the base of her tail. Little else is known of their behavior or ecology. Pangolins are frequently found in markets; the meat is consumed and the scales used for traditional medicines. The IUCN categorizes both Chinese and Sunda Pangolins as Near Threatened, and they are listed on CITES appendix 2.

INSECTIVORES (ORDER INSECTIVORA)

Along with rodents, insectivores are among the least known of Southeast Asia's mammals. This stems in part from a lack of systematic studies, which has resulted in taxonomic confusion over the number of species and their identification, and in part because many species are elusive and hard to trap. The most comprehensive early review of Indochina's mammals was the work of Wilfred H. Osgood, who in the 1930s examined material collected by the Kelley-Roosevelts and Delacour Expeditions. The renewal of small mammal surveys using improved trapping techniques in the 1990s has uncovered more richness in Vietnam's insectivores than previously thought, both through new species and new distributional records.

The Order Insectivora has historically been treated as a catchall group, a phylogenetic dumping ground for mammals sharing a few primitive traits representative of the ancestral placental mammals that originated 90 million years ago. These included a small and simple brain, relatively non-specialized dentition, and (in most species) intra-abdominal testes and a common chamber and outlet for both reproduction and all metabolic waste called a cloaca. Species such as the treeshrews were once grouped within the Insectivora because they shared these traits and could not easily be placed in any other order. Current genetic analyses of the roots of the mammalian tree and the evolutionary relations of groups within it will likely further subdivide this order.

With roughly 425 species, the Order Insectivora ranks third behind rodents (roughly 2,000) and bats (roughly 1,000) in size. Eighteen insectivore species have been reported from Vietnam. These fall into three groups: gymnures (two species), shrews (twelve species), and moles (four species). Gymnures, strictly Asian relatives of hedgehogs (Family Erinaceidae), are somewhat ratlike in appearance and do not have spines. The head and muzzle are elongated, and the top lip extends over the lower one. Vietnam's two species, the Lesser Gymnure (*Hylomys suillus*) and the Shrew Gymnure (*H. sinensis*), weigh 0.5–3 ounces (15–80 g) and measure 4–6 inches (10–15 cm) along the head and body. Shrews are similar but far smaller, more mouse-like, and generally covered with short gray or brown fur. The Pygmy White-toothed Shrew (*Suncus etruscus*), a widespread species found in Vietnam, is the world's smallest terrestrial mammal, weighing under an ounce (2–2.5 g) with a body length of 1.5–2 inches (3.5–5 cm). Moles are easily identified by their radically modified and powerful forearms, with large, almost circular hands turned permanently outward and tipped with five large claws.

The Insectivora contains the smallest mammalian predators, and the species are extremely diverse in habit and habitat. Most feed primarily on invertebrates, although a number appear to eat most anything organic. They are extremely active, with outsized appetites and high metabolic rates; a few shrew species must eat every few hours or they will die. All shrews likely ingest their feces to gather trace elements and vitamins. Most insectivores are terrestrial and forest-dwelling, though a small subset have adapted to arboreal, burrowing, or semi-aquatic lifestyles. The semi-fossorial, burrowing Mole Shrew (*Anourosorex squamipes*) and the Himalayan Water Shrew (*Chimarrogale himalayica*), which prefers mountain streams, are two specialized insectivores found in Vietnam.

The behavior, ecology, and distribution or conservation status of most insectivores, especially in Asia, are not well known because of their secretive manners. Distributions of tropical shrew species appear to be fairly circumscribed and their population densities low, making them vulnerable to forest conversion. The IUCN lists the Small-toothed Mole (*Euroscaptor parvidens*) as Critically Endangered. It is currently known from only two locations in the world.

TREESHREWS (ORDER SCANDENTIA)

Despite their common name, species in the Order Scandentia are neither shrewlike nor particularly well adapted for a tree-dwelling lifestyle. Instead, they most closely resemble squirrels in behavior, and in appearance are distinguishable by their smaller, fleshier ears, shorter and sparser tail hairs, and lack of facial whiskers. Originally classified within the Order Insectivora, from the 1920s to the 1960s treeshrews were placed within the Order Primates based on shared, primatelike traits, including forward-facing eyes and a relatively large brain. Now in their own order, they are considered a sister group to the flying lemurs (Order Dermoptera) by some scientists and to the Order Lagomorpha (rabbits, hares, and pikas) by others.

All nineteen species of treeshrew are confined to South and Southeast Asia, and their highest richness (ten species) is concentrated on the island of Borneo. Two species live in Vietnam: the semi-terrestrial Northern Tree-shrew (*Tupaia belangeri*) and the largely arboreal Mainland Slender-tailed Treeshrew (*Dendrogale murina*). Although it is diurnal and not especially shy, until recently the Mainland Slender-tailed Treeshrew was known only from a scattering of historical locations in extreme southeastern Thailand and central and southern Vietnam. A summary of survey records from 1998 through 2002 indicates a much wider albeit still highly localized distribution that includes Cambodia, southern Laos, and parts of northern Vietnam. The Northern Treeshrew is found throughout Indochina.

Little is known of treeshrew behavior and ecology, though all are apparently daytime creatures and largely solitary. The most astonishing treeshrew habit is the extremely limited amount of parental care provided by the mother (the only active parent) in three species studied (including the Northern Treeshrew). After giving birth in a separate nest, she visits her one to three offspring once every two days, feeding them milk high in protein and fat. The young emerge after a month and are then on their own. Treeshrews inhabit forests (including somewhat degraded ones) across a wide altitudinal range.

FLYING LEMURS OR COLUGOS
(ORDER DERMOPTERA)

The two species of flying lemurs (also known as colugos) in the Order Dermoptera are neither lemurs nor can they fly. Instead, they are among a number of tree-dwelling organisms (including some frogs, lizards, and snakes, as well as other mammals) with extensive morphological adaptations for gliding. A large, thin membrane extending from the sides of the colugo's neck, out along the limbs, and to the very tips of the fingers, toes, and tail enables them to glide more than 230 feet (70 m) without appreciable loss of height.

The Sunda Colugo (*Cynocephalus variegatus*) is found in Southeast Asia's Sunda Islands and across the southern mainland, including central and southern Vietnam. Individuals weigh 2–4 pounds (1–1.75 kg) with a head and body length of 13–16.5 inches (34–42 cm) and membrane width of 28 inches (70 cm); females are slightly larger than males. The second species, the Philippine Colugo (*C. volans*), which is restricted to that island, is slightly smaller. Colugos are completely arboreal and nocturnal, feeding on leaves, shoots, buds, and flowers (their digestion is adapted for processing leafy vegetation) supplemented occasionally with sap and fruit. The two front pairs of incisors have up to twenty comblike projections (called tooth combs) sprouting from each tooth root. The exact function of tooth combs remains unknown, but they may act as scrapers or strainers when feeding or aid in grooming. Vulnerable to birds of prey while gliding, colugos spend daytime hours in tree hollows or holding fast to trees with their sharp claws, camouflaged against detection by their dappled gray and brown fur. Young are born underdeveloped and are carried on the mother's belly at all times, even during flight; they are weaned at six months. When resting, the mother can fold her gliding membrane into a small pouch near her tail that also holds the infant. The potentially slow growth of colugo populations leaves their conservation status an open question.

BATS (ORDER CHIROPTERA)

Bats are the only mammals capable of using muscle-generated power to fly, in contrast to colugos and others that exploit winds and gravity to glide. The wing bones of bats correspond to a primate's hand and fingers and are highly modified to support a thin membrane of skin, leaving only the thumb free and functional, represented by a small claw at the first wing joint. Perhaps because flight reduces mortality due to predation, bats are remarkably long-lived for their size. There are multiple records of wild bats surviving to at least twenty years, with a few into their thirties. Bats have evolved low rates of reproduction (a single offspring per year for most species), slow development of the young, and extended maternal care. This assemblage of traits more closely resembles those of primates and other larger mammal species than small mammals closer to their size.

Bats are separated into two quite divergent suborders: the Megachiroptera (around 170 species) and the Microchiroptera (around 800 species). Megachiropterans, also known as flying foxes for their canine faces, are restricted to the Old World tropics and subtropics. On average they are larger than microchiropterans, with some species achieving wingspans of 5 feet (1.5 m) and weights over 2 pounds (1 kg). All species have large eyes and good vision, which they combine with their sense of smell to locate fruits, nectar, and flowers.

Microchiropterans as a group are both more ecologically diverse and more widely distributed, occupying all continents except Antarctica. Much smaller than megachiropterans, they range in weight from about 7 ounces (200 g) down to less than a tenth of an ounce (2 g) in the case of Thailand's endemic Hog-nosed or Bumblebee Bat (*Craseonycteris thonglongyai*), which may be the world's smallest mammal. Most species eat invertebrates caught in flight, while others specialize on nectar, pollen, fish and other small vertebrates, and blood. A trait characteristic of microchiropterans, and one closely tied to the group's high species richness, is a universal ability to echolocate using sound to detect objects. Individuals emit rapid pulses of ultrasonic sound and can interpret the resulting echoes and disruptions to detect and classify objects (including prey) and to navigate. The often ornate and bizarre elaborations of the nose are thought to help direct and focus these sounds, and the enlarged ears may be designed to detect echoes. Only one genus of megachiropterans, the rousettes (*Rousettus*), can echolocate, but they employ an independently evolved and far cruder system of tongue clicks used only for navigation in caves.

Of Vietnam's ninety-one recorded bat species, eleven are megachiropterans and the remaining seventy-nine represent five families of microchiropterans. Even given the undersurveyed state of the country's bat community, there is evidence of its richness. A 1997 survey of northern Vietnam's Cuc Phuong National Park determined that it harbors 3.5 percent of global bat species richness, a value that may reach 5 percent with intensive surveying. Bats play important ecological roles in the community as pollinators and seed dispersers. The loss of forests and caves (particularly in karst formations) for roosting is the primary threat to their survival. The IUCN lists four bat species as globally threatened. One of these, the Vietnam Leaf-nosed Bat (*Paracoelops megalotis;* Critically Endangered) has been recorded only once, in 1947. Vietnam's other endemic bat species is the diminutive 0.15 ounce (4 g) Annamite Mouse-eared Bat, described from Quang Binh Province in the northern Truong Son Range in 2001.

PRIMATES (ORDER PRIMATES)

Vietnam hosts three of Asia's five nonhuman primate families: the gibbons (Family Hylobatidae), leaf monkeys and macaques (Family Cercopithecidae), and lorises (Family Lorisidae). Two remaining groups, tarsiers (Family Tarsiidae) and orangutans (Subfamily Ponginae in the Family Hominidae), once occurred on the mainland but migrated southward and are now restricted to the wet evergreen forests of the Sunda Islands. A 2004 review of Asian primates recognizes nineteen species and eight subspecies in Vietnam, but the taxonomy remains very much in flux, especially for the gibbons.

In addition to both high richness and a large number of endemic species, many of Vietnam's primates are globally threatened. A 2002 review of primate conservation status worldwide included four of Vietnam's endemic primates among the top twenty-five threatened with extinction worldwide: Delacour's Leaf Monkey (*Trachypithecus delacouri*), Cat Ba Leaf Monkey (*T. poliocephalus poliocephalus*), Gray-shanked Douc (*Pygathrix nemaeus cinerea*), and Tonkin Snub-nosed Monkey (*Rhinopithecus avunculus*). A fifth, a poorly known complex of Eastern Black Crested Gibbon (*Hylobates [Nomascus] nasutus*) taxa, lives only in northeastern Vietnam and China's Hainan Island. The IUCN lists four Vietnamese primates as Critically Endangered, two as Endangered, and six as Vulnerable. All of the primates are listed on either CITES appendix 1 or appendix 2.

Lorises (Family Lorisidae)

The lorisids of the Old World tropics belong to Suborder Strepsirrhini, the same evolutionary lineage of primates as Madagascar's lemurs (Infraorders Chiromyiformes and Lemuriformes) and Africa's galagos or bush babies (Family Galagonidae). Together with the tarsiers, all three were once referred to collectively as prosimians based on shared primitive characters. Only a single loris genus (*Nycticebus*) is found in Vietnam and, until 1961, all the country's lorises were classified together as a single species (*N. coucang*). Two separate species are now recognized, the Northern Slow Loris (*N. bengalensis*) and the smaller Pygmy Loris (*N. pygmaeus*); a third, as yet unidentified taxon is also believed to exist. The Northern Slow Loris is widely distributed from northeastern India through Thailand's southern peninsula. The Pygmy Loris is far more restricted, found only in Indochina and southernmost China.

Lorises have short, thick, woolly fur, rounded heads with large eyes and small ears, and an extremely abbreviated tail, if present at all. The Northern Slow Loris weighs 2.5 pounds (1.2 kg), and its coat is buff-orange tipped with gray. The Pygmy Loris is notably smaller at around 1 pound (500 g), and its fur has a reddish rather than orange tinge. Both have dark circles around the eyes, and in the Pygmy Loris a broad, medium dark brown stripe runs up the back, forking at the forehead and running down toward the eyes. Both species are nocturnal and arboreal, creeping slowly along branches and tree trunks in search of invertebrates (including unpalatable and poisonous species), a diet they supplement with fruit. Pygmy Lorises also consume gum, gouging trees with their comblike lower teeth, and it is quite possible that other loris species also feed on this. Although they are primarily solitary, lorises may live in stable social groups whose members are dispersed. During the day, lorises sleep in tree forks and branch tangles. The female generally bears a single young that is weaned at six to nine months. Lorises' primary threat is exploitation, mainly for use in traditional medicine but also as household pets. The IUCN classifies the Pygmy Loris as Vulnerable.

Old World Cheek-pouched Monkeys
(Family Cercopithicedae: Subfamily Cercopithecinae)

Old World monkeys in the Subfamily Cercopithecinae behave much as monkeys are expected to, being generally loud, gregarious, curious, and brash. Of the group's eleven genera, only the macaques (*Macaca*) made it to Asia. Five species and one subspecies are found in Vietnam: the Bear Macaque (*M. arctoides*), Assamese Macaque (*M. assamensis*), Long-tailed

Macaque (*M. fascicularis fascicularis*) and a subspecies restricted to the Con Dao archipelago (*M. f. condorensis*), Northern Pig-tailed Macaque (*M. leonina*), and Rhesus Macaque (*M. mulatta*). They are the easiest to see of all primates in Vietnam and probably the most common in the wild. Nevertheless, few field studies of macaques have been carried out in the country.

Vietnam's macaques are stout-bodied, medium-sized monkeys with strong limbs, naked faces, and an elongated snout with powerful jaws. Coat color varies from yellowish gray through olive and chestnut to dark brown. The most noticeable differences between species are in tail length and body size. Tails range from the Bear's abbreviated 0.5–4 inches (1–10 cm) up to the Long-tailed's 26 inches (66 cm), equal to their body length. Vietnam's macaques vary in body size, females ranging from 8 to 18.5 pounds (3.6–8.4 kg) and males 12 to 27 pounds (5.4–12.2 kg). Most macaques live in relatively large groups that are organized around matrilines of related females. Males emigrate from their natal troop as they pass out of adolescence and spend the rest of their lives associating with a sequence of other groups and on their own. Within this structure, competition among males for matings is high, fostering larger size and sharper teeth.

Macaques primarily consume fruit but are highly opportunistic and adaptable, and their eclectic diets encompass virtually anything edible. This flexibility allows them to survive in modified environments, and they readily incorporate human foods and garbage into their diets. The Rhesus Macaque, the most widely distributed nonhuman primate, has been called a weedy species because it can live near human habitations (if not hunted) and tolerate highly disturbed habitats, often raiding crops for food. Four of Vietnam's macaques form two species pairs whose distributions overlap geographically between 14° and 17° N; the Assamese and Rhesus Macaques range north of this zone and the Pig-tailed and Long-tailed Macaques to the south. Coexistence may be facilitated by ecological segregation: the first member of each pair is restricted to broadleaf evergreen forests, whereas the second member inhabits a wide variety of other forested habitats, including mangroves and peat swamp forests. The fifth, the Bear Macaque, is found in forested areas throughout the country. Macaques are hunted as crop pests, for use in traditional medicines, and kept as pets when young.

The IUCN lists the Bear, Assamese, and Pig-tailed Macaques as Vulnerable.

Old World Leaf-eating Monkeys
(Family Cercopithicedae: Subfamily Colobinae)

The leaf-eating branch of Old World monkeys, the colobines, reaches its highest species richness in Asia, where roughly 80 percent of the species can be found. Eight species and four subspecies in three different genera, representing 44 percent of the country's primate taxa, can be found from the Sino-Vietnamese border south to the Mekong Delta. The taxonomy of most remains in flux, and their distributions (current and historic) are poorly known. Leaf-eating monkeys are perhaps Vietnam's most threatened primate group, with the IUCN listing one as Vulnerable, two as Endangered, and three as Critically Endangered.

Colobines feed predominantly on leaves, supplemented with some fruit and seeds; adaptations to an abundant diet of low nutritional quality are reflected in their physiology, ecology, and behavior. To accommodate and process the considerable quantities of foliage eaten, these primates have large stomachs partitioned into a number of sacks. Along with specialized salivary glands, stomach compartmentalization allows colobines to break down toxic leaf compounds and to extract nutrients via gut-dwelling microorganisms able to ferment indigestible cellulose, the major structural component of plant cell walls. In this respect, leaf-eating monkeys resemble deer, cattle, and antelopes (Suborder Ruminantia), which also exploit foregut fermentation to process large quantities of bulky, low-nutrient vegetation. Unlike ruminants, colobines also have a large, pouched colon or hindgut where fermentation takes place as well.

Leaf-eating monkeys are long-tailed, arboreal, and generally slender. Some assume a paunchy appearance because of their large stomachs, a character noticeable in Vietnam's doucs (genus *Pygathrix*). Species are usually identified by coat color and the varied whorlings, crests, and fringes of hair adorning their heads. The infant's coat often contrasts with that of adults, sometimes quite strikingly, as in the bright orange offspring of the largely black Delacour's Leaf Monkey. Leaf-monkey troops are organized around groupings of a male with one or two females and juvenile offspring, from which multimale, multifemale troops of widely varying sizes are formed. Snub-nosed leaf monkey species have been seen in bands of hundreds; such large groupings are facilitated by abundant food sources and specialized physiology. Vietnam's three doucs, eight leaf monkeys, and the single snub-nosed monkey species differ widely in appearance, body size, potential troop size, distribution, and habitat. Almost all are threatened by exploitation for meat, medicine, and use as pets and are now represented by fragmented and drastically reduced populations.

Gibbons (Family Hylobatidae)

The gibbons are the most diverse and, except for modern humans (*Homo sapiens*), the most widespread and abundant members of the Superfamily Hominioidea, a grouping that also includes the orangutans, chimpanzees (genus *Pan*), gorillas (genus *Gorilla*), and humans (genus *Homo*). They are largely creatures of Old World tropical wet evergreen forests, ranging from extreme eastern India through southern China and mainland Southeast Asia to the islands of Sumatra, Java, and Borneo. Evolutionary relationships among gibbons remain one of the most challenging taxonomic problems among Southeast Asia's larger land mammals. All of Vietnam's species are crested gibbons and belong to the subgenus *Nomascus* within the genus *Hylobates*.

Gibbons are slender and graceful, with long and powerful arms and no tail. Although they are almost entirely arboreal, gibbons are the most efficient of all apes at walking upright when moving along wide tree branches or, infrequently, the forest floor. Large, dark inquisitive eyes are set in bare black facial skin, and their heads are topped by an upright brush of crown hair that on males forms a crest, hence the English common name. Though the sexes differ little in size, averaging 12.5 pounds (5.7 kg) across the group, all crested gibbon taxa have characteristic differences in coat coloration identifying males, females, infants, and juveniles. Males are generally black, with cheek pouches ranging from white in the White-cheeked Crested Gibbon (*H. [N.] leucogenys;* fig. 21) to reddish yellow in the Yellow-cheeked

Figure 21. White-cheeked Crested Gibbon (*Nomascus leucogenys*)
male (left) and female with infant (right)

Crested Gibbon (*H. [N.] gabriellae*) to black in the Black-cheeked Crested
Gibbon (*H. [N.] concolor*). Females are light-colored, pale yellow through
buffy brown, with black caps. Infants are born with light-colored coats, resembling their mother but lacking her darker crown coloration. Their coats
change to all black during the first or second year. Females go through a

subsequent color change at sexual maturity, assuming the full adult female coat shortly before they leave the family troop.

Gibbons are distinguished from other primates by a combination of three traits: their method of locomotion, a monogamous social structure, and elaborate bouts of singing. Gibbons travel through forested habitats by brachiating, swinging and pivoting forward from hand to hand while suspended from branches and tree limbs, and they generally remain suspended when stopped. A specialized anatomy, including long, hooked fingers, flexible shoulder joints, and upright posture, enables these behaviors. Brachiation and upright suspension are likely adaptations to arboreal habitats and a diet dominated by ripe fruit and supplemented with shoots and leaves. Gibbons are monogamous, their groups consisting of the adult pair accompanied by one to three offspring born at three-year intervals and remaining with the family group until around eight years of age. The pair is territorial, guarding a home range of 100–1,240 acres (40–500 ha) that contains trees capable of providing a year-round food supply.

All gibbon species sing, producing loud, elaborate vocalizations varying between both species and sexes. Crested gibbon pairs usually sing in unison, producing duets from before dawn through midmorning; the frequency of these singing bouts ranges from twice per day to once every five days, depending on season, weather, and density of gibbons. The female produces the great call, an ascending, somewhat eerie, yet high-spirited whistling call that the male accompanies with more staccato vocalizations, usually adding a coda after the female finishes. Heard for more than a mile (several kilometers), these calls advertise the pair's presence, curtailing trespassing and reducing confrontations with other gibbon groups. Unmated males may perform solo song bouts, while juvenile vocalizations, which young gibbons add to the group's as they mature, resemble the female's great call.

Vietnam's four species and two subspecies of crested gibbon live in largely nonoverlapping ranges from the country's north to the southern Truong Son Range. They prefer primary or mature secondary evergreen forests with largely closed canopies; the southernmost species, the Yellow-cheeked Crested Gibbon, also occupies semi-evergreen communities. The major threat is hunting by humans for food and medicine or as trophies or pets. They are relatively susceptible to habitat degradation because of their reliance on relatively intact forests. The IUCN lists most as globally threatened, including the Critically Endangered Eastern Black Crested Gibbon (*H. [N.]* sp. cf. *nasutus nasutus*), an endemic northern Vietnamese species with only one known extant population.

CARNIVORES (ORDER CARNIVORA)

Carnivores have fascinated humans for millennia with their speed, power, stealth, efficiency, intelligence, and complex and flexible behavior. Translated from its Latin roots, the word *carnivore* means flesh (*carni-*) devouring (*-vorous*). Although most carnivores consume some vegetation and a few, like the bamboo-eating Red Panda (*Ailurus fulgens*) of the Himalayas, have abandoned meat entirely, all members of the Order Carnivora share a common ancestor that consumed flesh. This evolutionary lineage is preserved in teeth modified for shearing and slicing and in fused wrist bones and greatly reduced collarbones, possibly to facilitate running and flexibility. Short pregnancies preserve agility and produce young that are both small and blind. Offspring remain with the mother, parents, or social group for extended periods, learning to hunt and survive.

Meat, although more nutritious and easier to digest than plant matter, is both less abundant and harder to acquire. Carnivores are always less numerous than their prey, and their numbers and densities are limited largely by the population sizes of their potential food. This imbalance between predator and prey places carnivores in competition with members of their own species as well as with other carnivores sharing the same habitat. This is likely why most carnivores are territorial and, where species coexist, they usually differ in body size, preferred prey, capture technique, and activity pattern. Carnivores have an acute sense of smell, which is used to find prey and to communicate with others through urine, feces, and (in most species) scent glands.

All twelve modern carnivore families evolved during the Eocene and Oligocene (54–26 million years ago). Around 50 million years ago, a major split occurred, separating the order into a catlike branch that now holds the cats, civets, hyenas, and mongooses and a more diverse doglike branch consisting of the dogs, bears, weasels, and raccoons. The second branch also contains the marine-adapted walruses and seals (Suborder Pinnipedia), which separated from the terrestrial carnivores (Suborder Fissipedia) around 25 million years ago.

Thirty-nine species in six of these families have been recorded in Vietnam. Next to primates, carnivores are among Vietnam's most threatened orders, with the IUCN classifying six species as globally threatened. Because of their predatory nature and the unique ability of some members of the order to kill an unarmed human, carnivores have often come into conflict with people. Because of their inherent potency they are also vulnerable to exploitation for consumption and use in traditional medicines.

Dogs (Family Canidae)

The Family Canidae is the oldest modern lineage of carnivores and the most widespread, with members found on almost every continent. Medium-sized carnivores with long legs, lanky and agile bodies, and bushy tails, canids are highly carnivorous animals adapted for chasing prey across grasslands and other open landscapes. Though they bear large canines and effective shearing teeth, canid dentition is relatively uniform and unspecialized, providing a good, general weapon but not a killing bite. Instead, canids attack the neck or the nose of their prey, immobilizing the animal and dragging it down before killing it.

Apart from a relatively unvaried morphology, the most characteristic canid trait is an opportunistic, versatile, and highly adaptive behavior. This flexibility is frequently revealed in often-complex social organizations. At the basis of canid societies is a strong trend toward monogamous behavior. When the advantages of living with additional individuals outweigh possible costs (such as increased competition for food and mates or greater exposure to parasites), larger groups can form around a breeding nucleus. This can lead to cooperative behavior in both hunting and rearing young, accompanied by strong dominance hierarchies, complex social communication through facial expression, body language, sound, and scent, delayed dispersal of juveniles from the group, and suppression of reproduction by other pack adults. One of Vietnam's four canids, the Dhole, lives in groups and hunts cooperatively. Both the Golden Jackal and Red Fox (*Vulpes vulpes*) are monogamous but where jackal pairs may hunt larger prey together, red foxes forage alone. The final species, the Raccoon Dog (*Nyctereutes procyonoides*), is among the oldest canids, diverging from its relatives some 8 to 12 million years ago. Resembling a Raccoon (genus *Procyon*) somewhat in appearance, dentition, and diet, it is the only canid known to hibernate. In Vietnam, both the Raccoon Dog and the Red Fox are restricted to the north, where they are at the southern limit of their respective ranges. The IUCN lists the Dhole as Endangered.

Bears (Family Ursidae)

Bears are the largest carnivores alive today, easily identified by their bulky torsos, short and thick legs, strong claws, diminutive tails, and large heads with small eyes and rounded ears. Over evolutionary time, this lineage of eight species has traded speed for strength and bulk and, with the exception of the Polar Bear (*Ursus maritimus*), a flesh-dominated diet for a more wide-ranging and omnivorous one. Larger body size protected bears from predation and allowed them to consume more, attack larger prey, and build up fat reserves to survive food shortages and cold weather. They lack the order's typical shearing teeth, but their skulls feature strong jaw muscles and enlarged molars for grinding food.

Two bear species differing in size, preferred habitat, and feeding ecology are found throughout Vietnam. The larger Asian Black Bear (*U. thibetanus*) consumes primarily vegetation while the smaller Sun Bear (*U. malayanus*) mixes plant matter with insects. Both species are listed in CITES appendix 1.

Weasels (Family Mustelidae)

The Mustelidae is the largest of the carnivore families, with sixty-five recognized species as of 2003. Its members inhabit a wide variety of habitats, and some have diverged extensively from the basic long-bodied, short-legged body plan. Most mustelids are highly carnivorous with prominent canines and sharp shearing teeth, and their diets can include small burrowing mammals, birds, lizards, frogs, fish, eggs, and invertebrates. They are relentless and tenacious predators, and many species regularly take prey larger than themselves. Mustelids are generally solitary and all (excepting the Sea Otter, *Enhydra lutris*) have anal glands that secrete strong, acrid, musky secretions used in combination with urine and feces to communicate presence, status, and intentions.

Thirteen mustelids representing three major groups have been recorded in Vietnam: weasels and martens (Subfamily Mustelinae), badgers (Subfamily Melinae), and otters (Subfamily Lutrinae). Vietnam's four weasels and single marten are restricted to the country's north and include the Siberian Weasel (*Mustela sibirica*), closely related to the Indonesian Mountain Weasel (*M. lutreolina*), which lives in the highlands of Sumatra and Java. The two evolutionary lineages were likely separated by climate and sea level fluctuations during the Pleistocene (1.8–0.01 million years ago) or earlier. The IUCN lists a second species, the Back-striped Weasel (*M. trigidorsa*) as Vulnerable. This poorly known weasel is found in a small region stretching from Bhutan to China's Yunnan Province and south to Thailand, Laos, and Vietnam.

Four badgers, a group originating in Asia's forests, are found in Vietnam, including the Large-toothed (*Melogale personata*) and Small-toothed (*M. moschata*) Ferret Badgers. With their longer, thinner bodies and striking facial masks, ferret badgers are actually more closely related to weasels and otters than to the other terrestrial, burrowing badgers.

Vietnam's otters are its most threatened mustelids. Evidence from Thailand suggests that the Smooth-coated (*Lutrogale perspicillata*), Eurasian (*Lutra lutra*), and Oriental Small-clawed (*Aonyx cinerea*) species are able to coexist by eating different aquatic foods, specializing on large fish, small fish, and freshwater crabs, respectively. The Hairy-nosed Otter (*Lutra sumatrana*), rediscovered in Vietnam in 2000, does not co-occur with the Eurasian Otter. Otters locate their underwater prey with long, stiff whiskers on their nose, snout, and elbows and, in the case of the Small-clawed, by touch. Because they are dominant wetland predators, they are sensitive to pollution and can accumulate toxic compounds in their tissues. They are also trapped for their pelts and medicinal uses. The IUCN considers the Smooth-coated Otter Vulnerable and the Oriental Small-clawed and Eurasian Otters Near Threatened; there is insufficient information to assess the conservation status of the Hairy-nosed Otter.

Civets (Family Viverridae)

The Family Viverridae contains seventeen species of civets, linsangs, and genets distributed across Asia, Africa, and Europe's Iberian Peninsula, ten of which are found in Vietnam. Often called civet cats in deference to their slender, agile builds and stealthy, secretive behavior, these small to medium-sized carnivores have elongated muzzles, resembling more a fox's than a cat's. Viverrids as a group may be the most evolutionarily conservative of all the carnivores, retaining many characteristics of the lineage's putative small, semi-arboreal, and nocturnal precursor. Unlike most other groups, they have no physical adaptations for coursing after prey and instead use ambush tactics, and their teeth show little specialization. Viverrids in general are solitary and nocturnal with buff to dark brown coats marked with darker bands and spots, retractile or semi-retractile claws for climbing, and strong-smelling perineal glands (located between anus and genitalia) for scent marking.

Of Vietnam's civets, only Owston's Civet (*Chrotogale owstoni*) is considered globally threatened by the IUCN, which lists it as Vulnerable. Lowe's Otter Civet (*Cynogale lowei*), an unusual, semi-aquatic species known from a single skin collected in northern Vietnam's Bac Kan Province in 1926, is not assessed but must be considered threatened if it is still extant. The Tay Nguyen Civet (*Viverra tainguensis*), first described in 1997 from the southern Truong Son, may not be a valid species and instead a representative (possibly a subspecies) of the Large Indian Civet (*V. zibetha*).

Cats (Family Felidae)

The cats are the most strictly carnivorous members of their order, eating little if any vegetation. This hypercarnivory has shaped and constrained the morphology, behavior, and social structure of the group. All felids are highly efficient stalk-and-ambush predators. Short, strong jaws coupled with enlarged canines enable cats to deliver killing bites to the neck, severing the spinal column, or to grip the throats of larger prey, suffocating them. Powerful forearms and retractile claws enable cats to grasp their prey before the kill, holding it or dragging it down. Cats also have large, forward-facing eyes set high in the skull and excellent binocular and peripheral vision, allowing them to detect movement and judge distances before striking. Feline fur is usually tawny, and in the many forest-dwelling species it is mottled with spots or stripes, camouflaging them in light-dappled environments. Modern cats have deviated little from the group's ancestral body plan; species differ largely in size and coat coloration.

Eight of Asia's ten felids are found in Vietnam. Historically most ranged widely across the country except for the Marbled Cat (*Pardofelis marmorata*), which is apparently restricted to the north. The two smallest species, the Marbled Cat and the Leopard Cat (*Prionailurus bengalensis*), weigh between 5.5 and 7.5 pounds (2.5–3.5 kg) and are roughly the size of the domesticated cat (*Felis sylvestris catus*). The Marbled Cat lives in forests and eats a variety of small vertebrates and insects; the poorly known Leopard Cat is more arboreal, feeding on birds supplemented by small mammals and possibly frogs and lizards. The largest cat in Vietnam is the northern Indochinese Tiger (*P. t. corbetti*); males can weigh 330–430 pounds (150–195 kg) and measure 8.5–9.5 feet (2.55–2.85 m) from head to tail base. Deer (Family Cervidae) and wild pigs (Family Suidae) form the bulk of the tiger's diet, though they may take prey as small as a frog and as large as 2,200-pound (1,000 kg) wild cattle (genus *Bos*). Vietnam is also home to an Indochinese subspecies of Leopard (*P. p. delacouri*) and to the beautiful yet secretive Clouded Leopard. The coat of the Clouded Leopard is distinguished by darker cloudlike blotches partially outlined by black against a lighter dark gray to yellowish brown background. This cat is an excellent climber, spending much of its time in trees, and it feeds on primates, birds, and deer.

Regardless of body size, Vietnam's cats are all threatened by exploitation for their coats and use in traditional medical preparations. Tigers are also threatened by the depletion of their prey base. They are thought to require at minimum 11–13 pounds (5–6 kg) of meat per day. In areas where hunting has reduced medium-sized prey populations, tigers are found at very low densities, if they persist at all. The IUCN lists four of Vietnam's cats as Vulnerable: Clouded Leopard, Marbled Cat, Asian Golden Cat (*Cato-*

puma temminckii), and Fishing Cat (*Prionailurus viverrinus*); the Tiger is considered Endangered. The populations of all five species are declining.

WHALES, DOLPHINS, AND PÓRPOISES
(ORDER CETACEA)

Of all the mammals adapted to a life led in water, members of the Order Cetacea are the most specialized for an aquatic existence with their streamlined forms, lack of fur, and complete independence from land. Their previously elusive evolutionary origins began to be clarified in the mid-1990s when genetic analyses suggested their closest relatives to be the hippopotamuses, from which they diverged some 55 million years ago. This places the cetaceans solidly within a group that contains (among others) pigs, camels, deer, antelope, and cattle (Order Artiodactyla).

Cetaceans are divided into two groups: toothed whales (Suborder Odontoceti), including the dolphins and porpoises, and baleen whales (Suborder Mysticeti). Toothed whales, with their elongated heads and beaklike skulls, feed on squid, fish, and other aquatic mammals (including other cetaceans). The forehead curves gently upward in an enlarged "melon" shape that focuses the ultrasonic clicks toothed whales produce in their nasal passages to locate their prey. In contrast, instead of teeth, baleen whales have large, continuously growing hornlike plates of baleen (also called whalebone) hanging from the upper jaws. Formed primarily from the protein keratin, the rows of triangular baleen plates form an intricate filtration system to strain plankton, other invertebrates, and small fish from ocean waters.

Of the eighty-six currently recognized cetacean species, approximately twenty inhabit Vietnam's waters. They vary in size from the 65–150-pound (30–70 kg) Finless Porpoise (*Neophocaena phocaenoides*) to the Blue Whale (*Balaenoptera musculus*), which, at up to 165 tons, is the largest animal ever to exist on earth. Cetaceans are notoriously hard to census, largely because they spend most of their lives below the water's surface and far from land. Information on Vietnam's whale, dolphin, and porpoise species richness stems in part from beached individuals and bones collected and stored in temples for veneration. The few systematic surveys undertaken have recorded remarkably few cetacean sightings. Cetacean densities may be naturally low along Vietnam's coast because ecological conditions, such as naturally low food availability or water temperature, may limit population sizes. Humans likely also play a role in producing these low numbers through cetacean entanglement in in-shore fishing nets; the effects of military operations, oil exploration, and fishing with explosives on their hearing; and prey declines due to overfishing.

DUGONGS AND MANATEES (ORDER SIRENIA)

The four surviving sirenians represent the third extant mammal lineage to have abandoned land for an aquatic existence. Slow moving, large (up to 3,500 pounds; 1,600 kg) and ungainly in appearance, sirenians bear only fore flippers and a tail on their streamlined bodies. These sea creatures first appeared some 55 million years ago during the relatively warm Eocene epoch, and their closest living evolutionary relatives are the elephants (Order Proboscidae). Unlike cetaceans and the aquatic carnivores, sirenians feed entirely on plants, grazing on floating plants and sea grasses in rivers, estuaries, and shallow coastal environments. To process large quantities of this low-nutrient food, sirenians have enormous digestive tracts, the intestines reaching over 150 feet (45 m) in manatees. Restricted to tropical waters, they require little energy to maintain body temperature, though they do build up blubber reserves to survive periods of food shortage.

The Dugong (*Dugong dugon*) is Vietnam's only sirenian, inhabiting shallow coastal waters off Con Dao and Phu Quoc Islands. Like the other species, it is classified as Vulnerable by the IUCN and is threatened primarily by hunting.

ELEPHANTS (ORDER PROBOSCIDEA)

Vietnam's Asian Elephant is one of three species in the Order Proboscidea to be found on Earth today. Along with Africa's Savanna (*Loxodonta africana*) and Forest (*L. cyclotis*) Elephants, they are remnants of a once highly diverse group (more than 160 species uncovered to date) that originated in

Africa about 60 million years ago and spread to all continents except Australia and Antarctica. Proboscids are united by their large body size, elongated limbs with flattened feet, and modifications of the head frequently tied to their diet.

Modern elephants are grazers; each day, adults can consume 275–500 pounds (125–225 kg) of fresh grasses, nonwoody plants, bamboos, and the leaves and twigs of shrubs, vines, and trees, along with fruit, bark, roots, and pith. They rely on their trunks to forage, using them to pluck single plants from the ground or pull down limbs and whole trees. Male Asian Elephants weigh 11,900 pounds (5,400 kg) and females 6,000 pounds (2,700 kg), 15 to 25 percent of which is accounted for by the skull. A single, high-crowned, ridged molar occupies the entire back half of the jaw. This tooth migrates forward as it becomes worn down along the front, to be replaced by a new molar emerging from the rear. These replacement teeth are limited in number; elephants have six per jaw segment. Tusks arise from a pair of highly modified upper incisors, not canines, as is sometimes assumed.

Asian Elephants once spanned modern-day Iraq to China, and as recently as 1980 between 1,500 and 2,000 elephants ranged across Vietnam. These numbers have plummeted, and as of 2002, only fifty-nine to eighty-one animals apparently survive in the wild. The decline is due to a variety of causes, all rooted in human activity: poaching for ivory, loss and fragmentation of habitat due to agricultural expansion (including crop trees planted in forests), and capture for domestication. Reduced habitat has also increased Asian Elephants' contact—and conflict—with human populations, with negative consequences for both. Elephants can destroy crops and dwellings and, rarely, kill people. This has led to the killing of elephants and efforts at translocation that are not always successful, sometimes ending in death. Vietnam's known elephants are concentrated in Yok Don and Cat Tien National Parks in south-central Vietnam and scattered along the country's western border with Laos and Cambodia; it is not clear how many of these populations are viable. As of 2000, roughly 150 domesticated elephants survived, largely in Dak Lak Province. The IUCN considers the Asian Elephant as Endangered. The species will likely soon become extinct in Vietnam.

ODD-TOED (ORDER PERISSODACTYLA) AND EVEN-TOED (ORDER ARTIODACTYLA) UNGULATES

Although they are neither as charismatic as primates nor as beguiling as carnivores, Vietnam's ungulates share one trait with these groups: their status as some of the country's most threatened mammals. Of the roughly twenty ungulate species known to have lived in Vietnam, three are extinct in the country and two others are quite likely extirpated. Of the remaining, only five are well-enough known to be considered globally nonthreatened: Eurasian Wild Pig (*Sus scrofa*), Lesser (*Tragulus kanchil*) and Greater (*T. napu*) Oriental Chevrotains, Sambar, and Red Muntjac (*Muntiacus muntjak*). Ungulates also dominate Vietnam's newly recognized mammalian fauna, with four species newly described and two more rediscovered since 1992. Not all new ungulates have survived closer inspection. The Khting Vor (*Pseudonovibos spiralis*), described in 1994 based only on horn specimens, is in truth a domestic cow whose horns were modified (box 11).

All ungulates are largish animals—none weigh under 2 pounds (1 kg) —and, with the exception of pigs (Family Suidae), are exclusively plant eaters. They are well equipped for rapid movement, bearing hooves instead of claws and fewer toes than their ancestral five-digit foot. The odd-toed ungulates (Order Perissodactyla), such as horses (Family Equidae) and rhinoceroses (Family Rhinocerotidae), retain one or three toes, while the even-toed ungulates (Order Artiodactyla), including pigs, deer (Family Cervidae), and cattle (Family Bovidae), bear their weight on two or four toes. Most species are capable of both speed and endurance.

Most artiodactyls are also distinguished from their odd-toed relatives by two additional traits: rumination and horns. To cope with the otherwise indigestible cellulose that forms the bulk of their plant diet, ancestral artiodactyls evolved a complex digestive process. Food is initially fermented in the stomach's first chamber, where bacteria breakdown the cellulose, then regurgitated and rechewed before being reingested and moved through the rest of the intestines. Nonruminant artiodactyls and all perissodactyls rely on hindgut fermentation, a less efficient process occurring between the small and large intestines. Most ruminants also bear horns, bony growths that are often complexly branched. Horns may be permanent or shed an-

BOX 11

Khting Vor

In 1994 a new species of artiodactyl was described from the open deciduous dipterocarp and semi-evergreen forests of southern Indochina. This description was based solely on horns purchased at markets in south-central Vietnam and adjacent areas of eastern Cambodia that were thought to have been collected in the early twentieth century. Given the scientific name *Pseudonovibos spiralis,* the animal was believed to be a large artiodactyl, similar to the sympatric Gaur (*Bos gaurus*) and Kouprey (*B. sauveli*) but carrying a lyre-shaped set of horns that are both annulated (ringed) and twisted at the tips, a combination unique among mammals. These trophies were thought to represent the remains of an elusive animal known in Khmer as the Khting Vor, a name derived from the words *khting* (gaur) and *vor* (liana or creeping vine), describing the shape of the horns. Regional oral traditions depict the Khting Vor as a snake-eating wild ox whose horns can be used as talismans to guard individuals and homes against snakes or ground into a powder for treating venomous snakebites.

Independent analyses of DNA recovered from the horns have placed the species at three different phylogenetic positions within the Family Bovidea: in the Tribes Caprini (goats, sheep), Bovini (oxen, bison, buffalo), and closely related to the common domesticated cattle, *Bos taurus.* Considerable debate broke out over whether the Khting Vor ever existed or if these specimens were produced by local craftsmen in the 1920s for ritual or medicinal purposes. The limited number of horns collected (sixty to seventy), contamination problems associated with ancient DNA recovery, and the extremely limited locality data associated with these specimens all made the Khting Vor's

legitimacy extremely difficult to resolve. In addition to the molecular work showing that the frontlets analyzed were derived
from common cattle, sophisticated examination of the horns
themselves indicate that their unique ringing patterns and tor-
sion were created by carving, heating, and twisting.

nually, and they may be born by males alone or by both sexes. Male chevrotains (genus *Tragulus*), musk deer (genus *Moschus*), and muntjacs (genus
Muntiacus), bearing quite small antlers or none at all, lack impressive weap-
onry with which to compete for (and possibly attract) females. Instead, they
are equipped with continuously growing upper canines that project over
the lower lip; in musk deer these teeth can reach 2–3 inches (7–10 cm).

Vietnam's ungulates are threatened by hunting and habitat loss. Loss
of habitat has been particularly hard on two species that prefer low-lying
grasslands and marshy country, Eld's Deer and the Hog Deer. The IUCN
classifies Eld's Deer as Vulnerable, and the Indochinese subspecies of Hog
Deer is on the brink of extinction worldwide; both are likely extinct in
Vietnam. The species known to be extinct in the wild in Vietnam are the
Critically Endangered Kouprey, Wild Water Buffalo, and the Vietnamese
Sika Deer (*Cervus nippon pseudaxis*), although 8,000–10,000 Sika Deer are
held in farms in Nghe An and Ha Tinh Provinces to harvest their antler
velvet for sale as medicine. Also globally threatened are Vietnam's single
perissodactyl, the Lesser One-horned Rhinoceros (Critically Endangered);
two wild cattle, the Gaur (Vulnerable) and the Banteng (Endangered); a
goat antelope, the Southern Serow (Vulnerable); and the Saola (Endangered). The Forest Musk Deer (*M. berezovskii*), heavily exploited for its aromatic musk, is considered Near Threatened. Too little is known about the
populations of the recently described Truong Son (*M, truongsonensis*) and
Large-Antlered (*M. vuquangensis*) Muntjacs and the rediscovered Heude's
Pig (*Sus bucculentus*) to assess their conservation status. Whether the Silver-
backed Chevrotain (*Tragulus versicolor*), described in 2004 from specimens

collected near Nha Trang and known only from Vietnam, persists is unknown.

RODENTS (ORDER RODENTIA)

With more than 2,000 species, rodents (Order Rodentia) are the largest mammalian order, accounting for over 40 percent of the world's mammal species. Rodent comes from the Latin verb *rodere,* to gnaw; all species bear continuously growing incisors in the front of their jaws. Most are small, weighing less than 3.5 ounces (100 g), and they feed on various plant parts such as buds, seeds, nuts, tubers, and leaves, along with small invertebrates. To maximize their digestive efficiency small-bodied rodents reingest partially digested food directly from the anus. Plant matter, particularly cellulose, is initially broken down by bacteria in the caecum, located at the juncture of the large and small intestines. The resulting soft fecal pellets are then eaten, allowing now-released sugars and starches to be absorbed in the small intestines and water in the large intestines and producing, finally, small, hard fecal pellets.

Rodents are intelligent, often highly social, and quite vocal in their communications. Vietnam's roughly sixty-five species are the nondomesticated animals most likely to be seen, especially the squirrels (Family Sciuridae). Squirrels, identified by their long, fluffy tails and habit of eating food from their forepaws while sitting on their haunches, can be conspicuous, active and chattering away during the daytime. Vietnam's nineteen species include ground-dwelling, tree-dwelling, and flying squirrels. The last group is less likely glimpsed as all are nocturnal. More than forty of Vietnam's remaining rodents belong to the enormous mouse and rat family (Muridae) whose 1,300 species are found in habitats from tundra to tropical forests on all continents except Antarctica. Diversified for a wide variety of ecological roles, these mouselike rodents can be tree- or ground-dwelling, aquatic, burrowing, and even jumping. Almost all are capable of rapid population growth, breeding early and frequently, often producing large litters.

The third rodent family found in Vietnam contains the Old World Porcupines (Hystricidae), represented by two species: the Asian Brush-tailed

Porcupine (*Atherurus macrourus*) and the larger and more densely quilled East Asian Porcupine (*Hystrix brachyura*). They are largely terrestrial and strictly nocturnal, digging for roots and tubers and feeding on fallen fruit, leaves, and occasionally carrion. Asian Brush-tailed Porcupines weigh 3–9 pounds (1.5–4 kg), and their backs and sides are covered with chocolate-brown quills with minutely saw-toothed edges. Their tail is scaled, except for a brushlike tip covered with bristles and modified quills that make a dry, rattling sound when vibrated. The crested porcupines of the genus *Hystrix* are quite large at 28–60 pounds (13–27 kg) and bear more formidable quills. Robust spines ringed in alternating bands of black and white cover the back and sides and are interspersed with longer, thinner, slightly curved, and flexible quills. The short tail bears specialized open-tipped quills that also produce a loud rattling noise. The rest of the body is covered by short, flattened black bristles with a longer, erectile crest on the head. When threatened, the East Asian Porcupine rattles its tail, stamps its feet, and flares out its quills, sometimes chattering and grunting. If further perturbed it may charge sideways or rearward toward the threat, trying to impale its enemy with its easily detachable quills. Old World porcupines are among the longest-lived rodents, reaching fifteen years or more in the wild, and bear small litters of one or two young.

Easily overlooked and often classified in their entirety as pests, rodents play important roles in the function of ecosystems. Their habits of digging and burrowing aerate soils, influencing physical and chemical properties and creating microenvironments; rodents' foraging on seeds and young seedlings shapes the distribution and survival of trees, often differentially between species; and their role in dispersing spores of fungi that form positive, species-specific symbiotic relationships with tree roots can partially determine the composition of forests. Rodents conflict with humans mostly through agricultural crop damage, though their sometime role as disease carriers (brush-tailed porcupines are hosts of malaria, *Plasmodium atheruri*) can also be problematic. The IUCN classifies three rodents in Vietnam as globally threatened: the Particolored Flying Squirrel (*Hylopetes alboniger;* Endangered), Sikkim Rat (*Rattus sikkimensis;* Vulnerable), and Chapa Pygmy Dormouse (*Typhlomys chapensis;* Critically Endangered). Both Osgood's Rat (*Rattus osgoodi*) and the Chapa Pygmy Dormouse are suspected Vietnamese endemics. The latter is known from only a handful of specimens collected at Sa Pa in northwestern Vietnam's Hoang Lien Son Range in 1932.

LAGOMORPHS (ORDER LAGOMORPHA)

Globally, the Order Lagomorpha includes both rabbits and hares (Family Leporidae) and their much smaller, mouselike relatives, the pikas (Family Ochotonidae); only leporids are found in Vietnam. Rabbits and hares are easily recognized by their large ears and long hind limbs, which are well suited for rapid running. They differ primarily in how they cope with predators: hares attempt to outrun the threat, while rabbits rely on concealment, either in cover or beneath the ground. Well known for their exceptional reproductive capacity, they reach sexual maturity early and breed frequently. Tropical species are thought to breed aseasonally, producing more litters of fewer young than their temperate counterparts. Probably to minimize predation, hares and rabbits visit their well-concealed offspring for less than five minutes a day, feeding them milk that is extremely rich in fat and protein.

Two species of lagomorph are found in Vietnam: the Siamese Hare (*Lepus peguensis*) and the Annamite Striped Rabbit (*Nesolagus timminsi*). Hares generally prefer more open areas and are colored some shade of brown with blackened ear tips. With a buff body, rust-red rump, and black markings, the two species in the genus *Nesolagus* (the other occurs in the mountains of Sumatra) are unique in being the only striped lagomorphs. These rabbits are strictly nocturnal and prefer tropical forest cover. First described in 2000, the Annamite Striped Rabbit's conservation status is unknown, though its congener, the Sumatran Striped Rabbit (*N. netscheri*) is listed as Critically Endangered by the IUCN. Like most threatened rabbits and hares, both are relict species, occupying a small subset of a once wider distribution.

BIRDS

Vietnam's birds are its best-known animal group. Birds are generally easier to observe and identify than mammals for a variety of reasons: almost all species are out during the day; species-specific songs and calls are critical features in detecting and identifying them; and, because they can fly, birds rely less on cryptic coloration and concealment to avoid predators. The group's presence is also well recorded; many surveys, both past and present, within Vietnam and Indochina have focused largely on the country's avifauna.

The birds (Class Aves) were the last major group to have evolved, appearing in their modern form, both feathered and capable of flight, some 140 million years ago. Plumage is the most obvious feature unifying the almost 9,000 or so living bird species. Feathers play functional roles in flight and insulation and communicate varied information, including age, sex, individual identity, physical condition, and reproductive state. Birds are warm-blooded creatures with beaks (though lacking teeth), strong bones filled with air cavities to lighten them, external and calcified eggs, complex mating and parental behaviors, and keen color vision. Of the twenty-eight extant avian orders, a single one, the Passeriformes, also known as perching birds or passerines, accounts for more than half the known species. This group contains the highly diverse and species-rich songbirds (Suborder Passeri), which possess specialized voice boxes capable of producing complex vocalizations.

To date, almost 850 bird species have been recorded in Vietnam. This number is not the final word on the country's avian species richness, as new species continue to be added through discovery, rediscovery, and their first sightings within the country's boundaries. In addition to Vietnam's three new babbler species (Black-crowned Barwing, *Actinodura sodangorum;* Golden-winged Laughingthrush, *Garrulax ngoclinhensis;* and Chestnut-eared Laughingthrush, *G. konkakinhensis*), the Mekong Wagtail (*Motacilla samveasnae*), newly described from Cambodia in 2002, is also present along the Mekong's lowland tributaries in south-central Vietnam. Another four species have been rediscovered in Vietnam, including the endemic Gray-crowned Crocias (*Crocias langbianis*) (appendix 3).

Various communities of resident and visiting birds are associated with Vietnam's differing habitats and regions. Using species richness as a guide, by far the most significant habitats in Vietnam are the country's evergreen forests. Lowland forests are critical habitat for Vietnam's pheasants (Family Phasianidae) as well as for a suite of medium-sized birds including pittas (Family Pittidae), magpies (Family Corvidae), and the Red-vented Barbet (*Megalaima lagrandieri*), an Indochinese endemic. Montane forests above 3,300 feet (1,000 m) are home to large and diverse communities of passerines, including the three new babblers and two Vietnamese endemics, the Orange-breasted Laughingthrush (*G. annamensis*) and Collared Laughingthrush (*G. yersini*). The wet grasslands and flooded forests of the Mekong Delta are home to large waterbirds, including storks (Family Ciconiidae), ibises (Family Threskiornithidae), herons (Family Ardeidae), and cormorants (Family Phalacrocoracidae), as well as large birds of prey such as the Gray-headed Fish Eagle (*Ichthyophaga ichthyaetus*). Mudflats and sandy stretches along the estuaries and islands of the northern coast are important stopover and wintering sites for many waterbirds, including ducks (Family Anatidae), gulls (Family Laridae), plovers (Family Charadriidae), and the Black-faced Spoonbill (*Platalea minor;* Endangered).

Vietnam's bird species richness is not spread evenly across avian taxonomic groups. Some groups, including the Old World flycatchers (thirty species; Tribe Muscicapini), laughingthrushes (twenty-six species; Tribe Garrulacinae), and babblers (seventy-nine species; Tribe Timaliini) account for a large proportion of the country's species richness. They also capture a large percentage (71, 67, and 63 percent, respectively) of each group's total species count in Southeast Asia. Members of other groups with fewer species, such as the barbets (ten species; Family Megalaimidae) and trogons (three species; Tribe Harpactini), are important contributors to countrywide species richness. Still other groups may be represented by only one or a few species, including the Bengal Florican (*Houbaropsis bengalensis*), the only bustard (Family Otididae) found in Indochina. Southeast Asia and the Philippines are home to two endemic bird families, the fairy bluebirds (Irenidae) and the leafbirds (Chlorposeidae), both of which have species present in Vietnam. What follows is a description of Vietnam's more prominent, interesting, typical, and threatened avian groups.

Pheasants (Order Galliformes:
Family Phasianidae: Subfamily Phasianinae)

Pheasants are exclusively Asian with a single African exception: the Congo Peafowl (*Afropavo congensis*), restricted to central Africa's Congo Basin. Related most closely to Southeast Asia's Green Peafowl (*Pavo muticus*), its ancestral type was likely driven south during the Pleistocene glaciations and subsequently isolated from the rest of the group. Pheasant species richness centers on the eastern Himalayas and western China, and the group now occupies a wide variety of habitats from lowland forests and plains to upland plateaus. Of the forty-nine species currently recognized worldwide, twelve can be found in Vietnam (fig. 22), including two familiar species: the Red Junglefowl (*Gallus gallus*), wild ancestor to domesticated chickens, and the Common Pheasant (*Phasianus colchicus*), which has been introduced around the world as a game bird.

As a group, the pheasants are largish, nonmigratory, fairly sedentary birds. They are cursorial, preferring to walk or run along the ground, though their short, rounded wings and well-developed breast muscles permit sudden bursts of flight. They have sturdy beaks and stubby claws that they use to scrabble along the ground for food. The pheasants' primary diet is plant matter (leaves, shoots, seeds), which they supplement with insects and small vertebrates such as frogs. Chicks, however, require an insect diet, needing the protein for rapid growth and development. All pheasant young are precocial, meaning that they can move on their own and can feed themselves immediately after birth. They must still be brooded for some time, since they cannot control their body temperature when very young.

Pheasants are extremely variable in two associated traits: the extent of size and plumage differences between the sexes and their mating systems. They can be notably eye-catching birds. In many species, males are ornamented with elongated, brightly colored feathers that they exhibit to smaller and drabber potential mates in stereotyped displays. The degree of dimorphism in size and feathering is related to the type of mating system: in general, the more mates available to a male, the greater the sex differences. With the exception of polyandry (one female, multiple males), pheasant mating systems cover the spectrum of those observed in birds.

Figure 22. Family Phasianidae: Crested Argus (*Rheinardia ocellata*, top),
Green Peafowl (*Pavo muticus*, center), and Temminck's Tragopan (*Tragopan
temminckii*, bottom). Of these three species, Temminck's Tragopan is
the most arboreal. All are male.

They may be monogamous, polygynous (one male, multiple females), or promiscuous, a system where females visit displaying males that may be aggregated (lekking) or dispersed. Because pheasant chicks are precocial, a single bird can perform the parental role, freeing the male to abandon his mate and seek opportunities elsewhere. Sexual selection—selection to increase mating success—leads to the amplification of traits that are most successful at acquiring matings. Why there is such a broad variety of mating systems in this group is not well understood, though it may relate to food availability and habitat structure.

Vietnam's pheasant species richness reflects its range of habitats. There are distinctly upland species, such as Temminck's Tragopan (*Tragopan temminckii*), and lowland species, including the endemic Edwards's Pheasant (*Lophura edwardsi*). There are also divisions between more northerly species, such as the Gray Peacock Pheasant (*Polyplectron bicalcaratum*), and more southerly ones, including the closely related Germain's Peacock Pheasant (*P. germaini*). Five are listed as threatened, including the Crested Argus (*Rheinardia ocellata*) and Green Peafowl. Taxonomic questions remain around a group of closely related endemic pheasants: Edwards's Pheasant, Imperial Pheasant (*L. imperialis*), and Vietnamese Pheasant (*L. hatinhensis*). The Imperial Pheasant now appears to be a hybrid of Edwards's Pheasant and Silver Pheasant (*L. nycthemera*), whereas the Vietnamese Pheasant may represent descendents of a highly inbred population of Edwards's Pheasant. Because they have yet to be removed from published lists, they are retained here as part of Vietnam's pheasant fauna. Despite their at times brilliant feathering, pheasants are generally shy, retiring birds that are difficult to glimpse in forest understories.

Asian Barbets (Order Piciformes: Family Megalaimidae)

Although barbets are found throughout the Paleotropics and Neotropics, the group's twenty-six species are concentrated in Africa and in Asia, where they are a prominent element of Southeast Asia's forests. They are most closely related to South America's toucans and, together with toucans, are placed in the Order Piciformes, which also contains the woodpeckers and honeyguides. Asian barbet species richness increases along an east-to-west gradient, from a low in India, across Peninsular Malaysia to the islands of Sumatra, Java, and Borneo, where it peaks. This pattern may reflect Neogene (23–1.8 million years ago) and Pleistocene climate, sea level, and habitat distribution fluxes that had profound consequences for separation and recolonization events in Southeast Asia. Barbets are generally poor fliers, which may help explain their apparently effective isolation on islands.

Although it lies well north of peak barbet species richness, Vietnam is home to ten barbets, all in the genus *Megalaima*. These stocky birds have stout, pointed bills, strong legs for clinging to bark, and short, rounded wings that make their flight seem labored. All are bright green with bold harlequin patches and stripes of red, yellow, blue, and black covering their heads. They also bear noticeable bristles at the beak's base, sometimes longer than the bill; their function is unknown. Variation in head color — along with body size — is the primary means of identification. There is little to no difference in plumage between the sexes, which may be linked to the strong, long-term pair bonds formed in this group; such bonds reduce opportunities for direct male competition over matings. Barbets are primarily birds of lowland evergreen forests. One species, the Coppersmith Barbet (*Megalaima haemacephala*), is a bird of deciduous dipterocarp forests and tolerant of modified habitats; it is also the most globally widespread barbet.

Asian barbets feed primarily on fruit, and much of their activity centers around ripe fruit trees. A large, heavily fruiting tree can draw many barbets from more than one species, and aggressive interactions are frequent. Barbets nest and roost in separate cavities dug high up in dead or dying trees. Both the male and the female excavate the nest site, creating a short entrance hole and a long downward tunnel, which reduces predation. Both fruit-eating and hole excavation contribute to forest diversity by dispersing seeds and creating cavities to be exploited later by other creatures.

Their feeding and housing preferences place barbets in direct competition with others for limited resources. This conflict is likely the reason for their pugnacious, even belligerent natures. During the breeding season, barbets may harass smaller species by enlarging nest holes to make them uninhabitable, ejecting eggs and nestlings, and even stealing fruit directly from their bills. When confronting aggressors at a fruit tree or nesting site, they display by bowing downward and swinging their heads side-to-side, highlighting their bold head patterns. Barbets are generally territorial around breeding or feeding sites, though almost none are capable of defending a large, rich fruiting tree.

Most of Vietnam's ten barbets are widespread, though some hold more northerly or southerly distributions. Both the Great (*M. virens*) and Blue-throated (*M. asiatica*) Barbets are restricted to northern Vietnam and the northern Truong Son Range, while the Lineated (*M. lineata*) and Copper-smith Barbets are found only in the country's center and south. The Black-browed Barbet (*M. oorti*) is restricted to the southern Truong Son, where it is a common resident; elsewhere it can be found in a disjointed, patchy distribution from southern China to Sumatra.

Because of their dependency on forests and mature fruiting trees, Asian barbets are threatened throughout their ranges by deforestation and de-graded habitats. Their reduced numbers in turn threaten the diversity of forested ecosystems through the loss of seed dispersers and excavated nest holes.

Asian Hornbills (Order Coraciiformes: Family Bucerotidae)

Hornbills are the most recognizable and conspicuous inhabitants of the Old World tropics, and their fate is closely tied to the health of their for-ested habitat. Fifty-four species of hornbills live in sub-Saharan Africa and South and Southeast Asia. Of these, all but the two ground-dwelling Afri-can species (the largest of the hornbills and now placed in their own family, Bucorvidae) are arboreal. They range in size from 3.5 ounces (100 g) to well over 9 pounds (4 kg); Vietnam's six representatives are at the larger end of the spectrum. For all hornbills, the body is relatively small when compared to the prominent bill and outsized, broad wings and tail. In flight, the long, slow wing beats of larger hornbills produces a whooshing sound that can be heard for over a half a mile (1 km) and is idiosyncratic enough to iden-tify the species.

The hornbill family's most distinctive external feature is the casque sur-mounting the oversized beak. At its least elaborate, the casque is merely a bony ridge running along the top of the bill and strengthening it. In many species, however, it is enlarged into a mostly hollow, helmetlike structure that juts forward from the base of the beak along the top of the bill. The degree of elaboration in size and shape and the brightness of the casque's coloring vary quite widely between species. Casques are believed to communicate information about species identity, sex, and age and may play roles in individual recognition or in resolving conflicts over food, nest sites, or mates.

The hornbills' most characteristic behavioral trait is their peculiar breeding biology. Like many birds, hornbills nest in natural cavities, mostly in trees. They form monogamous pairs, and as nesting time approaches both sexes become increasingly territorial. Once the female has identified an acceptable nest site, she walls herself into it, building a barrier first from the outside with mud and then from the inside with her droppings and food remnants. A vertical slit is left open through which the male feeds her, regurgitating items one by one and passing them individually to her in the tip of his beak. Egg laying does not begin immediately, and the staggered clutch, once started, can take up to twenty days to produce. This attenuated egg production is possible because of the extraordinary longevity of the sperm stored internally by the female; its fertility can remain high for three weeks after the last copulation. After laying begins, the female molts, shedding first her tail and then flight feathers. The male continues to feed her and the chicks until they emerge. The length of the female's confinement can be extensive; females of one species found in Vietnam, the Wreathed Hornbill (*Aceros undulatus*), have remained sealed in the cavity for more than four months. Up to a third of all hornbills breed cooperatively; helpers (likely immature offspring) aid in feeding the female and rearing the young.

Vietnam's hornbills are largely fruit-eaters, supplementing this diet with small animals. Species vary in their preferred foods, though all are selective in what they eat, favoring fruits with high nutritive value and high water content (hornbills do not drink). They are predominantly found in evergreen forests, though they may roam large areas in search of fruiting trees. The IUCN lists the Rufous-necked Hornbill (*A. nipalensis*) as Vulnerable and two other Vietnamese species, the Great Hornbill (*Buceros bicornis*) and Brown Hornbill (*Anorrhinus tickelli*), as Near Threatened. Vietnam's hornbills are threatened by loss of the mature forests they depend on and by hunting for food (their meat is considered delicious) and medicinal use. None of Vietnam's hornbill populations is healthy, and all should be considered threatened within the country.

Asian Frogmouths (Order Caprimulgiformes: Family Batrachostomidae)

Asian frogmouths are in the small minority of bird species that are active mainly at night, making it unlikely that they will be glimpsed in the wild. The continent's twelve frogmouths belong to the Order Caprimulgiformes, a widespread group that also contains the cosmopolitan true nightjars (Family Caprimulgidae) and Neotropical potoos (Family Nyctibiidae). These families share an unusual combination of concealing plumage, largely silent and solitary behavior, nighttime activity, and foraging behaviors specialized for capturing insects on the wing.

Asia's frogmouths (genus *Batrachostomus*) are nocturnal and secretive, clothed in camouflaging feathers to seem a part of the surrounding forests. Although these traits provide effective concealment from predators, they handicap observers; species are most readily identified by their calls and songs. Frogmouths have large heads with well-developed facial bristles, a massive, wide, and slightly hooked beak with an enormous gape, rounded wings for maneuverability, and extremely short legs. The feathers are drab: grays, browns, chestnuts, and brownish red tones finely patterned to resemble scaling bark. Some species exhibit different color morphs, subtle but clearly recognizable variations in plumage color that earlier researchers initially misinterpreted as sex differences. When disturbed, frogmouths assume the dead branch posture, a characteristic frozen position where they remain motionless, perched at a slight angle with their head erect, feathers sleeked against their body, and eyes narrowed to small slits. Against a background of branches and snags, they become almost impossible to see.

Frogmouths feed on invertebrates and small vertebrates they collect during short flights or sallies from the ground, tree trunks, and foliage. They are extremely sedentary and live year-round either alone or in pairs on relatively large territories defended with threat calls and songs. Frogmouths usually lay a single egg in a well-crafted but abbreviated cup nest placed atop a branch and built out of cobwebs, lichens, leaves, and down plucked from their underparts. The sexes appear to rotate incubation and brooding duties, with males on during the day and females at night, to reduce predation and the risk of dislodging the egg or nestling.

Asian frogmouths are birds of lowland to submontane evergreen forests. Two species live in Vietnam: Hodgson's Frogmouth (*B. hodgsoni*) in the central Truong Son and the Javan Frogmouth (*B. javensis*) in the south. Hodgson's Frogmouth was not recorded from Vietnam until 1997, though it was doubtless always present; neither historic explorers nor Vietnamese scientists knew its call.

Storks (Order Ciconiiformes: Family Ciconiidae: Subfamily Ciconiinae)

The health of Vietnam's stork populations is intimately tied to the status of the country's diverse wetlands, from the large open grasslands of the Mekong Delta to seasonal forest pools. Of the world's nineteen species, ten are known historically from Vietnam, though at least one is no longer present and a number of others have ceased to breed there. Found on all continents except Antarctica, storks are placed alongside other large wading birds, including the ibises and spoonbills, in the Order Ciconiiformes. Recent genetic work and examination of fossil remains now suggest that their closest living relatives are the New World vultures (Family Cathartidae). The stork family is divided into three groups depending on body size and bill shape, which relates directly to their feeding strategies: the woodstorks and openbills (Tribe Mycterinii), the typical storks (Tribe Ciconiini), and the giant storks (Tribe Leptoptilini).

Woodstorks and openbills are relatively small storks, roughly 2.5–3.5 feet high (80–100 cm), and they bear highly specialized bills. Three species were known from Vietnam, but only the Asian Openbill (*Anastomus oscitans*) is still resident, breeding in the south; the status of the Milky Stork (*Mycteria cinerea*), which the IUCN lists as Endangered, is unknown but likely extirpated, while the Painted Stork (*M. leucocephala*) is now a rare visitor. The term *openbill* refers to the gap that remains between the bill's upper and lower mandibles when the beak is closed. Openbills are specialized for feeding on snails and freshwater mussels. Instead of using their gaped beaks as shell crackers, the openbill will hold a snail against the ground with its upper mandible, delicately slip the razor-sharp tip of its lower mandible under the snail's protective plate, and cut the muscle that holds the snail in its shell. The openbill's saliva contains a narcotic that flows into the snail, relaxing the muscle and further easing extraction. Openbills use a similar feeding technique on mussels. Because few other animals can overcome their defenses, openbills lack strong competitors for such wide-spread resources. As colonial breeders, they nest in groups of a few to several thousand.

All seven of the typical storks belong to the genus *Ciconia*. Slightly larger than the openbills, they are opportunistic and generalist carnivores with unspecialized bill morphology. One species nests in Vietnam, the downy-naped Woolly-necked Stork (*C. episcopus*). It is a scarce and highly localized resident in the southern Truong Son and the south, where it is a solitary nester. The Woolly-necked Stork has also been called the Bishop Stork (*episcopus* means "bishop" in Latin) because it appears to wear a black cloak and cap. A second species, the Black Stork (*C. nigra*), breeds in South Africa and across northern Eurasia and is a rare winter visitor to northeastern Vietnam.

The six species of giant storks are huge birds, standing 3.5–5 feet (110–150 cm) tall with massive bills and wingspans reaching 9.5 feet (290 cm). The largest Vietnamese species, the Greater Adjutant (*Leptoptilos dubius;* Endangered), was formerly a southern resident but is now a rare, non-breeding visitor. Specializing on carrion, its huge bill presents a formidable weapon for threatening other scavengers but is quite ineffective at cutting meat off carcasses. Greater Adjutants feed by tearing off large chunks and can swallow whole pieces weighing over 2 pounds (1 kg). Its naked head and throat, combined with the large, bulbous, wrinkled air sacs on the throat and back of the neck that are used for cooling and displays, make the Greater Adjutant a less than attractive bird. Two other resident giant storks, the extremely scarce Lesser Adjutant (*L. javanicus;* Vulnerable) and the Black-necked Stork (*Ephippiorhynchus asiaticus*), specialize on fish.

Despite differences in feeding strategies, storks are largely similar in most other areas: they are carnivorous, they build large bulky nests almost exclusively in trees, they prefer to be near water, and they all depend on a combination of physical adaptations and behavior to shed excess heat. Many accomplish this partly through urohydrosis, defecating on their legs and losing heat through evaporative cooling. All storks are declining throughout their southern Vietnamese ranges due to a combination of habitat loss, pesticide use, disturbance or destruction of colonies, and direct exploitation of eggs and birds.

Pittas and Broadbills (Order Passeriformes: Families Pittidae and Eurylaimidae)

Pittas and broadbills are characteristic songbirds of Southeast Asia's tropical forests. Both are relatively retiring and can be difficult to spot. Vietnam's nine pittas are shy ground-dwellers that prefer rich forest understories near streams or rivers. They hop along the forest floor, flicking their wings and tail as they search the leaf litter for earthworms and the occasional small vertebrate. All pitta species build similar, well-concealed ground nests: a flattened dome loosely constructed of sticks, leaves, grass, and moss with a neat cup nest of fine roots and fibers inside.

Despite the name broadbill, the grouping of these species is actually based on a distinctive leg musculature used to bend the toes that is not seen in any other group of passerines. Broadbills feed mostly on insects, capturing their prey either in short, often ungainly sallies or by actively gleaning foliage and bark. Unlike pittas, they build gourdlike nests suspended from branches, palm-leaf tips, and other conspicuous sites. Camouflaged with lichens, leaves, spider egg-cases, and caterpillar cocoons, the nests are well disguised to resemble hanging vegetation.

Birds in both families are rather stout and thickset, and there can be wide variation in plumage color and flashiness among each group. Pittas are usually outfitted with solid patches of brightly contrasting greens, blues, reds, and chestnuts, though in a few species these tones are muted. Most broadbills are strikingly colored blue, red, yellow, and green in discrete patches, spots, and bars, with females tending to be slightly duller. Vietnam's most distinctive broadbill is the 8.5–9.5-inch (21.5–23.5 cm) Long-tailed Broadbill (*Psarisomus dalhousiae*). Males and females are similar, with green bodies, a long blue tail, and blue flight feathers. The head is black except for a blue patch in the center of the crown and a yellow throat, narrow collar, and ear patches. In the pitta family, the candidate is the Bar-bellied Pitta (*Pitta elliottii*), a bird nearly endemic to Indochina, stretching marginally into Thailand. Males are vivid green above with a black stripe across the eyes, a pale green breast, a yellow belly marked with narrow, dark bars except for a dark blue center, and a blue tail. Females are similar except that the head and breast are buff and they lack the blue abdomen spot. The Bar-bellied Pitta is a fairly common resident throughout the lower-lying parts of the country.

Fairy Bluebirds and Leafbirds (Order Passeriformes: Families Irenidae and Chloropseidae)

The fairy bluebirds (Irenidae) and leafbirds (Chloropseidae) are the only bird families endemic to Southeast Asia (including the Philippines). Each contains only a single genus: *Irena* and *Chloropsis,* respectively. Of the two species of fairy bluebirds, a single one is found in Vietnam, whereas three of the eight leafbirds live in the country. Both families are small to medium-sized arboreal birds with slender bills and short tails, and all have sexually dimorphic plumage. Fairy bluebirds feed mostly on fruit such as figs, while leafbirds eat fruit supplemented with nectar they extract with specialized forked tongues. With the exception of the Orange-bellied Leafbird (*C. hardwickii*), which ranges between 2,000 and 7,000 feet (600–2,135m), these birds inhabit lowland forests.

The Asian Fairy Bluebird (*Irena puella*) is among Vietnam's more distinctive birds and is frequently easy to spot in the appropriate habitats. The male is a deep, shiny blue on the crown, nape, and upperparts with black on the sides of the head and the tail, flight feathers, and underparts. The female, while still striking, is a lighter and duller blue all over, except for her black tail and flight feathers. Both have red eyes and measure about 10 inches (25 cm) long. The leafbirds are smaller (6.5–8 inches; 17–20 cm) and bright green overall to which the males add a variety of darker facial markings. The Orange-bellied Leafbird has a yellowish orange chest and belly and (on the male only) deep bluish purple feathers in the tail and along the outside of the wings.

Babblers (Family Timaliidae)

Southeast Asia is renowned for its richness in babblers, a sprawling group of around 240 songbirds placed by some taxonomists within the Family Sylviidae and by others in the Family Timaliidae. The group is defined more by how its members differ from other Old World insect-eating birds (including thrushes, flycatchers, and warblers) than by a set of distinctive, shared traits. Babblers are characterized by the lack of a distinct juvenile plumage, a relatively heavy size and shape when compared to members of these other groups, and by their nonmigratory behavior. They are generally insectivorous and live in a variety of habitats from grasslands to the middle story of montane forests. Babblers differ from each other widely in plumage, size, and bill shape. All are extremely gregarious, and they are frequently seen foraging in mixed-species flocks.

Researchers have started applying genetic techniques to this untidy group in an attempt to refine their taxonomy and understand how the different groups are related. Results indicate that some species placed within the babblers actually belong to such other groups as the shrike babblers (genus *Pteruthius*) and that some taxa thought to be distantly related to the group are in fact much closer relatives, as is the case with warblers in the genus *Sylvia*. Within the babblers, the laughingthrush genus (genus *Garrulax*), originally believed to represent a single evolutionary lineage, now appears to contain more than one.

This taxonomic confusion does not decrease the real species richness of the babbler group. It is difficult to count the number of babblers in Vietnam, though it does harbor over half of mainland Southeast Asia's species. Five species are endemic to Vietnam and an additional seven to Indochina. These totals include the three species described from the Kon Tum Plateau in 1999, the Golden-winged Laughingthrush, Chestnut-eared Laughingthrush, and Black-crowned Barwing.

HERPETOFAUNA (CLASS AMPHIBIA AND CLASS REPTILIA)

Herpetology encompasses the study of two quite distinct vertebrate lineages, the amphibians (Class Amphibia) and the reptiles (Class Reptilia), collectively referred to as herpetofauna. Their union in one discipline reflects the early tendency to combine all "creeping things," *herpetos* in Greek.

Amphibians and reptiles are often the least-known group of terrestrial vertebrates, and their status in Vietnam is no exception. They are generally smaller than birds and mammals, secretive in their habits, largely nocturnal, and often spend much of their time underground. Taxonomic issues — the correct identification and assignment of individuals to recognized species and higher groups — have also been problematic for some herpetofaunal groups. This situation changed abruptly in the mid-1990s, when interest in documenting and mapping herpetofaunal species richness in Vietnam (and Indochina as a whole) was renewed. From 1997 through 2004, fifty-eight new species were described: thirty-three frogs and twenty-five reptiles (four snakes, eighteen lizards, and three turtles; see appendix 3). One source of this novel biodiversity is the identification through morphological and genetic analyses of distinct species (known as cryptic species) previously presumed to be undifferentiated populations of a single, widespread species. Researchers have uncovered hidden richness in the species complexes of the Green Cascade Frog (*Rana livida*), Indochinese Box Turtle (*Cuora galbinifrons*), and Asian Leaf Turtle (*Cyclemys dentata*). A second source for this rapidly expanding country list are species not previously known from Vietnam, such as the Chinese Crocodile Lizard (*Shinisaurus crocodilurus*), a limestone karst specialist noted from northeastern Vietnam in 2003 and previously known only from China's Guangxi Province.

As of 2004, nearly 500 amphibians and reptiles have been recorded from Vietnam. They are widely distributed across the country, occupying mountains, low-lying areas, islands, and freshwater and marine environments. The country's most species-rich environments, however, are its lowland and montane broadleaved evergreen forests. Their structural complexity provides many ecological niches in the multistoried forest canopy, the understory, and both on and beneath the soil. A variety of water environments, which amphibians depend on for reproduction, exist in these habitats, from tree holes and stagnant ponds to torrents. Some of Vietnam's reptiles are adapted to more challenging habitats, such as limestone karst outcroppings and brackish estuarine environments. Herpetofaunal species richness drops in drier environments, such as south-central Vietnam's deciduous dipterocarp forests, where aridity makes it difficult to manage evaporative heat loss and poses severe problems for amphibian reproduction. A few species are able to exploit human-modified environments and are widespread: many species of rice frogs (genus *Microhyla*) breed in the standing water of rice paddies; the Common House Gecko (*Hemidactylus frenatus*) uses well-lit walls to hunt insects; and the Flowerpot Snake (*Ramphotyphlops braminus*) occupies gardens and other damp areas.

A high percentage of Vietnam's herpetofauna is endemic, though this is not spread evenly across the taxonomic groups, ranging from 6 percent in turtles and 9 percent in snakes to 30 percent in lizards and 37 percent in amphibians. Many of these endemic species are newly described and currently known from only one location.

Amphibians (Class Amphibia)

Amphibians appeared 350 million years ago and were the earliest tetrapods (four-limbed vertebrates) to adopt a terrestrial life. Almost all species are tied to water (or at least a moist environment) by their reproductive requirements; the term *amphibian* derives from the Greek *amphibios,* "living a double life." Much like fish, they lay externally fertilized, mucous-covered aquatic eggs that hatch into gilled larvae. Metamorphosis, which in frogs encompasses the radical transformation of an eyedrop-shaped tadpole into large-eyed, four-limbed, lunged adult, converts an organism restricted to aquatic environments to one equipped for life on land. The amphibian class includes frogs (Order Anura), salamanders (Order Caudata), and blind, limbless burrowers named caecilians (Order Apoda).

Vietnam's amphibian communities, especially frogs, have benefited more from the recent expansion of in-country research than any other vertebrate group. A review in 1999 of Vietnam frog species richness enumerated 100 species; by the end of 2004 the total had increased by more than half to 157 known species. Almost all these new descriptions have come from submontane and montane wet evergreen forests in northern Vietnam and along the Truong Son Range. This pattern reflects real spikes of species richness and endemism in these regions, but it also marks the degraded quality of Vietnam's lowlands. Many northern frog species are part of amphibian communities that stretch across the border into southern China; this is the case for the Earless Toad (*Bufo cryptotympanicus*) and the Chinese Bubblenest Frog (*Philautus rhododiscus*), both recently spotted in Vietnam.

As with all other Vietnamese vertebrates, the country's amphibians are threatened with exploitation for consumption and trade and by loss of habitat. They are also especially susceptible to the loss or pollution of the freshwater habitats required for reproduction. The IUCN lists fifteen amphibians as globally threatened, including the endemic Vietnamese Warty Newt or Tam Dao Salamander (*Paramesotriton deloustali*; Endangered).

True Frogs (Family Ranidae)

The true frogs are called such because they are a common group in Europe, where much of the early taxonomic work occurred. A cosmopolitan family, its species richness peaks in South and Southeastern Asia. In Vietnam, it is the most species-rich group (fifty-five species) and the most diverse in morphology and breeding behavior. Ranid frogs can be terrestrial, arboreal, aquatic, or burrowing, and they may breed in swift torrents, slower streams, temporary pools, or stagnant water. Color is varied but never bright, ranging from greens to browns, solid or patterned with spots or variegations, depending on the habitat. Male paa frogs (*Paa*) and wart frogs (*Limnonectes*) may have stiff belly spines, fanglike lip projections, and enlarged heads associated with breeding periods.

Although most ranids are smaller than 2 inches (5 cm), the paa frogs of northern Vietnam frequently reach lengths of 4 inches (10 cm) and weights of 11 ounces (300 g). It is not unusual in ranid frogs for females to be larger than males. Female reproductive success, roughly measured by the number of eggs she can produce, generally increases with body size, whereas male reproductive success often does not (or at least not to as great an extent). In the waterfall-dwelling Grass Frog (*Rana graminea*) of northern Vietnam, females can reach almost 4 inches (9.4 cm), whereas males measure less than 2 inches (4.6 cm). Small male size in this species may also be favored by their mating behavior; males clasp themselves to the backs of females, and together they swim through torrents, where the eggs are laid under rocks and then fertilized.

Figure 23. Species complex of the Green Cascade Frog
(*Rana livida,* Family Ranidae): Morafka's Cascade Frog (*R. morafkai,* top),
Green Cascade Frog (*R. chloronota,* center), and Ba Na Cascade Frog
(*R. banaorum,* bottom). All are male.

Cascade Frogs (genus *Amolops*) also live and breed in the swift waters
of mountainous northern and central Vietnam. Adults have powerful legs
with long hind limbs and extensively webbed feet with large discs on all the
digits to help them grasp rocks (and for males the females while mating).
Eggs are laid in the swiftest part of the rapids, attached to the bottoms of
rocks or stones with sticky jelly. To survive in these torrent environments,
the tadpoles have a large sucker on the abdomen that holds them firmly in
place, with a grip strong enough that collectors must pry them off the rocks.
Another species, Penang Taylor's Frog (*Limnonectes hascheanus*), does not

require a body of water to breed. Instead, males dig holes in the muddy forest floor where females (attracted by the male's calling) lay their eggs. Development and metamorphosis takes place completely within the egg, and after about a month a small, yet maturely formed froglet emerges.

Not all amphibian species richness is readily detected. This is clear from ongoing research into the true richness of the Green Cascade Frog complex (fig. 23). Members are generally characterized by a green back and large finger and toe pads. Their skin produces strong-smelling, toxic secretions that can kill other frogs and cause human eyes to burn. Despite this, people eat them throughout their range in South and Southeast Asia. Recent genetic and morphological studies have revealed that the Green Cascade Frog, originally described in 1856, has mistakenly comprised a number of separate and distinct species. Although resembling the general description, these new species differ subtly in such traits as eye size, skin color, and spotting and marbling on body and limbs. Genetic analyses have confirmed these diagnostic morphological differences. To date more than fifteen cryptic species in the complex of *Rana livida* frogs have been identified from eastern India to southern China, mainland Southeast Asia, and the Sunda Islands. These discoveries have important implications for conservation, since a single, widespread species is inherently more stable than multiple ones with smaller ranges. Other ranid species complexes include Boie's Wart Frog (*Fejervarya limnocharis*), Asian Peters Frog (*Hoplobatrachus chinensis*), and Blyth's Wart Frog (*Limnonectes blythii*).

Asian Tree Frogs (Family Rhacophoridae)

Asian tree frogs are creatures of the Old World tropics, reaching their highest species richness in the Southeast Asia, where they generally outnumber ranids by a ratio of almost three to one. Vietnam, however, with forty-three tree species, actually has fewer tree frogs than true frogs. They are highly arboreal; large adhesive discs on their fingers and toes enable them to climb vertical surfaces and cling to branches. Both hands and feet are webbed, sometimes extensively, and such species often have flattened bodies and flaps of skin lining the limbs. These traits allow frogs like north and central Vietnam's Rheinwardt's Flying Frog (*Rhacophorus reinwardtii*) to parachute (or glide) from higher perches to lower in the canopy or the forest floor. Splotches of hidden color (oranges, purples, blacks, and yellows) are a common feature in rhacophorids, which otherwise are green to brown. Asian tree frogs can vary greatly in size. The bubble-nest frogs (genus *Philautus*) are quite small, measuring about an inch (2.5 cm), while the Annam Flying Frog (*Rhacophorus annamensis*), a Vietnamese endemic, can grow to 3.5 inches (8.5 cm) in length.

Like true frogs, Asian tree frogs have many different modes of reproduction. Species in the largest genus, flying frogs (*Rhacophorus*), construct foam nests by beating excretions from the reproductive tract into a froth with their hind feet. The foam then hardens on the outside, maintaining a moist environment for the eggs within and protecting them from predation. The foam nests are placed over standing water; when the eggs hatch, the tadpoles fall or are washed into the water below. Vietnam's five species of bug-eyed frog (genus *Theloderma*) attach their eggs to trunks and branches above water-filled tree holes, into which the hatched larvae drop to undergo metamorphosis. Bubble-nest frogs lay their eggs on leaf tops or in the crevices of epiphytes, where they develop directly into froglets.

Reptiles (Class Reptilia)

Vietnam's reptiles come from four orders: the species-rich snakes (172 species) and lizards (110), both in the Order Squamata, and the less diverse turtles (thirty-four; Order Testudines) and crocodiles (two; Order Crocodilia). Though vastly different in form, reptiles share two adaptations that free them from dependence on moist environments: a skin covered with horny scales preventing desiccation, and the evolution of a protected egg that can be laid almost anywhere, except in water. First appearing over 280 million years ago, reptiles had become the dominant terrestrial life form 50 million years later.

Patterns of species richness and endemism vary between these groups. Like frogs, the number of endemic snakes appears to peak in montane areas, whereas for lizards there seem to be more endemics in the south, including eight on the Con Dao Archipelago off southeastern Vietnam. Snake and lizard species richness is evenly distributed across Vietnam's lowlands and uplands, whereas turtles are generally lowland species, and peak species richness is found in this habitat in both the north and the south. Among the most species-rich reptile lineages are the geckos (Family Gekkonidae: thirty-two species) and skinks (Family Scincidae: forty-two species), both families of lizards, and the colubrids (Family Colubridae: 130 species), something of a catch-all group for snakes. Groups with a low number of species but a high percentage of their global species richness in Vietnam include the sunbeam snakes (Family Xenopeltidae: both species) and the blind skinks (Family Dibamidae: six out of nineteen species).

Reptiles make up a significant portion of Vietnam's vertebrates whose survival in the wild is threatened by exploitation for the wildlife trade. The IUCN lists over three-quarters of turtle species as globally threatened, including three endemics, the Annam Leaf Turtle (*Mauremys annamensis*), Bourret's Indochinese Box Turtle (*Cuora bourreti*), and the Painted Indochinese Box Turtle (*Cuora picturata*), which is known only from southern markets. The Siamese Crocodile (*Crocodylus siamensis;* Critically Endangered) is now effectively extinct in Vietnam, though a reintroduction program is under way in Cat Tien National Park. Although not globally threatened, Vietnam's two monitor lizards, the Bengal Monitor (*Varanus bengalensis*) and Water Monitor (*V. salvator*), are a source of concern since they are under pressure for both their meat and hides. The fate of Vietnam's cobras (Family Elapidae) and pythons (Family Boidae) is also uncertain.

Sunbeam Snakes (Family Xenopeltidae)

Only two species belong to the Family Xenopeltidae, and both reside in Vietnam: the Common Sunbeam Snake (*Xenopeltis unicolor*) ranges across mainland and island Southeast Asia and is found throughout Vietnam, and the more restricted Hainan Sunbeam Snake (*X. hainanus*) lives in northern and north-central Vietnam and southern China. The hard, shiny scales that cover the backs of sunbeam snakes are pigmented a dark purplish brown, but microscopic structures within them reflect back all the colors of the light spectrum, so that they appear brilliantly iridescent, scattering a rainbow of colors. Sunbeam snakes spend much of their time underground, burrowing in leaf litter, under logs, and in moist soil, often using tunnels created by other creatures. Like many burrowing reptiles, their bodies are quite rounded, with blunt heads and short tails, and they can measure more than 4 feet (1.3 m) in length, though most are less than 2.5 feet (80 cm) long.

Sunbeam snakes have unusual dentition. Instead of being firmly fixed, their many small, sharp teeth are attached to the jawbones with flexible tissue fibers, creating a hinge. They can be folded down, but only in a backward direction. Hinged teeth, which appear in at least five other snake genera, seem to be an adaptation for swallowing hard-bodied prey, including skinks (Family Scincidae), the largest of the lizard families (more than 1,400 species worldwide). Skinks have muscular torsos, either greatly reduced limbs or none at all, and a slippery covering of hard, smooth scales. These three characteristics make them a challenging food item, since they are quite capable of wriggling out of a predator's grasp. Unidirectional folding teeth let sunbeam snakes swallow hard-bodied prey rapidly and lock the prey in place if it tries to escape. In addition to skinks, sunbeam snakes feed on other lizards, rodents, birds, and snakes. The Hainan Sunbeam Snake is found between 660 and 3,600 feet (200–1100 m) in forests of northern and north-central Vietnam. More ecologically tolerant, the Common Sunbeam Snake lives throughout the country in damp agricultural and garden environments and forests between 330 and 6,600 feet (100–2,000 m).

File Snakes (Family Acrochordidae)

The three file snakes that compose the aquatic Family Acrochordidae are highly specialized for life in the water. Loose, roughened skin, combined with strong musculature, lets them flatten themselves vertically, creating an efficient, ribbonlike shape for moving through water. File snakes also have small belly scales that point downward along the midline of the belly to form a sort of keel. They can remain submerged for several hours, abetted by a low metabolic rate, a large blood supply, and the ability to exchange oxygen and carbon dioxide with water through the skin.

Their roughened skin helps file snakes to grasp their fish prey firmly. They react to a fish's touch by quickly looping their body around the prey, trapping it firmly in their coils. Wavelike contractions then move the fish along the snake's body to its mouth, where it is quickly swallowed. Such quick action is possible because of tiny hairlike bristles located between the snakes' granular scales that appear to be very sensitive to touch. These sensors may also help the snakes in environments where visibility is usually low.

Two species of file snakes are found in Vietnam's central and southern lowlands and coasts. Little File Snakes (*Acrochordus granulatus*) are primarily marine, though they can tolerate a wide range of salinities, including freshwater. Most typically found in shallow coastal waters of mangroves and estuaries a couple of feet (m) deep, they have been collected more than 6 miles (10 km) out to sea and at depths of up to 66 feet (20 m). Javan File Snakes (*A. javanicus*) are found in lagoons, streams, and other permanent bodies of fresh water. They are less tolerant of salt water, though they can apparently endure brackish environments and even enter the sea. Though they are adept swimmers, file snakes usually crawl along the muddy bottoms. They forage actively at night, secreting themselves during daylight hours amid mangrove roots and in burrows and holes in banks, where Javan File Snakes can sometimes be found in large aggregations. All three members of the family have been described as "astonishingly homely" with a baggy, flabby appearance (Greene 1997, 167); Little File Snakes are a mottled gray, black, and white and can reach lengths of 20–28 inches (50–70 cm), while Javan File Snakes are dull brown or grayish and can grow to nearly 6.5 feet (2 m) in length.

Blindskinks (Family Dibamidae)

Because of the secretive lives of blindskinks (Family Dibamidae), which they lead almost entirely underground, little is known of either their diversity or their ecology and behavior. Measuring 2–10 inches (5–25 cm) in length, they are blunt-headed, burrowing lizards covered with shiny, smooth, overlapping scales. Their eyes are vestigial and hidden under immoveable scales, and they have no external ear openings. Both sexes lack forelimbs, and only males have hind limbs, shrunken to tiny, flaplike appendages possibly used in courtship or copulation. Blindskinks can be found in a variety of forested and scrubland environments but require moist soil conditions and often burrow deep under rocks or fallen logs during the dry season. Scientists assume that they eat insects and they lay sequential clutches of single eggs.

All but one of the nineteen known blindskinks belong to the genus *Dibamus*, which is restricted to Southeast Asia, the Philippines, and western New Guinea. The final species, the Mexican Blind Lizard (*Anelytropsis papillosus*), is found on the other side of the Pacific Ocean in a small region of northeastern Mexico. The evolutionary relationship of blindskinks to other lizards is unknown; these two genera may be the last remnants of an old, formerly more widespread group. The number of known blindskink species has been increasing rapidly, with seven new species described since 1997, two of these from Vietnam. Six blindskinks live in the country, one of which (*D. kondaoensis*), the Con Dao Blind Skink, is endemic to the southeastern island of Con Dao.

FRESHWATER FISH

Freshwater fish are an important source of protein for the Vietnamese people but remain poorly known throughout the country. This is the function of a number of factors, including historically poor surveying and a situation of taxonomic chaos throughout mainland Southeast Asia and southern China that makes it difficult to identify specimens accurately and interpret published survey results. Extremely rough estimates of Vietnam's inland waters suggest there are some 450 species, possibly representing 80 percent of the total ichthyofauna; around half of these are known from single locations. Almost 50 percent of species recorded during surveys of southern Vietnam's Dong Nai River in 1990 and 1999 were new species records for the drainage.

Their restriction to waterways causes freshwater fish to diverge from their terrestrial relatives in patterns of species richness and the primary threats to their continued existence. Biogeographically, three distinct fish faunas occur in Vietnam: one associated with the Red River, one with the Mekong River, and a third with the rivers draining the Truong Son Range's eastern slopes. The fish associated with the Red River are a distinct group, similar to those found in southeastern Chinese rivers, whereas the Mekong's ichthyofauna is widespread across much of mainland Southeast Asia. Though not particularly rich in species, the Truong Son's middle reaches, headwaters, and rapids have a high percentage of endemic taxa, often with specialized suckers and flattened bodies, adaptations for swift-flowing waterways.

Threats to inland fish include dams that alter flow patterns, deforestation in drainages leading to erosion and siltation, removal of forest cover over streams affecting water temperature, changes in oxygen levels, and pollution. Overfishing, including the use of dynamite, is also a danger. Species considered most threatened today are the large fish of the Mekong; this assessment is biased by the currently poor knowledge of the rest of the freshwater ichthyofauna. It is quite possible that species restricted to one or a few streams may go extinct with comparatively little pressure, some of them before scientists have the chance to name them.

Catfish (Order Siluriformes)

The Siluriformes is an enormously diverse, cosmopolitan order containing almost 3,000 catfish species grouped into thirty-one families. The best-known characteristic of catfish is their barbels, thin, whiskerlike feelers that occur in pairs around the mouth. Equipped with taste buds and sensitive to touch, barbels help catfish gather food in dim or cloudy waters. Catfish are largely nocturnal freshwater bottom-dwellers that feed on invertebrates, though many eat fish or plants and a few are even parasites on other fish. They often bear sharp spines at the base of their back and pectoral fins, and most species lack scales, leaving their leatherlike skin bare. Catfish have adapted to a variety of habitats and feeding ecologies, and species can be found in waters ranging from highly oxygenated, swift waterways to stagnant, almost anoxic pools and both brackish and marine environments.

Catfish, especially the larger species living in the Mekong River, are a major source of fish protein in Vietnam. Many of these species are migratory, shifting during the year between locations for spawning, maturation, and feeding, and often crossing international boundaries. They are easily targeted by fishermen during these simultaneous mass movements. New catfish species are being uncovered in Vietnam at a rapid rate, including from the Mekong, with eight new species described between 2000 and 2004.

Hillstream or River Loaches (Family Balitoridae)

The 115 or so species of hillstream loaches are specialized for life in waters with strong currents. Their bodies are elongated and flattened in the horizontal plane, and some species have modified pectoral and pelvic fins forming a sucking disk on the belly that helps them survive in swift-flowing streams. Small-bodied—the largest species reaches a length of about 6 inches (14 cm)—and quite reclusive, hillstream loaches are usually not targeted by fishermen but are killed incidentally. Balitorids are potential indicators of stream health, since they are sensitive to small environmental changes. Their species richness in Vietnam is only beginning to be understood. Twenty new species were described, mostly from the central Truong Son Range, between 2000 and 2004.

INVERTEBRATES

The animals referred to as invertebrates are grouped by a single common trait: the lack of a backbone. Otherwise they share little else, and their collection under one name does not imply a shared evolutionary origin, unlike the other taxonomic terms used so far. Invertebrates are a diverse group that includes insects (Superclass Hexapoda), spiders and ticks (Class Arachnida), many different worms (such as the Phyla Nematoda and Annelida), crabs and shrimp (Subphyllum Crustacea), mollusks such as snails, clams, and squid (Phylum Mollusca), and moss animals (Phylum Ectoprocta). Invertebrates are by far the largest group of living animals in both species number and biomass. They are also the least well known. Some have characteristics, such as limited mobility of snails and other mollusks, that make the evolution of endemic species more likely. Vietnam's karst hills and caves, likely high in endemic species, house unexplored communities of such organisms. Little is known about the conservation status of invertebrates in Vietnam.

Butterflies and Moths (Family Lepidoptera)

Butterflies and moths are often among the first invertebrates to be surveyed in an area. They are relatively large, often colorful, active during the day in

Figure 24. Order Lepidoptera: morpho butterfly species male (*Zeuxidia masoni,* upper left), Indian Fritillary female (*Argyreus hyperbius,* upper right), and swallowtail butterfly species male (*Graphium mandarinus,* bottom)

the case of butterflies, and among the best studied and most readily identifiable of the insect groups. Vietnam's recorded species richness currently stands at over 250 species, though lepidopterists believe this to be only a quarter of the country's species richness (fig. 24). Elaborate wing patterns are the primary identifying traits, though within a species these may differ between the sexes, seasonally, and with geographic distribution.

Food sources of adult butterflies include nectar, fruit, sap, animal droppings, and rotting organic matter whereas caterpillar larvae eat leaves. Based on larval food requirements most lepidopteran species can be classified as either specialists, generally rare and dependent on a limited range of habitats and food plants, or generalists, frequently widespread and with broader ecological requirements. A study of butterfly communities in northern Vietnam's Tam Dao National Park found that rarer species dependent on the older, less disturbed, primary forests had smaller geographic ranges than those tolerating disturbed areas. When gaps appeared in the canopy by tree felling, only these restricted-range, specialist species were affected.

Coral (Class Anthozoa)

Corals belong to the Phylum Cnidaria, an exclusively carnivorous group of invertebrates that includes sea anemones, jellyfish, sea pens, and hydra. Corals are sexual reproducers; they release sperm and eggs into the water, and the resulting larvae establish new corals on free surfaces such as rocks. Many coral species are single, solitary individuals; however, the corals most people are acquainted with also reproduce asexually and form expanded, sometimes huge, colonies of genetically identical individuals. The most familiar of these colony-forming species are the hard or stony star corals (Order Scleractinia), which build up into reefs, a characteristic component of many tropical coasts. Reefs are slowly built out of the coral's hardened calcium carbonate exoskeleton, which persists long after the individual organism has died. Hard corals are the most diverse and important cnidarian order in Vietnam, with more than 300 recognized reef-building species. Vietnam's marine environments also contain more than twenty species of gorgonian sea fans and seventeen species of soft coral (Order Alcyonaria).

Vietnam's overall coral fauna is less diverse than expected when compared with other regions of Southeast Asia (the Philippines harbor about twice as many species). Near shore, corals are not extensive, limited mostly to low fringing reefs. There are several natural possible causes of reduced coral abundance and species richness. Freshwater runoff, especially from the Red and Mekong River Deltas, lowers salinity and deposits sediments, both of which can inhibit coral growth. Lower-than-expected coral species richness may occur because the prevailing ocean currents during coral spawning periods do not flow from the regions of high richness (the Sunda Islands), limiting recruitment of a diverse coral assemblage.

SIX

Northern Vietnam
Termination of the Himalayas

Northern Vietnam is geologically and environmentally complex, a mixture of granite and limestone, uplands and delta, jagged peaks and humid lowlands, and tropical and subtropical species. This diversity reflects northern Vietnam's position near the intersection of the tropical and subtropical zones and the biotic influence of three biogeographic units: Indochina, south China, and coastal Indochina. During the French colonial period northern Vietnam formed the administrative district of Tonkin; the Vietnamese refer to the area as Bac Bo. It is bordered by China's Guangxi Province to the northeast and Yunnan Province to the northwest, and by Laos along its western border (fig. 25). An extensive and ecologically significant coastal region stretches along the Bac Bo (Tonkin) Gulf to the southeast, beyond which lies China's Hainan Island in the East Sea. The Red River (Song Hong) flows from the Chinese border through the middle of northern Vietnam and fans into a large, heavily populated, and predominantly agricultural floodplain before draining into the gulf. Unlike the unifying role the much larger Mekong plays in the south, the Red River bisects northern Vietnam. The Ca River (Song Ca), running through the middle of Nghe An Province, forms the southwestern boundary of this region. It coincides with biotic, geological, and ethnographic transitions and roughly marks the beginning of the Truong Son Range in Vietnam.

The people of northern Vietnam come from a diversity of ethnic groups and range from ancient inhabitants to recent immigrants. People have lived

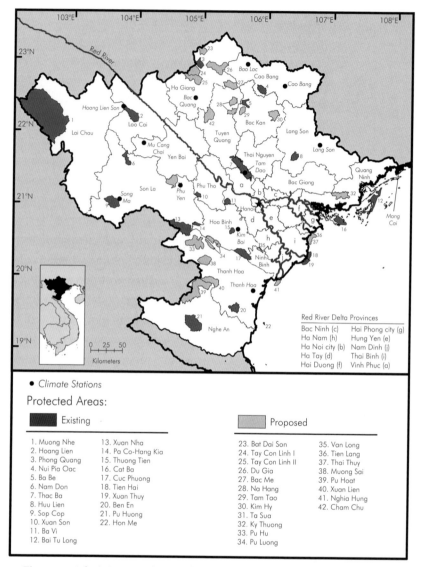

Figure 25. Administrative features and protected areas of northern Vietnam

in the rich floodplains of the Red River Delta for at least 20,000 years; in the twenty-first century, it is the most densely populated region of Vietnam, with an average of 3,056 inhabitants per square mile (1,180/km²) as compared to 598 per square mile (231/km²) for the country as a whole. The population here is overwhelmingly Viet, the dominant ethnic group in Vietnam.

Of Vietnam's fifty-three other ethnic groups, at least thirty live in the north, concentrated in the twelve highland provinces ringing the central delta region. Population density in this region is far lower than in the lowlands, averaging about 207 people per square mile (80/km²) but it continues to rise owing to high birth rates and internal migration to the region. Some of the larger ethnic groups in the north, such as the Hmong, are relatively recent arrivals to Vietnam, having migrated from southern China starting in the late eighteenth and early nineteenth centuries. Others, such as the Tay, have lived in these areas since before written records.

TOPOGRAPHY

Hilly and montane areas form a rough semicircle around the northern boundary of Vietnam, though these upland areas are higher and the width of the arc is thicker to the north and west (fig. 26). Within this semicircle lies the extensive Red River Delta. Low, rounded hills 500–650 feet (150–200 m) above sea level and narrow river valleys form a transition zone of midlands between the upper reaches of the delta and upland areas. The uplands are also cut by a broad depression in the east, running from Cao Bang Province near the Chinese border south toward the coast.

Geologists describe the northern half of Vietnam as a "tectonic mélange" (Findlay 1999, 359), because it was assembled from many geological elements and then transformed, deformed, and rearranged over hundreds of millions of years. Formed out of the collision of the South China and Indochina blocks and subsequently transformed by the energy of the India-Eurasia collision, it remains a seismically active region to this day. East of the Red River, northern Vietnam's geology is of largely south Chinese origin. West of the Red River, a broad subduction zone extends far south, to Da Nang in central Vietnam, where elements of south China and Indochina as

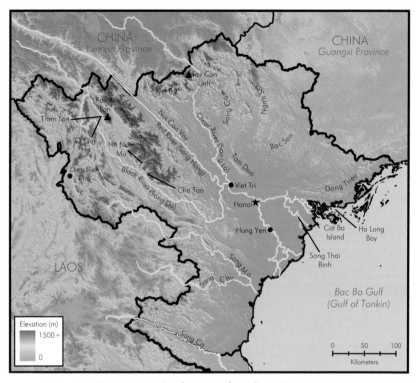

Figure 26. Major features of northern Vietnam

well as other microblocks are mingled. Extensive faulting and folding has occurred in this region, largely during the period after India's impact with Asia 50 million years ago, creating a series of parallel northwest–southeast-oriented ridges and valleys. The accumulation of long-term tectonic movements and deformations has produced both a complicated topography and a mixture of geologic origins underlying northern Vietnam.

The Red River Delta is a broad, flat, roughly triangular region anchored at Viet Tri, 34 miles (55 km) northwest of Hanoi. Bounded to the northeast by the Thai Ninh River and to the southwest by the Red River, the delta covers 6,688 square miles (17,321 km²), with a coastline of nearly 190 miles (300 km). Estuaries, mudflats, dunes, and beaches line this coast where numerous aquaculture ponds (primarily for farming shrimp) have replaced the natural mangrove forests. Short hills roughly 30 feet (10 m) high ring a vast alluvial plain no more than 10–16 feet (3–5 m) above sea level. The coastal regions to the north and south resemble the delta's, with the addition of limestone cliffs and lagoons. Thousands of offshore islands dot Vietnam's northeastern coastline, ranging in size from tiny pinnacles to the 110-square-mile (285 km²) Cat Ba Island, part of the 970-square-mile (2,500 km²) Ha Long Bay Archipelago.

A prominent feature of northern Vietnam's topography is its extensive karst formations, areas of irregular limestone eroded into towers, hills, caves, and passages (fig. 27). From the late mid-Devonian (370–360 million years ago) to the early Triassic (245–224 million years ago), much of northern and central Vietnam was covered by shallow seas that left behind extensive limestone deposits, up to 9,800 feet (3,000 m) thick in some areas. When exposed to rain by soil erosion and tectonic uplift, the rock surfaces slowly dissolve. Ha Long Bay's flooded limestone hills off the northeastern coast are perhaps Vietnam's best-known and most striking karst formations. Cat Ba Island is the center of this now mostly submerged massif, which is visible only as scattered emergent hilltops of various heights, on a flat sea bottom 6–80 feet (2–25 m) below. Vietnam's northeastern karsts are more complex than the northwestern ones and include a greater variety of formations, such as jagged towers, loaf-shaped mountains, cones, flat-floored depressions, and caves. Here, two large karst formations, Cao Bang and Bac Son, stand at 3,300 feet (1,000 m) above sea level, their hilltops rising between 330 and 2,000 feet (100–600 m) over the intervening lowland valleys and flat depressions. Northwestern Vietnam also contains significant karst features, including an extensive but highly dissected plateau that runs along the Black River (Song Da) from the Chinese border to the coast. Highly eroded karsts are also found in the provinces of Lai Chau, Son La, Hoa Binh, Thanh Hoa, and Nghe An.

The dominant feature west of the Red River is the Hoang Lien Son Range, the southeasternmost extension of the Himalaya Range. This granite formation runs parallel to the river's west bank for approximately 420 miles (675 km) southeast from the Chinese border. Much of it lies above 6,600 feet (2,000 m), with a number of peaks reaching from 8,200 to more than 9,800 feet (2,500–3,000 m), including Fan Xi Pan, the tallest mountain in Vietnam at 10,312 feet (3,143 m). The Hoang Lien Son granites date from 80 to 29 million years ago, and uplift of the range by tectonic ac-

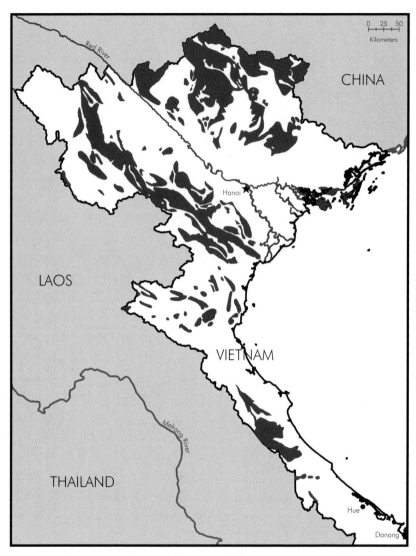

Figure 27. Distribution of limestone formations across northern
and central Vietnam (After Dang Hung Vo 1996)

tivity began around 65 million years ago and continues to this day. Sharp pinnacles, needle-pointed heights, and deeply incised gorges indicate that uplift was fairly rapid and erosion began only recently. South and west of Hoang Lien Son lies the Black River valley and another band of karst mixed with older rocks. The Viet Bac Massif, a granite formation adjacent to the Chinese border, includes Tay Con Linh at 7,936 feet (2,419 m), northeastern Vietnam's highest peak. Also of note is the isolated Tam Dao Massif, which rises over 4,900-foot (1,500 m) on the edge of the delta and includes one of the better studied ecosystems in Vietnam.

The uppermost soils of the Red River Delta are young, deposited from the Quaternary (2.6 million years ago) to the present, and contain high levels of both alluvium and sand. Alluvium contains fine, muddy, and slightly acidic sediments deposited by the region's swiftly flowing rivers and is suitable for growing rice. Sand, however, has a low organic content and is slightly alkaline, making it less suitable for agriculture. The delta's fertility varies from place to place, largely due to the source of the alluvium. Unfortunately, the extensive dikes protecting the croplands from flood have also prevented the deposition of the rich sediments originally responsible for the delta's fertility. Presumably there were once peat formations in the delta as well, before agricultural conversion. Most upland soils are heavily weathered, low in nutrients, and highly vulnerable to erosion when the land is cleared. This poor soil quality limits crop growth and is likely responsible for the region's high rate of goiter, a condition caused by insufficient iodine in the diet. Iron and aluminum oxides give the soils a reddish color, from which the Red River derives its name.

Northern Vietnam holds the lion's share of the country's coal; the large anthracite coal beds in Quang Ninh Province represent 98 percent of the country's deposits of this high-quality coal. The north is also rich in iron, tin, graphite, and apatite.

CLIMATE

Most of northern Vietnam experiences temperatures that are strongly seasonal, more so than in the rest of the country, and subtropical, especially in the interior (table 2). This (relative) coldness and seasonality is caused

Table 2. Climate stations in northern Vietnam

Name	Elevation (ft/m)	Temperature (C/F) Annual average	Temperature (C/F) Range monthly averages	Rainfall (in/mm) Annual average	Rainfall (in/mm) Range monthly averages	Dry months (N)	Wettest month
Bao Lac	846 (258)	72 (22.2)	58–82 (14.5–27.6)	49 (1,247)	1–9 (20–232)	4	July
Cao Bang	846 (258)	71 (21.6)	57–81 (14–27.3)	57 (1,443)	1–11 (16–267)	3	Aug.
Bac Quang	243 (74)	73 (22.6)	59–82 (15.1–27.7)	189 (4,802)	3–35 (68–901)	0	June
Hoang Lien Son	7,119 (2,170)	55 (12.8)	45–62 (7.1–16.4)	140 (3,552)	3–27 (64–680)	0	July
Mu Cang Chai	3,199 (975)	66 (18.7)	54–73 (12.4–22.6)	71 (1,813)	1–15 (17–371)	2	July
Lang Son	846 (258)	70 (21.2)	56–81 (13.3–27)	55 (1,392)	1–10 (23–258)	3	July
Mong Cai	23 (7)	73 (22.7)	59–83 (15.1–28.4)	108 (2,749)	1–24 (38–599)	0	July
Tam Dao	2,943 (897)	64 (18)	51–74 (10.8–23.1)	104 (2,631)	1–21 (38–525)	0	Aug.
Phu Yen	597 (182)	73 (22.8)	60–82 (15.7–27.8)	61 (1,537)	0–12 (12–305)	4	Aug.
Song Ma	991 (302)	72 (22.4)	61–80 (16.1–26.4)	47 (1,185)	0–10 (10–255)	5	Sept.
Hanoi	16 (5)	74 (23.5)	62–84 (16.5–28.9)	66 (1,674)	1–12 (18–314)	6	Sept.
Hong Gai	285 (87)	73 (23)	61–83 (16–28.5)	75 (1,894)	1–17 (20–430)	4	Aug.
Kim Boi	328 (100)	73 (22.8)	60–82 (15.7–28)	89 (2,256)	1–17 (23–433)	3	Sept.
Thanh Hoa	16 (5)	74 (23.6)	63–84 (17.1–29)	69 (1,742)	1–16 (25–395)	4	Sept.

Source: After Nguyen Khanh Van et al., 2000

by the northeast monsoon winds that bring cold air from the edge of the
Tibetan Plateau into Vietnam in the winter (December through February or
March). Average daily temperatures in Hanoi are 62°F–68°F (16.5°C–20°C)
during these months, rising to 81°F–84°F (27.3°C–29°C) from May through
August. Unlike the other major deltas in mainland Southeast Asia (Mekong,
Chao Phraya, Irrawaddy), the winter climate is cold enough to interfere
with year-round rice cultivation. The winter monsoon winds are also quite
arid, and most of northern Vietnam experiences a dry season during these
months. Toward the end of winter (February to March) persistent drizzling
rains fall in the lowlands, preceding the hot, humid, and rainy summer
months. The shift in climate results from the arrival of warm southwestern monsoon winds blowing in from southerly oceans. Typhoons (tropical
Pacific cyclones) arrive during the rainy season, from April to October, and
can cause severe flooding in the Red River Delta.

   Within this basic pattern, northern Vietnam's rainfall and temperature
regimes vary considerably. Above 6,600 feet (2,000 m) the Hoang Lien Son
Range experiences no dry season, and temperatures regularly drop below
freezing during December and January, with snowfall one to three days of
the year. These conditions are closer to temperate Chinese climates than
subtropical ones and are partly responsible for the distinctive plant communities found on these slopes. Rainfall tends to increase as one moves
northeast up the coast from Hanoi toward the Chinese border where Mong
Cai, located at northern Vietnam's easternmost point, receives on average 108 inches (2,749 mm) of rain and experiences three dry months each
year. Throughout the region, average annual rainfall varies from a low of 44
inches (1,127 mm) at Nam Dinh, located southeast of Hanoi near the coast,
to a high of 189 inches (4,802 mm) at Bac Quang at the foot of the Viet Bac
Massif in Ha Giang Province.

HYDROLOGY

The Red River and its tributaries dominate northern Vietnam's terrain and
the lives of most of its inhabitants. The Red River itself rises in the Van Nam
highlands in China's Yunnan Province, where it is called the Yuan Chiang,

and then flows southeast into Vietnam along the Red River fault zone. Two major tributaries also originating in Yunnan, the Clear River (Song Lo) to the east and the Black River (Song Da) to the west, join the Red River 6 miles (10 km) apart and approximately 34 miles (55 km) northwest of Hanoi. All three rivers are swift-flowing, and the Red and Black descend to the delta through deep, narrow gorges. In 1998, the Hoa Binh Dam blocked the Black River's flow before its juncture with the Red River, creating Vietnam's largest reservoir and supplying a significant proportion of the country's electricity. Two other major rivers, the Song Ma and the Song Ca, parallel the Red River's course to the south. Both are fast-flowing in their upper reaches, and the Song Ca has a wide delta similar to the Red River's, though far smaller.

Despite its relatively short course (at 750 miles or 1,200 km, it is outranked by more than 100 other rivers worldwide) and limited drainage area of 46,000 square miles (120,000 km^2), the Red River has a disproportionately high flow rate and sediment load. The river undergoes dramatic changes between the wet and dry seasons. Annual rainfall in the delta averages 60–70 inches (1,600–1,800 mm), 80 to 85 percent of which falls between April and October. Combined with the swift Black and Clear Rivers, the Red River swells and is in flood from June to October. During these months, the river carries 73 percent of its total volume, and flow rates can reach 46,000 cubic yards per second (35,000 m^3/sec); the annual average is 5,100 cubic yards per second (3,900 m₃/sec). Partly because of high flow rates and partly due to upstream erosion caused by continuing tectonic uplift and deforestation, the Red River carries a high load of sediments, five times more per square mile (km^2) of drainage area than the Mekong. The accumulation of these sediments and other matter transported by the river has filled in what was once a shallow inlet of Bac Bo Gulf to form the expansive delta.

Flooding is an unpredictable but serious threat to people and their crops in the delta; the high-water mark can be as much as 46 feet (14 m) above the surrounding lands in some areas. The delta's residents have built an extensive system of inland and coastal dikes over the centuries to protect crops and people and for irrigation. In addition to the Red River, the delta includes the mouths of the Day, Thai Binh, and Van Uc Rivers.

VEGETATION AND HABITATS

Northern Vietnam's forests lie at the northern distributional limit of tropical plants and the southern distributional limit of subtropical and temperate ones. Transitions between plant communities are seen here as one moves south to north, east to west, and from lowlands to uplands. The dominant forest type in northern Vietnam is evergreen, including both broad-leaved and coniferous plants, with pockets of semi-evergreen forest. Coastal mangrove formations and forests growing on limestone are also important elements of the north's natural landscape diversity.

The Red River Delta was once covered with freshwater swamp forest inland and a wide band of mangroves along its estuaries and coast. Essentially none of this native vegetation is left as all potentially arable land has been transformed to wet rice paddies and other croplands and the coastline greatly modified for aquaculture, saltpans, and protection from flooding. Land conversion and subsequent loss of diversity here is not recent. Modification of the delta dates back centuries. The first recorded large-scale dike was 5.3 miles (8.5 km) long and constructed at the end of the ninth century C.E. Northern Vietnam's natural mangrove forests are shorter and not as diverse as those in the south. Thick, closed-canopy stands once clustered around the delta, wide and strong enough to connect the mainland to Cat Ba and other islands in Ha Long Bay. Now less than 32 square miles (82 km²) remains, distributed in narrow strips 15–30 feet (5–10 m) wide, of which only 0.3 square miles (0.8 km²) are more than thirty years old. The rest is scrubby, open, and most often plantations of only a single species.

Outside the delta and coastal regions, northern Vietnam's natural vegetation is forest. Lowland broad-leaved evergreen forests once covered much of northern Vietnam up to elevations of 2,000–2,600 feet (600–800 m). These are now rare and greatly threatened. People have cleared the vast majority of these forests for crops and pasture, and many are replaced now by scrub and secondary forest.

At 2,000–2,600 feet (600–800 m) in northern Vietnam the vegetation transitions from wet lowland to montane evergreen forests. The montane forest is distributed roughly between 2,000 and 6,600 feet (600–2,000 m)

Figure 28. Rhododendron (genus *Rhododendron*) forest from higher slopes of Mount Fan Xi Pan (Photograph by Eleanor J. Sterling)

and is a mix of broad-leaved trees and conifers. Subtropical and temperate tree families replace previously dominant tropical ones, largely due to lower temperatures. Most tropical dipterocarps (Family Dipterocarpaceae) are not found above 2,000–3,000 feet (600–900 m) in the north and many montane species find their lower distributional limits at 3,000–3,900 feet (900–1,200 m). Dominant families at this elevation include beeches (Fagaceae), magnolias (Magnoliaceae), and laurels (Lauraceae) alongside a diversity of conifers, including Fokienia (*Fokienia hodginsii*), which often emerge above the canopy. At higher altitudes, moisture in the form of fog, clouds, heavy dew, and rain is near constant along ridges and mountain peaks, forming ideal conditions for cloud forests. The trees in these distinctive communities are mostly conifers and heaths (Family Ericaceae), which includes the rhododendrons (genus *Rhododendron;* fig. 28). Stunted, twisted, and often quite old, they are heavily laden with lichens, mosses, and orchids.

On the upper slopes and ravines of the Hoang Lien Son Range are forests whose taxa are indicative of the strong affinity between Vietnam's highlands and the forest communities of southern China. Growing between 6,600 and 9,200 feet (2,000–2,800 m) are conifer forests dominated by tall Himalayan Hemlock (*Tsuga dumosa*) and Delavay's Fir (*Abies delavayi fansipanensis*). These forests are the sole Southeast Asian occurrence of a temperate hemlock-fir community more typical of southwestern China, and they include species found nowhere else in Vietnam. Also present are a wide variety of temperate species, including birches (Betulaceae), walnuts (Juglandaceae), willows (Salicaceae), and blueberries (genus *Vaccinium*). Their diversity and uniqueness confers national conservation significance to this upland forest type. Unfortunately, even at these heights, much of the forest has been removed for agriculture and is now mainly shrub and grassland.

A final important component of northern Vietnam's vegetation is the extensive and quite distinctive plant communities rooted on and over limestone (fig. 29). Here, these forests are found at altitudes up to 5,600 feet (1,700 m), most commonly 1,000–3,000 feet (300–900 m). With increasing altitude they pass from closed-canopy evergreen forests to shorter, more open semi-evergreen formations featuring twisted and bent vegetative forms. Northern Vietnam's limestone communities are often dominated by a rich mix of conifers, including the rare pine *Pinus kwangtungensis,* which is restricted to a few locations in southern China and northern Vietnam. Increased light reaching toward the forest floor encourages a thick and diverse community of smaller trees and shrubs, including mountain ashes (*Sorbus*), bittersweets (*Celastrus*), and rhododendrons. Above 4,000 feet (1,200 m), limestone forest canopies become even more open and dominated by conifers.

Vietnam's orchids reach their greatest variety among the extensive limestone formations east of the Red River. As of 2004, botanists had identified 296 species from limestone and other areas of northeastern Vietnam. Of these, 14 percent are believed endemic to Vietnam (though this may change

Figure 29. Logged primary broad-leaved evergreen forest with the linden
Burretiodendron hsienmu (Family Tiliaceae) dominant on limestone karst,
Na Hang District, Tuyen Quang Province (Photograph by Phan Ke Loc)

with further surveying). By contrast, there are 117 species in the highland
areas of the Hoang Lien Son Range and Ha Giang Province, of which 9 percent are endemic. Orchid diversity on limestone is concentrated on upper
slopes and ridges where the many habitats and light regimes result in high
diversity of ground-rooted, epiphytic, and lithophytic species. Also present
are unusual species of saprophytic orchids, life-forms that derive their nutrients from decaying organic matter. The richness of Vietnam's limestone-
growing orchids is found in Cao Bang Province. Here, the endemic orchid
Renanthera citrina, whose delicate, bright yellow petals bear random purple
splotches, was discovered in 1997.

FAUNA

Like its vegetation, northern Vietnam's animal communities are a mixture
of tropical and subtropical species, many of which are unique to the northern third of the country. Within the region, the Red River may be an effective barrier to movement (or coincide with one) for some groups, such as

gibbons (Family Hylobatidae), resulting in different species and communities in the northeast and northwest. For others, such as birds, the Red River appears less critical than such factors as climate in shaping diversity patterns.

The Red River Delta, despite its radical transformation under human pressures, remains a critical passage stopover and overwintering spot for migratory birds, though almost all of its native mammals, a suite of wetland and swamp forest species, are now gone. Limestone outcroppings host specialized communities, including a group of closely related leaf-eating monkeys (genus *Trachypithecus*). However, the bulk of the region's diversity is associated with its evergreen forests, including large ground birds, songbirds, squirrels, shrews, deer, and primates. Unfortunately, both habitat loss and exploitation have taken their toll—the Asian Elephant (*Elephas maximus*) is now nearly extinct here, and the Lesser One-horned Rhinoceros (*Rhinoceros sondaicus*), which once roamed the southwestern part of the region, has vanished.

From a historical perspective, northern Vietnam has been relatively well surveyed for mammals and birds, including the 1928–1929 expedition to Vietnam, Laos, and Siam (now Thailand) led by Theodore Roosevelt, Jr. Biological surveys have uncovered previously unknown (though not unexpected) populations of the Tonkin Black-cheeked Crested Gibbon (*Hylobates [Nomascus] concolor concolor;* Endangered), Tonkin Snub-nosed Monkey (*Rhinopithecus avunculus;* Critically Endangered), and Rufous-necked Hornbill (*Aceros nipalensis;* Vulnerable). One of the best-studied areas of Vietnam, Tam Dao, is located in the northeast, roughly 50 miles (80 km) north of Hanoi. This isolated granite ridge was the site of a French hill station during the colonial period and is now partly incorporated into Tam Dao National Park. The list of species known to occur there is among the highest in the country and includes less well studied groups such as the butterflies and other invertebrates.

Mammals

Almost forty mammal species in northern Vietnam are found nowhere else in the country. One subset of this group is the region's endemics: the Tonkin

Snub-nosed Monkey, Delacour's Leaf Monkey (*Trachypithecus delacouri*), Cat Ba Leaf Monkey (*T. poliocephalus poliocephalus*), the newly described Cao Van Sung's Mountain Shrew (*Chodsigoa caovansunga*), and the Chapa Pygmy Dormouse (*Typhlomys chapensis*).

The majority are mammals whose geographical ranges extend southward into the region from China and the Himalayas. Some are common in temperate regions, including the Forest Musk Deer (*Moschus berezovskii*), which is widely distributed through south and central China and Tibet, and the Raccoon Dog (*Nyctereutes procyonoides*), whose natural distribution includes most of East Asia. Some are less widely distributed such as the Assamese Macaque (*Macaca assamensis*), East Chinese Hare (*Lepus sinensis*), and a number of shrews and moles (Order Insectivora). Conversely, fewer species from central and southern Vietnam intrude into the north. An isolated Saola (*Pseudoryx nghetinhensis*) population may persist just north of the Song Ca, an area included in Pu Huong Nature Reserve. Also near or at its northern limit here is the Sun Bear (*Ursus malayanus*), though this may reflect hunting pressure rather than zoogeography.

The ranges of large mammals are generally less restricted by altitude than those of birds and amphibians. One exception is the strong association between leaf-eating monkeys in the François's Leaf Monkey (*T. francoisi*) species group and forests on limestone hills. There is also some turnover in the small mammal communities with elevation, such as squirrels, mice, and rats. Most large mammals here are on the verge of becoming locally extinct if they are not already, including the Forest Musk Deer and Gaur (*Bos gaurus*).

Tonkin Snub-nosed Monkey (Rhinopithecus avunculus)

In the late 1860s, Père Armand David transported the first snub-nosed monkey (genus *Rhinopithecus*) specimens to Europe, catalyzing a century-and-a-half discussion on their proper taxonomic placement. Not until 1912 did scientists describe the Vietnamese representative of the genus, the Tonkin Snub-nosed Monkey (fig. 30), placing it with three already known Chinese species, the Golden (*R. roxellana*), Yunnan (*R. bieti*), and Guizhou (*R. brelichi*) Snub-nosed Monkeys. The name describes their remarkable

Figure 30. Tonkin Snub-nosed Monkey (*Rhinopithecus avunculus*)

upturned noses, which seem to be pressed back against the face so that the nostrils point directly outward. The four snub-nosed monkey species live along a spectrum of relatively cool climates from subtropical forests below 4,900 feet (1,500 m), where temperatures never dip below freezing (Tonkin Snub-nosed Monkey), to coniferous forests at 14,000 feet (4,500 m) that are frost-bound for 280 days a year (Yunnan Snub-nosed Monkey). These cold, temperate environments are among the harshest of all nonhuman primate habitats.

Snub-nosed monkey species vary in diet, coat color, body size, degree of sexual dimorphism, whether they are primarily tree- or ground-dwelling, and group size, which can reach as high as 600 members in the Golden Snub-nosed Monkey. Some of this variation may relate to their different environments. The Tonkin Snub-nosed Monkey eats a seasonal diet of leaves and fruits, whereas the Guizhou Snub-nosed Monkey diet is non-seasonal and composed primarily of lichens. The constant availability and (compared to fruit) broad distribution of lichen may allow the Guizhou species to live in larger groups, where more males vie for access to fertile females. This favors the evolution of traits such as large body size and long canines that help males compete with other males for mates.

Until 1993 the snub-nosed monkeys were often placed within the douc genus, *Pygathrix*, and scientists still consider them most closely related to the doucs. Morphologically, the Tonkin Snub-nosed Monkey is intermediate between the Red-shanked Douc (*P. nemaeus nemaeus*) and the three other snub-nosed monkeys. It is smaller and more slender than the Chinese species, males and females are more similar in size, and they are almost completely arboreal. Yet it is still Vietnam's largest primate, with males averaging 30 pounds (13.8 kg) and females 18 pounds (8.3 kg). The fur is black on the upper parts and creamy white below. The face is bluish white, blue-black around the muzzle, and in adults the pink lips are enlarged to clown-sized proportions. The Tonkin Snub-nosed Monkey dwells in limestone forests up to 3,300 feet (1,000 m) in northeastern Vietnam, living in bands of up to thirty individuals (formerly possibly as high as 100). Groups often associate with each other, forming larger bands. Little else is known of this species except that in ecology and behavior it resembles other leaf monkeys more than its Chinese relatives.

The Tonkin Snub-nosed Monkey was never widespread and was likely always endemic to the area that is now northeastern Vietnam. Once found in Tuyen Quang, Yen Bai, Bac Thai, and adjacent provinces, it is now restricted to Na Hang and Cham Chu Nature Reserves and a few nearby sites. The Na Hang reserve was created specifically to conserve this species, and it houses the largest known population. Unfortunately, the reserve is split into two sectors, each encompassing a reproductively isolated subpopulation. Vietnamese scientist Le Khac Quyet discovered a new population in 2002 in the Du Gia Nature Reserve, bringing estimates of the number remaining in the wild from fewer than 200 to fewer than 260. Hunting for meat and medicine is the main threat to the species; in China snub-nosed monkey bones are believed to cure a variety of ills, including rheumatism.

Crested Gibbons (Hylobates [Nomascus] concolor and H. [N.] sp. cf. nasutus)

North Vietnam's black crested gibbons provide a glimpse into how geographic distribution, evolutionary relationships, and conservation status are often intimately intertwined. Northern Vietnam is home to four taxa: three distinct black crested gibbons and the Northern White-cheeked Crested Gibbon (H. [N.] leucogenys leucogenys). They seem to occupy non-overlapping ranges and are often separated by rivers. Defining the relationships among Southeast Asia's gibbons is among the more challenging problems in current primate taxonomy, and researchers continue to debate the number of species and subspecies and their position within the group.

One species, the Tonkin Black-cheeked Crested Gibbon, is found in northwestern Vietnam between the Red and Black Rivers. The males are completely black and the females are yellow with black hairs covering a large part of the chest and stomach and a patch of black on their head running from front to back. A second species, the Eastern Black Crested Gibbon (H. [N.] sp. cf. nasutus), lives only east of the Red River and on China's Hainan Island. There is great confusion about how many distinguishable forms exist within this species. In Vietnam there appear to be two. In one, the H. (N.) sp. cf. nasutus population, the males are all black and the females are a brownish yellow-gray all over with a dark crown patch. This fur color pattern closely resembles that of their sister population restricted to Hainan Island, H. (N.) sp. cf. nasutus hainanus. The other Vietnamese form, H. (N.) sp. cf. nasutus nasutus, is represented by only a single female acquired in 1962 from Hong Gai (coastal Quang Ninh Province) for the Berlin Tierpark. Her coloration is very different: buff-brown all over, much darker brown on the chest, with a wide black cap on the head. However, her calls (a distinguishing trait among gibbons) are virtually identical to those of the Hainan females.

This situation presents an intriguing set of questions: How many subspecies are there? What is the evolutionary relationship between the non-overlapping taxa? Why does gibbon diversity appear so high in a relatively small area? These might seem academic riddles if not for the dire conservation status of the gibbons. The Eastern Black Crested Gibbon is perhaps the most threatened primate in the world. Until a group of about thirty was discovered in a 7,400-acre (3,000 ha) forest in Cao Bang, the only known population consisted of sixteen (possibly fewer) individuals on Hainan Island. Though there has been no research, it is likely that the mainland and island groups are subspecies, while the taxon represented by the 1962 Hong Gai female may be extinct. The Tonkin Western Black Crested Gibbon's Vietnamese population numbers less than 100, with a group of seventy at Che Tao (Yen Bai Province) and twenty at Ho Nam Mu (Lao Cai Province). Similar taxa in China (*N. c. furvogaster* and *N. c. jingdongensis*) and Laos (*N. c. lu*) are currently considered different subspecies from the Vietnamese one.

The distinctness and distribution of these three gibbon taxa must be clarified before effective action to conserve them can be undertaken. Ranges should be more accurately mapped (if possible) and variation in morphology, vocalizations, and genetics analyzed. This research is crucial for managing wild populations, for breeding programs in zoos or rescue centers, and for the relocation of any confiscated animals. When species hybridize and produce offspring with a member of another taxon, biodiversity in the form of genetic diversity is effectively lost.

François's Leaf Monkey species group (Trachypithecus delacouri, T. francoisi francoisi, *and* T. poliocephalus poliocephalus)

All five of Vietnam's black-and-white leaf-eating monkeys are closely related and placed, along with one species in Laos and another in China, in a grouping referred to as the François's Leaf Monkey group or superspecies. By gathering these seven taxa together, scientists acknowledge their close evolutionary relationships and current uncertainty about the structure of these links. All live on limestone hills and cliffs, inhabit nonoverlapping geographic ranges, and replace each other sequentially from the Chinese border to the north-central Truong Son Range. Three dwell in Vietnam's north, the Delacour's Leaf Monkey (*Trachypithecus delacouri*) and the Cat Ba Leaf Monkey, both of them endemic to Vietnam, and François's Leaf Monkey (*T. francoisi francoisi*).

The northernmost species, François's Leaf Monkey, is all black except for a narrow band of slightly longer white hairs running from the corners of its mouth up to the ears. Like all monkeys in this group, the head is crowned with a high, pointed crest. This combination of crest and extended handlebar moustache lends individuals a handsome, reserved, almost wise appearance. Historically, François's Leaf Monkey resided on northeastern Vietnam's karst formations from Thai Nguyen Province northward and in eastern sections of the northwest's Lao Cai and Yen Bai Provinces. It has now largely disappeared from this range, and a report from 2002 estimated that fewer than 300 remained. Fortunately, it is also found in China's adjacent Guangxi Province, though this larger population (3,200–3,500) is also highly fragmented.

Delacour's Leaf Monkey resides in a 2,000-square-mile region (5,000 km^2) located south and east of the Red River in the karst hills of Ninh Binh, Ha Nam, Hoa Binh, and Thanh Hoa Provinces. White fur replaces black from the middle of the back down to the knees, and the monkey's common name in Vietnamese, *vooc mong lang,* translates as "the leaf monkey with white trousers." As in François's, long white hairs run from the mouth, here ending in a patch of white behind the ears. Although described in 1932, no subsequent sighting emerged until one in Cuc Phuong National Park in 1987. In the wild there are now 270–300 individuals in nineteen isolated subpopulations, only two of which (in Van Long and Pu Luong Nature Reserves) have 30–35 individuals and are thought to be marginally self-sustaining.

North Vietnam's third François's group member is also its most threatened. The Cat Ba Leaf Monkey's dark chocolate–brown body is capped by striking yellowish to creamy white fur on its head and neck. The Cat Ba Leaf Monkey is known only from Cat Ba Island in Ha Long Bay. Its range was likely larger when lower sea levels exposed the bay's surrounding limestone. The island's entire population now numbers only fifty to sixty, and the reproductive rate is extremely low. The IUCN lists the Cat Ba Leaf Monkey as Critically Endangered.

One of the most interesting questions about this entire group is why the species are so closely associated with limestone. Suggestions include a diet specializing on limestone vegetation, retreating to caves as protection from predators, and using caves to buffer the climate in both summer (when they are relatively cool) and winter (when they are warm). It is also possible that limestone is not an essential habitat but a refuge from human disturbance, as seems to be the case with close relatives (White-headed Leaf Monkey, *T. p. leucocephalus*) in China.

The primary cause for these drastic population declines is hunting for food, medicine, and export. Habitat loss and fragmentation are also concerns; the north's limestone hills are isolated islands amid a sea of agriculture. François's Leaf Monkey is also threatened by regional mining, which disturbs the monkeys and attracts miners who hunt in the surrounding lands. The reproductive isolation of the fragmented populations and their dwindling numbers are further threats. Small, isolated populations suffer from loss of genetic exchange and low birthrates, as well as susceptibility to chance environmental events that could cause them to go extinct. As the demography of this species suggests, it is critical not to use overall population estimates to assess conservation status; more important are the number of subpopulations that are actually viable.

*Asian Black Bear (*Ursus thibetanus*) and Sun Bear (*U. malayanus*)*

Two bears live in Vietnam: the temperate Asian Black Bear, sister species to the American Black Bear (*U. americanus*), and the tropical Sun Bear (fig. 31). The Asian Black Bear is much larger than the Sun Bear, 4–6 feet (1.2–1.9 m) in length from head to tail, and the males are much heavier at 132–441 pounds (60–200 kg) than females, 88–309 pounds (40–140 kg). The Asian Black Bear is marked by a prominent white chevron on the chest stretching out to the shoulders and a ruff or mane of long hair on the back and sides of the neck. The Sun Bear is noticeably smaller, 3.5–5 feet (1.1–1.5 m) in length

Figure 31. Family Ursidae: Asian Black Bear (*Ursus thibetanus,* left)
and Sun Bear (*U. malayanus,* right)

and weighing 60–143 pounds (27–65 kg). Sun Bears have a variable ocher-to-white colored chest patch that may be U-shaped or a complete circle. Because of its small stature and extremely short fur it is called the Dog Bear in parts of its range. Both bears move about with an ambling gait that places the front and back feet on one side of the body forward simultaneously.

Asian Black Bears prefer hilly and mountainous forests along a range extending from Iran east to Siberia and south to mainland Southeast Asia. In Vietnam they are recorded from forests throughout the country. Accomplished climbers active during the day, they subsist on a wide-ranging, seasonally variable, and largely vegetarian diet. In one study, the food of Asian Black Bears living in China's mountainous Sichuan Province was dominated by young leaves, stalks, and bamboos shoots in the spring, berries and fruits in the summer, and nuts in the fall, supplemented by insects and small amounts of carrion. To satisfy their dietary needs these black bears foraged across areas in excess of 47.5 square miles (123 km²), shifting between different altitudes and habitats. Unfortunately, little is known of Asian Black Bear habits and behavior in Vietnam's warmer, more stable climate. Bears are generally quite flexible in their ecology and behavior, so diet and movements here likely reflect local availability of similar food resources. The length of hibernation is probably much shorter or nonexistent compared to more northerly-dwelling bears. Like their close evolutionary relatives in North America, coat color may be brown or even a bright blonde in rare individuals.

Of the world's eight bears, the Sun Bear is the most poorly known. A truly tropical species, its range includes lowland to lower montane forests in eastern India, southern China, mainland Southeast Asia, and the islands of Sumatra and Borneo. Despite their relatively small stature, Sun Bears are considered quite dangerous, rising up on their hind feet, lunging, swatting, and barking when startled. The Sun Bear is highly arboreal, spending much of its time aloft, and its front feet are rotated inward and equipped with long, heavy claws for climbing. Its diet is dominated by invertebrates such as termites (Order Ispotera) and beetles (Order Coleoptera) and fruit. Sun Bears forage largely in trees by ripping or breaking apart limbs and trunks with their claws and massive teeth and extracting insects and honey with a tongue that can extend 8–10 inches (20–25 cm). Like Asian Black Bears, when they experience fluctuations in food availability, they respond by switching both diet and foraging areas, though not as drastically, and they appear to use smaller home ranges. Once thought to be primarily nocturnal, instead they are mainly active during the day, switching to nighttime activity in areas disturbed by humans. Sun Bears do not hibernate; when sleeping they use hollow logs and tree nests made of bent and broken branches. Mating appears to occur during any season, but gestation of the one or two young varies widely, from three to eight months. This is likely caused by delayed implantation, known to occur in bears, where embryonic development is halted until birth can occur when food is plentiful.

Exploitation is the largest threat to Vietnam's bears. Asia's bears have been hunted for more than 3,000 years for their paws, considered a delicacy, and gall bladder bile used in traditional medicines. They also come into direct conflict with humans when they raid commercial crops, including pineapple, corn, and jackfruit. The IUCN lists the Asiatic Black Bear as Vulnerable; the data are insufficient to assess the conservation status of the Sun Bear.

Birds

Of Vietnam's 844 bird species, 675 have been recorded in northern Vietnam, 154 of which are not found in the rest of the country. Most of this unique avifauna is concentrated in one of two distinct communities: birds overwintering in coastal areas, and montane forest-dwelling residents allied with China, the Himalayan foothills, and the Palearctic, a vast region stretching across Europe, Iceland, and temperate Asia.

Most of northern Vietnam's coastal visitors are waterbirds, such as geese and ducks (Family Anatidae), snipes (Family Scopacidae), lapwings and plovers (Family Chradriidae), gulls and terns (Family Laridae), egrets (Family Ardeidae), and ibises and spoonbills (Family Threskiornithidae). But overwintering species are not restricted to the coastal wetlands. The north's upland forests are overwintering areas for birds such as warblers in the genus *Phylloscopus,* many of which breed far to the north in Asia, and the Wood Snipe (*Gallinago nemoricola*; Vulnerable).

The north's characteristic residents are largely songbirds (along with some pheasants) living above 3,300 feet (1,000 m) in the region's temperate and subtropical forests. Distinctive members of this community include the Spot-breasted Scimitar Babbler (*Pomatorhinus erythrocnemis*), Streak-throated Fulvetta (*Alcippe cinereiceps*), and Spot-breasted Parrotbill (*Paradoxornis guttaticollis*), which all inhabit subtropical evergreen, semi-evergreen, coniferous, and cloud forests. Above 6,500 feet (2,000 m) the species composition changes and truly temperate species begin to appear, such as the Long-tailed Thrush (*Zoothera dixoni*) and a striking crimson pheasant, Temminck's Tragopan (*Tragopan temminckii*). These temperate species occur in the Hoang Lien Son Range and, just as with the vegetation, are far more common and widespread in similar habitats in China.

No birds endemic to Vietnam live in the north, though two Indochinese endemics are found here, the Red-vented Barbet (*Megalaima lagrandieri*) and the Short-tailed Scimitar Babbler (*Jabouilleia danjoui*), as is one of the country's two limestone karst specialists, the Limestone Wren Babbler (*Napothera crispifrons*). Avifauna conservation efforts here focus on protecting coastal regions and mid- to high-elevation forests. Mount Fan Xi Pan and adjacent peaks, along with northern Laos, are recognized as important areas of bird diversity, home to four restricted-range species whose individual global ranges fall below 20,000 square miles (50,000 km²): Ward's Trogon (*Harpactes wardi*), Red-winged Laughingthrush (*Garrulax formosus*), Broad-billed Warbler (*Tickellia hodgsoni*), and Yellow-billed Nuthatch (*Sitta solangiae*). Worryingly, Ward's Trogon—a gorgeous bird, the male unmistakably marked by a dark pink forehead, lighter pink underbelly, and overall pinkish wash; the female equally distinctive with yellow forehead and pale yellow belly and outer tail feathers—has not been recorded in Vietnam since 1930 despite repeated surveys. It was once considered common on Mount Fan Xi Pan.

Overwintering Coastal Birds (Families Anatidae, Scolopacidae, Laridae, Threskiornithidae, and Others)

The Red River Delta's coastal zones lie along one of the world's largest, most complex, and most threatened bird migration routes, the East Asian–Australasian Flyway. Birds using this flyway cross a wide belt of land, sea, and ocean from temperate breeding grounds as far north as Siberia and Alaska to tropical and subtropical wintering areas as far south as Australia and New Zealand. It is a challenge to estimate the number of birds flying this path twice each year, though the vast majority of the region's 4 to 6 million shorebirds (such as plovers, sandpipers and snipes) and 15 to 22 million geese and ducks are migratory. This list excludes the large number of inland migratory birds such as raptors and songbirds also moving seasonally between Palearctic Eurasia and Southeast Asia, Australia, and New Zealand.

Vietnam's Red River Delta is a critical link along this flyway, providing both stopover areas for rest and feeding and more permanent wintering grounds. Visiting birds depend on its coastal and estuarine habitats, primarily intertidal mudflats, mangroves, salt marshes, and offshore islands, for food and refuge. Among these winter visitors are globally significant

Figure 32. Black-faced Spoonbill (*Platalea minor*)

numbers of the Black-faced Spoonbill (*Platalea minor;* Endangered; fig. 32). Standing 2 feet, 6 inches (75 cm) tall, these birds have a uniformly white nonbreeding winter plumage. When breeding, both sexes display a yellowish patch at the base of their necks and a crest of yellow feathers flaring out and up from the back of their heads. Black-faced Spoonbills were common along coastal China until the 1930s. Today they nest on a few rocky islands scattered along the Yellow Sea's coasts and off Korea's western shore. The most important breeding locations — and probably the least disturbed — lie in the Demilitarized Zone separating North and South Korea. The Red River Delta is one of the spoonbill's three main wintering grounds; the others are Taiwan's Tsengwen Estuary and Hong Kong's Deep Bay. In Vietnam they wade in the brackish wetlands of mudflats and mangroves, sweeping their slightly ajar bills back and forth through the water, closing on prey such as aquatic insects, shellfish, mollusks, and fish when they sense vibrations from detectors located inside the spoon. When not feeding, Black-faced Spoon-

Figure 33. Spoon-billed Sandpiper (*Calidris pygmea*)

bills roost in flocks on sandy islands or in other isolated areas where they can avoid human disturbance. Winter counts, begun in the 1980s, have recorded up to 104 Blackfaced Spoonbills from Vietnam's northern coastline.

A second threatened shorebird wintering in the delta with a similarly flattened, spatulate bill is the Spoon-billed Sandpiper (*Calidris pygmea*; Endangered; fig. 33). Spoon-billed sandpipers are roughly 5.5 inches (14–16 cm) tall, and females are slightly larger than males. When wintering in the delta, Spoon-billed Sandpipers are far less conspicuously dressed than during the breeding season, when the head is a dark cinnamon red with bold black streaks on the crown, the breast is reddish with white underparts, and the rump is a dusky brownish gray. Both sexes bear the same plumage. The birds walk slowly forward, swinging their heads from side to side in shallow water and soft mud and relying on the bill's nerve endings to detect worms, insect larvae, small crabs, and other prey. Come spring, Spoon-billed Sandpipers migrate far to the north, seeking the coasts of northeastern Siberia and the Chukotski Peninsula, which lies across the Bering Strait from Alaska's Seward Peninsula. Arriving, they settle amid sparsely vegetated sandy ridges and adjacent wet meadows, marshes, and lakes. Females abandon their chicks when they are only four to six days old and sometimes immediately after hatching when it is late in the season. The male continues to tend the brood for fifteen to twenty days, shepherding them to independence.

These two spoon-billed shorebirds are far from the only migratory birds whose uncertain futures rely on the preservation of the Red River Delta's coastal zone. Other globally threatened winter visitors include the Nordmann's Greenshank (*Tringa guttifer;* Endangered), a relative of the sandpipers, and a black-headed gull, Saunders's Gull (*Larus saundersi;* Vulnerable). Rarely seen are Baer's Pochard (*Aythya baeri;* Vulnerable), a green-headed member of the duck family (Anatidae) and the Black-headed Ibis (*Threskiornis melanocephalus;* Near Threatened). Many other non-threatened birds visit here, too, among them the Greylag Goose (*Anser anser*), Common Snipe (*Gallinago gallinago*), Eurasian Curlew (*Numenius arquata*), Tufted Duck (*Aythya fuligula*), Pallas's Gull (*Larus ichthyaetus*), and Black Stork (*Ciconia nigra*). Because migration concentrates birds along flyways, it increases their vulnerability to a variety of threats. People erect mist nets (stretches of fine, virtually invisible netting to entangle and capture birds) during spring and fall migration, capturing birds for consumption and sale. For threatened birds, the loss of even a handful of breeding adults can jeopardize population survival. When birds are concentrated in small wintering areas, their exposure to disease can also increase. This happened in the winter of 2002–2003, when seventy-three Black-faced Spoonbills died during an outbreak of botulism in Taiwan's Tsengwen Estuary. The dependence of many individuals on small wetland areas magnifies the impact of any habitat loss.

And yet, because migration funnels birds along a limited number of flyways and stopover or wintering sites, it is feasible to monitor populations and protect important migratory sites. This is particularly true for species, such as the Spoon-billed Sandpiper, that breed in inaccessible regions. For migratory or winter counts to be useful, survey techniques must be tailored to the biology of each species. The vagaries of timing, triggered by the weather or breeding success, and location, affected by wind patterns and other factors, can cause counts to fluctuate widely between years. The four-fold increase in known Black-faced Spoonbill global population to nearly

1,200 individuals over the past fifteen years points to the importance of these research methods.

Northern Pheasants and Partridges (Family Phasianidae)

Most of northern Vietnam's eight resident pheasants and partridges (Family Phasianidae) are restricted to forests above 3,300 feet (1,000 m)—in two cases above 6,500 feet (2,000 m). Though none of these species are endemic or considered globally threatened by the IUCN, they do offer a glimpse into the great diversity of pheasants and partridges found in Southeast Asia's mountains.

Temminck's Tragopan has been recorded at 7,000 feet (2,135 m) and above in the Hoang Lien Son Range (see fig. 22). It can be found up to 14,000 feet (4,270 m) elsewhere in an extensive range stretching from the eastern Himalayas to northwestern Vietnam. In Vietnam these large, heavily built birds (average weight 2.25 pounds; 980–1,120 g) prefer cool, damp broad-leaved evergreen, semi-evergreen, and rhododendron forests with thick undergrowth. Their behavior is secretive, shy, and wary, and they are quite hard to either see or hear in the field. Unlike most pheasants, Temminck's Tragopans are highly arboreal, spending nearly all their time in trees feeding on buds and leaves supplemented by berries, seeds, and insects. They prefer to nest 3–26 feet (1–8 m) above the ground, sometimes in the abandoned nests of crows or other birds. The hen lays a clutch of three to five eggs (typical for forest-dwelling pheasants), and the chicks can safely fly to aboveground perches when only two or three days old. They are likely monogamous, males and females occurring singly, in pairs, or in small family groups.

The two sexes may be similar in size and weight, but they are strikingly different in appearance. Males are unmistakable: bright crimson all over, marked with gray spots ringed in black on the upper parts, naked blue skin on the face and neck, black feathering above the eyes, and a crimson crown. The female has a blue ring around the eyes but is otherwise grayish brown all over with brown to buff streaking that grows lighter on the undersides. All male tragopans have two unusual head ornaments. One is the lappet, a thin piece of skin that is usually completely retracted beneath the beak, making it invisible. When the male displays for his mate, he unfolds it over his chest much like a shield-shaped, brightly colored bib some 4–6 inches (10–15 cm) long and 2–3 inches (5–7.5 cm) wide. In Temminck's Tragopan, the lappet is a brilliant blue with a lighter turquoise coloring the spots scattered across its center and outlining the eight intense red bars lining the sides. The male also erects his second lure, a pair of light turquoise fleshy horns 2–3 inches (5–8 cm) long, which are normally folded back and hidden amid the crown feathers. Male tragopans perform a display quite different from most pheasants, described by Jean Delacour (Indochina's most prominent early ornithologist and a specialist in pheasants) as "altogether weird and beautiful" (Delacour 1977, 71). Often emerging from behind a rock, the male moves rapidly toward the female, beating his wings, fanning his tail feathers, and expanding his lappet and horns. Once in front of the female he stops abruptly, stands erect on his toes, pushes his half-extended wings outward and downward, fluffs out the lower body feathers, and lowers head to chest, displaying the now fully extended lappet and horns.

Three partridges are found in the northern forests above 3,300 feet (1,000 m): the Rufous-throated (*A. rufogularis*), Hill (*A. torqueola*), and Mountain Bamboo (*Bambusicola fytchii*) Partridges. The Silver Pheasant (*Lophura nycthemera*)—a highly variable species—occupies a complicated range depending on the extent of competition with other *Lophura* species. In their presence, it usually ranges above 3,300 feet–6,500 feet (1,000–2,000 m) but can drop to sea level when alone as it is in the country's north. The Gray Peacock Pheasant (*Polyplectron bicalcaratum*)—very similar in appearance and behavior to its close relative, Germain's Peacock Pheasant (*P. germaini*)—occupies evergreen forests up to at least 6,600 feet (2,000 m). And the familiar Common or Ring-necked Pheasant likely ranges from 3,300 feet (1,000 m) and up, though its Vietnamese distribution is poorly known. One species, the Chestnut-necklaced Patridge (*A. charltonii*), is restricted to lowland and submontane elevations below 3,300 feet (1,000 m); it is considered Near Threatened. All other species have large distributions spread across the eastern Himalayan foothills. Habitat loss is the biggest threat to their survival, followed by hunting and indiscriminant capture in ground snares of these large, mostly terrestrial birds.

Yellow-billed Nuthatch and Beautiful Nuthatch
(Sitta solangiae *and* S. formosa*)*

Nuthatches (genus *Sitta* in the Family Sittidae) are instantly recognizable in their forest (or, for two species, rock) habitats. Small, compact birds with short legs and long claws, they scuttle along tree trunks and branches, sometimes hanging upside down to glean insects, seeds, and other food items from the bark. Other birds can cling upright to tree trunks—woodpeckers are one example—but nuthatches are the only group that do not need to use the tail as a prop. They are also the only birds able to clamber facedown along trunks. Described as "'agile,' 'jolly,' and 'good-humored'" (Matthysen 1998, 3), nuthatches derive their common English name from a habitat of wedging larger food items, such as insects and nuts, into cracks in the bark and then hammering them apart with their long, sturdy bills. They are also scatter hoarders, hiding nuts and seeds individually in crevices about their territories.

Nuthatches are primarily creatures of mature temperate and subtropical forests, where they can exploit existing holes for their nests. Their diversity is highest in the Himalayas and mountains of mainland Southeast Asia. Of the twenty-four nuthatch species worldwide, six (25 percent of global diversity) can be found in Vietnam. All six are present in the north and two are particularly interesting: the Beautiful Nuthatch for its conservation status, and the Yellow-billed Nuthatch for its restricted range and a distribution typical of many montane birds in Vietnam.

The Beautiful Nuthatch is indeed as advertised. Most *Sitta* species hew closely to the same basic plumage pattern: blue-gray above and white to deep chestnut below, sometimes with a dark eye-stripe and lighter patch under the chin. Its upperside is black, streaked with brilliant blue and white; the wings flash two white bars, and there is pale bluish lavender edging along the long flight feathers. A faint dark eye-stripe is highlighted against the pale rufous-brown sides of the head and neck above a creamy throat and cinnamon-buff underbelly. Compared to Vietnam's other nuthatches, the Beautiful Nuthatch is relatively large at 6.5 inches (16.5 cm) long, whereas the other five species range between 4.75 and 5.25 inches (12–13.5 cm) in length. Beautiful Nuthatches are monogamous, laying four to six eggs within a tree cavity, often constricting the entrance hole with a plastering of mud to reduce predation. Like other nuthatches, they are sedentary, though they may move to lower altitudes outside the breeding season.

The Beautiful Nuthatch is difficult to observe. It appears alone or in small groups of four or five, often in foraging flocks mixed with other species such as babblers. It also lives at low densities in localized populations scattered across a wide range from the eastern Himalayas to Myanmar and Indochina's Truong Son Range. In Vietnam, it is known from a number of sites in and around the Hoang Lien Nature Reserve in Lao Cai Province and from mountains in the Viet Bac Massif, east of the Red River in Ha Giang Province. Oddly, although it occurs along the western slopes of the Truong Son in Laos, it has yet to be seen on the eastern flanks in Vietnam. This overall scarcity and low abundance appear to be the bird's natural state, though the underlying reasons are unclear. Although it favors dense evergreen forests, the nuthatch has also been seen in disturbed forests and open country habitats. It does not appear limited in its altitudinal range either, having been recorded at 2,000–7,900 feet (600–2,400 m), though apparently preferring elevations of 3,300–6,500 feet (1,000–2,000 m). Competition with other nuthatches also seems an unlikely cause, since the Beautiful Nuthatch's larger size reduces overlap in foraging sites and techniques. Its scarcity, even if natural, increases the risks posed by habitat fragmentation and loss.

The Yellow-billed Nuthatch (*S. solangiae*) is one of a group of three closely related violet-blue nuthatches, two from continental Southeast Asia and one found in the Philippines. In Vietnam it inhabits submontane and montane evergreen forests at 3,000–8,000 feet (900–2,500 m). The bird's upperparts — including the crown — are a dark violet-blue in color and paler on the nape, sides of the neck, and behind the ears. The forehead is a velvety black, and the bill, eye, and eye ring are all a contrasting yellow. Its chin and throat are off-white, with the remaining underparts a pale lilac. The Yellow-billed Nuthatch has a small, restricted geographic range split among three isolated populations: the subspecies *solangiae* in northwestern Vietnam; *fortior* from the uplands of the central and southern Truong Son; and *chienfengensis* from China's Hainan Island. The three subspecies vary in the strength of colors on the head, back, and underbelly.

A number of montane bird species in Vietnam share the Yellow-billed Nuthatch's distribution: resident in the northern mountains and the uplands of central and southern Troung Son. Other species with this range include a number of babblers: the Rufous-chinned Laughingthrush (*Garrulax rufogularis*), Chestnut-tailed Minla (*Minla strigula*), Golden-breasted Fulvetta (*Alcippe chrysotis*), Rusty-capped Fulvetta (*A. dubia*), Black-headed Sibia (*Heterophasia desgodinsi*), and Stripe-throated Yuhina (*Yuhina gularis*). Their disjunct populations are frequently distinct enough to be considered subspecies and the differences among them can be quite marked. The crown and crest of the Sultan Tit (a large bird, black above and yellow below) subspecies from northern Vietnam (*Melanochlora sultanea sultanea*) are a bright, contrasting yellow, whereas the crown and crest of the subspecies from the central Truong Son (*M. s. gayeti*) are the same glossy black as the upperparts.

The IUCN classifies the Beautiful Nuthatch as Vulnerable and the Yellow-billed as Near Threatened. The major hazard both face is forest destruction. The Beautiful Nuthatch in particular is associated with the oldest and largest trees in mature evergreen forests, including the cypress Fokienia (*Fokienia hodginsii*).

Migrating Raptors (Families Acciptridae and Falconidae)

Compared to the coastal migrations of the Black-faced Spoonbill and Spoon-billed Sandpiper, little is known about migrations across the north's inland forests and mountains. Birds of prey are frequently migratory, including a number of buzzards, hawks, and eagles (Family Accipitridae) and falcons (Family Falconidae). There have been occasional records of small raptor groups passing through Vietnam, but the size and timing of these movements were unclear. How much this phenomenon had gone unnoticed was made clear in a report of fall bird counts at the Tram Ton (6,400 feet; 1,950 m) and O Quy Ho (5,750 feet; 1,750 m) passes in the Hoang Lien Son Range (see fig. 25). Over a period of thirteen days (13–25 October 1997), 1,884 raptors were recorded moving south through the pass. This is by far the largest raptor migration event yet recorded in Vietnam. Only three of the thirteen species identified breed in Vietnam.

Among the birds on passage were more than 1,400 Amur Falcons (*Falco amurensis*). This insect-eating falcon is small, 11–12 inches (28–31 cm) in length, and as in other birds of prey, the female (4–6.5 ounces; 111–188 g) is larger than the male (3.5–5.5 ounces; 97–155 g). Both are slaty gray above and paler below, although the female is marked all over with darker bars. In flight, adult males are unmistakable, identified by large white patches on the wings' undersides contrasting strongly with black on the remaining surface.

The remarkable migratory route of the Amur Falcon connects breeding sites in Siberia, northern China, and perhaps North Korea with wintering areas in southern Africa from Malawi to the Transvaal. Amur Falcons undertake this journey of roughly 6,800 miles (11,000 km) twice a year but use different routes, depending on the season. In autumn they leave the breeding grounds in the latter half of September and fly along the southern border of the Himalayas to India, arriving in November. There they feed, fattening themselves for the demanding flight of 1,900–3,000 miles (3,000–4,800 km) across the breadth of the Indian Ocean to Africa. During this crossing, which must last several days, they are aided by the autumnal northeastern monsoon winds at their tails. Arriving in southern Africa in December, they spend the winter feeding on termite and ant alates—winged reproductive forms of these insects—as well as on grasshoppers and locusts. Amur Falcons leave again in March for the north, this time apparently using a different, poorly mapped route that may cross the Arabian Peninsula to take a northerly path around the Himalayas.

Before these records, Amur Falcons had been seen only twice before in Vietnam, and never in double-digit numbers. The Hoang Lien Son Range may be a migration bottleneck for Amur Falcons and other birds of prey that previous researchers overlooked. From the perspective of the watcher, migration is often a transient phenomenon, with most birds passing through rapidly in a short time. In the 1997 survey, three-quarters were recorded over only three days (13–15 October). These sporadic bursts may be caused by changes in the weather. A cold front passed through the Hoan Lien Son Range on 9–13 October. If the birds required warmer weather and thermals to cross the passage, unfavorable weather may have stalled their migration until it changed, causing them to build up before the pass.

Herpetofauna

As of 2004, more than 100 amphibians and 150 reptiles have been recorded from Vietnam's north, a sharp rise since the early 1990s. As the known number of species rises and distributions are better documented, the number of endemic species has fallen. This in turn has clarified amphibian and reptile diversity patterns and provided some clues to the factors that structure them. One factor that has fallen in prominence is the Red River. Surveys in northeastern mountains from the late 1990s and early 2000s indicate that there is more similarity with the better-studied communities in the northwest than previously thought.

Much of northern Vietnam's herpetofaunal diversity centers on the region's mountains, which emerge as fragments of habitat above a sea of largely degraded lowlands. A number of northern mountain-dwelling amphibians and reptiles, such as the brightly marked Hubei Firebelly Toad (*Bombina microdeladigitora*), are also found over the border in southern China. Not all northern species, however, are found in such temperate climates. About twenty of northern Vietnam's reptiles, including the Rhinoceros Snake (*Rhynchophis boulengeri*), are also native to the warmer, more tropical climates of southeastern China's coastal Guangxi Province and Hainan Island. These species are not found in cooler conditions to the north and west.

Limestone forests may harbor specialized herpetofaunal species and communities. Surveys of nearshore karst islands off the coast of Quang Ninh Province found relatively rich communities, including Anderson's Mountain Keelback (*Opisthotropis andersonii*), previously thought to be endemic to Hong Kong. The relatively undisturbed nature of these islands —their cliffs rising steeply 1,000–2,000 feet (300–600 m) above sea level from narrow beaches—partly accounts for the persistence of these communities. The endemic north island gecko Lichtenfelder's Gecko (*Goniurosaurus lichtenfelderi*) probably once also occurred on the mainland when land bridges linked the two areas. Karst specialists on the mainland include the Chinese Crocodile Lizard (*Shinisaurus crocodilurus*), an otherwise-endemic Chinese species first observed in Vietnam in 2002 at Yen Tu Nature Reserve, Quang Ninh Province.

Roughly twenty-four endemic amphibians and reptiles are found in the north of the country. Extreme caution should be taken in assuming that these are endemic to Vietnam since many, especially the thirteen newly described frog species, are still known only from where they were first collected. The IUCN lists all turtles and seven amphibians as globally threatened.

Vietnam Warty Newt (Paramesotriton deloustali)

Also known as the Vietnamese or Tam Dao Salamander, this rare amphibian is endemic to northern Vietnam, where its range is poorly known. From René Bourret's initial description in 1934 until 2001 it had been sighted only in higher elevation forests along the Tam Dao mountain ridge. In 2002, researchers reported strikingly similar warty newts from two other areas: Xin Man District, in Ha Giang Province, to the north and Van Ban District, in Lao Cai Province, east across the Red River. Specimens collected from both localities closely resemble Tam Dao's endemic newt, though final determinations await detailed morphological and genetic studies.

The Vietnamese Warty Newt is solidly built, with a large, triangular head, heavy limbs, and a long, vertically flattened tail (fig. 34). It is the largest species in the warty newt genus *Paramesotriton*: there are records of wild adults reaching over 8 inches (21 cm) in length, and they quite possibly grow even larger. Viewed from above the Vietnamese Warty Newt is unremarkable. The muddy olive-brown (almost black) skin on the back is covered with many small granules and bumps; this pairing of tint and texture blends well with stream bottoms and forest floors. But when its undersides are exposed, any camouflaging effects are lost as the mundane upper parts give way to flamboyant harlequin patterns and colors beneath. The Vietnamese Warty Newt's entire throat, belly, and tail down to its tip are covered with large, irregular splotches of bright orange to carmine red and separated by a network of black webbing.

Rather than attracting unwanted attention, this vivid and conspicuous design functions as a warning sign. When threatened, Vietnamese Warty Newts flip onto their backs and remain immobile—feigning death and exposing their memorable bellies. To provide any deterrence, a signal such

Figure 34. Vietnamese Warty Newt (*Paramesotriton deloustali*)

as this must evolve alongside a system or character that provides protection against predation. In the Vietnamese Warty Newt's case, this defensive mechanism is tetradotoxin, a potent nonprotein neurotoxin secreted from rows of wartlike glands running along its sides. When a predator tastes a newt, it associates the unpleasant experience with the colorful warning pattern. Experiments using birds as predators showed their speedy ability to learn adverse stimuli (here insects modified to be both brightly colored and toxic) and subsequently avoid the noxious prey. To minimize the number of such experiences needed for a predator to learn, clear and unambiguous warning signals have been favored through evolution. Such warning signals are part of many invertebrate and vertebrate antipredation repertoires, though they are not always visual. North American rattlesnakes use an acoustic signal, their distinctive rattle, to warn potential predators, whereas New World skunks enhance their odorous threat behaviorally by displaying their distinctive black-and-white coat with highly stereotyped dance-like movements. Similarly, Vietnamese Warty Newts use behavior to make their signal more effective, rolling on their backs to flash their belly pattern.

Vietnamese Warty Newts inhabit undisturbed forests at elevations above 1,650 feet (500 m) and are most often found along bottoms of the clear-flowing brooks and streams where they breed. All life stages, from egg to adulthood, are toxic. Juveniles are terrestrial, and until 1989, adults were believed to be entirely aquatic. Recent examination of hind limb functional morphology indicates adaptation for long-distance overground movement, an observation consistent with the collection of a single adult more than 1.25 miles (2 km) from the nearest stream. The largest specimen studied, however, did not have limb morphology capable of terrestrial locomotion. This suggests a number of possibilities: there may be two forms in the population, possibly representing different species. Alternatively, limb morphology may change under certain ecological conditions or when the newt reaches a certain body size.

The IUCN considers the endemic Vietnamese Warty Newt as Vulnerable. Uncontrolled development at Tam Dao National Park—almost entirely to encourage tourism—has meant both logging within the protected area's boundaries and the diversion and capture of water from stream habitats. The existence of potentially two additional populations is a hopeful development, however, and highlights our extremely limited knowledge of the species's distribution.

Paa Frogs (Genus Paa)

Species in the genus *Paa* go by a variety of common names in English, including paa frogs, spiny frogs, and mountain bullfrogs. Found in the Himalayan regions from northern Pakistan to southern China and northern Vietnam, they are members of the globally distributed Family Ranidae. Paa frogs are both large and edible, an ill-fated combination that exposes the group to intense hunting pressure from people throughout most of its range. As a group, paa frogs may constitute a substantial portion of locally consumed protein in montane areas of Vietnam and China, where they are at times called green chickens or mountain chickens.

As of 2004, five paa frogs were included on Vietnam's herpetofauna lists: Boulenger's Paa Frog (*Paa boulengeri*), Bourret's Paa Frog (*P. bourreti*), Spiny Paa Frog (*P. spinosa*), Warty Paa Frog (*P. verrucospinosa*), and Yunnan Paa Frog (*P. yunnanensis*). A sixth Southeast Asian species, the Kakhien Paa Frog (*P. feae*), is reported from single locations in Myanmar and Yunnan Province. Paa frogs prefer montane forests from elevations below 3,300 feet up to 13,100 feet (1,000–4,000 m) and are most commonly found in or on the banks of swiftly flowing, rocky streams with cascades and torrents. All are stout, bearing large, flattened heads and bulky limbs. Male and female adult length is similar, hovering around 4 inches (10 cm), though individuals measuring near 5 inches (13 cm) are not uncommon. Weights have been less frequently recorded, though a single male Boulenger's Paa Frog collected in China's Sichuan Province during the breeding season weighed over 13 ounces (370 g). The upper sides are mottled dark gray, brown, or olive and roughened with small granules and larger round or elongated warts. Beneath, the skin is whitish, marbled, and spotted variously with brown and black.

The main distinguishing characteristic of paa frog species is the pattern and extent of the black, horny spines present on the fingers, limbs, and undersides of mature, breeding males. During breeding season all males undergo radical morphological changes in response to elevated testicular activity. Increased muscle mass dramatically swells and thickens their forearms, which in some species can attain the diameter of their robust thighs. They also develop nuptial excrescences, patches of modified dermal and epidermal tissues on their fingers, undersides, and sometimes thighs. In paa frogs these take the form of small projecting cones or spines, heavily pigmented to appear black. This combination of enlarged forearms and extensive nuptial excrescences is commonly observed in frogs that breed in swift, torrential streams. Herpetologists believe that both features help males mating in these environments to maintain amplexus, the copulatory embrace where the male grasps the female from above, his belly to her back, before she deposits her eggs and he fertilizes them externally. Paa frog eggs are also adapted to swiftly flowing aquatic environments. Each ovum is tightly bound to a submerged rock or branch by a strong, thick cable of jelly.

Identification of all paa frogs remains challenging because the spines are both seasonal and restricted to mature males (though some adult female Yunnan Paa Frogs also have spines on their fingers). Complicating matters, the current taxonomy of the *Paa* genus is probably inaccurate. Species definitions and limits vary among authors, evolutionary relationships among species are unknown, and undescribed taxa remain hidden owing to incomplete surveys, incorrect identifications in museum collections, or both. The Global Amphibian Assessment of 2004 considered three species to be of conservation concern—Giant Spiny Frog (Vulnerable), Warty Paa Frog

Figure 35. Chinese Softshell Turtle (*Pelodiscus sinensis*)

(Near Threatened), and Yunnan Paa Frog (Endangered)—because of habitat loss and overcollection for consumption. There is not enough information to assess a fourth, Bourret's Paa Frog, a Vietnamese endemic known only from Sa Pa and Mount Fan Xi Pan.

Softshell Turtles (Family Trionychidae)

Four of Vietnam's five species of softshell turtle are found in the north: the Wattle-necked Softshell Turtle (*Palea steindachneri*), Asian Giant Softshell Turtle (*Pelochelys cantorii*), Chinese Softshell Turtle (*Pelodiscus sinensis*; fig. 35), and Shanghai Softshell Turtle (*Rafetus swinhoei*; box 12). Their appearance, ecology, and habitat preferences are similar; body size is the primary difference among them. A fifth species, the Asiatic Softshell Turtle (*Amyda cartilaginea*), lives in central and southern Vietnam's lowlands.

Softshell seems an odd description for a reptilian order (Testudines) best known for its hard, encasing armaments. Both the upper (carapace) and lower (plastron) shells in the Family Trionychidae are covered with a layer of thick, leathery skin instead of horny plates. The layers of bone lying beneath the skin are reduced in size compared to other turtles, and the individual bony sections forming the plastron are only loosely connected in-

BOX 12

The Sacred Turtles of Hoan Kiem Lake

Located in Hanoi's crowded center, Hoan Kiem is not much of a lake. Barely 660 feet (200 m) wide and 2,300 feet (700 m) long, its murky green waters are at most 6.5 feet (2 m) deep. Polluted by urban runoff and ringed by heavily used walking paths, it is probably the last place one would expect to find a massive rare reptile. Even before the presence of the Hoan Kiem turtles was established by scientists, Vietnamese schoolchildren learned a legend featuring the creature. During the decade-long struggle in the fifteenth century between Ming invaders from China and Vietnamese defenders, heroic King Le Loi acquired a magic sword from a local fisherman. After the Ming enemies were repulsed — with the aid of the sword's magical powers — Le Loi went boating on Hanoi's central lake. A talking turtle surfaced to request the return of the sword, and the king complied. From then on, the lake was called Hoan Kiem, Lake of the Returned Sword.

The giant softshell turtle that lives in Hoan Kiem Lake, long thought to be the Asian Giant Softshell Turtle (*Pelochelys cantorii*), is in fact a member of the softshell turtle genus *Rafetus*. Although scientists agree on its generic name, its status as a species is debated. Based on shell morphology, most scientists believe that Hoan Kiem's turtles are Shanghai Softshell Turtles (*R. swinhoei*), possibly the world's largest and rarest softshell turtle. Others suspect that the turtle is a species new to science. The question of its taxonomic identification cannot be solved at present because of the handful of available specimens.

According to figures displayed next to a dry specimen turtle in a temple on one of the lake's two islands, this turtle weighed 550 pounds (250 kg) when it died in the 1960s. The specimen measures roughly 5 feet (about 1.45 m) long, though measurements based on a dry specimen can underestimate the living turtle's size due to shrinkage of its leathery skin. Estimates based on photographs of a basking turtle place its length at more than 6 feet (1.9 m), making it the world's largest softshell turtle. It is unclear how many individuals live in the lake, though recent estimates suggest between one and three. Apparently, these turtles can remain under water for long periods by absorbing oxygen through their skin and membranes of their throat and cloaca. Once seen on average about four times a year, increased attention has brought sightings to around thirty annually.

It is widely thought that viable populations of this species no longer exist in the wild. The Hoan Kiem Lake turtles may be unable to find a mate or nesting place, and pollution may interfere with their hatching and growth. Favored nesting sites around the lake and on the middle island are no longer available because of cemented pavements and banks. Nevertheless, surveys undertaken in 2000 revealed small populations in several northern provinces in Vietnam and the collection of one juvenile in 1999 indicates that at least one population in Vietnam can still reproduce. It is still uncertain where Hoan Kiem's turtles originated, though they may have migrated from the Red River when it was still connected to the lake four hundred years ago.

stead of sutured into a single inflexible plate. The carapace and plastron are joined at the sides by ligaments, not the usual scale-covered bony bridge. These structural differences lend softshell turtles a flattened, pancake-like appearance. Softshells also have webbed feet, long necks, jaws covered by fleshy lips, and snouts ending in a narrow, delicate nose.

Structural elasticity is one of a suite of specializations for life on the muddy bottoms of streams, rivers, ponds, lakes, and other slow-moving water bodies. Softshell turtles are exclusively aquatic and almost as exclusively carnivorous, capturing a variety of fish, crabs, mollusks, frogs, insects, and other animal prey depending on body size and habitat. Usually soft-shells hide themselves in silt and mud along the bottom, ambushing their prey with a sudden, swift strike of their long, flexible neck. This sinuous neck can extend to the water's surface, allowing the turtles to breathe from their hiding places, only the tubelike proboscis's small tip showing above the surface. Because of the shell's flexibility, softshells can retract both head and neck completely within the body. Swift, powerful swimmers, they are considered voracious, ferocious—even irascible—and larger species can inflict serious bites on fishers.

All four of northern Vietnam's softshells are dull-colored above, distinguishable by variation in warts on the carapace and neck and the shape, size, and color of the head and proboscis. The Chinese Softshell Turtle is a relatively small species, reaching a carapace length of 10 inches (25 cm) or less. The Wattle-necked is larger, reaching maximum lengths of 17–20 inches (43–50 cm). Both the Asian Giant and Shanghai Softshell Turtles are considered giants, growing as large as 39–51 inches (100–129 cm) and 41 inches (104 cm), respectively. Variation in body size may allow softshell species to coexist in the same aquatic habitats by facilitating differentiation in feeding niches (such as prey size). All live in lowland aquatic environments except the Wattle-necked, an upland species of hills and mountains that has been recorded at 5,000 feet (1,500 m) in northern Vietnam.

Vietnam's softshell turtles are threatened by collection for consumption—the flesh is considered a delicacy—and use in traditional Asian medicine. These northern four are considered globally threatened by the IUCN: the Chinese Softshell Turtle as Vulnerable, the Wattle-necked and Asian Giant Softshell Turtles as Endangered, and the Shanghai Softshell Turtle as Critically Endangered.

Jerdon's Pitviper and Rhinoceros Snake
(Protobothrops jerdonii *and* Rhynchophis boulengeri)

Though both are found in northern Vietnam, Jerdon's Pitviper and the Rhinoceros Snake share few traits other than this coincidence. Jerdon's Pitviper is a colorful, highly venomous snake in the Family Viperidae (vipers, adders, and pitvipers). The Rhinoceros Snake, a nonvenomous green snake well camouflaged for its arboreal habitats, belongs to the Family Colubridae (colubrids). Further differences in ecology, behavior, appearance, habitat, and range parallel their extremely modest evolutionary connection.

Jerdon's Pitviper, also known as the Yellow-speckled Lancehead, belongs to a group of approximately thirty closely related Asian pitvipers, including seven in the genus *Protobothrops*. It is a high-altitude snake of the Himalayan Mountains. The known distribution extends from northeastern India, Nepal, and Tibet through northern Myanmar and southwestern China. In Vietnam, Jerdon's Pitviper is restricted to forests at 6,200 feet (1,900 m) and above in the Hoang Lien Son Range. Its entire body, which can reach 43 inches (110 cm), is strongly patterned with black and yellow. The conspicuously triangular head bears symmetrical yellow and black spots and stripes, and a single black band runs from the eye to the corner of the mouth. Its back is covered with a series of black diamonds and the sides with vertical black spots, fashioning an intricate pattern against a yellowish background. Underneath, the skin is yellow mottled with black that becomes solid along the anterior belly and tail.

Viperids are distinguished from other venomous snakes (excepting Africa's stiletto snakes in the genus *Atractaspis*) by their enlarged fangs, which are highly mobile, hollow, and positioned at the rear of the mouth. Jerdon's Pitviper is armed with a potent hemotoxin that immobilizes and kills its prey (mostly forest rats and frogs). It is semi-arboreal and primarily nocturnal, occasionally seen along stony streamsides. All pitvipers—a large and behaviorally confrontational group of sixteen genera and 157 species—possess a pair of pitlike sensory organs. In Jerdon's Pitviper they appear gray and are positioned below and to the front of the eye. Sometimes referred to as heat sensing, each organ is in essence a crude eye sensitive to infrared radiation, electromagnetic energy with wavelengths longer than visible light. Pitvipers use them to locate prey by detecting thermal radiation (heat) emitted by potential quarry.

The Rhinoceros Snake (or Asiatic Vine Snake) is the only snake in Vietnam with a scale-covered appendage attached to the front of its snout. It bears a conical, sharply pointed projection (much like a small horn) that extends forward and turns gently upward at the narrow tip. The function of this horn is unknown; possibly it further camouflages the snake against branches and vines. The Rhinoceros Snake is green above and slightly paler below, with barely visible white and black margins on some scales. The head is long, triangular, and swollen at its base so that it is quite distinct from the neck. The body is streamlined and compressed, wider along the belly than the back, and can reach 54 inches (138 cm) in length.

The co-occurrence of these two distinctive snakes in Vietnam's north reflects the intersection of the Indochinese and South Chinese biogeographic regions in this small area. Like Jerdon's Pitviper, the Rhinoceros Snake is a creature of northern Vietnam's montane forests. Unlike the pitviper, it is associated with the flora, fauna, climate, and habitats of tropical and subtropical northeastern Vietnam and southern China. Vietnamese records come from Tam Dao, Ba Be, and Hon Nor Way (the Norway Islands lying off the northeastern coast near the Sino-Vietnamese border). In China it has been identified at a number of sites in Guangxi Province and on Hainan Island. This region is warmer, milder, lower, and often wetter than the more elevated, westerly, and Himalayan region where Jerdon's Pitviper is found. The north's mixture of species from the Himalayas and sections of southern China is paralleled in other groups; paa frogs and torrent-dwelling sucker frogs (genus *Amolops*) have respectively similar affinities.

Neither snake is considered globally threatened, but both are harvested. Like all venomous snakes, Jerdon's Pitviper is valued for its blood, meat, and the making of medicinal snake wine—thought to cure many ills from a flagging male libido to rheumatism and skin diseases. Although the Rhinoceros Snake is not venomous, its resemblance to the venomous green tree vipers has meant that it is also exploited owing to the ignorance of collectors and consumers.

Chapa and Tonkin Bug-eyed Frogs
(Theloderma bicolor *and* T. corticale)

Bug-eyed frogs in the genus *Theloderma* inhabiting northern Vietnam's mountain forests are members of the Family Rhacophoridae, also known as flying frogs or Old World tree frogs. The more than 300 Asian species occupy a range of habitats in the Old World tropics, though most live, mate,

and breed aboveground along trunks and branches and in hollows, epiphytes, and other arboreal microhabitats.

Like many tree frogs, the north's *Theloderma* species have a lean, compressed shape with long, slender legs, and they grow to a length of about
3 inches (70 mm). Their fingers are free, but the toes are webbed and both
sets of digits end in oval-shaped disks that help these frogs maneuver
around their arboreal habitats. The head is broad, triangular, and flat, and
rising from the forehead are large, golden-green-flecked eyes centered with
black irises. Both species are well camouflaged by the color and texture
of their mossy, barklike skin. Their upper sides (including the eyelids and
tympani, or ears) are roughened by large, irregular glandular bumps scattered among the more numerous, smaller granules that dot the skin. This
roughening extends across the limbs, backs of the thighs, and undersides.
The two species differ in coloration: the Chapa Bug-eyed Frog is largely
dark olive above, whereas the Tonkin species is yellowish to dark green with
reddish brown splotches on its uppersides.

As with virtually every amphibian species, Chapa and Tonkin Bug-eyed
Frogs must have access to water at some point during reproduction. Both
are tree-hole specialists, depending on pools of rainwater and dew trapped
in the hollows, cups, and holes of trees to hold their developing larvae (tadpoles). A few eggs (four to eight) are deposited above these pools in small
gelatinous lumps; after hatching, the tadpoles fall or are washed into the
water below. Stagnant, acidic, low in oxygen, and usually both small and
ephemeral, these puddles offer scant protection and food for the developing
tadpoles. Bug-eyed frogs appear well adapted to exploit these harsh conditions. Unlike many other frogs their tadpoles do not seem to be dietary
specialists: they can consume both microscopic plankton filtered from the
water and larger invertebrates and frog eggs. This flexibility frees them from
dependence on a predictable diet, which tree holes do not provide. *Theloderma* tadpoles are also capable of extremely rapid development when the
pools dry up and in fact fare less well under typically ideal amphibian conditions. In a lab setting with clean, well-aerated running water, Tonkin Bug-
eyed Frog development is halted. Metamorphosis begins only after the tadpoles are placed in their natural, stagnant aquatic environment.

Chapa and Tonkin Bug-eyed Frogs live in the montane forests of northern Vietnam, with their ranges separated by the Red River. The Chapa resides in the Hoang Lien Son Range of the northwest; the Tonkin is known only from Mao-Son Mountain near the Chinese border in the northeast. The nonoverlapping distributions may reflect a dispersal barrier (either formed by the Red River or coincident with it), subtle differences in habitat and climate between the two montane environments, or interspecific competition. So little is known about their evolutionary history and habits that these questions are unanswerable. Three other bug-eyed frogs are found in northern Vietnam: Hill Garden (*T. asperum*), Gordon's (*T. gordoni*), and Taylor's (*T. stellatum*) Bug-eyed Frogs. In 2004, the Global Amphibian Assessment classified the Tonkin Bug-eyed Frog as Vulnerable because of habitat loss in the Hoang Lien Son Range.

Fish

The freshwater fish of northern Vietnam are more closely related to those found in southern China's Yangtze and Pearl Rivers than to the broad Mekong basin's ichthyofauna. This is consistent with the theory that the upper Yangtze once flowed into the Red River and then to the Bac Bo Gulf. Although none of northern Vietnam's roughly 270 native species are recognized as threatened by the IUCN, the Red Data Book of Vietnam includes eighteen on its national list, seven from the delta and eleven inland. Species richness and the number of endemics are both certainly significant underestimates, especially for the smaller species of minnows and carps (Family Cyprinidae) that dominate mainland Southeast Asia's freshwater fish fauna. New species continue to be identified here, ten since 1995. One of these, the catfish *Pterocryptis verecunda*—a genus found in fast-flowing mountain streams—is known only from a single stream on Cat Ba Island in Ha Long Bay.

Invertebrates

As with all areas of Vietnam (and the world), the north's invertebrates remain generally understudied. The only exception to this trend is the butterflies. Work on this group has been concentrated in northern Vietnam,

Figure 36. Golden Kaiser-I-Hind Butterfly (*Teinopalpus aureus*)
male (left) and female (right)

particularly in the uplands of Tam Dao, from which some 300 species of butterfly have been recorded.

Golden Kaiser-I-Hind (Teinopalpus aureus)

The Golden Kaiser-I-Hind is a stunning member of the swallowtail butterfly family (Papilonidae), so named for the tail-like hindwing extensions displayed by most (but not all) members of the family (fig. 36). It is the only insect in Vietnam on the IUCN's Red List and so little is known about its status that it is classified as Data Deficient. The Golden Kaiser-I-Hind inhabits montane forests throughout a range that covers southeastern China (including Hainan Island), Laos, and Vietnam. Until 1991 all Vietnamese records were from the northern mountains (including Tam Dao). The identification of a new subspecies (*T. aureus eminens*) extended its range almost 600 miles (1,000 km) south to south-central Vietnam's Lam Dong and Kanh Hoa Provinces. It almost certainly occurs patchily in appropriate habitats along the intervening region. Research into the effects of local disturbances (forest gaps) on the butterfly communities at Tam Dao suggests that species confined to mature forest understory are preferentially lost. The habitat preferences of the Golden Kaiser-I-Hind are still not known, but it is likely to be one of these vulnerable species.

VIEWING WILDLIFE IN NORTHERN VIETNAM
Cuc Phuong National Park
(Ninh Binh, Hoa Binh, and Thanh Hoa Provinces)

Cuc Phuong is the oldest (established in 1962 by President Ho Chi Minh) and quite possibly the most accessible national park in northern Vietnam. Enormous buttressed trees dominate a forest teeming with creepers, lianas, and epiphytes and the limestone karst formations provide caves for exploring with numerous orchids growing near the cool entrances. The best place to view primates in the park is surely the Endangered Primate Rescue Center, with black-and-white leaf monkeys and eerily serene doucs, among other Vietnamese species. Operatic gibbon duets can be heard during an early morning walk along the road next to the center. There are also captive breeding programs for Owston's Civet (*Chrotogale owstoni*) and freshwater turtles in the park.

Cat Ba National Park (Hai Phong Province)

Cat Ba National Park was established as a park in 1986 and in 2003 was included in United Nations Development Programme's Man and the Biosphere Reserve network. Located in Ha Long Bay, it includes half of Cat Ba Island as well as some smaller islands to the east. A proposed marine protected area (Dao Cat Ba) also centers on the archipelago.

Ha Long Bay's scenery has become almost iconographic for Vietnam: jagged limestone karst formations towering over waters dotted with fishing boats. Underneath its green surface are an estimated 160 species of coral, their rainbow of colors quite unlike the dead bleached chunks for sale in the tourist trade. Other marine and coastal habitats include sea-grass beds, mangroves, and sandy beaches. The island's main terrestrial habitat is evergreen forest, home to a number of endemic plants, including orchids and a palm. Freshwater swamp forests are also present, and the islands hold many small lakes, waterfalls, and caves.

Cat Ba Island is the only site where the fifty to sixty remaining Cat Ba Leaf Monkeys live. They can occasionally be seen on the cliffs, most readily by boat. Only a few other larger mammal species remain: Southern

Serow (*Naemorhedus sumatraensis*), Eurasian Wild Pig (*Sus scrofa*), and Red Muntjac (*Muntiacus muntjak*). Cat Ba lies along a major migration route for waterfowl and during these periods is a haven for such birds as the Little Grebe (*Tachybaptus ruficollis*), Spot-billed Duck (*Anas poecilorhyncha*), White-breasted Waterhen (*Amaurornis phoenicurus*), Light-vented Bulbul (*Pycnonotus sinensis*), and Blue Rock Thrush (*Monticola solitarius*).

Cat Ba Island is a popular tourist destination, in particular because it is easily accessible by boat.

Ba Be National Park (Bac Can Province)

Ba Be is a relatively easy excursion northward from Hanoi. Set aside in 1992, it is visited by tens of thousands of (mostly Vietnamese) tourists each year. The primary attraction is Ba Be Lake, the largest natural lake in Vietnam at 5 miles (8 km) long and up to 2,600 feet (800 m) wide. The lake is surrounded by four limestone peaks and a dense evergreen forest that is fast disappearing. Numerous caves and odd karstic formations can be reached from its shores, and boat rides through one of the caves into the lake can be arranged. The total area is relatively small, only 30 square miles (7,610 ha), and the elevation ranges from 500 to 3,600 feet (150–1,100 m).

Two endemic species can be found here: Owston's Civet and François's Leaf Monkey. A third, the Tonkin Snub-nosed Monkey, is now extinct at this site, though it persists in neighboring Na Hang Nature Reserve. Wetland habitats support a variety of kingfishers (Families Alcedinidae and Halcyonidae), herons (Family Ardeidae), and other waterbirds and beautiful Short-billed (*Pericrocotus brevirostris*) and Scarlet Minivets (*P. flammeus*) grace the lake's shores. Butterflies are the park's best-known group. In 1997 and 1998 entomologists recorded 332, twenty-two of which were new records for Vietnam.

Ba Vi National Park (Ha Tay Province)

Perhaps owing to its proximity to Hanoi 35 miles (50 km) away, the French developed Ba Vi as a hill station, and in 1992 the Vietnamese government established a national park there. The park centers on Mount Ba Vi, an isolated, often fog-enshrouded mountain rising above flat plains. The highest of its three peaks is 4,250 feet (1,296 m). Although long overused by humans, this small park of 26 square miles (6,786 ha) has several picturesque waterfalls and a modest variety of bird life. Some natural, evergreen forest remains on slopes higher than 2,000 feet (600 m).

Tam Dao National Park
(Vinh Phuc, Thai Nguyen, and Tuyen Quang Provinces)

Tam Dao National Park (established in 1996) is located along an isolated mountain ridge that rises from the surrounding agricultural lowlands 45 miles (75 km) northwest of Hanoi. Its 85 square miles (21,982 ha) are mountainous; several peaks surpass 4,300 feet (1,300 m) and the highest, Mount Tam Dao Bac, is 5,223 feet (1,592 m). This area served the French as a hill station in the early twentieth century, and several luxurious villas from that period remain.

Tam Dao may be the best-inventoried protected area in Vietnam. Recent bird records include two migratory species considered Vulnerable by the IUCN: Imperial Eagle (*Aquila heliaca*) and Fairy Pitta (*Pitta nympha*). A strenuous hike might reveal a variety of subtropical Chinese and Himalayan birds known from only a few other sites in Vietnam, such as the Blue-rumped Pitta (*P. soror*), Purple Cochoa (*Cochoa purpurea*), Chestnut-headed Tesia (*Tesia castaneocoronata*), Pale-footed Bush Warbler (*Cettia pallidipes*), and Greater Rufous-headed Parrotbill (*Paradoxornis ruficeps*). Almost 4 percent of the world's snake species have been recorded here (though this number is likely bolstered by the frequent release of animals confiscated from the wildlife trade).

Sadly, one of the best places to see wildlife up close in Tam Dao is in the restaurants, which are famous for selling wild game, including endangered species. Tam Dao draws thousands of domestic and foreign tourists annually.

Hoang Lien Nature Reserve (Lao Cai Province)

Many tour groups and independent tourists travel from Hanoi to Sa Pa, principally to visit the market, where many of the region's minority ethnic groups gather. From a naturalist's point of view, however, the journey's highlight is a chance to visit the Hoang Lien Nature Reserve, established in 1986. At 97 square miles (25,000 ha), it is a large reserve for Vietnam. Although less than half the area is still naturally forested, the remaining flora is noteworthy and includes more than a quarter of Vietnam's known endemic plants. The nature reserve also supports almost 350 bird species, including some found only in these high northwestern mountains. Unfortunately, heavy hunting pressure has drastically reduced populations of the larger mammals.

Hardier types should trek up Fan Xi Pan, where changes in altitude bring a turnover in the fauna and flora. In the river valleys of the foothills, there are kingfishers and Brown Dippers (*Cinclus pallasii*). Farther up are Crested Finchbills (*Spizixos canifrons*), Red-faced Liocichlas (*Liocichla phoenicea*), and Spot-breasted Scimitar Babblers. Reaching 6,600 feet (2,000 m), you may see Gould's Shortwing (*Brachypteryx stellata*), the Black-faced Laughingthrush (*Garrulax affinis*), and the Dark-breasted Rosefinch (*Carpodacus nipalensis*). Birds found only at the highest elevations include Temminck's Tragopan, the Red-winged Laughingthrush, and the White-browed Bush Robin (*Tarsiger indicus*). Habitat also changes, from montane evergreen forest to distinctive fir-hemlock stands at 6,600 feet (2,000 m) and rhododendrons, conifers, and temperate hardwoods at higher elevations.

Hanoi Botanical and Zoological Parks

Though not mentioned in many guidebooks, there are both botanical and zoological gardens in Hanoi. The botanical gardens offer a pleasant and informative respite to the bustle of the city. They are located west of Hanoi's center in Binh District between West Lake and the Ho Chi Minh Mausoleum. Birders can spot many wading birds near the lake. The Hanoi Zoological Gardens are located in Thu Le Park, a western suburb of Hanoi. The zoo does its best to keep animals despite a limited budget and is one of the few places outside of a market where one can see a Binturong (*Arctitis binturong*) up close.

SEVEN

Central Vietnam and the Truong Son Range
From Wet Mountains to Dry Forests

Vietnam's central region circumscribes a curving ribbon of mountains, lowlands, and coastal plains that offers the country's widest range of habitats, including both its wettest and driest regions. Bounded by the Nghe An Province's Ca River to the north and by the eastern edges of Binh Phuoc, Dong Nai, and Ba Ria Vung Tau Provinces to the south, it comprises most of the area known to the Vietnamese as Truong Bo (fig. 37). During the eighteenth and early nineteenth century, central Vietnam formed the majority of Annam, an administrative district of colonial France.

Central Vietnam's dominant geological feature is the Truong Son Range. This string of mountains and plateaus intersected by passes and lowlands is roughly 750 miles (1,200 km) long and 30 to 50 miles (50–75 km) wide. For much of this distance, it runs parallel to the central coastline, straddling the border with Laos (where it is called the Saiphou Louang), with the southern third running into south-central Vietnam. Most of its hills lie between elevations of 1,600 and 6,500 feet (500–2,000 m), and their lower sections serve as transit points for both people and clouds and damp winds from the eastern slopes. This entire chain of uplands is also known as the Annamite Mountain Range or Annamese Cordillera. Four wide passes divide the range north to south: Ngang, Hai Van, Mong, and Ca.

Low areas lie next to and are interwoven with the Truong Son Range. Evergreen forests dominate the upland areas, and habitat diversity occurs largely at elevations below 3,300 feet (1,000 m), including semi-evergreen

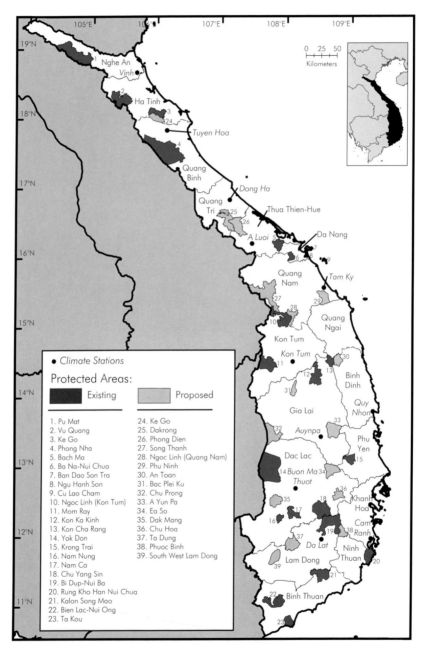

Figure 37. Administrative features and protected areas of central Vietnam

and deciduous forests dominated by dipterocarps (Family Dipterocarpaceae). A narrow, irregular coastal plain nestles between the Truong Son and the East Sea, broken by dunes, lagoons, and estuaries of the many rivers that drain the Truong Son to the west. South of the Hai Van Pass (c. 16° N), many islands lie offshore, some now-submerged extensions of mainland ridges, others still connected and forming peninsulas and bays. Off this eastern shore lie fringing coral reefs, sea-grass beds, and other marine habitats.

As with the rest of Vietnam, active scientific research along the Truong Son was interrupted for much of the later twentieth century. This inattention was exacerbated by the Truong Son's relative inaccessibility and position astride Vietnam's borders with Laos and Cambodia. Renewed research beginning in the 1990s has produced both new species, including the Annamite Muntjac (*Muntiacus truongsonensis*), and records of animals not seen since their initial descriptions dating from before World War II, such as Edwards's Pheasant (*Lophura edwardsi*). Much of this newly uncovered or recovered diversity appears to be endemic to the Truong Son Range and surrounding areas. The Truong Son also supports four regions with high bird endemism, two upland and two lowland.

In addition to its natural diversity, central Vietnam holds great cultural and historical significance. Archaeological remains of the Dong Son, a culture that emerged in Vietnam about 3,000 B.C.E. and known for its bronze drums, have been found in Thanh Hoa Province. Between 1802 and 1945, the city of Hue was the capital of a united Vietnam and seat of the Nguyen Dynasty, Vietnam's last precolonial rulers; their majestic mausoleums still stand south of Hue's citadel. The central region has been an important theater in Vietnam's struggles for independence and unity. From 1885 to 1895, Phan Dinh Phung led a broad anticolonial resistance movement and rebellion in central Vietnam, at times hiding in the forests of what is now Vu Quang Nature Reserve in Ha Tinh Province. The provisional boundary between North and South Vietnam established by the 1954 Geneva Accord followed the Ben Hai River upstream and then ran due west to the border with Laos. The demilitarized zone extended 3 miles (5 km) to each side. Central Vietnam also contains large sections of the Vietnam-American War's Ho Chi Minh Highway, a mountainous network of paths and roads used by North Vietnam to ferry troops and supplies southward. Its namesake,

President Ho Chi Minh, was born in a small village 9 miles (14 km) from the north-central coastal city of Vinh.

Central Vietnam's overall population density is lower than the rest of the country, and as elsewhere, fewer people live in the mountains. Figures vary from a high of 1,419 people per square mile (548 people/km^2) in the municipality of Da Nang down to 83 people per square mile (32 people/km^2) in Kon Tum Province. Government internal migration processes continue to alter the demographics of many upland regions as people move from higher-density areas in the country's north and south. This phenomenon is largely responsible for a population increase of 63 percent in the Central Highlands (the Kon Tum, Play Ku, and Dac Lac Plateaus). Twenty-one ethnic groups are found in the region, most living in the central and southern reaches of the Truong Son Range; among the largest groups are the Gia-rai, Ba Na, and Cham peoples. The Muong ethnic group, which dwells here and in the north, comprises descendents of some of the earliest peoples in Vietnam. Unfortunately, these minorities are among those most negatively affected by the ongoing agricultural conversion of the region's forests.

TOPOGRAPHY

Much in keeping with the region's elaborate history of peoples, conquerors, cultures, and states, the Truong Son Range has had a long, complex, and turbulent geological past. Composition of the underlying rocks is highly variable throughout central Vietnam and includes sedimentary rocks such as limestone and sandstone, granites extruded from the Earth's crust, and basaltic lava flows. These have been mixed, transformed, and overlain by extensive uplift, folding, and volcanic activity over hundreds of millions of years. The result is a diversity of rocks and soils underlying central Vietnam that vary in depth, acidity, moisture content, richness of organic material, and nutrient and mineral content.

Vietnam's Truong Son can be divided into three regions, and scientists often use these divisions to delineate species distributions. Starting in Nghe An Province, the range's northern stretch terminates at a break in the ridge at Khe San (fig. 38). The mountains here are quite low; few exceed 4,300 feet (1,300 m), though to the west in Laos they can exceed 9,200 feet (2,800 m).

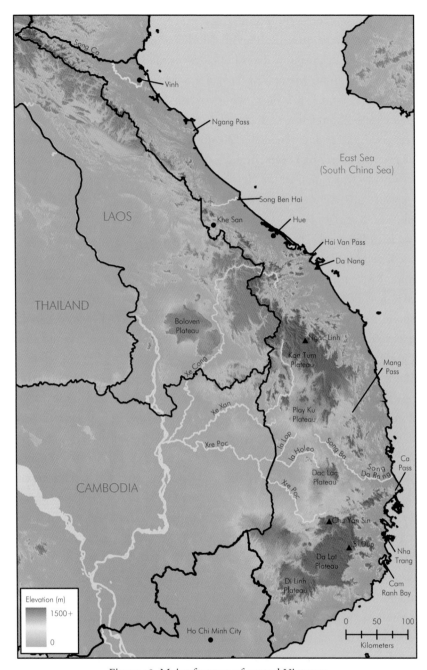

Figure 38. Major features of central Vietnam

Much of this region is composed of ancient sea basins (more than 400 million years old) that have been uplifted and now are heavily eroded. A widespread swath of limestone deposited 290–255 million years ago cuts across the Truong Son in Quang Binh Province. Contiguous with extensive areas in Laos, it is among the most extensive tracts of limestone karst habitat in Indochina. Phong Nha-Ke Bang National Park is centered here and protects both the region's characteristically sharp karst ridges and peaks and an extensive system of caves, tunnels, and underground rivers and streams.

Below Khe San, near the Hai Van Pass, a spur ridge of the Central Truong Son runs east to the sea while the rest of the range continues south along the Laos-Vietnam border to the Song Ba-Da Rang River (roughly coinciding with the southern border of Gia Lai Province). Its dominant feature is the Kon Tum Massif, an enormous, largely granite formation stretching 155 miles (250 km) north to south and 125 miles (200 km) inland, composed of now-exposed crystalline basement rocks formed over 560 million years ago in the Precambrian. It is among the oldest uncovered rocks in Southeast Asia. Mount Ngoc Linh on the northwestern border of the massif is the highest peak in central Vietnam at 8,523 feet (2,598 m). Extending westwards and southwards from here the massif's foothills reach into extreme northeastern Cambodia. To its south is the lower 2,600–4,600 feet (800–1,400 m) Play Ku Plateau made of basalts deposited by volcanic activity beginning some 20 million years ago.

From the Song Ba-Da Rang the Truong Son extends south to include Vietnam's remaining uplands, a series of eroded granite and basalt plateaus dotted with isolated peaks. First encountered is the 1,300–2,600 foot (400–800 m) Dac Lac Plateau at the southern end of which lies the city of Buon Ma Thuot, the region's largest city. The large Da Lat Plateau stretches from the Cambodian border eastward nearly to the coast. Lying mostly at elevations between 4,000 and 7,000 feet (1,200–2,200 m), the peaks of Bi Doup (7,096 feet; 2,163 m) and Chu Yan Sin (7,906 feet; 2,410 m), the plateau's highest, stand along its northeastern edge. Southwest of Da Lat is the 3,300–5,000-foot (1,000–1,500 m) Di Linh Plateau.

Central Vietnam's lowlands are far smaller than the large, fertile delta regions of the north and south; along the northern Truong Son they are particularly limited, squeezed between the mountains and coast. The narrow coastal plains of central Vietnam widen in its southern half, extending inland for 12 to 19 miles (20–30 km) around Nha Trang and south. Both picturesque and botanically interesting, they include one of Vietnam's most beautiful sights, the unusual red sand habitats and unique coastal forests that cluster around Cam Ranh Bay.

CLIMATE

Compared with the north, central Vietnam experiences a generally wetter monsoon climate, though the seasonality of both temperature and rainfall vary widely throughout the region (table 3). This climatic range is generated by large differences in latitude, elevation, surrounding topography (which can create rainshadows), and the steepness and exposure of the slopes. Lowlands and foothills of the northern and central Truong Son experience temperatures resembling northern Vietnam's, with warm summer highs around 86°F (30°C) and winter lows reaching 60°F (16°C). Rainfall is higher, however, at 80–100 inches (2,000–2,500 mm), and the wet season is later, with rains most frequent between August and November. The coastal lowlands at Nha Trang and south experience a far drier, semi-arid climate. Lying in the shadow of the Da Lat Plateau, the lowlands have a mean rainfall below 53 inches (1,350 mm), and annual averages below 30 inches (750 mm) have been recorded. Temperatures are less seasonal at 75°F–85°F (24°C–29°C) throughout the year, and the wet seasons are shorter and later, peaking October through December. The interior lowlands and foothills south of the Kon Tum Plateau are also drier than farther north, with rainfalls more in the range of 60–80 inches (1,500–2,000 mm) and distinct wet and dry periods.

The Truong Son's uplands are cooler and wetter than the lowlands, and its eastern and windward slopes usually receive more rain than the western and leeward ones. Across the Kon Tum and Da Lat Plateaus at elevations above 3,300 feet (1,000 m) there is usually more than 80 inches (2,000 mm) of rain annually, and this figure increases with altitude. Along the Da Lat Plateau's eastern edge, annual rainfall reaches 150 inches (3,850 mm) and there is essentially no dry season. Temperatures in these upland mountain areas are less seasonal and can be quite cool; on Da Lat the annual aver-

Table 3. Climate stations in central Vietnam

Name	Elevation (ft/m)	Temperature (C/F)		Rainfall (in/mm)			
		Annual average	Range monthly averages	Annual average	Range monthly averages	Dry months (N)	Wettest month
Vinh	20 (6)	75 (23.9)	64–85 (17.6–29.6)	78 (1,968)	2–19 (44–479)	0	Sept.
Tuyen Hoa	82 (25)	75 (23.8)	64–85 (17.5–29.2)	89 (2,267)	1–23 (35–582)	1	Oct.
Dong Ha	13 (4)	77 (25)	67–85 (19.7–29.6)	88 (2,245)	1–29 (25–724)	2	Oct.
A Luoi	1,804 (550)	71 (21.6)	63–77 (17.3–25.1)	134 (3,405)	2–36 (40–911)	1	Oct.
Tam Ky	69 (21)	78 (25.6)	71–84 (21.4–28.9)	102 (2,586)	1–28 (37–709)	3	Sept.
Kon Tum	1,759 (536)	74 (23.4)	69–78 (20.4–25.7)	70 (1,783)	0–13 (2–328)	4	Aug.
Quy Nhon	16 (5)	80 (26.8)	74–86 (23.1–29.8)	67 (1,697)	1–19 (29–476)	5	Oct.
Auynpa	492 (150)	78(25.6)	72–83 (22–28.3)	49 (1,231)	0–9 (2–224)	5	Sept.
Buon Ma Thuot	1,608 (490)	75 (23.7)	70–78 (21.2–25.8)	70 (1,789)	0–12 (2–302)	4	Aug.
Cam Ranh	52 (16)	80 (26.9)	76–84 (24.3–29)	45 (1,151)	0–11 (9–270)	6	Nov.
Da Lat	4,964 (1,513)	65 (18.2)	62–67 (16.4–19.7)	73 (1,865)	0–12 (9–314)	3	Sept.
Dong Phu	292 (89)	79 (26.2)	75–83 (24.1–28.4)	97 (2,469)	0–17 (7–433)	4	Sept.
Ham Tan	49 (15)	80 (26.4)	76–83 (24.7–28.3)	65 (1,645)	0–12 (0–297)	5	Sept.

Source: After Nguyen Khanh Van et al., 2000

age temperature is 65°F (18.2°C). At the highest elevations, fogs, mists, and dew contribute to some of the highest recorded rainfalls in Vietnam. The summit of Mount Bach Ma, at 4,750 feet (1,448 m), receives on average 315 inches (8,000 mm), or more than 26 feet, of rain a year. The Di Linh Plateau (the region's southernmost uplands) lies in the rainshadow of southwestern Cambodia's Cardamom and Elephant Mountains and experiences a drier and more seasonal climate than areas to the north.

HYDROLOGY

Central Vietnam lacks a single dominant river and drainage such as the Red and Mekong Rivers provide to the north and south, respectively. Instead, hundreds of rivers and streams descend from the Truong Son's eastern slopes carrying freshwater that eventually drains into the East Sea. A drive along coastal Highway 1 south from the Song Ca through Quang Nam Province brings an encounter with a river crossing every 12 miles (20 km) or less.

Originating along the western edge of the central Truong Son Range and from the southern Truong Son are rivers flowing into the Mekong in northern Cambodia, including the Xe Cong, Xe Xan, and Xre Pac. The Xre Pac (also transliterated as Srepok) is a major Mekong tributary, and within the southern Truong Son many rivers drain into it. As the only permanent waterway in Yok Don National Park, it provides critical habitat for river and shoal birds, including the newly described Mekong Wagtail (*Motacilla samveasnae*).

VEGETATION AND HABITATS

It is in the Truong Son's uplands and lowlands that the mixing of Vietnam's subtropical and tropical biota becomes most apparent; forest composition changes abruptly across latitudes and especially across elevations. This is a function of both the amount and regularity of rainfall, temperature range, and soil type coupled with local topographic features. Vegetation on the northern Truong Son's limestone areas is similar to that in the north: largely semi-evergreen and rich in endemic species.

Figure 39. Broad-leaved evergreen forest in the watershed of the Rao An River, Huong Son District, Ha Tinh Province (Photograph by Cal Snyder)

Evergreen forests grow on the Truong Son at all elevations from its northern tip to around 14° N (fig. 39). At elevations up to about 2,600 feet (800 m), central Vietnam's evergreen forests are largely broad-leaved, with canopies dominated by tropical families such as the dipterocarps, and with many palms and lianas in the understory. Although there is low diversity of dipterocarps in this northern section, these ecologically important trees are often seen emerging above the forest canopy. As elevation increases and the climate becomes cooler and wetter, more temperate families such as the beeches (Fagaceae) and magnolias (Magnoliaceae) begin to dominate. The transition is often abrupt, occurring over a gradient of 660–1,000 feet (200–300 m). Wet, submontane, and montane forests are found at elevations of 3,300 feet (1,000 m) or more throughout the Truong Son. Windswept upper montane forest formations grace exposed peaks and narrow ridges at the highest points along the mountain range, sometimes as elfin forest or moss forest formations. Rhododendrons (genus *Rhododendron*) are an important component of these communities, which can be found as far south as Bi Dup-Nui Ba Nature Reserve on the Da Lat Plateau.

Figure 40. Primary submontane evergreen forest with Da Lat (*Pinus dalatensis*) and Krempf's (*P. krempfii*) Pines dominant near Bi Dup-Nui Ba Nature Reserve, Lac Duong District, Lam Dong Province (Photograph by Phan Ke Loc)

Evergreen trees bearing cones are an important component of central Vietnam's forests, and the number of conifer species here is second only to karst regions in the northeast (fig. 40). Two fairly common pines usually dominate drier coniferous forests below 5,000 feet (1,500 m): the Benguet Pine (*Pinus kesiya*) can be found around 3,300–5,000 feet (1,000–1,500 m), sometimes mixed with Evelyn's Pine (*Keteleeria evelyniana*); the Tenasserim Pine (*P. latteri*) replaces it at lower elevations and on drier soils. The highest diversity and most interesting species are concentrated in the Truong Son's wetter, montane areas, usually above 4,000 feet (1,200 m), where they grow in highly diverse, mixed broad-leaved and coniferous forests. The endemic Da Lat Pine (*Pinus dalatensis*) can be found in these habitats, including ridges and summits, in the center and south of the range, whereas the unusual flat-needled and endemic Krempf's Pine (*P. krempfii*) is restricted to the southern Truong Son's Da Lat Plateau. A third endemic, the yew *Amentotaxus poilanei,* is known only from cool, wet evergreen forests on Mount Ngoc Linh, which experience mean temperatures below 54°F (12°C)

Figure 41. A nearly pure stand of a young loosestrife *Lagerstroemia calyculata* (Family Lythraceae) in secondary deciduous forest near Chu Mom Ray National Park in Say Thay District, Kon Tum Province (Photograph by Phan Ke Loc)

and more than 120 inches (3,000 mm) of rain a year with no dry months. Other conifers include Fokienia (*Fokienia hodginsii*) and members of the podocarp (Podocarpaceae), yew (Taxaceae), and plum-yew (Cephalotaxaceae) families. These species are restricted to upper-elevation forests because of their moisture requirements.

In the southern half of the Truong Son, areas below 3,300 feet (1,000 m) are covered with a variety of forest types depending on local conditions. At these elevations the lowland evergreen forests of the northern Truong Son give way to drier semi-evergreen and deciduous dipterocarp formations (fig. 41). Soil moisture and climate can vary over small areas, so these three forest types are often present in a patchwork without clear boundaries. Lining the moister banks of such smaller streams and rivers as the Xre Pac, Ia H'Leo, and Ia Lop are narrow ribbons of evergreen and semi-evergreen forests. These riverine or gallery forests are among Southeast Asia's most

fragile habitats since waterways are among the first and most heavily modified landscapes.

Semi-evergreen forests form a transition between wet evergreen forests and the drier, dipterocarp-dominated deciduous forests of the plains
south of the Kon Tum Plateau and west of Dac Lac's uplands. These deciduous dipterocarp forests are widespread and link central Vietnam ecologically with similar regions from Cambodia through Myanmar. Though
Southeast Asia's eastern forests once extended uninterrupted to India, agricultural conversion in Thailand has isolated them from India's western forests. These open forests with a largely grass understory are crossed by temporary streams and dotted with seasonally inundated grasslands.

This habitat harbors large mammals such as Eld's Deer (*Cervus eldii*)
and Banteng (*Bos javanicus*) and provides important habitat for birds, including the Giant Ibis (*Pseudibis gigantea*), White-shouldered Ibis (*P. davisoni*), and Lesser Adjutant (*Leptoptilos javanicus*). In 2004 active eastern
Sarus Crane (*Grus antigone sharpii*) nests were found in deciduous dipterocarp forest within Yok Don National Park in Dak Lak Province. Both semi-
evergreen and deciduous dipterocarp forests often grow interspersed with
open, savannah-like woodlands. This usually occurs where humans have set
fires extensively.

Plant communities along Vietnam's south-central coastline experience
the lowest rainfall in Southeast Asia. Strong winds, little precipitation, and
dusty soils support thorny vegetation, and the region is home to several
cycads, including the endemic *Cycas inermis.* A unique, dry coastal dune
forest grows on the stabilized red sands found near Cam Ranh Bay south
of Nha Trang; two of Indochina's five endemic dipterocarps grow only in
these dune forest stands. Few scientists have studied this area, and more intensive research may uncover other endemic species, though the vegetation
is fast disappearing as development encroaches.

FAUNA

Many endemic and near-endemic vertebrates are associated with the Truong Son Range (see appendix 2). Living amid its lowlands, foothills, and

upper slopes are both new species, including the Saola (*Pseudoryx nghetin-hensis*), Annamite Striped Rabbit (*Nesolagus timminsi*), and Black-crowned Barwing (*Actinodura sodangorum*), and endemic ones, such as the Red-shanked Douc (*P. nemaeus nemaeus*), Edwards's Pheasant (*Lophura edwardsi*), and Annam Flying Frog (*Rhacophorus annamensis*). As of 2004, the geographic ranges of fifteen mammals and sixteen birds are either entirely or largely confined to these evergreen forests, and there is some evidence for an elevated number of endemic species among amphibians, reptiles, and fish. Although it is difficult to quantify rates of endemism and compare them among areas and groups of organisms, these observations suggest that central Vietnam's uplands and associated lowland areas may be a focal point or hotspot of endemism within mainland Southeast Asia.

If true, a possible explanation is that the Truong Son Range remained climatically and ecologically stable as the surrounding forests and other habitats contracted, expanded, or turned over during long-term climate fluctuations. Its forests may have served as a refuge for forest-dwelling species during cooler, drier periods when their evergreen forested habitats disappeared from lower elevations. Under these long-term, stable conditions, older species were preserved and the evolution of new species may have been facilitated. The persistence of more primitive or relict species such as the Saola, Annamite Striped Rabbit, and Krempf's Pine in its forests could be attributed to long-term habitat stability in the Truong Son. Many endemic species here, such as the doucs (genus *Pygathrix*), have overlapping but distinct range boundaries. This patchy distribution may be due to barriers (climatic, geographic, or ecological) or interspecific competition that prevent effective dispersal out of the patches. It could also be that species have not yet recolonized other areas since the last glacial maximum 18,000 years ago, even though they may be capable of doing so.

Mammals

Vietnam's mammalian diversity and endemism are richest in the breadth of forested habitats of the country's central portion. Among the species found here are crested gibbons (genus *Hylobates [Nomascus]*) and doucs (genus *Pygathrix*) dependent on undisturbed broad-leaved evergreen forests, large wild cattle (genus *Bos*) that flourish in the patchwork of open drier forests, grasses, and pools, and top predators such as tiger (*Panthera tigris*) and Dhole (*Cuon alpinus*) that require large ranges and healthy prey populations to survive. Central Vietnam is home to three-quarters of the country's carnivores (Order Carnivora), including almost all of its civets (Family Viverridae) and cats (Family Felidae), and is particularly rich in even-toed hoofed mammals (Order Artiodactyla) with sixteen out of nineteen of Vietnam's native deer and cattle species. Other species-rich groups are the primates (Order Primates) and the rats and mice (Family Muridae).

None of central Vietnam's forests, wet or dry, support either the number or diversity of mammals of former years. Scientists and big-game hunters who visited northern and eastern Cambodia's dry forests, which extended into central Vietnam early in the twentieth century, described the habitat as second only to the Serengeti in game abundance. In 1936, however, the American Museum of Natural History's Fleischmann-Clark Indo-China Expedition reported a decline in Wild Water Buffalo (*Bubalus arnee*) numbers and wholesale shooting of both Eld's Deer (*Cervus eldii*) and Hog Deer (*Axis porcinus*) for medicinal purposes. Today the Wild Water Buffalo is extinct in Vietnam, and both of these deer species may be as well. Other globally threatened species, such as the Asian Elephant (*Elephas maximus;* Endangered), Gaur (*Bos gaurus;* Vulnerable), Tiger (Endangered), and Asian Black Bear (*Ursus thibetanus;* Vulnerable), hang on by a thread.

Doucs (Genus *Pygathrix*)

Doucs, also called Douc Langurs, are Vietnam's most colorful and emblematic monkeys (fig. 42). Three forms exist, and all have gray bodies with a white triangle on the rump, gray upper arms, and black shoulders and chest. Gray heads sport a black band across the forehead, and the delicate fringe of their snow-white beards contrasts with a chestnut throat. Doucs have long, graceful limbs, with the arms slightly longer than the legs, and long, slender white tails. Their striking faces, almond-shaped slanted eyes, and multi-hued coloration make them one of the world's most beautiful primates.

Each of the three taxa have characteristic color patterns, most noticeably on their lower legs or shanks. The Red-shanked Douc has deep red-

Figure 42. Red-shanked Douc (*Pygathrix nemaeus nemaeus,* bottom), Gray-shanked Douc (*P. n. cinerea,* top left), and Black-shanked Douc (*P. nigripes,* top right)

dish, almost rust-colored shins, black thighs, white forearms and hands, and porcelainlike pale yellow-orange facial skin. The Gray-shanked Douc (*P. nemaeus cinerea*) resembles the Red-shanked but has gray limbs, black hands and feet, and a narrower black band across its forehead. The Black-Shanked Douc (*P. nigripes*) has all-black legs, gray arms, black hands, and bluish gray facial skin with yellowish eye rings.

The three forms are found in overlapping ranges running north to south along the Truong Son Range. The Red-shanked Douc lives furthest north, in the northern and central Truong Son in Vietnam and Laos. The Gray-shanked Douc lives in the central Truong Son Range, and its known range lies within Vietnam. Scientists know little about this taxon; it was discovered only in 1997, and its description was based largely on individuals confiscated from the wildlife trade. The third form, the Black-shanked Douc, ranges through Vietnam's southern Truong Son into Cambodia. Analyses indicate that genetic differences between the three are consistent with species-level status; the northern (Red) and central (Gray) forms are more closely related to each other than either of these is to the southern (Black). Observations by scientists in Cambodia in 2001 called into question the identity of some of these forms, and more research is needed to determine the relationship among the Black, Red, and Gray-shanked Doucs.

Scientists have undertaken few studies of doucs in the wild, but they appear to be highly arboreal, living in groups of up to fifty individuals, though three to ten is more likely. As leaf monkeys they feed mostly on leaves with occasional buds, fruit, flowers, and seeds. They inhabit primarily evergreen forests, though the southernmost Black-shanked are also found in semi-evergreen formations. Nothing is known of ecological or behavioral differences among the taxa. Doucs are particularly susceptible to hunting because they often react to disturbance by remaining motionless rather than fleeing; a ship's crew putting in at Da Nang in 1819 was able to shoot more than 100 Red-shanked Doucs between five in the morning and breakfast. Today they are hunted for food, for traditional medicine, as pets, and for taxidermy. Stuffed Black-shanked Doucs adorn hotel lobbies and roadside stands throughout the Da Lat region. The IUCN lists the Red- and

Black-shanked Doucs as Endangered; too little is known to assess the Gray-shanked Douc.

Golden Jackal and Dhole (Canis aureus and Cuon alpinus)

Central Vietnam's two canid species, the Golden Jackal and Dhole, differ markedly from each other in social behavior, hunting methods and prey, and preferred habitat. The Golden Jackal, a midsized dog weighing 15–22 pounds (7–10 kg), is related most closely to the wolf (genus *Canis*). It is slimly built, with pointed, erect ears, long hair, and a relatively short tail. The coat is usually a pale grayish or gold-brown speckled with black and white on the back and flanks, and the back is marked with a black saddle. The limbs and head are a sandy rufous brown, the underparts are pale, and the tail is largely black. Identification in the field can be problematic, for Golden Jackals closely resemble some domestic dog (*Canis familiaris*) types. The larger Dhole is distinguished by its size (22–37 pounds; 10–17 kg), overall sandy red coat (paler on the undersides), and shorter, broader muzzle. It, too, can be hard to distinguish from other dogs, particularly at night.

The Golden Jackal's wide distribution spans sub-Saharan Africa, southeastern Europe, the Middle East, and large parts of South and Southeast Asia. It can thrive in a variety of habitats, from desert to evergreen forest and from sea level to at least 13,000 feet (4,000 m), due in part to an omnivorous diet and in part to a tolerance for arid environments and some human disturbance. Golden Jackals hunt alone, relying on their excellent senses of smell, hearing, and sight to locate their prey of small mammals, birds, reptiles, amphibians, and carrion. They are monogamous, and males protect den sites, while both parents chew and disgorge food for their young, starting when the pups are about three weeks of age. They prefer sandy soils for denning and proximity to pools. Threats to the Golden Jackal are unclear, though its nose is reportedly sold in markets for traditional medicine. Historical sources omitted reference to Golden Jackals in all of Indochina, despite existing museum specimens and records from Vietnamese zoos. In Vietnam, its distribution seems to be limited to the south-central region, especially in or near Yok Don National Park in Dak Lak Province.

Dhole are large, social carnivores, pack animals, and communal hunters that take ungulate prey in both open and closed forested country. They live in groups of generally fewer than ten individuals (rarely up to twenty) that are probably organized around a set of either male or female kin. They hunt cooperatively, which allows them to bring down large animals, including Eurasian Wild Pig (*Sus scrofa*), Sambar (*Cervus unicolor*), and Gaur. They also will hunt alone and are known to take quite small prey, including rodents and beetles. Their social structure is poorly understood and potentially complex. It appears that only one female in the multi-male, multi-female pack breeds and that all members guard, play with, and feed the young indiscriminately. Dhole are well known for their unique whistling cries used to make contact with other group members and reassemble the pack in forested hunting environments.

Although Dhole were once common in forests across Vietnam, they are seldom seen today, in part because their prey populations have declined considerably. Scientists believe that effective conservation of this species will require extremely large protected areas of more than 390 square miles (1,000 km²). The IUCN lists the Dhole as Endangered because of its shrinking distribution, now restricted largely to South and Southeast Asia. Because of its wide distribution and flexible ecology, the Golden Jackal is less of a conservation concern.

Binturong (Arctitis binturong), Owston's Civet (Chrotogale owstoni), and Spotted Linsang (Prionodon pardicolor)

Ten civet species representing three subfamilies are known from Vietnam, and all but one can be found in the central region. The Binturong is a member of the palm civets (Subfamily Paradoxurinae), though with its large size (20–31 pounds; 9–14 kg) and all-black coat it is not representative of this largely tree-dwelling group (fig. 43). The only carnivore besides the Kinkajou (*Potus flavus*) of Central and South America to have acquired a prehensile tail, the Binturong uses its tail to hold onto branches, leaving the forefeet free to handle ripe fruit. Along with enlarged, grinding cheek teeth, the tail is an adaptation for a specialized tree-dwelling, fruit-eating lifestyle, which the Binturong supplements with rodents and birds. The females of these solitary, slow-moving animals are roughly 20 percent larger than the

Figure 43. Family Vivveridae: Spotted Linsang (*Prionodon pardicolor,* top), Owston's Civet (*Chrotogale owstoni,* center), and Binturong (*Arctictis binturong,* bottom)

males and are usually dominant when the sexes encounter each other. Binturongs require forested habitats and are found from India through mainland Southeast Asia to the islands of Sumatra, Java, Borneo, and the Philippines. In Vietnam, they dwell primarily in the country's central region as well as a bit to the north and south.

Owston's Civet, a 4.5–6.5-pound (2–3 kg) banded civet (Subfamily Hemigalinae) also appears to be a specialist, in its case on a diet of invertebrates. The stomachs of two individuals, when opened, contained chiefly earthworms. Owston's Civet is more terrestrial than most Asian civets, using its long snout to root along the ground for worms and other insects, though it also hunts in trees. Unfortunately, these ground-dwelling habits make it more vulnerable to snaring. Owston's Civet is a globally threatened (Vulnerable), restricted-range species and until five years ago was known from a handful of locations in northern Vietnam, northern Laos, and southern Yunnan and southwestern Guangxi Provinces in China. Recent surveys have recorded it as far south as Gia Lai Province in the central Truong Son. It prefers damp, forested environments, often near rivers.

The Spotted Linsang is placed in the Subfamily Viverrinae, the largest group of viverrids and home to the true civets and genets. Linsangs are the most catlike of the viverrids; small, delicate, and quick, they depend on stealth to stalk the small mammals and birds that make up the bulk of their diet. They are also among the rarest and most poorly known members of the group. The Spotted Linsang weighs 1.3 pounds (600 g), with a head and body length of 15.5 inches (39 cm) and a tail almost as long (13.5 inches, 34 cm). Active at night, it spends the day resting in a leaf-lined nest under roots or hollow logs. The Asiatic linsang genus *Prionodon* differs from other civets in lacking both their typical scent-marking perineal glands and a pair of upper molars. Recent genetic analyses indicate that this evolutionary lineage is quite old and distinct from the rest of the civets, its sister group being the cats (Family Felidae) from which it separated roughly 33 million years ago. The African Linsang (*Poiana richardsoni*), with which the Spotted Linsang was formerly grouped due to shared coat pattern, skull morphology, dentition, and an arboreal nature, originated more than 20 million years later. Their close resemblance is due to convergent evolution, where similar adaptive pressures (here small-bodied, arboreal, forest-dwelling carnivory) have caused the independent evolution of like characters and function. The Spotted Linsang is found in submontane forests up to elevations of at least 9,000 feet (2,700 m) from Nepal through northern mainland Southeast Asia. In Vietnam it is restricted to the country's north and the northern Truong Son.

All three species of civets bear an average of two young per litter and may breed twice a year. They all experience intense hunting pressure in Vietnam, as do the rest of the members of their family. Civets are highly valued in the wildlife trade both for their meat, considered a delicacy by some, and for their use in traditional Asian medicine. Their perineal glands secrete an oily substance sometimes referred to as civet oil, which the animals use to communicate information such as territorial boundaries and reproductive status. Medicinal uses of this musk include the treatment of skin conditions and excess perspiration. Civet oil has long played an important role in perfumery as both scent and base, and there are records of its importation from Africa by King Solomon dating to the tenth century B.C.E. Although now largely replaced by synthetics, it is still harvested (mostly from live animals) for this use.

Fishing Cat (Prionailurus viverrinus)

The Fishing Cat is a small, wild cat (Family Felidae) strongly associated with wetland areas in South and Southeast Asia. Unlike most other small cats, the Fishing Cat has a stocky build with a powerful chest and short legs—more similar to a Leopard (*Panther pardus*) than the closely related and slimmer Leopard Cat (*Prionailurus bengalensis*). Males (24–27 pounds; 11–12 kg) are much larger than females (13–15 pounds; 6–7 kg), and both sexes have relatively short tails of less than half their body length. The Fishing Cat's short olive or gray-brown fur is covered with small black spots that merge into short streaks on the head, neck, and back; the tail is marked with black rings and a black tip. Its feet are moderately webbed, possibly an adaptation to living in wet areas, and the claw sheaths are shortened so that the claw tips protrude partially even when retracted.

Fish prey have dominated this cat's diet in what few detailed studies have been made. Other prey taken include birds, small mammals, frogs, snakes, and crustaceans, as well as young deer fawns and smaller domestic animals (such as goats, dogs, and poultry). Fishing Cats hunt by crouching along riverbanks, scooping out fish with their paws or pouncing on other prey. They are also strong swimmers and will enter the water to capture both fish and aquatic birds.

Little is known of their social organization. They may be primarily nocturnal and solitary, and limited radio-tracking data suggests that larger male ranges overlap those of several females. They bear two to three kittens and apparently den in rough nests built in dense reeds. Fishing Cats are found in a variety of wetland habitats with thick vegetation cover, including mangroves, swamps and marshes, tidal creeks, and streams and rivers in evergreen, semi-evergreen, and deciduous dipterocarp forests. Despite this, their occurrence tends to be patchy and localized, and they are discontinuously distributed across northern India through mainland Southeast Asia and south to Sumatra and Java.

The distribution and status of the Fishing Cat in Vietnam is poorly known, and they are considered rare and secretive. Historically this cat has been recorded at five locations, including Yok Don National Park. The primary threat to Fishing Cats throughout their range in Vietnam is hunting for their meat and fur. As with all wetland-dependent species, Fishing Cats are also threatened with destruction of their habitats, primarily for conversion to agriculture.

With the exception of the Marbled Cat (*Pardofelis marmorata*), all of Vietnam's eight felids are found in the country's center, including two other small cats, the Jungle Cat (*Felis chaus*) and Asian Golden Cat (*Catopuma temminckii*; Vulnerable). The IUCN lists the Fishing Cat as Vulnerable.

Finless Porpoise (Neophocoena phocoenoides)

The Finless Porpoise is the only porpoise species (Family Phocoenidae) that is not restricted to a saltwater environment (fig. 44). Ecologically flexible — described as a facultative freshwater species — it resides in fresh, brackish, and marine waters along a narrow coastal band running from Iran in the Persian Gulf to the waters of Japan and south to northern Java. It can also be found up to 1,060 miles (1,700 km) upstream in China's Yangtze River and associated water bodies.

Finless Porpoises are so named because they lack a back fin. Instead there is either a narrow (about an inch, or 2 cm), raised ridge running the length of the back or, in some populations, a wider, 4–6-inch (10–14 cm), slightly V-shaped back groove that tapers to a ridge for the last third. Short, bumpy projections called tubercles are usually present along these ridges and grooves. Unlike other porpoises, the forehead rises into a distinctly rounded curve called a melon, a formation seen also in toothed whales. Size varies geographically: the tropical populations from southern China

Figure 44. Finless Porpoise (*Neophocaena phocoenoides*)

are smaller than northern ones, adults typically reaching body lengths of 5–6 feet (1.4–1.6 m) and maximum weights of less than 130 pounds (60 kg).

Finless Porpoises prefer river systems and nearshore habitats such as semi-enclosed bays, coastal shallows, and mangrove forests, where they feed on squid, crustaceans, and small fish. Almost nothing is known about their social behavior, though like other porpoises, they may live in relatively small groups.

Little is known about the Vietnamese population, though they likely resemble the more tropical forms from south China and Pakistan. One important source of information is Finless Porpoise bones that fishermen have deposited, along with those of other stranded cetaceans, in whale temples. Vietnamese fishers worship these marine mammals because they believe that the animals will aid them when they are in distress at sea (box 13). The presence of more than seventy skulls at temples in south and south-central Vietnam suggests that Finless Porpoises once occupied coastal areas and river systems in these regions.

Because Finless Porpoises require the same riverine and marine habitats subject to intensive human activity, their populations are highly threatened. The primary cause of death is accidental entanglement in fishing nets and other tackle. Intensive fishing has greatly reduced their available prey base and likely their abundance. It has also brought them into conflict with humans, whose gill nets they sometimes raid. The reverence in which fishermen hold them has provided them with some protection, though this attitude appears to be fading. There is evidence that chemical pollutants such as pesticides deposited in rivers and nearshore areas also have damaging effects on the animals.

The Finless Porpoise is the only porpoise in the Indo-Malayan region. One other facultative freshwater marine mammal is known from the region, the Irrawaddy Dolphin (*Orcaella brevirostris*), whose tiny Indochinese population hangs on in a small stretch of the Mekong River in Cambodia and Laos. There is insufficient information for the IUCN to assess the conservation status of the Finless Porpoise.

Muntjacs (Genus Muntiacus)

Muntjacs are an ancient lineage of small deer native to South and Southeastern Asia plus Tibet and China (fig. 45). They bear simple, spiky, slightly branched antlers rooted on long, bony, fur-covered bases known as pedicles. Solitary forest dwellers, muntjacs are territorial to a degree, marking their ranges with droppings and glandular secretions produced before their eyes and under the chin. They feed on browse (herbs, sprouts, and other easily digested vegetation), as well as eggs, young birds, and small mammals, which they dispatch by hitting them with their front legs and biting. Muntjacs are commonly known as barking deer for the barking sound that males emit when alarmed. Males have been known to spar both with their antlers and with their unusually large, enamel-covered canine teeth.

Despite their diminutive size, Southeast Asia's muntjacs attracted

BOX 13

Central Coast Fish Festival

Along the central and southern coasts of Vietnam, fishermen revere the spirit of the whale, called Ngu Ong, or "Sir Fish." Sir Fish protects fishers as they navigate the open seas, and many recount stories of harrowing mishaps that resulted in their rescue by Sir Fish. At the start of the spring-summer fishing season, villagers celebrate the Cau Ngu Festival, a tradition that dates back at least to the early 1800s. The mere sight of a whale, living or dead, is thought to bring good luck to fishermen. The first person to see a whale carcass not killed by being caught in a fisherman's net becomes Sir Fish's eldest son and must go into a period of mourning for the departed whale. This brings good luck to the mourner and his village for many years. Villagers practice elaborate rituals with the whale's carcass, according it the respect they would give to a departed relative. Mausoleums shelter bones of beached whales and are open only on festival days and during New Year's festivities. Dolphins, however, are another story in some areas of central Vietnam. Here dolphins signify bad luck, for the dolphin is believed to incarnate the soul of a drowned man transformed into an evil spirit who brings harm to fishermen.

worldwide attention beginning in the 1990s, when scientists began to survey the Truong Son Range. As a group, the muntjacs are genetically complex and poorly understood. Their chromosome numbers range widely, differing not just between species but also between the sexes of the same species. For many years scientists thought there were just five or six muntjac species, with only one, the relatively widespread Red Muntjac (*M. muntjak*), known from the Truong Son Range.

Figure 45. Large-antlered Muntjac (*Muntiacus vuquangensis,* upper left),
Annamite Muntjac (*M. truongsonensis,* upper right), and Red Muntjac
(*M. muntjak),* female (lower left) and male (lower right)

Scientists have now identified eight muntjac species, with four known from the Truong Son Range: one expected, one rediscovered, and two species new to science. This picture will undoubtedly change with further research. The four muntjac species living in the Truong Son Range differ in size, ranging from the Large-antlered Muntjac (*M. vuquangensis*) at 75 pounds (34 kg) to the midsized Red Muntjac at 57 pounds (26 kg) to the two smallest species, which weigh closer to 33 pounds (15 kg).

The Red Muntjac, found from India through Tibet, mainland Southeast Asia, Sumatra, Java, and Borneo and introduced into England, shows considerable variation in coat color at different altitudes and latitudes. More northerly populations and those living at higher elevations are darker red with a varying amount of black on the legs, whereas populations further south and in the lowlands have a more reddish yellow coat. Male canines can reach 1 inch (2.5 cm) in length, and females have small bone knobs and tufts of hair instead of antlers on their foreheads.

The first new muntjac uncovered along the Truong Son was the Large-antlered Muntjac, described from central Laos in 1996. It is now known as far south as northeastern Cambodia and Vietnam's Lam Dong Province, and it is clear that hunters of the Da Lat Plateau knew of it in the early twentieth century. The Large-antlered Muntjac has a gray-brown to tan grizzled coat, a short, triangular tail, and relatively massive antlers for a muntjac set on short, stout antler bases. The Large-antlered Muntjac occurs only in the Truong Son Range, preferring primary or old-growth evergreen forests of the foothills and upper slopes.

Harold Coolidge, a scientist on the Kelley-Roosevelts Expedition undertaken in 1928–1929, collected a single young specimen of a distinct muntjac in northern Laos. This turned out to be a new species, Roosevelts' Muntjac (*M. rooseveltorum*), and the expedition's collection was deposited in the Field Museum in Chicago. No additional record of this species surfaced until 1994, when local Laotians informed scientists that an additional muntjac they had not yet seen lived in the Truong Son's forests. Genetic analyses using new samples and the old specimen confirmed the rediscovery. Roosevelts' Muntjac has an auburn to brown coat with white-tipped hair, and a white throat, a short brown tail, and prominent chin glands. Its preferred habitat seems similar to the Large-antlered's, though its distribution is not well known.

Again in the 1990s, scientists discovered an unusual muntjac in Laos, this time in a menagerie. They were able to locate further individuals in Vietnam, and in 1998 a description of the Truong Son or Annamite Muntjac (*M. truongsonensis*) was published. Its dark appearance makes it distinctly different from the Truong Son's other muntjacs. The crown is bright orange, the coat dark brown deepening to black on the limbs, with a black tail edged with white and white bands above each hoof. Long hairs cover the bases of the short, spiky antlers. The Vietnamese specimens came from central Vietnam, and the species was thought to be restricted to the Truong Son Range. In 2001, however, a small, dark muntjac was photographed in the forests of Van Ban District, Lao Cai Province, in the Hoang Lien Son Range. Both the distribution and the taxonomy of this species remain unclear.

Muntjacs are hunted for their meat and for use in local and traditional medicines, especially of the antlers and feet; the conservation status of the newly discovered and rediscovered species is unknown. A fourth, tiny muntjac, the Little Leaf Deer (*M. putaoensis*), was described from northern Myanmar in 1999.

Wild Cattle or Oxen (Genus Bos)

All twelve species of wild cattle (Tribe Bovini) are at risk of extinction; nine live in Asia. The semi-evergreen and dry deciduous forests covering southern Laos, southeastern Thailand, Cambodia, and south-central Vietnam form the world's only region where the ranges of four wild cattle overlap: Gaur, Banteng (*B. javanicus*), Kouprey (*B. sauveli*), and Wild Water Buffalo.

Larger than any other oxen, Gaurs can reach 6.5 feet (2 m) or more in height, with males weighing over 2,600 pounds (1,200 kg). The males have dark, rich coats, whereas the females are reddish brown, and both sport a distinct white raised ridge between the horns and whitish hair around the nose and on the lower legs. Their eyes are generally blue. Formerly distributed across India and mainland Southeast Asia, Gaur lived in diverse habitats, particularly semi-evergreen or wet evergreen forests up to about 6,600

Figure 46. Banteng (*Bos javanicus*) male (left) and female (right)

feet (2,000 m). Their range is now greatly reduced in all countries as people hunt them for trophies and for their bile and other parts for use in traditional medicine. Probably a few hundred Gaur remain in Vietnam, in Gia Lai and Dak Lac Provinces, as well as in the central and northern Truong Son.

The smaller Banteng measures 60–69 inches (1.5–1.75 m) in height and weighs 1,300–2,000 pounds (600–900 kg). It has slim, slightly curving horns, a white rump, and white stockings on the lower legs (fig. 46). Like Gaurs, male and female Bantengs differ in color: males are dark brown or black, whereas females and immatures are more ocher in color. Banteng seem to have stronger habitat preferences than their larger relations, selecting more open habitats, particularly deciduous dipterocarp forests. The Banteng is experiencing some of the highest rates of population decline among mammals. It is still present in Vietnam, but only in smaller, more fragmented populations. The largest herds occur in Dak Lak Province, in the open, grassy plains, deciduous forests, and nearby denser forest habitats that the species prefers.

The Kouprey or Gray Ox lies between the Gaur and the Banteng in size. The distinguishing features of adults are an overall gray color and in the males a large dewlap (folds of skin hanging from the neck). Males bear horns twice as long as those of the females and with distinctly fraying ends that create a splintered fringe. Scientists first described the Kouprey in 1937, remarkably late for such a large-bodied animal, and for the next twenty years, researchers all but ignored the species. A two-month study undertaken in 1957 remains the pinnacle of our understanding of the Kouprey. It apparently has a strong preference for open habitats and feeds on grasses rather than browsing on leaves and stems. During the 1957 study scientists located populations of Kouprey relatively easily, though individuals apparently were never common. As of 2004, despite twenty years of concerted effort, no individuals had been seen throughout their range, which formerly extended from Cambodia to parts of Thailand, Laos, and Vietnam. The Kouprey, listed as Critically Endangered, is most likely extinct in Vietnam, and perhaps in the world.

Birds

The avifauna of the Truong Son Range is rich in species and high in endemism. All three newly described songbirds and more than half of the restricted-range species found in Vietnam are limited to the country's central section (see appendixes 2 and 3). With two exceptions, the Vietnamese Greenfinch (*Carduelis monguilloti*) and Mekong Wagtail (*Motacilla samveasnae*), they are either pheasants (Phasianidae) or babblers (Timaliidae). One distinct habitat specialist, the Sooty Babbler (*Stachyris herberti*), is found among the central Truong Son's limestone karst areas. Largely missing from central Vietnam are the habitats of specialized waterbird communities found in the country's north and south.

Although knowledge of the number of endemic pheasants in the Truong Son remains somewhat opaque, the two well-accepted species, the Annam Partridge (*Arborophila merlini*) and Edwards's Pheasant, are tied to lowlands below 660–990 feet (200–300 m). And although the Crested Argus (*Rheinardia ocellata*) has been sighted at 6,200 feet (1,900 m) in the southern Truong Son, these montane populations may depend on movement from lower areas, where they are more numerous, to survive. Babbler diversity, in contrast, is concentrated in the hills and mountains areas, and endemic diversity especially so. Together with sunbirds (Family Nectariniidae), sparrows (Family Passeridae), and finches (Family Fringillidae), this enormous group forms the bulk of a diverse suite of perching birds that is perhaps the Troung Son's most characteristic avian community. Most restricted-range birds are found at 3,300 feet (1,000 m) and higher, while three, the Golden-winged (*Garrulax ngoclinhensis*) and Collared (*G. yersini*) Laughingthrushes and the Spectacled Fulvetta (*Alcippe ruficapilla*), live only above 5,900 feet (1,800 m).

The Truong Son's birds are threatened mainly by habitat loss. Especially hard-hit are its lowland species since much of their evergreen forests have vanished. But logging and clearing for such crops as coffee has penetrated high up the range's eastern flanks, threatening montane communities, too. Large ground birds are collected, sometimes by indiscriminant snaring. Although songbirds are caught for the wildlife trade, few if any of central Vietnam's endemic species are specifically targeted.

Pheasants (Subfamily Phasianinae)

Central Vietnam is home to nine species of pheasants, of which four are endemic to Vietnam, one is endemic to Indochina, and six are listed as globally threatened by the IUCN. Species here are a mixture of birds restricted to the lowlands and ones that can range upward of 6,600 feet (2,000 m) in elevation.

Probably the most elegant of central Vietnam's (possibly the world's) pheasants is the Crested Argus, a species that prefers submontane and montane evergreen forests up to 6,200 feet (1,900 m) in elevation (see fig. 22). Both sexes are deep brown all over, and the male is stippled with small whitish and light brown spots, while the female is more darkly barred. Both combinations help conceal them in the gloomy forest understory. Males carry an astonishingly long tail that is strongly compressed from the sides so that it appears very wide in profile. The tail feathers of the male Crested Argus are the longest of any bird, reaching 5 inches (13 cm) in width and up to 67 inches (1.73 m) in length on mature individuals. The female's tail is far shorter, measuring 14–17 inches (35–43 cm), and is heavily barred. Both have drooping, feathered crests that are brownish black and white on the male and simply black on the female. Males are territorial and display for females on dancing grounds, spreading their tails vertically to make them appear even larger. They also produce loud, far-carrying calls from these dancing grounds. There are two highly disjunct populations of Crested Argus, both restricted to damp, mature forests. One lives in the hills of Vietnam's central Truong Son, the other in a small area of montane forest in Peninsular Malaysia.

Less exotic in appearance but far more enigmatic in distribution and taxonomic status is the suite of three *Lophura* pheasant species living in central Vietnam's rapidly disappearing lowland forests. Edwards's Pheasant was the first to be described in 1896, followed by the Imperial Pheasant (*L. imperialis*) in 1925. The Vietnamese Pheasant (*L. hatinhensis*), sometimes considered a subspecies of Edwards's Pheasant, was informally described much later, in 1975 by Vo Quy, Vietnam's leading ornithologist. Male Imperial Pheasants are a dark purplish blue all over, with a dark crest and red facial skin. Edwards's differs in having a white crest, smaller tail, and glossy green highlights on the wings. The Vietnamese Pheasant is quite similar to Edwards's, with the addition of white central tail feathers. Females of all species are a dull brown. Both Edwards's and Imperial Pheasants were thought lost from the forests until rediscovered in 1996 and 1990, respectively. Genetic research on Imperial Pheasants indicates that they are in fact rare hybrids produced by naturally occurring crosses between Edwards's Pheasant and the Silver Pheasant (*L. nycthemera*). It is also quite likely that the Vietnamese Pheasant is the result of inbreeding within small, isolated populations of Edwards's Pheasant. This confusion over taxonomic identity is not so surprising since the entire *Lophura* genus is complex and variable and many pheasant species are known to hybridize in the wild. Edwards's Pheasant is listed as Endangered by the IUCN and should be considered one of the rarer birds in the world.

Other pheasants here include the Green Peafowl (*Pavo muticus*), a close relative of the Indian Peafowl (*P. cristatus*), which inhabits open woodlands and forests up to 3,000 feet (915 m) in central and southern Vietnam (see fig. 22). The male's spike-like crest, glossy green upperparts, and long train of tail feathers dotted with ocelli, or eyes, are unmistakable. The species is classified as Vulnerable because it has become rare and its range in Southeast Asia has become increasingly fragmented. Also present up to 4,600 feet (1,400 m) in the central and southern Truong Son is Germain's Peacock Pheasant (*Polyplectron germaini*), a smaller, darker, crestless relative of the north's Gray Peacock Pheasant (*P. bicalcaratum*). This restricted-range species is classified as Vulnerable by the IUCN.

Red-collared Woodpecker (Picus rabieri)

The tropical and subtropical forests of Southeast Asia are rich in woodpeckers (Family Picidae), and the Red-collared Woodpecker is one of twenty-seven species in Vietnam, representing more than 12 percent of global diversity. Found in the country's north and the northern and central Truong Son, its global distribution is limited to northern Indochina and China's southern Yunnan Province.

Both male and female Red-collared Woodpeckers are a dark green above, fading to a slightly drabber, more olive tone on the slightly mottled underparts with a red collar circling the neck and running up the back of the head. The female crown is black, whereas males are more conspicuous with a red crown, moustache, and upper chest. Measuring about a foot in length (30 cm), Red-collared Woodpeckers spend much of their time on the forest floor, where they forage for the ants that dominate their diet. Pointed beaks probe ground nests, and the ants uncovered are gathered up by the woodpecker's highly specialized tongue. Unusually long and sticky, with a tip covered with backward-pointing barbs, the tongue functions as an adhesive strip. Ant-hunting in leaf litter is one of many foraging techniques, forest layers, and habitats woodpeckers make use of. Despite woodpeckers' shared adaptations for foraging on hidden insects, these subtle specializations allow as many as thirteen species to coexist in the same areas.

Red-collared Woodpeckers are lowland forest dwellers, living in broad-leaved and secondary forests up to 2,300 feet (700 m). They are often found in mixed flocks with babblers such as the laughingthrushes (genus *Garrulax*) and other woodpeckers. Twenty other woodpeckers occur in central Vietnam, and most, like the Red-collared, are residents. Three species are known only from the Truong Son: the Gray-headed Woodpecker (*P. canus*) from the north, the Stripe-breasted Woodpecker (*Dendrocopos atratus*) from the central, and the Yellow-crowned Woodpecker (*D. mahratten-sis*) from the south. All are more widespread than the Red-collared Wood-pecker, and the Gray-headed is found as far away as Scandinavia and France.

Although it can apparently survive in disturbed habitat if enough large trees remain, the Red-collared Woodpecker is considered Near Threatened by the IUCN due to lowland habitat loss throughout its restricted range. None of Vietnam's other woodpeckers are considered either globally threat-ened or Near Threatened.

Rufous-necked Hornbill (Aceros nipalensis)

Vietnam's most beautiful and most threatened hornbill is the Rufous-necked Hornbill. A bird of evergreen and semi-evergreen hill forests at ele-vations of 2,300–6,600 feet (700–2,000 m), this hornbill once ranged from eastern Nepal through northern and north-central Vietnam. Listed as Vul-nerable by the IUCN, it can be found only in small, isolated forest pockets in a subset of its former range.

The Rufous-necked Hornbill is a large bird, with males weighing 5.5 pounds (2.5 kg) and females 5 pounds (2.3 kg), and both sexes stand about 3 feet (1 m) tall. The male has a bright rufous-red head, neck, and under-parts and is glossy black elsewhere except for white on the latter third of the tail and the tips of the flight feathers. The bill is heavy and yellow, ridged along the upper mandible, where it is marked with dark vertical bars. The casque surmounting the bill is quite small. Pale blue naked skin surrounds the eyes, and inflatable scarlet skin covers the throat. The female is black where the male is rufous, and the coloring of her bare skin patches is duller. Their long tails and long and heavy wings make their substantial bodies seem relatively small.

Like other hornbills, Rufous-neckeds are cavity nesters with a twist. Selecting a natural tree hole and crevice some 30–100 feet (10–30 m) off the ground, the female enters and seals herself in with a mix of matted plant pulp and feces. She lays one or two eggs, incubates the clutch, and remains with the chicks until they are judged mature enough to emerge;

this involved process can take four months. The male attends her and the brood during this time. Rufous-necked Hornbills feed mostly on fruits in the canopy and rarely forage on the forest floor, where they move with awkward shambling hops. During the breeding season, males broaden their dietary horizons, and one study collected the remains of twenty animals from nest sites, including beetles, earthworms, frogs, lizards, fish, and other birds.

Rufous-necked Hornbills likely never occupied a large range in Vietnam, which lies at the southeastern edge of their distribution. Early-twentieth-century explorers recorded the species from the upper section of northwestern Vietnam, including Mount Fan Xi Pan. Even then they were considered scarce, and until 2001 they were confirmed only from the northern Truong Son's Pu Mat National Park. That spring a second population was uncovered at Che Tao, a remote commune in the Hoang Lien Son Range. A larger population of Rufous-necked Hornbills is known from across the border in Laos, and it is quite possible that the species survives elsewhere in the hills of north-central Vietnam.

Babblers (Family Timaliidae)

The babblers are the most species-rich bird group in Vietnam, and much of this diversity is centered along the Truong Son Range (fig. 47). This includes species with restricted ranges, species that are endemic to the country, and ones that have only recently been described.

The Short-tailed Scimitar Babbler (*Jabouilleia danjoui*) is the only member of its genus and is actually more closely allied with the six genera of wren babblers than with the typical scimitar babblers (*Pomatorhinus, Xiphirhynchus*). It shares its long, downwardly curving bill with the other scimitar babblers, but its tail is far shorter. Both sexes are dark brown above and almost white below, with dark, black streaking on a reddish breast. Short-tailed Scimitar Babblers are observed along the ground and in the undergrowth of evergreen, secondary, and bamboo forests at elevations of up to 6,900 feet (2,100 m). The species is restricted to northern and central Vietnam and central Laos, though a recent record from Ha Giang Province in

Figure 47. Grey-faced Tit Babbler (*Macronous kelleyi*, top), White-browed
Shrike Babbler (*Pteruthius flaviscapis*, second from top), Sooty Babbler
(*Stachyris herberti*, third from top), and Short-tailed Scimitar Babbler
(*Jabouilleia danjoui*, bottom). All four are males.

far northeastern Vietnam suggests that it probably also lives over the border in China.

The Sooty Babbler is one of the few babblers known to have specific ecological requirements, in this case restriction to areas of karst. The initial description in 1920 was based on five specimens from a location in central Laos. Then in 1995 it was reported for the first time since its description from what is now the Phong Nha–Ke Bang National Park in the central Truong Son Range. Sooty Babblers are a rich, dark, sooty brown touched with purple bronzing all over except for paler plumage on the throat. Adults have a blue-gray eye ring that is diagnostic of the species. Sooty Babblers appear to be locally common in their Vietnamese range and are exclusively associated with lowland evergreen forests on limestone substrates. The species is endemic to these two habitats in Laos and Vietnam.

The Gray-faced Tit Babbler (*Macronous kelleyi*) is endemic to Indochina, living in broad-leaved evergreen forests and some secondary forests at elevations of up to 3,800 feet (1,165 m) in central and southern Vietnam, central and southern Laos, and eastern Cambodia. The adults are rather unremarkable in appearance, 5.5 inches (14 cm) long with rufous-brown upperparts and light yellow underparts with barely visible brown streaking primarily on the chest. The gray coloring referred to in the common English name is visible above the eye and along the sides of the head. This species occupies a range less than 20,000 square miles (50,000 km²), though it has been recorded as far north as Cuc Phuong National Park in the country's northwest.

Shrike babblers are sturdy, strongly patterned, and sexually dimorphic birds of montane forests. The White-browed Shrike Babbler (*Pteruthius flaviscapis*) is an extremely variable species that ranges from northeastern Pakistan to Sumatra, Java, and Borneo. In general males have black heads (except for a broad white stripe above the eye), wings, and tails, gray upperparts, and pale gray underparts with some chestnut feathering on the upper part of the wings. Females are gray above and pale gray below with a white stripe above the eye and light olive wings and tail. The White-browed Shrike Babbler is a common resident in Vietnam outside of the south. In 2003, a genetic study removed the shrike babbler genus *Pteruthius* from the babblers; its actual position within Old World songbirds is unclear.

Other babbler genera in central Vietnam's forests include the laughing-thrushes, medium-sized, stocky, long-tailed, gregarious birds with highly variable plumage; scimitar babblers, with their downward-curving beaks; floppy-crested barwings (*Actinodura*); the small and noisy fulvettas (*Alcippe*), largely colored chestnut, brown, and gray; and the compact, soft-feathered parrotbills (*Paradoxornis*), with their distinctive short, sharp-edged bills.

Three new babbler species have been described from the central Truong Son since 1999: the Golden-winged Laughingthrush, Chestnut-eared Laughingthrush (*G. konkakinhensis*), and Black-crowned Barwing. The two laughingthrushes are currently known only from Vietnam's Kon Tum Plateau, while the barwing has also been sighted on the Bolovens Plateau in southern Laos. All are birds of montane evergreen forests, and all are classified as Vulnerable. An additional two endemic Vietnamese babblers, the Collared Laughingthrush and Gray-crowned Crocias (*Crocias langbianis*) are restricted to southern Vietnam's Da Lat Plateau. Both are listed as Endangered by the IUCN because of decline and fragmentation of their montane evergreen habitats. The Short-tailed Scimitar Babbler and Sooty Babbler are currently classified as Near Threatened by the IUCN.

Amphibians and Reptiles

Although the Truong Son is receiving the most attention for its new mammal discoveries, it has proved equally rich in novel herpetofauna. From 1992 through 2004 one turtle, four snake, ten lizard, and nineteen frog descriptions were published from diverse habitats (see appendix 3). The lizards include a karst specialist from the northern Truong Son, the Phong Nha–Ke Bang Bow-fingered Gecko (*Cyrtodactylus phongnhakebangensis*), and a coastal forest dweller from Nha Trang, the Vietnamese Leaf-toed Gecko (*Dixonius vietnamensis*). Most of the new frogs are upland species from the central Truong Son, including four species in the Cascade Frog (*Rana livida*) complex. All these new herpetofauna are known so far from at most a handful of locations.

As they are throughout Vietnam, turtles are the central region's most threatened herpetofauna. Critically Endangered species include the endemic Annam Leaf Turtle (*Mauremys annamensis*), the extraordinarily valuable Chinese Three-striped Box Turtle (*Cuora trifasciata*), and a newly described member of Indochinese Box Turtle (*C. galbinifrons*) complex, Bourret's Indochinese Box Turtle (*C. bourreti*). The Estuarine Crocodile (*Crocodylus porosus*) hangs on in central Vietnam's lowlands, but its smaller relative, the Siamese Crocodile (*C. siamensis;* Critically Endangered), has been extirpated. Eight frog species are currently considered Vulnerable by the IUCN.

Annam Flying Frog (Rhacophorus annamensis)

First described in 1924, the endemic Annam Flying Frog is still known only from central and southern Truong Son Range. It is an enormous frog, one of the largest found in Southeast Asia; the females, which are larger than the males, can reach 3.5 inches (8.5 cm) in length. Annam Flying Frogs, though common where they occur, are found exclusively in the canopies of relatively undisturbed forests. Another frog described in the early 1920s, the Annam Spadefoot Toad (*Brachytarsophrys intermedia*), shares this limited distribution. Many of central Vietnam's newer frog species are also, strictly speaking, endemic to the country even though they may be known from only a single location. More survey work should help determine if the Truong Son is a center of frog endemism, as suggested by these longer established species. Clarifying the ranges of all the frog species found in this mountain range will shed light on how diversity is distributed along its 750-mile (1,200 km) length.

Annam Flying Frogs do not in fact fly; rather, they glide among trees using their large webbed hands and feet. Small flaps of skin attached to the top of their backend are believed to help them steer. These features are observed in another member of the genus, the aptly described Spinybottom Tree Frog (*R. exechopygus*). Some reptiles are also capable of gliding flight. In the spectacular flying lizards (genus *Draco*), a thin membrane stretches over highly specialized folding ribs that, when extended, form a wide, often beautifully marked gliding surface perpendicular to the body. Parachute geckos in the genus *Ptychozoon* are aided by often-prominent flaps of skin under the jaw, on the neck and tail, and between the fingers so that they almost appear webbed. Flying snakes (genus *Chrysopelea*) have no apparent morphological adaptations for gliding. Instead they flatten their bodies horizontally, almost doubling their width, and pull their undersides upward to form a concave surface. They are able to control their in-air movements to a remarkable degree given the fact that they have no apparent steering mechanism. Three flying lizards and one flying snake are known from Vietnam, and all are found in its central region. The Annam Flying Frog, Annam Spadefoot Toad, and Spinybottom Tree Frog are all listed as Vulnerable by the IUCN.

Sievers' Three Horned-scale Pitviper
(Triceratolepidophis sieversorum)

Like the Annamite Striped Rabbit (*Nesolagus timminsi*), Sievers' Three Horned-scale Pitviper was first noticed by scientists after it had been collected for the wildlife trade, in this case preserved in rice liquor. Subsequent surveys in nearby Phong Nha–Ke Bang National Park uncovered an additional live animal, and a new genus and species of pitviper was described in 2000. The eyes are cream-colored with a vertical orange-yellow stripe. Horns surmount the head, and the body is colored to camouflage it against a background of algae, moss, and lichens. Unlike other pitvipers, this species lacks a prehensile tail for climbing on vegetation. This, along with its defensive tail-vibrating behavior, suggests that the species is mostly terrestrial.

Sievers' Three Horn-scaled Pitviper lives in low- to mid-elevation semi-evergreen forests on limestone. It is one of a suite of animals strongly associated with central Vietnam's karst habitats. Others include the Annamese Leaf Monkey (*Trachypithecus francoisi hatinhensis*), Sooty Babbler, and Phong Nha–Ke Bang Bow-fingered Gecko.

Bengal Monitor (Varanus bengalensis nebulosus)
and Water Monitor (Varanus salvator)

The monitors (Family Varanidae) are a group of approximately sixty lizards found in the Old World tropics. All but one belong to the genus *Varanus*, and they share a long-necked, robust, flattened body plan that has remained largely unchanged over the past 65 million years. Varanids are generally active predators, especially when compared to other cold-blooded species, and use sharply serrated teeth to rend and tear prey that can range in size from earthworms to large vertebrates. Many are the dominant predators in their communities. Almost all males engage in ritual fights during the breeding season, rising up on their hind legs and wrestling. Two species are found in Vietnam, both of which are widespread globally: the Bengal Monitor, sometimes called the Clouded Monitor in Vietnam, and the Water Monitor.

The Water Monitor is the second largest lizard in the world behind the giant Komodo Dragon (*V. komodoensis*); wild specimens have been reported reaching 55 pounds (25 kg) and over 8 feet (2.5 m) in length. They are dark brown or black above with horizontal yellow splotches beneath that generally fade with age. Water Monitors spend much of their time on land, but they remain close to water and reach their highest densities in mangrove forests. Their ability to swim long distances makes Water Monitors frequent island colonizers; in Vietnam they can be found on islands off the northeastern coast's Quang Ninh Province and in the south on the Con Dao Archipelago. (Alternatively, these distributions may reflect movement over land when sea levels were lower.) They have enormously broad diets, eating mollusks, crustaceans, all vertebrates, carrion, and human waste (including feces). Active during the day, they often rest partially in the water, and spend their nights in trees, bushy vegetation, or burrows that can reach 33 feet (10 m) in length.

The Bengal Monitor is somewhat smaller, with males reaching lengths of approximately 5 feet (1.5 m) and a weight of 6 pounds (2.7 kg); females are somewhat smaller. The Clouded subspecies that lives in Vietnam is lightly colored, ranging from gray to dingy yellow with some speckling over the back. These monitors are more terrestrial and frequent drier areas than do Water Monitors and are agile climbers despite their bulk. They seem to feed mainly on small, invertebrate food items such as beetles, snails, and ants, which they locate by rooting around in the ground and then scoop up with their forked tongue. Vertebrate prey is rare, though they do feed on carrion. Clouded Monitors use burrows at night, basking after their morning

Figure 48. Annam Leaf Turtle (*Mauremys annamensis*)

emergence to raise their body temperatures for the hunt. The young of both species spend all their time in trees eating insects.

The Clouded Monitor is found mainly in central Vietnam; the Water Monitor is more widely distributed, though it is now believed to be extirpated in the country's northeast uplands. Although neither is considered threatened on a global scale, both species experience enormous hunting pressure in Vietnam for both their meat and their hides, and there is evidence of range contractions and fragmentation. The Water Monitor has also suffered from loss of its preferred mangrove habitats.

Annam Leaf Turtle *(*Mauremys annamensis*)*

Scientists first described the Annam Leaf Turtle in 1903, and it remains Vietnam's only confirmed endemic turtle (fig. 48). Smallish and rather uncompelling in appearance, it can attain shell lengths of just under a foot (30 cm). It is best identified by three or four yellow stripes running along the side of its dark brown or black pointed head. The upper shell has three raised keels running parallel front to back, and the toes are fully webbed. Annam Leaf Turtles belong to the largest of the turtle families, the Geoemydidae, which is distributed widely across tropical and subtropical areas of the Americas, Europe, Africa, and Asia. Leaf turtles of the genus *Mauremys* occur in two isolated patches, with three widespread species found in Europe, Africa, and the Middle East, and the remaining three, including the Annam Leaf Turtle, restricted to East and Southeast Asia. The habitat that covers the intervening stretch is quite dry; during wetter periods leaf turtles may have been distributed more continuously throughout the range.

Most geoemydids are aquatic or semi-aquatic. Although the ecology and behavior of the Annam Leaf Turtle is still unclear, its shell and foot morphology and lowland habitat suggest that it inhabits sluggish or still waters. It is thought to be omnivorous, and in captivity it consumes both vegetables (fruit and lettuce) and animals (fish and worms). For a long time, this endemic turtle was thought to be restricted to a small area in Quang Nam Province. New information, largely from the wildlife trade, suggests that its range extends south at least to Binh Dinh Province. During the 1930s and 1940s, Annam Leaf Turtles were abundant in the lowland marshes and slow-moving water bodies near the cities of Hoi An and Da Nang. It is clear that its numbers have declined dramatically, and at present, it is rare in the trade and virtually impossible to locate in the wild.

Fish

The rivers that flow off Vietnam's eastern flank of the Truong Son Range to the East Sea form a separate set of drainages than those that feed into the Mekong. The characteristic ichthyofauna of these relatively isolated upland watersheds, though thought to be less species-rich than the Red River's and the Mekong's, is expected to have a high proportion of endemic species, particularly those associated with headwaters and rapids.

Hill Stream Loach Species (Sewellia lineolata)

Scientists originally believed that there was one species of hill stream loach in the genus *Sewellia* in Vietnam, *S. lineolata*. First described in 1846,

Figure 49. *Sewellia lineolata,* a species of hill stream loach (Family Balitoridae)

S. lineolata eluded scientists until its rediscovery on the mountain slopes near Hue more than 140 years later. Between that rediscovery and 2004, an additional five new *Sewellia* species have been described from the streams and coastal rivers of central Vietnam. The fish in this genus are extensively adapted for life in fast-flowing freshwater streams, riffles, and waterfalls. Both the body and head are flattened, and the pectoral and pelvic fins have been highly modified into adhesive disclike organs on the bottom of the body to help the fish hang on to horizontal and vertical surfaces of rocks and stones in this difficult environment (fig. 49). Individuals are active during the daytime, hiding and foraging among gravel or other debris at the river bottom for aquatic invertebrates. *S. lineolata,* which scientists distinguish from other *Sewellia* by a set of four distinctive longitudinal stripes on the side of the body, is found in streams and small rivers of the central Truong Son Range.

Invertebrates
Spiders (Class Arachnida: Order Aranea)

The terms *predators* and *prey* are used most often to describe the ecological roles played by vertebrates: mammals, birds, amphibians, reptiles, and fish. But similar roles and relationships exist within the world of species without backbones. Spiders (Arachnida: Aranea) are infamous predators of other invertebrates and often a major limiting influence on populations of pest species. As is the case with many invertebrate groups, the best information about the spiders of Southeast Asia comes from agricultural surveys. Even given this focus, the few studies undertaken have led to the discovery of many new species. Scientists researching spiders of the cultivated rice lands of Southeast Asia in the early 1990s described 258 new spider species, constituting about 75 percent of the species found in the survey.

It is no surprise, then, that the spiders in central Vietnam are virtually unknown. Diana Silva, a Peruvian biologist studying at the American Museum of Natural History, conducted a survey in 1998 of spiders at several locations in the northern Truong Son Mountains. What she found was surprising: almost all of the thirty-eight families of spiders she collected were never before recorded from anywhere in Vietnam. Among the spiders Silva examined were new species whose closest known relatives reside in Thailand and even Australia.

VIEWING WILDLIFE IN CENTRAL VIETNAM

Central Vietnam's protected areas fall predominantly within the Truong Son Range and are isolated and difficult to reach. Extremely important areas, such as the Vu Quang and Pu Mat National Parks, are world treasures, but ones appreciated from afar. Several areas, however, are relatively easy to get to and provide opportunities for wildlife viewing in both terrestrial and marine habitats.

Bach Ma National Park (Thua Thien Hue Province)

Bach Ma National Park is located on a mountain ridge in central Vietnam where the country tapers to a narrow belt. Reaching from the mountains of Laos eastward to the coast, this high ridge cuts across Vietnam's coastal plain, dividing northern and southern flora and fauna and marking the separation between two climatic zones. This location, topography, and climate support a great richness of species at Bach Ma. The park, inaugurated in 1991, is characterized by dense forests studded with rhododendrons (*do quyen* in Vietnamese) that blossom toward the end of March, a startlingly white display amid lush greens. There is also the possibility of coming across some of the region's spectacular pheasants, such as the Gray Peacock Pheasant. Masked Palm Civets (*Paguma larvata*) prowl around the station bungalows at dusk.

Phong Nha–Ke Bang National Park (Quang Binh Province)

Now recognized by the United Nations as a World Heritage Site, Phong Nha–Ke Bang's spectacular karst hills, caves, and underground rivers are perhaps Vietnam's most awe-inspiring geological site. The entrance to Phong Nha cave or Cave of Teeth (after its spectacular stalagmites), 60 feet (18 m) high and 100 feet (30 m) wide, is one opening to an underground system measuring over 25 miles (60 km). These tunnels and caves have served as sanctuaries for centuries. Altars and inscriptions attest to Cham use of the caves as Buddhist refuges in the ninth and tenth centuries, and during the Vietnam-American War they served as a hospital, as an ammunition storage area, and as key entrances to the Ho Chi Minh Trail. Until recently the local Chut people lived in the caves; they have now been resettled into villages.

There is plenty to see above ground in Phong Nha–Ke Bang as well, though these areas are much harder to reach. Because of the harsh terrain, the karst outcroppings here have remained largely forested and are home to both the Annamese and Black (*T. f. ebenus*) Leaf Monkeys, along with Red-shanked Doucs and Crested Argus. The park has become a popular tourist attraction, and a large area has been set aside for tourism development that, it is hoped, will not damage the limestone ecosystems that make the reserve so special.

Nha Trang (Hon Mun) Marine Protected Area
(Khanh Hoa Province)

At Nha Trang, scuba divers and snorkelers can explore extensive reef systems and marine life in the clear offshore waters, which land-based visitors can also appreciate in tanks at the nearby oceanographic institute. Boating trips are also available to explore the dozens of islands off the coast. Hon Mun Island is part of a new Marine Protected Area (MPA), established in 2001, which includes several neighboring islands and surrounding waters. The MPA was established to conserve the reefs, which with more than 350 hard coral species host the richest coral diversity in Vietnam, and other marine habitats; to restore the surrounding fisheries; and to establish sustainable tourism. Fish diversity is lower than expected due to overfishing and other environmental threats, but still numbers in the hundreds of species. A few of the islands, including Hon Mun, support edible nest swiftlet (*Collocalia germani*) colonies, whose nests are harvested to make bird's nest soup (see box 22 and fig. 69).

Yok Don National Park (Dak Lak Province)

Established in 1991, Yok Don is Vietnam's largest national park at 285,515 acres (115,545 ha). In 2001, the government began to consider a proposal that would almost double its size. This relatively flat protected area sits on a plateau about 655 feet (200 m) in elevation, with a couple of peaks rising to 1,555 feet (474 m). The park encompasses a large area of deciduous forest and is internationally known for its plant diversity. It is one of the last places in Vietnam to harbor such large mammal species as Asian Elephants, Gaur, Banteng, and Tiger, though these populations continue to decline steeply. Several globally threatened bird species, including the Lesser Adjutant (*Leptoptilos javanicus*), White-rumped Falcon (*Polihierax insignis*), and Rufous-winged Buzzard (*Butastur liventer*), live within the park's boundaries, and it is one of the only established protected areas to harbor the Green Peafowl. Yok Don is, unfortunately, not easily accessible for most tourists. Buon Don District, where the park is located, is renowned for its long history of elephant domestication, and small tour operations have begun to bring tourists into the reserve on elephant back.

EIGHT

Southern Vietnam
Ascendancy of the Mekong

 Southern Vietnam is dominated by the vast Mekong Delta, a broad, fertile plain that blankets the southern two-thirds of the region. Called Nam Bo in Vietnamese and Cochinchina by the French, southern Vietnam stretches from south of the Truong Son to the tip of Ca Mau Peninsula, the country's southernmost mainland point (fig. 50). The Mekong is Southeast Asia's largest river; scientists estimate that in its number of fish species it ranks third globally, behind only the Amazon and Congo Rivers. The biodiversity of the delta and southern Vietnam as a whole depends on cycles of water and resources originating upstream and flowing into the Mekong River.

When the Mekong River swells during the rainy season, one of the world's most spectacular natural phenomena takes place. The vast quantity of water flowing down the Mekong forces one of its tributaries in Cambodia to reverse its normal southeastern direction. It then flows backwards into mainland Southeast Asia's largest freshwater body, the Tonle Sap Lake. The shallow lake quickly expands from its dry-season low of 1,050 square miles (2,700 km²) to around 4,000 square miles (10,360 km²), and its depth increases from 3–10 feet (1–3 m) to 30–45 feet (9–14 m). This flooding brings a large volume of nutrients into the lake's system, ensuring healthy populations of fish and supporting spectacular gatherings of waterbirds as well as a substantial fishing industry and rice cultivation along its shores.

North and east of the Mekong Delta lies a mix of evergreen, semi-evergreen, deciduous, and coastal forests often dominated by dipterocarps

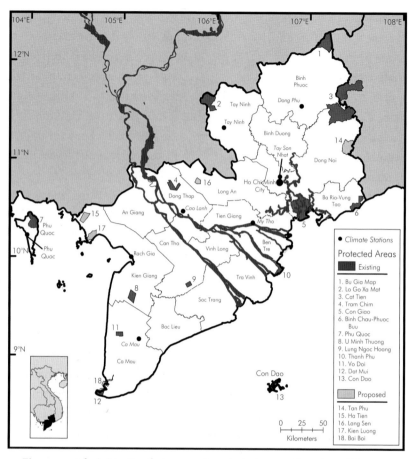

Figure 50. Administrative features and protected areas of southern Vietnam

(Family Dipterocarpaceae). These habitats are quite similar to the lower-elevation areas described for south-central Vietnam, since they grow on similar soils and experience the same climatic regime. As in south-central Vietnam, available ground moisture is the main determinant of forest type. Lowland habitats along waterways and small forest lakes are critical for such species as the rare Lesser One-horned Rhinoceros (*Rhinoceros sondaicus annamiticus*) and Germain's Peacock Pheasant (*Polyplectron germaini*). Because these forest habitats have been described for central Vietnam in chapter 7, this chapter focuses on Southern Vietnam's unique wetland environments.

The people who live in southern Vietnam outside Ho Chi Minh City are predominantly from the Viet, Hoa, and Khmer ethnic groups. The Khmer, Vietnam's sixth largest ethnic group, have lived for centuries in the Mekong Delta region of both Vietnam and Cambodia. The country's fifth largest group, the Hoa began coming to Vietnam from southern China at the start of the Common Era, but the largest waves of immigration occurred just before and after World War II. Population densities in the Mekong Delta were historically low and large areas began to be settled only in the seventeenth century. Today, however, southern Vietnam is the second most densely populated region in the country (after the Red River Delta), with 6,200 people per square mile (2,400 people per km²) in Ho Chi Minh City. The greater delta region has a lower density than the Red River Delta, with just over 1,000 people per square mile (400 people per km²).

TOPOGRAPHY

The flat Mekong Delta has an average elevation of only about a dozen feet (a few meters) above sea level, with a small number of isolated hills rising out of the flatlands. Most are granite, with occasional limestone outcroppings; the tallest hill is Cam Mountain at 2,330 feet (710 m). Along the border between Cambodia and Vietnam, ancient terraces of sediment deposited by the Mekong River cover about 370,000 acres (150,000 ha) of the delta. Alternating periods of marine flooding and seawater retreat over tens of thousands of years have shaped the delta's topography. Three major landforms comprise the delta: the floodplain, the coastal complex, and the broad depression, defined by their topography, hydrology, climate, and soil characteristics.

The most widely distributed landform type in the delta by far is the floodplain, located in the northern and central regions (fig. 51). The high floodplain in the northwest (the area inundated by the deepest floodwaters) consists of natural levees, sandbars, and back swamps. A closed section of this area, known as the Plain of Reeds, drains slowly and with difficulty, remaining inundated up to 10 feet (3 m) most of the year. An open section in the southwest, known as the Long Xuyen Quadrangle and including the Ha Tien Plain, drains down to the Gulf of Thailand and floods to 5–6 feet

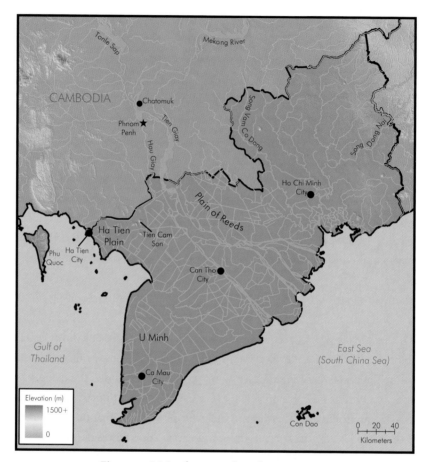

Figure 51. Major features of southern Vietnam

(1.5–2 m). Both the open and closed sections of the high floodplain contain highly acidic soils. In contrast, the tide-affected floodplain at the center of the delta floods to lower levels, at 1–3 feet (0.5–1 m), and the rivers keep the soil from becoming too acidic.

In the southern and eastern regions, marine and river environments combine to influence the coastal complex of flats, sand ridges, and mangrove forests. At 3–5 feet (1–1.5 m) above sea level, the low flats along the coast are not directly inundated by seawater, though some salt water does seep into the soil from adjacent areas. Sand ridges rising to 8 feet (2.5 m) parallel the Mekong Delta's coastline along the East Sea. Saltwater inundates the flats lying between them during the dry season; it is replaced by freshwater during the wet season. Mangrove swamps and forests ring the Ca Mau Peninsula and river mouths in east-facing coastal areas.

A broad depression occupies much of the inland areas of the southern delta. This region is the most isolated from the effects of the Mekong River, and saltwater floods much of it in the dry season. Peat swamps, including U Minh Thuong and U Minh Ha, dominate the lowest areas in the broad depression. During the wet season, when 120 inches (3,000 mm) of rain can fall, peat swamps are inundated to 3–5 feet (1–1.5 m). During the dry season, peat soils retain large quantities of water and become a key source of irrigation for surrounding agricultural areas.

The majority of the soils in the Mekong Delta are alluvial. Highly acidic soils cover over 40 percent of the Mekong Delta. These soils develop in tidal swamp and marsh areas, where the soil is waterlogged and flushed by seawater, and organic matter is rich. The process of decomposition produces compounds in the soil (such as sulfides) that can lead to acidic conditions in certain situations. When kept moist, they remain neutral. Under drier conditions, however, they become acidic. As sulfuric acid leaches out of the soil, plants are exposed to toxic or damaging elements. Often, contiguous waters can also become acidic. Water draining from these soils is one of the main reasons why surface water in the delta can be highly acidic (with a pH of less than three). These changes, which can affect areas well downstream, interfere with plant growth and may be toxic to fish; one can imagine the difficulty that fish or plants would have living in water with the same acidity as vinegar.

CLIMATE

Southern Vietnam exhibits a tropical, strongly monsoonal climate, and the typical annual rainfall range is 60–80 inches (1500–2000 mm). Because of local variations in climate, the northern regions receive barely half the annual rainfall (50 inches, 1,250 mm) of the southwestern regions (92 inches, 2,350 mm). Rain falls during a fairly uniform wet season beginning in May, with the most rain falling in September and October. The winter season (December to March) is extremely dry, with four to six months of rainfall below 4 inches (100 mm) and some areas reporting virtually no rainfall in a month (table 4).

The Mekong Delta region is the warmest and most humid part of Vietnam, particularly in April. During the coldest time of the year (around January), temperatures hover around 68°F–73°F (20°C–23°C) across the region, whereas during April, they creep up to 90°F–95°F (32°C–35°C).

HYDROLOGY

The Mekong River originates at an elevation of 16,400 feet (5,000 m) in the Tanghla Shan Mountains in the Tibetan Himalayas, and winds 2,700 miles (4,350 km) through or along the borders of six countries (China, Myanmar, Thailand, Laos, Cambodia, and Vietnam) before reaching the East Sea (fig. 52). At the source of the Mekong River in the Tibetan Plateau, the climate is harsh, with long winters, cool summers, and low annual precipitation (10–20 inches, 250–500 mm). Upland pasture and semi-tundra vegetation dominate this region. Here the river is known as Dza Chu, or Water of Stone, in Tibetan.

As the Mekong River passes through southeastern Tibet, it is in extraordinary proximity with two of Asia's other great rivers. In one compressed region just 40 miles (60 km) wide, the Salween, Mekong, and Yangtze Rivers flow in parallel for more than 200 miles (300 km) through a series of steep, forested river gorges. The rivers lie at 3,300–5,000 feet (1,000–1,500 m) above sea level and are separated by towering mountain ranges over 16,500 feet (5,000 m) high. They then suddenly diverge, the Salween flowing west into the Bay of Bengal, the Yangtze twisting circuitously eastward through the mountains and plains of China to the Pacific Ocean, and the Mekong coursing southeast toward Laos, Cambodia, and Vietnam. Whereas in southern Tibet these great rivers converge to within tens of miles (kilometers) of one another, their mouths discharge 2,500 miles (4,000 km) apart.

In China's Yunnan Province, the climate becomes milder, with greater annual rainfall (more than 67 inches; 1,700 mm) per year and winters generally free of frost. In this region of southwest China, the Mekong is known as Lancang Jiang, or Turbulent River. Leaving Yunnan Province, the Me-

Table 4. Climate stations in southern Vietnam

Name	Elevation (ft/m)	Temperature (C/F)		Rainfall (in/mm)		Dry months (N)	Wettest month
		Annual average	Range monthly averages	Annual average	Range monthly averages		
Tay Ninh	33 (10)	80 (26.9)	77–84 (25.2–28.9)	71 (1,813)	0–12 (8–313)	4	Sept.
Tan Son Nhat	30 (9)	81 (27.1)	78–84 (25.7–28.9)	76 (1,931)	0–13 (4–327)	5	Sept.
Cao Lanh	7 (2)	81 (27)	77–84 (25.2–28.7)	54 (1,359)	0–10 (4–245)	5	Oct.
My Tho	3 (1)	81 (27)	78–83 (25.5–28.5)	55 (1,407)	0–10 (2–265)	5	Oct.
Rach Gia	7 (2)	81 (27.4)	78–84 (25.7–28.9)	83 (2,108)	0–14 (5–366)	4	Aug.
Ca Mau	10 (3)	80 (26.7)	78–82 (25.2–28)	92 (2,344)	0–14 (8–348)	3	Aug.
Con Dao	10 (3)	81 (27)	78–83 (25.4–28.3)	82 (2,069)	0–13 (5–337)	5	Oct.
Phu Quoc	7 (2)	81 (27.1)	78–83 (25.6–28.4)	119 (3,024)	1–20 (31–516)	3	Aug.

Source: After Nguyen Khanh Van et al., 2000

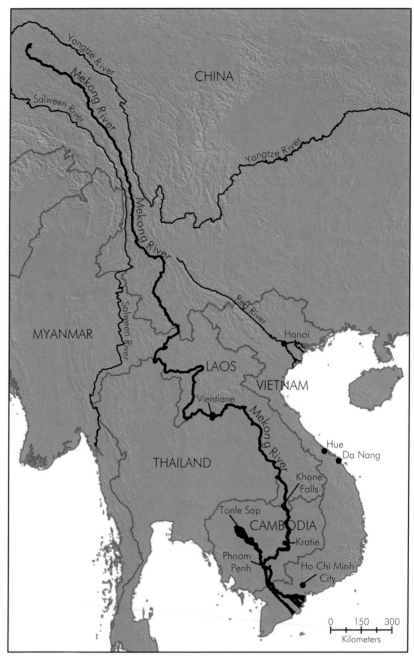

Figure 52. Current course of the Mekong River

kong first flows along the border between Myanmar and Laos. Then, having already descended 14,750 feet (4,500 m) over the course of 1,100 miles (1,800 km), it slows slightly and heads eastward into Laos. Nearly all of Laos's river drainages (most of which drain the Truong Son's western slopes) join the Mekong River as it travels 1,000 miles (1,600 km) across the country, cutting a gorge through the sandstone rim of the Khorat Plateau. Waterfalls and rapids abound through these upper reaches of the Mekong. At the Cambodian border, the Mekong, 8 miles (13 km) wide at this point, cascades over the 65-foot (20 m) Khone Falls. Below this point, Vietnam's major Mekong tributaries flowing from the western and southern Truong Son join the river. At Kratié the Mekong begins to slow, completing its metamorphosis from a swift, upland river into a broad, lowland one with many oxbows and swamps.

In south-central Cambodia, the Mekong River receives water from its last major tributary, the Tonle Sap River. Opposite Phnom Penh, at a place called Chatomuk, the river splits in two. The Mekong (Tien Giang in Vietnamese) flows to the east and the Bassac (Hau Giang) courses west. The rivers then braid into numerous streams to form the 25,000-square-mile (65,000 km²) Mekong Delta, 80 percent of which lies in Vietnam.

The delta, formed predominantly by ancient sediments from the Mekong River, drains into the East Sea through nine mouths. These mouths give the Mekong its Vietnamese name, Song Cuu Long, or River of Nine Dragons. The river's silt load has produced a continually expanding delta; over the past century sediment deposited into the East Sea has expanded the delta outward at the rate of 165–500 feet (50–150 m) per year. The delta region currently encompasses about 2,500 miles (4,000 km) of waterways, including rivers, creeks, and canals (see fig. 51).

Seasonality of rainfall across Southeast Asia causes large fluctuations in the Mekong's volume and in the extent of flooding experienced by the surrounding lands. Flooding is caused by increased flow during the wet season and is exacerbated by high tides that occur simultaneously. Annual peak flow at Kratié is 2 million cubic feet per second (56,800 m³/sec). This is forty-eight times the recorded minimum, a greater seasonal flow change than in any other of the world's large rivers. In contrast, when flows are at their lowest, saltwater tides infiltrate upstream areas, flooding a full third of the delta. During the wet season, saltwater tides may also inundate parts of the southeast.

At peak water flow, large parts of the delta are completely flooded; in the north, waters as deep as 10 feet (3 m) can last four or five months (fig. 53). Along certain stretches of the river, water can rise as much as 65 feet (20 m). In Vietnam's Mekong Delta, these waters flood over 4,600 square miles (12,000 km²) of forests, grasslands, and fields.

VEGETATION AND HABITATS

Forests in the northern spur of southern Vietnam range from lowland evergreen to semi-evergreen forests, as well as widespread secondary grassland and bamboo habitats. Deciduous trees in the genus *Lagerstroemia*, a loose-strife, dominate the 115–150-feet-high (35–45 m) canopy of the region's semi-evergreen forest, while a mix of evergreen and deciduous trees grows in the understory. Interspersed in the forested regions are small areas of freshwater wetlands, including lakes, seasonally inundated grasslands, and flooded forest.

Although evidence such as very large tree stumps indicates that considerable areas of the Mekong Delta were once forested, little of its original vegetation remains. Three main forms of natural vegetation now characterize the region: freshwater swamp forests, mangroves, and grasslands. Which form dominates in an area depends on the amount of rainfall, salinity levels, depth and duration of standing water, and soil characteristics.

The remaining semi-natural wetland areas in the Mekong Delta are the Plain of Reeds, the Ha Tien Plain, and the U Minh wetlands (see fig. 51). Freshwater vegetation includes swamp forests and nonwoody, riverbank and aquatic vegetation in waterways and other bodies of water. Freshwater swamp forests grow in areas where soils remain perpetually saturated with water. These forests probably once covered large areas of the delta, but human activities have significantly reduced their range and changed their composition. Little is known about the composition and structure of freshwater swamp flora in Vietnam. Paperbark swamps, characterized by Caje-put (*Melaleuca cajuputi*), a member of the myrtle family (Myrtaceae), grow in seasonally inundated areas of the delta where salinity is low, decomposed

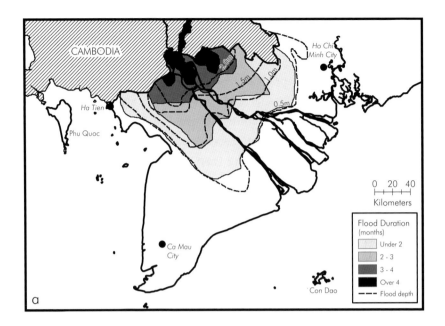

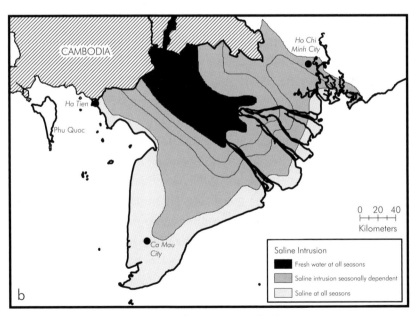

Figure 53. Duration of flooding (a) and salinity intrusion
(b) across the Mekong Delta (After Akira 2003)

organic matter accumulates, and floodwaters deposit seeds. Cajeput is a slight, evergreen tree papered in thick, white, shaggy bark that produces bottlebrush-like white flowers. The fruits release seeds a few days after heating from brush fires. Cajeputs can grow in infertile quartz sands as well as in degraded grasslands, but prefer swampy riverbanks and coastal alluvium. They usually dominate their community, growing in relatively pure stands. Such stands currently cover 75,000 acres (30,000 ha) in Long An Province and 17,000 acres (7,000 ha) in Dong Thap Province, with the largest stands found in U Minh wetlands and smaller areas located in the Plain of Reeds and the Ha Tien Plain.

Although they are low in plant diversity, these forests are an essential part of the greater ecosystem. They temper water flow in the wet season, store fresh water in the dry season, reduce soil acidification, and serve as habitat for aquatic organisms and a variety of wild animals, including bees. Honey from wild bees visiting Cajeput trees is highly valued, and the tree flowers profusely year-round. Paperbark formations also provide wood for fuel, construction, and fodder; plant parts for rope, fishnets, and floats; and oils distilled from their leaves for fertilizer, insect repellent, aromatics, and treatment of a diverse set of ills (rheumatism, hepatitis, skin diseases, fever, and respiratory problems). Because Cajeput trees do not need to be planted in raised beds, they are highly suited for cultivation in acid sulfate soils and were a logical choice for forest restoration efforts after the Vietnam-American War.

The U Minh wetlands are among the Mekong Delta's most important wetlands for biodiversity conservation because, in addition to containing the most extensive paperbark formations, they harbor the only peat swamp forests. Peat is formed when the accumulation of dead vegetation in an area exceeds the rate of its decomposition. In tropical climates this usually occurs in flat, waterlogged areas with high rainfall and natural barriers that block drainage. As partially decomposed vegetation accumulates, the plants rooted on it are moved away from the underlying soils, and their growing environment becomes increasingly acidic and poor in oxygen and nutrients. Eventually the peat surface rises above the level of the groundwater, forming a dome and acting as a water reservoir. Restricted water flow is critical in the development of peat, because it prevents external nutrients and minerals from entering the system. At this stage, plants can acquire these nutrients and minerals only from the peat layer or rainfall, both of which are poor sources. Additionally, decomposing vegetation produces both organic and inorganic acids that are no longer neutralized by the calcium carbonate in groundwater. The resulting environment is low in oxygen, poor in nutrients, and highly acidic, all features that hinder decomposition and decay and favor the accumulation of additional peat. Unlike temperate peats, which are formed mostly from mosses and sedges, tropical peats contain partially decomposed tree limbs, trunks, and roots embedded in a structureless organic matter also derived from plants. The spongy black peat at U Minh is up to 3–10 feet (1–3 m) deep, and its domes are the highest non-man-made structure in the region.

Uncontrolled cutting between 1975 and 1985 and other perturbations led to the near extinction of peat swamp forests. Subsequently, the government restricted access to the area and implemented better management strategies, including maintenance of water levels with a system of canals and dikes surrounding the core zone. Then a devastating fire in the spring of 2002 burned nearly 500 acres (200 ha) in U Minh all the way down to clay soil, destroying the overlying peat. Peat layers are quite sensitive to change and highly flammable during the dry season. When peat dries out, it becomes thin and oxidizes, leading to the production of sulfuric acid. The water in the forested core area is almost neutral with a pH of six to seven compared to an acidic pH of three to four in the denuded buffer zone. Fortunately, regeneration began within six months over a significant portion of this area.

Mangrove forests grow in flooded areas that experience higher salinity than swamp forests occurring along the coastlines and estuaries of southern Vietnam (fig. 54). One species, *Avicennia alba*, dominates mangrove communities that are closest to the sea and almost permanently inundated by salt water. Red mangrove species in the genus *Rhizophora* are found just inside, to the landward side of the formation. On drier ground, the community composition changes again. Brackish areas closest to fresh water support stands of palms in the genus *Nypa*.

Mangroves form an ecological link between marine and terrestrial systems. Functioning as ecological analogs to kidneys, they filter freshwater

Figure 54. Mangrove forest in the Can Gio Biosphere Reserve,
Ho Chi Minh City. Mangroves in the front are *Avicennia alba,* at
the rear *Rhizophora apiculata.* (Photograph by Tran Triet)

runoff before it reaches the ocean, provide nurseries for newly hatched fish,
and help prevent erosion and inundation by tides and storm surges. Mangroves are directly related to the livelihood of local people; 2.5 acres (1 ha)
of mangrove forest may contribute to approximately 44 tons of offshore fish
catch per year.

Mangrove communities up to 20 miles (30 km) wide once crowned
the Ca Mau Peninsula. Although changes in mangrove communities over
time are difficult to estimate because mangroves were rarely mapped in detail, losses of up to 75 percent have been recorded in the Ca Mau Peninsula, and the remaining mangrove formations are largely degraded. Mangrove decline here results from three main causes. First, napalm bombing
and defoliant spraying during the Vietnam-American War wiped out large
tracts. In the last decades of the twentieth century, mangrove formations
were cleared in order to construct aquaculture ponds for shrimp, causing

Figure 55. Seasonally inundated grassland at Tram Chim National Park,
Dong Thap Province (Photograph by Jeb Barzen)

such considerable problems as in-shore erosion and potential loss of fish
owing to the eradication of their nursery areas. As the mangroves have been
cleared, larger boat fleets and increased effort have been required to harvest the shrinking wild fish populations. Last, the immigration of landless
people from other regions of Vietnam has added to local overexploitation
of trees for timber, fuelwood, and charcoal. Fortunately, some areas are
undergoing natural colonization by mangroves, and others are now actively
managed for replanting.

Several types of grasslands—communities dominated by sedges (Family Cyperaceae) and grasses (Family Poaceae)—grow in the delta, in both
acid sulfate and alluvial soils (fig. 55). Although grasslands are often overlooked in conservation considerations and deemed wasteland in development planning, they support diverse plant and animal species that are important components in the region's biodiversity. In one study of the Ha Tien
Plain, the most diverse plant communities were grasslands, encompassing
ninety-four species of grasses and sedges.

The coastal and marine areas of southern Vietnam harbor many types of habitat, from low-diversity sea-grass beds in the shallow regions on the Sunda Shelf that sustain Dugong (*Dugong dugon*) populations to coral reefs, particularly in the Con Dao Archipelago.

FAUNA

In contrast to north and central Vietnam, few animals found in the south are restricted to this part of Vietnam, none are endemic to the country, and only a handful are endemic to Indochina. The deciduous lowland forest habitats that dominate the region are widespread in mainland Southeast Asia, reaching across Cambodia to Thailand and north into Laos and Myanmar. Animals in this part of Vietnam are thus very likely to be found in these habitats elsewhere. In general, fewer endemic species come from lowland than upland regions. This may be because lowland populations are less easily isolated than their mountain-dwelling relatives, reducing the probability of divergence and increasing the likelihood of dispersal through contiguous habitat. Of the few Vietnamese species found only in the south, such as the Sunda Colugo (*Cynocephalus variegatus*), a nocturnal, arboreal mammal capable of gliding flight, most also range south to Peninsular Malaysia, Sumatra, Java, and Borneo.

Another important albeit nonbiological reason for the low species richness and paucity of endemics in the south is that almost the entire landscape, particularly the dominant Mekong Delta, has been highly modified for agriculture for more than 200 years. This has meant the loss of much of the wetland habitats before even basic biological inventories took place. Combined with strong hunting pressures, habitat loss has led to a reduction, and in some cases complete loss, of wetland-dependent species. Resident wetland birds breeding in the delta have been particularly hard hit. The Critically Endangered Giant Ibis (*Pseudibis gigantea*), though never common, is now in all practicality extinct in the country. There have been only two recent records from Vietnam, and neither population is thought to be viable. Hunting has also permanently altered the large-mammal community here. The Lesser One-horned Rhinoceros, whose preferred habitat is wet lowland forest, particularly along watercourses, once ranged throughout the south. It remains in only a single locality, Cat Tien National Park, possibly the only population surviving in mainland Southeast Asia.

Mammals

Very little is known about southern Vietnam's mammals. Scientists have recorded more than fifty terrestrial mammals (excluding bats) and thirty-one truly aquatic mammals from the south since expeditions began visiting the region in the late nineteenth century. This list includes mammals adapted to life in a semi-inundated landscape and aquatic mammals frequenting marine, estuarine, and freshwater environments along the Mekong River, coastline, and offshore islands. Today the Mekong Delta supports few large mammal species. The Tiger (*Panthera tigris*), Dhole (*Cuon alpinus*), Asian Elephant (*Elephas maximus*), Sun Bear (*Ursus malayanus*), and Wild Water Buffalo (*Bubalus arnee*) are all now locally extinct (and nationally extinct, in the case of the Buffalo). Only two primates are found here: the Long-tailed Macaque (*Macaca fascicularis*) and Silver Leaf Monkey (*Trachypithecus villosus*). Reports that the Pileated Gibbon (*Hylobates [Nomascus] pileatus*) ranged on Phu Quoc Island (located off Cambodia's coast in the Gulf of Thailand) have been refuted.

Although the south has no endemic mammal species, there are three endemic subspecies on the Con Dao Archipelago off the coast to the southeast. One is a subspecies of the Long-tailed Macaque (*M. f. condorensis*) and two are squirrels, the Con Dao Black Giant Squirrel (*Ratufa bicolor condorensis*) and Con Dao Variable Squirrel (*Callosciurus finlaysonii germaini*). Another subspecies of Variable Squirrel (*C. f. harmandi*) is restricted to southern Vietnam's other major island, Phu Quoc.

Hairy-nosed Otter (Lutra sumatrana)

The rarest of Vietnam's four otter species, the Hairy-nosed Otter is a Southeast Asian endemic (fig. 56). Otters are the only truly amphibious members of the weasel family (Mustelidae), and although different species are superficially similar, they often have strong social and behavioral specializations that allow them to co-occur without competing. The Hairy-nosed Otter de-

Figure 56. Hairy-nosed Otter (*Lutra sumatrana*)

rives its name from its unusual nose pad, which is completely covered with hair except for a small rim around each nostril (most otters' noses are at least partially hairless). Its fur is dark chocolate brown above and subtly lighter on the underparts, with contrasting yellow-white on the lips, chin, and throat. Its body is 2–2.7 feet (0.6–0.82 m) long, and its tapered tail is about half the length of its body. A medium-sized otter with well-webbed feet and strong claws, the Hairy-nosed Otter has footprints that cannot be reliably separated from those of Vietnam's two other large-clawed otter species, the Eurasian (*Lutra lutra*) and Smooth-coated (*Lutrogale perspicillata*) Otters.

The ecology and behavior of the Hairy-nosed Otter remain almost completely unknown. It appears to be an opportunistic predator, taking fish as well as frogs, crabs, and other prey as it encounters them. The Hairy-nosed Otter may share similarities with the other members of its genus. These species are mouth-oriented predators, chasing fish underwater and catching them in their jaws. In detecting their prey they are helped by stiff tactile whiskers on their snouts and elbows that are sensitive to water turbulence. *Lutra* species are primarily solitary; males and females pair up temporarily for breeding but form no stable pair-bond. Scent marking is extremely important in all otters, and areas they inhabit generally have a strong musky odor. Paired scent glands at the tail base are used for both communication and territorial marking, and spraint (feces) piles and urine markings are used to mark territory as well.

The Hairy-nosed Otter was historically found in Cambodia, southern Thailand, Peninsular Malaysia, Sumatra, and northern Borneo, as well as in Vietnam's central and southern regions. Within Vietnam it is currently known only from the Mekong Delta's U Minh region, where it was recently resighted in the country for the first time in several decades (box 14). The habitat preferences of this elusive species remain poorly known, but a 1991 record from Peninsular Malaysia as well as subsequent reports from Cambodia, Thailand, and Vietnam suggest that these otters may be associated with slow-moving forested water bodies, including peat swamp forests. Because they are largely aquatic, Hairy-nosed Otters could be extremely vulnerable to water-borne pollutants that can reduce available prey populations and become concentrated in the otters' tissues. They are also strongly affected by agricultural conversion, logging, and fires, activities that remove their forested habitats and can result in erosion and siltation of waterways. Otters are also hunted, mainly for their pelts.

The Oriental Small-clawed Otter (*Aonyx cinerea*) is also found in the Mekong Delta, and it is possible that the Smooth-coated Otter (*Lutrogale perspicillata*) still occurs there. Too little is known of the Hairy-nosed Otter to assess its conservation status.

BOX 14
Rediscovery of the Hairy-nosed Otter

The Hairy-nosed Otter (*Lutra sumatrana*) is identified by the IUCN's Otter Specialist Group as one of five otter species meriting top global conservation concern; its worldwide status is uncertain. In Vietnam, investigation of the Hairy-nosed Otter dates back to 1925, but the species has been recorded in only a few instances, indicating its rarity. Scientists first sighted the Hairy-nosed Otter in Vietnam in 1932, and it was seen several times after that before 1941. With the start of the First Indochinese War it became impossible to survey effectively, and thirty-six years followed with no records. When the Vietnam-American War ended, Vietnamese scientists again conducted wildlife studies in southern Vietnam, and in 1977 two Hairy-nosed Otters were found, one in the Ngoc Hien District of Ca Mau Province, and the other in the Phung Hiep District of Can Tho Province. No confirmations of the otter's presence followed until 2000, when Vietnamese scientists conducted two otter surveys in the Mekong Delta and located a Hairy-nosed Otter population in what was then U Minh Thuong Nature Reserve (now a national park) in Kien Giang Province.

This time, in addition to using traditional survey methods (interviewing forest guards and local hunters, examining tracks and droppings, and direct observation), researchers used camera trapping. In this method, strategically placed cameras with infrared motion detectors are positioned to photograph animals as they pass by. This noninvasive technique is being used with increasing frequency in many areas to detect the presence of rare, elusive species. In this case, it confirmed the existence of a species feared extinct in Vietnam for several decades. The survey also documented the scarce Small-clawed Otter (*Aonyx cinerea*) in these wetlands.

The rediscovery of the Hairy-nosed Otter in Vietnam is significant for conservation planning. Despite the strong efforts of forest guards, human impact on the nature reserve remains extensive and includes hunting and fishing, plant collecting, and declining water quality. Because U Minh Thuong National Park supports populations of the extremely rare Hairy-nosed Otter, the establishment of an otter-monitoring program and a campaign for increased public awareness of otter conservation are high priorities. Otter conservation is dependent on successful management of Vietnam's wetlands. The best opportunity at present appears to be one that allows local communities to derive sustainable benefits from these areas.

Nguyen Xuan Dang, Institute of Ecology and Biological Resources, Hanoi

Lesser One-horned Rhinoceros
(Rhinoceros sondaicus annamiticus)

Five species of rhinoceros persist in the world, two in Africa and three in Asia. Two of these, the Hairy Rhinoceros (*Dicerorhinus sumatrensis*) and the Lesser One-horned Rhinoceros, may have roamed Vietnam, but the evidence for the Hairy Rhinoceros's presence in the country is thin. The Lesser One-horned Rhinoceros is relatively small for the group, weighing 3,300–4,400 pounds (1,500–2,000 kg). Its three well-defined skin folds give it an armored appearance (fig. 57). Males of this species have a single horn, about 8 inches (20 cm) in length. Females are similar in appearance to males but do not have a well-developed horn and appear to be larger than males.

The Lesser One-horned Rhinoceros probably formerly ranged in Java and Sumatra, mainland Southeast Asia, and parts of the Indian subconti-

Figure 57. Hairy Rhinoceros (*Dicerorhinus sumatrensis,* top) and Lesser One-horned Rhinoceros (*Rhinoceros sondaicus annamiticus,* bottom). The Lesser One-horned Rhinoceros persists in two isolated populations, one each in southern Vietnam and on the island of Java. The Hairy Rhinoceros is known to survive in Peninsular Malaysia and on the islands of Sumatra and Borneo; it is unclear if this species was ever present in Vietnam.

nent. Populations persisted across Vietnam until the 1930s and 1940s. In spite of anecdotal evidence to the contrary, many presumed the Lesser One-horned Rhinoceros to be extinct after the Vietnam-American War. People were therefore stunned in 1988 when a hunter tried to sell the fresh horn and skin of a Lesser One-horned Rhinoceros. Local sightings, footprints, and a dung sample confirmed that a small population remains in the Cat Loc sector of Cat Tien National Park. The first photographs of these elusive mammals came in 1999 from remotely triggered cameras in the park. This population is one of only two known populations of Lesser One-horned Rhinoceros in the world, each representing separate subspecies: *R. s. annamiticus,* with a population of five to eight animals in Vietnam, and *R. s. sondaicus,* represented by fifty to sixty animals in Java.

The animals in Cat Tien live in thick, bamboo-dominated, semi-evergreen and evergreen forest at elevations of 1,000–2,000 feet (300–600 m), though historically they lived in a wider variety of forest habitats. Although rhinoceroses are generally solitary animals, they sometimes congregate at mud flats, where they wallow to regulate their temperature and limit parasites. They also frequent salt licks for their mineral-rich waters. Preferred food appears to be saplings and shrubs, which they harvest with their prehensile, grasping lips, but food availability in the marginal habitats they now inhabit is inadequate. Major threats to these animals include poaching and habitat loss and fragmentation, though poaching has decreased with the extremely low population size, in part because hunters do not often encounter rhinoceroses. The creation of the Cat Tien National Park in 1998 has stemmed habitat loss somewhat, but lack of coordination of development activities within the park and a wide strip of intensive agricultural development separating its two sections continue to pose problems. The IUCN lists the Lesser One-horned Rhinoceros as Critically Endangered.

Dugong *(Dugong dugon)*

The Dugong is one of four extant members of the Order Sirenia, a group that includes the three manatee species found in rivers and coastal waters of West Africa and the Americas (fig. 58). Along with elephants (two species in the Order Proboscidea) and hyraxes (three species in the Order Hyracoidea), sirenians are the last living representatives of an ancient group of hoofed mammals, the Paenungulata, which originated around 65 million years ago. The Dugong is unique in being the only herbivorous mammal that is a true saltwater species, though they are occasionally reported from

Figure 58. Dugong (*Dugong dugon*)

river mouths. Dugongs feed almost exclusively on sea grasses that grow in the shallow coastal waters of tropical and subtropical Africa, Asia, and Australia.

Dugongs are large, ungainly looking animals that somewhat resemble a cross between a plump dolphin and a walrus. Adults average 9 feet (2.7 m) in length and 550–660 pounds (250–300 kg) in weight, with uniformly gray skin scattered with small hairs. They lack both hind limbs and a dorsal fin; their forelimb flippers are short and nail-less, and the tail fluke is split, similar to a dolphin's. The Dugong's most notable feature is its massive head, which shows distinct adaptations to a plant-eating, bottom-feeding ecology. The large snout turns downward in a flexible disc that has rows of bristles used for rooting along the bottom. Males, and occasionally older females, have tusklike incisors that erupt through the upper lip of the disc. The function of these teeth is unclear—apparently they are not used for feeding. They may be used in social interactions, including courtship, mating, territorial defense, and conflicts with other Dugongs.

Dugongs spend the greatest part of their time foraging in sea-grass beds. They are selective feeders, typically consuming fewer than a dozen sea-grass species, with greatest preference for weedy or colonizing species. This selectivity results in a diet low in fiber and high in available nitrogen, which is broken down with the help of microorganisms in their long digestive tract. Dugongs prefer to uproot entire plants from the sea floor when possible. This foraging behavior results in distinctive winding feeding trails in the sea-grass beds that can often be observed at low tides. Because of their habitat preference and feeding behavior, Dugongs are often found in turbid waters, making it exceedingly difficult to observe them and count their numbers. Mating behavior varies among geographical areas; in some populations multiple males scramble violently to engage an estrous female, and in others the males lek, defending tiny adjacent territories, which females visit solely for mating, since these areas provide no other resources. Females bear their first calf relatively late, between the ages of ten and seventeen, although a few breed as young as six. Gestation takes thirteen to fifteen months and lactation lasts fourteen to eighteen months, resulting in long, two-and-a-half to seven-year intervals between births. The oldest recorded wild Dugong was a seventy-three-year-old female.

Dugong distribution historically has coincided closely with the distribution of their food plants. Their range includes coastal areas in thirty-seven countries and territories, extending from Africa's east coast through Asia and northern Australia to New Caledonia. Their distribution is not uniform across this range, reflecting both uneven habitat quality and the effects of human activities. Dugongs appear to be declining throughout their range. In Vietnam, the only verified population is a small group of more than thirty Dugongs observed at Con Dao National Park, though evidence suggests that they exist in additional suitable habitat around Phu Quoc Island and in neighboring Cambodian coastal waters. The primary threat to Dugongs is hunting; they are easy to capture, their meat is considered delicious, and they have value in traditional medicine. They are also vulnerable to incidental by-catch in fishing nets and loss of sea-grass beds to both bottom trawling and typhoons. Because of their slow reproductive rate, Dugong populations are threatened by any increase in adult mortality. The IUCN lists the Dugong as Vulnerable.

Birds

The Mekong River and its delta region are important habitats for resident and migratory birds. Records compiled from the region since 1988 list 247 species, twenty of which the IUCN considers either globally threatened or Near Threatened. Roughly a third of the birds are migratory, and half are dependent on wetlands (including reed warblers, *Acrocephalus*). Diversity is highest in seasonally inundated grasslands and swamps located in U Minh, the Ha Tien Plain, and the Plain of Reeds. These areas encompass some of the last remaining habitats for a variety of specialist and tree-nesting waterbirds, such as the Lesser Adjutant (*Leptoptilos javanicus;* Vulnerable), Woolly-necked Stork (*Ciconia episcopus*), Chinese Egret (*Egretta eulophotes;* Vulnerable), and Glossy Ibis (*Plegadis falcinellus*). Some visiting bird species that once bred in the delta now no longer do so, including the eastern Sarus Crane (*Grus antigone sharpii;* Vulnerable), Painted Stork (*Mycteria leucocephala;* Near Threatened), and Spot-billed Pelican (*Pelecanus philippensis;* Vulnerable).

The Mekong and its lowland tributaries in Vietnam, Cambodia, and southern Laos are critical habitat for a distinctive guild of riverine birds, including the River Lapwing (*Vanellus duvaucelii*), Black-bellied Tern (*Sterna acuticauda*; Near Threatened), and Black Kite (*Milvus migrans*).Within Vietnam, however, these habitats have been largely degraded, with the possible exception of regions in central Vietnam's Dak Lak Province. All three species were once resident in southern Vietnam; now their status there is uncertain.

Interestingly, four of the five Indochinese avian endemics in the south are found in evergreen, semi-evergreen, and (in a few cases) bamboo forests. One of these, the Orange-necked Partridge (*Arborophila davidi*; Endangered), was until recently classified as endemic to forests in the northeastern section of southern Vietnam. In early 2002, a camera-trap set in a remote region of eastern Cambodia's Mondulkiri Province near the Vietnamese border captured this bird on film. It now appears to be locally common up to an elevation of 820 feet (250 m) in its tightly circumscribed range. Two other restricted-range species are found here, Germain's Peacock Pheasant (*Polyplectron germaini*) and the Near Threatened Grey-faced Tit-babbler (*Macronous kelleyi*). The one regional endemic associated with wetland areas found in these open forests, the Giant Ibis, teeters on the verge of extinction in Vietnam.

Southeast Asian Bengal Florican
(Houbaropsis bengalensis blandini)

The Bengal Florican is a specialist of moist grassland areas that do not undergo extended periods of flooding (fig. 59). It is the only species of bustard (Family Otididae) known to breed in mainland Southeast Asia. The size of large ducks, breeding males are predominantly black, with mostly white wings that stand out in flight and when tucked against their bodies. The elongated black feathers on the head, neck, and back are fluffed during aerial displays, giving the birds a slightly moplike look. Adult females by contrast, though larger than males (3.75–4.2 pounds versus 2.75–3.3 pounds; 1.7–1.9 kg versus 1.25–1.5 kg) are more cryptically colored, with a white wing patch seen only in flight. Juveniles look much like adult females but are paler. Though good fliers, Bengal Floricans prefer to walk or run along the ground. Their diet varies with food availability and can include insects, berries, young grass shoots, and flowers.

The sexual variation in feathering reflects the different roles that males and females play in the Bengal Florican's promiscuous mating system. During the dry season and before breeding, males establish individual territories (5–70 acres, 2–28 ha) with a small central core area of shorter grass where they forage and perform displays. The most striking of these is an exaggerated aerial display during which the male flies 10 to 13 feet (3–4 m) above ground, descends, and then rises again before diving to the ground, covering a distance of 50–80 feet (15–25 m). This display flight is accompanied by *chik, chik, chik* calls beginning at the first peak and loud wing clapping during the first descent. Performed infrequently (approximately one to three times per hour) at dawn and dusk, these displays can be triggered by the presence of females or males and the calls of other birds. Other male

Figure 59. Bengal Florican (*Houbaropsis bengalensis*)
male (front) and female (back)

displays include a standing display with the neck feathers fluffed (which frequently precedes the flight display) and a walking and head-pumping courtship display.

Female behavior is far more secretive, so much so that it is almost impossible to measure a given population's sex ratio. Females visit male territories singly and briefly for breeding as well as foraging. They typically lay a clutch of two glossy, olive-green eggs with purple-brown flecks directly on the ground amid dense vegetation at a distance from the male's territory. Male Bengal Floricans provide no parental care to the chicks, which are precocial, able to walk (and run) and to feed themselves shortly after hatching. The breeding season ends with the coming of the summer monsoon rains, when the birds may move locally to higher grasslands or migrate short distances to avoid flooding.

Two subspecies of Bengal Florican inhabit Asia. The Indian subspecies (*H. b. bengalensis*) numbers 300–400 individuals, surviving in highly fragmented populations in northeastern India and Nepal. The Southeast Asian subspecies occurs in Cambodia and in Dong Thap Province and the Ha Tien Plain of Vietnam's Mekong Delta. Although the Cambodian population may number as many as a thousand birds, in Vietnam the bird is far rarer, with studies having only recently uncovered indications of breeding in the country. The key threats to their survival are loss and degradation of this distinctive wet grassland habitat and hunting for both food and egg collection.

Other grassland-dependent birds found in the Mekong Delta include the Grass Owl (*Tyto capensis*), a poorly known, very localized species in Indochina, and the White-headed Munia (*Lonchura maja*) in Lo Go Xa Mat National Park in Tay Ninh Province. The IUCN lists the Bengal Florican as Endangered.

Eastern Sarus Crane (Grus antigone sharpii)

The Sarus Crane is the tallest flying bird in the world; adults can stand almost 6 feet (1.75 m) tall with a nearly 10-foot (3 m) wingspan. In addition to its massive size, the Sarus Crane's most distinctive feature is the naked red skin on the sides and back of the head, extending slightly down the neck. Sarus Cranes can vary both the brightness and amount of skin exposed depending on outside stimuli and their internal motivational state; generally the skin is brighter during the breeding period and while displaying. The rest of the body is lead gray and uniformly feathered, including a cap on the crown and small spots behind the ears. Males and females appear almost identical, though males tend to be taller than females. Juveniles are brownish gray with fully feathered heads and necks, more cryptic coloration that may offer protection against predators. The Southeast Asian subspecies, the eastern Sarus Crane, is found in Vietnam and in small areas of Cambodia, Laos, and Myanmar. Sarus Cranes are generalist feeders, consuming roots and tubers dug up with their bills, as well as small vertebrates (frogs and lizards), invertebrates, and occasionally fish.

The Sarus Crane's most distinctive behavior is its elaborate dance displays and trumpeting duets. All cranes dance, performing long and highly coordinated sequences of leaps and bows, runs, and short flights while tossing grass, twigs, and other small objects in the air. They begin performing these stylized movements when young and continue throughout their lives. Dancing appears to perform a variety of functions, including socialization, formation and maintenance of male-female pair-bonds, and displacement of tension. Cranes often begin dancing for no apparent reason, however, and the dancing, once begun, can spread throughout the flock. The loud trumpeting duets performed by mated pairs are known as unison calls. Most frequently heard early in the breeding season, they are one component of the pair-bond and also function to mark territories and respond to intruders. These calls are one of the few ways male and female Sarus Cranes can be distinguished in the field: females emit two to three calls for each male call, and unlike females, males raise their wings over their back, drooping the long primary feathers on their wings while calling. The Sarus Cranes produce their distinctive trumpeting sounds from a specially modified and coiled windpipe; the loudest of all the cranes, they can be heard for distances of more than 0.5 mile (1 km).

Sarus Cranes are monogamous breeders, and if a pair is successful, they can develop lifelong pair bonds. Monogamy has shaped both their morphology (the lack of variation between the sexes) and behavior (unison calls) and is in turn related to their ecology, longevity, and requirements for successful breeding. Breeding in the eastern Sarus Crane is tightly linked to the Southeast Asian monsoons, and in Cambodia breeding likely occurs from late May to late November. During the breeding season, eastern Sarus Cranes defend territories in seasonally flooded wetlands and glades bordered by dry dipterocarp forests, and they will not breed if water levels are too low. The pair builds an enormous, low, messy nest by uprooting the surrounding vegetation, accumulating a vast pile with a ring of open water around its approximately 10-foot-diameter (3 m) base. Females lay two, occasionally three, whitish eggs that both sexes incubate. Sarus Crane chicks leave the nest soon after hatching but continue to be fed by their parents even after they can feed themselves. Despite a rapid growth rate, chicks do not fledge until they are almost three months old (85–100 days). The young remain with their parents during the move to dry-season overwintering areas, where the birds occupy a mixture of shallow wetlands, wet grasslands, and dried sedge meadows. At this time they form loose flocks, though the family unit generally remains together. At the start of the next breeding season, the juveniles either leave on their own or are driven off by their parents.

Sarus Cranes historically were found from Pakistan to the Philippines and Australia. Populations of the eastern Sarus Crane subspecies have drastically declined to only 500–1,500 birds. At some point during the Vietnam-American War, they apparently disappeared from the delta as their wetland habitat was drained and deforested to reduce available cover for the North Vietnamese fighters. In 1984, however, the birds were resighted for the first time in rehabilitated wetlands on the Plain of Reeds. To protect the cranes and their fragile habitat, Tram Chim District Reserve, now a national park, was created in 1986. Efforts continue to restore this area by re-creating the natural hydrological flows that underlie the ecosystem's productivity and diversity.

The distribution and movements of eastern Sarus Cranes remain poorly known, but they appear to breed primarily in northern and northeastern Cambodia and extreme southern Laos. They also attempt to breed in extreme southern Gia Lai and Dak Lak Provinces. The birds overwinter during the dry season predominantly in Cambodia and Vietnam's Mekong Delta. There is also a small population breeding in Myanmar. Vietnamese records within the past five years include Tram Chim National Park in Dong Thap Province, Kien Luong Proposed Nature Reserve in Kien Giang Province, Cat Tien National Park in Dong Nai Province, and Dak Lak Province. The primary threat to eastern Sarus Cranes is continued hunting and low breeding success owing to egg-stealing.

No other crane species are known from southern Vietnam. Other large waterbirds can be found in the same delta habitats as the eastern Sarus Crane's habitat, including the Painted Stork, Woolly-necked Stork, Asian Openbill (*Anastomus oscitans;* another stork), and White-shouldered Ibis (*Pseudibis davisoni*). The IUCN lists the Sarus Crane species as Vulnerable.

White-shouldered Ibis (Pseudibis davisoni)

The White-shouldered Ibis is thought to be the most threatened large waterbird in Indochina. Although never abundant, this large, stout bird was once locally common throughout its range from Myanmar across to southwest Yunnan and south to Indochina and Borneo. Its population has dropped precipitously since 1950, and it is now known from only a few scattered locations in extreme southern Laos, northern Cambodia, southern Vietnam, and along rivers in interior Borneo.

The White-shouldered Ibis is a member of the Family Threskiornithidae (ibises and spoonbills), a group known for distinctive bill morphology. This ibis has a long, downwardly curving, grayish bill, which it uses to probe for aquatic insects, crustaceans, mollusks, small fish, and amphibians in shallow waters. A solid, thickset bird, 30–34 inches (0.75–0.85 m) tall, it has sturdy red legs and feet and walks with ease. The plumage is brown overall, with greenish blue sheen bronzing the wing feathers. The head is naked and almost black, with a collar of bare bluish white flesh around the upper neck and nape. The common English name comes from a distinctive patch of white feathers on the inner forewing that is visible in flight but usually hidden while standing. Males and females are indistinguishable in the field, and juveniles are duller and browner, with fully feathered heads.

White-shouldered Ibises were probably once found in a variety of wetland habitats. Now they are restricted to pools, lakes, streams, marshes, and seasonally inundated wetlands in semi-evergreen, deciduous dipterocarp, and paperbark swamp forests. Unlike most other ibises they are not particularly gregarious and are usually seen either alone or in pairs and small flocks. They also nest either on their own or in small aggregations, with the pair constructing a large, somewhat unkempt nest composed of sticks, grasses, rushes, and other vegetation in a tree about 20–40 feet (6–12 m) above the ground. Females lay two to four whitish eggs, and in the early weeks chicks require extensive care, including brooding and the provision of semi-digested, regurgitated food. White-shouldered Ibises are resident and largely sedentary, apparently making only small shifts with changes in water level. In the past, when populations were larger, they may have made seasonal movements.

The IUCN classifies the White-shouldered Ibis as Critically Endangered. The current global population is estimated at fewer than 500 individuals and possibly as few as 150 birds. The ibises are threatened by direct exploitation (hunting for meat, eggs, and the live bird trade), human disturbance, and modification of their preferred habitat, freshwater wetlands in forest. Although rare in Vietnam, this habitat is still extensive in Cambodia.

In Vietnam, the White-shouldered Ibis is known from only two locations: Kien Luong District, in Kien Giang Province in the Mekong Delta, and Cat Tien National Park in Dong Nai Province. Both these groups are likely too small to be viable, breeding populations. Additional small remnant populations may exist in suitable habitats in Indochina, including Tay Ninh, Gia Lai, and Dak Lak Provinces. In 2003 a small population (roughly thirty birds, the largest known on mainland Southeast Asia) was sighted in Stung Treng Province in northeastern Cambodia, and apparently suitable but unoccupied habitats are present in both Cambodia and Laos. Despite the potential for recolonization and the existence of previously undetected populations, this species will probably go extinct in the next decade.

Two other ibis species can be found in the Mekong Delta, the Glossy Ibis (*Plegadis falcinellus*) and the Black-headed Ibis (*Threskiornis melanocephalus*). A fourth species, the aptly named Giant Ibis, was recently resighted in Vietnam for the first time in sixty-eight years.

Oriental Darter *(Anhinga melanogaster melanogaster)*

Also known as the Snakebird for its serpentine appearance while swimming, the Darter is a widely distributed Old World species found in tropical, subtropical, and warm temperate wetlands from sub-Saharan Africa and Madagascar through southern Asia to New Guinea and Australia. Despite this extensive geographic range, the IUCN lists the Darter as Near Threatened because of sharp population declines in the past thirty years. Southeast Asian populations have been particularly hard hit, and in spite of previously widespread records, its numbers have plummeted everywhere except in sections of Cambodia. Formerly resident in central and southern Vietnam, the Darter now breeds only in the Mekong region with sporadic nonbreeding records from around the southern Truong Son.

Darters are one of two species in the Family Anhingidae, the other one being the strikingly similar Anhinga (*A. anhinga*), which occupies a similar niche in the New World. The Darter is usually divided into three subspecies (occasionally recognized as full species); Vietnam's Oriental Darter (*A. m.*

melanogaster) is found from India to the Philippines and Sulawesi. Darters closely resemble cormorants in their appearance and feeding ecology. They are distinguished by a long, thin neck, long tail, and slender, daggerlike bill that lacks the cormorant's hook. The plumage is dark brown, becoming glossy and almost black in breeding males, with a pale stripe running from the ear down the side of the neck and silvery white feathers that stand out on the upper wings. A distinctive feature of Darters and Anhingas is the evolution of two modified vertebrae in the neck, forming a hinge that allows the neck to be bent backward in an S-shape. The head can then be thrust forward rapidly and with great force, impaling fish on the bill—hence its common English name. Darters are found mostly in calm, sheltered, shallow fresh waters—especially open areas such as lakes, slow-flowing rivers, marshes, and swamps. They require vegetation along water edges or on islets for breeding, roosting, and perching.

Darters feed primarily on small fish 4 inches (10 cm) or less in length, supplemented by aquatic reptiles (turtles, snakes) and invertebrates (insects, mollusks, crustaceans). They usually dive from the water's surface, stretching their long head and neck forward and quietly slipping beneath the surface, much like a submarine, though they can also drop from above-water perches. Darters are not active hunters, instead waiting for prey to come to them and stabbing it with slightly open, serrated mandibles. They then surface, shake the fish loose from the bill, toss it into the air, and swallow it whole, headfirst. Diving is made easier by the fine-scale structure of their feathers, which causes them to rapidly absorb water, thus reducing buoyancy. Darters become completely soaked while in the water, and after a dive, they perch with their wings spread to dry their feathers and warm up. This water-logging is one reason why the Darter swims snakelike with only the head and upper neck showing above the water's surface.

Darters can nest solitarily, in loose groups, or colonially with ibises, herons, egrets, and cormorants. The male attracts the female to a nest site he has selected near water, and together the monogamous pair builds a large tree nest of sticks and reeds, lining it with green leaves and branches. Although they nest within a few feet of one another, Darters are territorial and can be aggressive toward birds that approach the nest. The female lays an average of four eggs; the eggs are greenish blue, covered with a chalky coating, and noticeably pointed at one end. The chicks are fed semi-digested and regurgitated fish, moving on to solid foods they pull from deep in their parents' throats as they grow. They leave the parents before they are two months old.

As few as 4,000 Darters may be left in all of South and Southeast Asia. In Vietnam, they remain in the Mekong Delta and are known to breed at U Minh Thuong and at Tram Chim, where 141 birds were counted in 1999. Reduced population size is attributed to hunting and egg-collecting, but other threats include habitat degradation and loss, disturbance at nest and roost sites, pollution (reproduction is known to be reduced by dichloro-diphenyl-trichloroethane [DDT], which is used in Vietnam), and possibly by-catch in fishing nets.

Vietnam White-headed Munia (Lonchura maja vietnamensis)

The White-headed Munia is a grassland-dwelling species that is a resident of Sumatra, Java, Peninsular Malaysia, and southern Thailand. Its range was not known to include Vietnam until 1994, when a few individuals were identified in international shipments of birds originating from Ho Chi Minh City. Subsequent surveys and interviews recorded the bird in the Mekong Delta and south-central Vietnam, and this population is considered a distinctive subspecies (vietnamensis). It is probably a rare resident in Vietnam, though nothing definitive is known of the population's status.

Munias are small, round-bodied birds with conical bills that feed mainly on seeds. Vietnam's White-headed subspecies is actually pale brownish colored on the head, with white restricted to the eye area, and has a brown bib and throat. The body is maroon-red to chestnut above and black below and on the legs; females are slightly duller than males in color. Apparently monogamous, the pair builds a globular nest with a slightly down-sloping side entrance out of grasses and long leaves, lined with finer vegetation. White-headed Munias probably breed from February to October, although breeding can occur whenever the weather and food supply are appropriate.

Southern Vietnam's White-headed Munias inhabit lowland grasslands, cultivated fields, and rice paddies, often in mixed-species flocks with the more numerous—but still scarce—Black-headed Munia (*L. malacca*). These two species, among many others, are under intense trapping pressure to supply domestic and international songbird markets. In addition to purchase for release as part of Buddhist ceremonies, munias form part of the increasingly popular caged bird trade. Owners display these songbirds in cages for their beauty and song and as a symbol of individual wealth and prestige. Intensive agriculture practices and loss of grasslands and marshlands may also contribute to the demise of both munia species.

The White-headed Munia is now very rare in Vietnam, and the Vietnam subspecies may be close to extinction and should be considered threatened in the country. Its only recent record is from reed habitats at U Minh Thuong.

Amphibians and Reptiles

Approximately 125 species of reptiles and amphibians can be found in the Mekong Delta, of which roughly half are snakes. This group is less diverse—especially among the amphibians—and has fewer endemic species than the herpetofauna found in Vietnam's other regions. Many of the reptiles are lowland species either found in association with water, such as the Water Monitor (*Varanus salvator*), Chinese Water Dragon (*Physignathus cocincinus*), and the kraits (genus *Bungarus*), or truly aquatic, including the Asian Giant Softshell Turtle (*Pelochelys cantorii*), White-bellied Mangrove Snake (*Fordonia leucobalia*), and the water snakes (genus *Enhydris*).

Three endemic reptiles are known from the Mekong Delta and southern Vietnam's islands. The Con Dao Bow-fingered Gecko (*Cyrtodactylus condorensis*) and a species of blind, limbless lizard, the Con Dao Blind Skink (*Dibamus kondaoensis*), described in 2001, are found only in the Con Dao Archipelago. Another new blind skink species, Deharveng's Blind Skink (*D. deharvengi*), was described in 1999 from the coastal forests of Ba Ria–Vung Tau Province and is known only from this location. Because these lizards live underground, they are extremely hard to survey, and the mainland species may eventually prove to have a broader distribution.

Reptiles that previously inhabited the delta but are now locally extinct include the Siamese Crocodile (*Crocodylus siamensis*) and the Batagur, or

River Terrapin (*Batagur baska*). The Critically Endangered Siamese Crocodile was generally acknowledged as extinct in Vietnam by 2000, driven out
by a combination of hunting for skins and meat and collection for crocodile farms. Managers released individuals into Cat Tien National Park in
2001–2002 in an attempt to reestablish a viable population in the wild. The
Reticulated Python (*Python reticulatus*) and Malayan Flat-shelled Turtle
(*Notochelys platynota*) are likely on the verge of local extirpation if they
have not already disappeared. Other rare and globally threatened reptiles
found in the Mekong Delta and the surrounding coastal waters include the
Asian Box Turtle (*Cuora amboinensis*), Giant Asian Pond Turtle (*Heosemys
grandis*), Malayan Snail-eating Turtle (*Malayemys subtrijuga*), and Yellow-
headed Temple Turtle (*Hieremys annandalii*), all of which the IUCN lists as
Vulnerable.

Pacific Hawksbill (Eretmochelys imbricata bissa)

In Vietnam, the Hawksbill was once found from Cat Ba Island in Bac Bo
Gulf south to the Mekong Delta and the Gulf of Thailand (fig. 60). Its current distribution is poorly known (few studies have focused on Vietnam's
marine turtles), and significant nesting populations are found only on the
Truong Sa and Hoang Sa Archipelagos off central Vietnam and the Con
Dao and southern Phu Quoc Archipelagos in the south. The eight extant
species of marine turtles, including the Hawksbill, are reptiles and therefore dependent on terrestrial habitats for egg laying. The rest of their lives,
however, is spent entirely in tropical marine waters, and largely because of
this, their life histories and behavior are poorly known.

The female Hawksbill lays her eggs on beaches and buries them in the
sand. When they hatch, the 0.16–0.2-inch-long (0.4–0.5 cm) hatchlings
make their tenuous way down the beach and into the sea at night. They
then drift passively in the open waters of the oceans for an unknown time,
feeding on seaweed, fish eggs, and other foods. When they reach around 14
inches (35 cm) in length, individuals of the Indo-Pacific subspecies found in
Vietnam settle in foraging areas on coral reefs and in shallow coastal waters
such as bays and estuaries. The turtle will subsequently spend most of its
life in this area, growing to about 35 inches (90 cm) in length. At three-year

Figure 60. Hawksbill Turtle (*Eretmochelys imbricata*)

(or longer) intervals, reproductively mature adult Hawksbills undertake a return migration of hundreds and possibly thousands of miles to the region where they hatched. After mating, males return to the distant foraging grounds while females move short distances to beaches, where they lay two to three clutches of 130 eggs (on average) at two-week intervals before also making the long migration back. The female will continue to return to within 3 miles (5 km) of these nesting beaches for the rest of her reproductive life.

Until the late 1980s, naturalists believed that Hawksbills fueled these complex migrations and reproductive cycles with a relatively indiscriminate, omnivorous diet. But in 1988, a careful examination of Atlantic Hawksbill (*C. i. imbricata*) gut contents from the Caribbean demonstrated a remarkable feeding specialty: marine sponges. This dietary specialization is an exceedingly rare vertebrate trait, and the only other known examples come from a handful of highly adapted fish. Why is this diet so rare? Sponges generally suffer little predation because of formidable defenses: the presence in their tissue of glasslike silicate spicules (needlelike structures) and toxic chemical compounds. As a result of this diet, Hawksbill stomachs can contain over 50 percent silica by dry weight, and the presence of toxins in their tissues may explain the occasional human deaths reported after consuming their meat. Interestingly, Hawksbills appear to have no specialized morphology or feeding behavior for processing this diet. The Hawksbill is not alone in making peculiar food choices. Leatherback Sea Turtles (*Dermochelys coriacea*), another marine turtle known from Vietnam's waters, have a diet dominated by jellyfish.

Hawksbill conservation efforts in Vietnam focus primarily on the nesting beaches of Con Dao National Park. Egg-bearing Hawksbill females are extremely sensitive to light, noise, and other human activities, and clutches are directly threatened by egg collection for food and captive breeding. The main nesting beaches in the archipelago are now monitored and protected, and more than thirty clutches per month have been recorded (with peak laying from March to August). Adult Hawksbills are exploited for their tortoiseshell, the translucent amber scales streaked with yellow, black, and red that are removed from the upper shell by heating. Both stuffed Hawksbills and tortoiseshell products, from eyeglass frames to cigarette lighters, are widely available in Ho Chi Minh City and elsewhere in the country, including duty-free airport shops. Effective Hawksbill conservation in Vietnam is further hindered by a poor understanding of migration patterns and connectivity between regions, making it harder to understand patterns of mortality and reproduction.

The Green Turtle (*Chelonia mydas*) also nests on Con Dao's beaches. Both Loggerhead (*Caretta caretta*) and Leatherback Turtles are found in the area but are not known to nest here. The Hawksbill is considered Critically Endangered by the IUCN. In 2002, Vietnam's government developed legislation outlawing the capture and sale of all marine turtles and their byproducts.

Saltwater Crocodile and Siamese Crocodile
(Crocodylus porosus *and* C. siamensis)

There are two species of crocodile known from Vietnam, the Saltwater Crocodile and the Siamese Crocodile. The Saltwater Crocodile, the largest living crocodilian in the world, averages 16–20 feet (5–6 m) long and can weigh more than 2,200 pounds (1,000 kg). It has a large head, heavy jaws, a characteristic pair of ridges running along the center of the snout, oval scales on the flanks, and rectangular scales on the belly. Sexually mature at ten to twelve years, adults are usually darkly colored with a light yellow or white belly. As its name implies, the Saltwater Crocodile is adapted to salty environments; its preferred habitat is near the sea, in river and canal mouths. Nevertheless, it can live in freshwater rivers, swamps, and lakes. It is believed to eat a wide range of foods, including fish, crustaceans, waterbirds, and snakes. The Saltwater Crocodile was formerly found in the Mekong Delta and on Phu Quoc Island and the Con Dao Archipelago. Natural populations probably no longer exist in the wild in Vietnam, mainly owing to extremely high hunting pressures. This species is under threat from hunting and habitat destruction in many other areas in its range. However, there are large populations in Papua New Guinea and Australia, with an estimated 100,000–150,000 crocodiles in Western Australia, Queensland, and Northern Territory.

The smaller-bodied (11.5–13 feet, 3.5–4 m) Siamese Crocodile bears a characteristic bony crest at the back of its head. Juveniles closely resemble Saltwater Crocodiles, but the adults have a broader snout and more scales running crosswise along the throat. The Siamese Crocodile lives in freshwater swamps and slow-moving rivers above tidal limits. What little is known of its ecology and behavior comes largely from captive animals, though it is thought in the wild to eat small animals such as fish, snakes, and crustaceans. Siamese Crocodiles reach sexual maturity at ten years, and the young may remain with the mother for at least two years. One of the world's most endangered crocodilians, the Siamese Crocodile was formerly common in Vietnam from the central region to the Mekong Delta; its previous distribution ranged across Southeast Asia with the exception of the Philippines. This species has disappeared from the wild over most of its range, though a few populations exist in remote areas of Laos, Cambodia, and possibly Thailand. Threats to the Siamese Crocodile include habitat destruction, egg collecting, hunting for skins and meat, collecting for crocodile farms, and drowning in monofilament gill nets. Crocodile farms for production of skins, hatchlings, and meat exist throughout the Mekong Delta. The IUCN lists the Siamese Crocodile as Critically Endangered.

Balloon Frog and Toumanoff's Wart Frog
(Glyphoglossus molossus *and* Limnonectes toumanoffi)

The lowland areas of mainland Southeast Asia have relatively low frog diversity, and Vietnam's Mekong Delta is no exception to this pattern. To breed, many groups of frogs in Southeast Asia require clear, flowing streams high in dissolved oxygen, and the lack of such habitats in most of southern Vietnam excludes these species. Nonetheless, interesting frogs inhabit southern Vietnam, including the Balloon Frog and Toumanoff's Wart Frog.

The Balloon Frog (Family Microhylidae) receives its name from its spectacularly ill-proportioned appearance. The tiny head, bearing a blunted nose and small, down-turned mouth, is attached to an oversized, bloated body; the frog is about 2.5 inches (7 cm) long. The almost indistinguishable neck disappears into a smooth expansion of the head toward the vast body. The wrinkled body skin is grayish to blackish brown flecked with lighter patches above and cream to white below. The Balloon Frog is fossorial, and the inner bone on each hind foot has a large and sharp digging edge for burrowing backwards underground. Burrowing into cooler, more humid substrates is a common dry-season defense against desiccation. Like many other plants and animals that breed in the delta, the reproduction of the Balloon Frog is tied to the monsoon rains. After a substantial rain, males call to attract breeding females, who lay eggs in temporary pools of rainwater. The Balloon Frog may be fairly common in suitable habitat from southern Vietnam (including the Mekong Delta) to peninsular Thailand and north to Myanmar.

Little is known about the equally odd-looking Toumanoff's Wart Frog, found in Cambodia and adjacent southern Vietnam. In many ways, Toumanoff's Wart Frog resembles a typical long-legged jumping frog with marbled reddish brown skin above and white below. Yet its head is very large relative to its body, and in its center a large bump, or knob, ramps up from between the eyes toward the back of the head, where it abruptly falls off. The function of this enlarged knob is unknown. The males of some Southeast Asian ranid stream frogs develop enlarged heads during the breeding season and engage in head-butting competitions for access to reproductive females and nest sites (both resources that may be in short supply). The enlarged knob on Toumanoff's Wart Frog may serve a similar function. The presence of secondary sexual characteristics on male frogs is not uncommon and can include spines and tusks as well as roughened patches of skin that may help males hold onto females during mating. René Bourret, the most influential of early Indochinese herpetologists, described Toumanoff's Wart Frog in 1942 from a single male specimen collected in Mimot, Cambodia, across the border from Vietnam's Tay Ninh Province; it is named after Constantin Toumanoff, who was then head of the medical entomology laboratory at the Pasteur Institute in Saigon. Except for its presence in Vietnam, little else is known of the frog. It probably breeds in quiet waters along clear streams outside the delta.

The Balloon Frog and Toumanoff's Wart Frog are much less common in southern Vietnam than species that have successfully colonized rice paddy environments, such as the Malaysian Narrowmouth Toad (*Kaloula pulchra*) and Java Whipping Frog (*Polypedates leucomystax*). They are unlikely to be seen unless actively searched for at night. All amphibians in natural areas of the delta are threatened by habitat modification and loss, especially agricultural conversion. In addition, some reports from Thailand indicate that people eat Balloon Frogs.

Kraits (*Genus* Bungarus)

The twelve kraits in the genus *Bungarus* are colorfully marked, highly venomous snakes found from Pakistan to Indonesia. They belong to the Family Elapidae (272 species in sixty-two genera), a large, cosmopolitan, and diverse assemblage that includes the cobras, New World coral snakes, and relatives. The Elapidae are grouped by the shared presence of immovable, venom-producing fangs at the front of the mouth. Of the five species of kraits known from Vietnam, three are found in southern Vietnam: the Malayan or Blue Krait (*Bungarus candidus*), the Banded Krait (*B. fasciatus*), and the Red-headed Krait (*B. flaviceps*).

Although the delta's three kraits are similar ecologically and behaviorally, they differ strikingly in coloration. The Malayan Krait, which can reach almost 5 feet (1.5 m) in length, is alternately banded with black and white stripes above, the white sections spreading as they descend the flanks until they form a solid white belly underneath. The head is gray-black with lighter lips and a white underside. The Banded Krait is also striped, almost completely encircled with equally wide pale yellow and black crossbands. Its head is black above with yellow upper lips and yellow mottling on the snout and sides of the head. This is the largest of all the kraits and can exceed 6.5 feet (2 m) in length. The beautiful Red-headed Krait, by contrast, is not striped. Its body is an iridescent blue-black except for a bright scarlet head and tail and an ivory belly. It can grow to 6.25 feet (1.9 m) in length. All three species have a raised ridge along their back that lends their bodies a triangular appearance in cross-section.

The Malayan, Banded, and Red-headed Kraits are nocturnal, partially aquatic creatures. Once thought to feed primarily on other snakes (ophiophagy), they are now known to include in their diet skinks, lizards, frogs, caecilians, small mammals, and snake eggs. All lay eggs, with clutch sizes for the Malayan and Banded Kraits ranging from four to fourteen eggs; the clutch size of rarer Red-headed Krait is not well documented. The three species can be found in lowland to montane forests, often near water; the Banded Krait also inhabits drier open country and rice paddies. The Malayan and Red-headed Kraits share roughly the same Southeast Asian distribution, from southern Myanmar and Thailand to Indonesia and Malaysia. The Banded Krait overlaps this geographic range and is found in southern China and the Tibeto-Himalayan region. A broad diet and varied habitat preferences may help explain how these three kraits can coexist in southern Vietnam.

Krait venom appears to function primarily as a neurotoxin, preventing communication across neuromuscular synapses and resulting in paralysis and death by asphyxiation because the victims can no longer breathe on their own. Despite this intrinsic deadliness, kraits are usually not considered of high risk to humans in the daytime. Variously described as sluggish, lethargic, and extremely inoffensive, they often remain hidden during the day and, when disturbed, press their head into the ground or hide it in the flattened or rolled coils of their body. During the night they are active hunters and can be aggressive and extremely dangerous. Kraits are considered medically significant snakes both for their dangerous bites and for the potential use of the varied neurotoxins present in their venom in research on neurotransmitter receptors. Unfortunately, their venomous nature also makes them a valuable component of traditional Asian medicines. The consumption of poisonous snakes or a tonic made by steeping them in alcohol is used to treat a variety of health problems, including rheumatism. Along with other venomous snakes, Vietnam's wild kraits are heavily hunted for both domestic use and a thriving international trade.

Fish

Estimates of the number of fish species present in the entire length of the Mekong River lie near 1,200. Approximately 260 species have been reported from the Mekong Delta in Vietnam, though certainly more occur there. Many of the fish in the Mekong River system are migratory, moving up and down the great river and its tributaries with seasonal changes in water flow. These usually nocturnal migrations are often an important part of the reproductive cycle as populations move between spawning and feeding grounds.

Mekong Giant Catfish (Pangasianodon gigas)

The Mekong Giant Catfish (Family Pangasiidae) is endemic to the Mekong River and its tributaries from Vietnam's delta north through Cambodia, Laos, and Thailand and into southern China's Yunnan Province (fig. 61). In the twentieth century, a combination of fishing pressure and habitat degradation along the developing Mekong brought this fish to the edge of extinction in the wild. Its range and abundance are drastically reduced, and it has been extirpated from Yunnan, northeastern Thailand, and Vietnam. Although many freshwater fish are threatened in the region, the Mekong

Figure 61. Mekong Giant Catfish (*Pangasianodon gigas*). The fish
pictured is a subadult, probably one or two years old.

Giant Catfish, as the largest, has become a prominent focus of conservation
efforts. Unresolved questions about its natural history, life cycle, and population structure also illustrate challenges facing the preservation of similar
species.

Although this giant catfish is one of the Mekong's better-known catfish, its ecology and behavior are still poorly understood. Its most obvious
characteristic is its monstrous size: the fish can attain 10 feet (3 m) in length
and exceed 660 pounds (300 kg) in weight; a 7.3-foot-long (2.2 m) specimen
caught in 1932 yielded 88 pounds (40 kg) of roe. Feeding primarily on algae

cropped from stones (and occasionally swallowing rocks in the process), these fish can reach 330–440 pounds (150–200 kg) in six years, placing them among the fastest-growing freshwater fish in the world. Like other members of their family, Mekong Giant Catfish have morphological and behavioral adaptations for maximizing growth rate, including voracious feeding habits and an alimentary canal and abdomen capable of remarkable expansion. Other than its size, this catfish is typical for its family: the smooth, scale-less skin is white to light gray in color, the dorsal, anal, and caudal fins are a darker gray, and there is a small, spineless, fatty fin on the lower spine. The barbels (sensory whiskers) on the upper and lower lips are well developed in juveniles but shrink and even disappear in older individuals.

The Mekong Giant Catfish was almost certainly migratory to some degree in the past, and it may still be, although natural patterns have been obscured and disrupted by the fish's precipitous decline and changes in the river's habitats and flow. It is thought to move upstream as the flood-waters recede (in late winter and early spring) and return downstream as the river swells again with snowmelt and the monsoon rains. The largest remnant populations of Mekong Giant Catfish appear to live in Cambodia (notably in the Tonle Sap River and Lake), Thailand, and Laos, where local fishermen occasionally catch individuals. Where and when the fish spawn is unclear. There is no recent evidence of spawning in northern Thailand, but the presence of smaller fish in Tonle Sap is consistent with natural spawning in the Mekong, although this conclusion is highly contested. In 1984, the Thai government began a captive breeding and reintroduction program, but catches in the area continue to decline. Because the distance and direction of movements, spawning ground locations, and ecology of larval development are unclear, the relationships among migration, reproduction, population status, and genetic structure remain virtually unknown.

Answering these questions is critical to conserving the Mekong Giant Catfish and other migratory fish in the river. Without knowing the fish's life cycle, it is difficult to choose and protect areas necessary for reproduction, monitor the status and size of the populations, and estimate the effects that the many planned hydroelectric dams will have on migratory movements and survival. Learning the genetic structure of the populations will determine whether the Cambodian and Thai fish represent one or two separate populations and what the effect of released fish on native stocks, if any, has been. A first step toward answering these questions has been made with the institution of a buy-and-release program at the Tonle Sap River fishery, where researchers purchase Mekong Giant Catfish from local fishermen, and measure, tag, and release them back into the waters. This program aims to save adult breeders and in the long run gather information on the fish's biology. A final challenge to saving the Mekong Giant Catfish from extinction is the necessarily transnational nature of the work. Effective conservation will require coordinating as many as five countries, each with its own priorities for conservation, development, and natural resources. The IUCN lists the Mekong Giant Catfish as Endangered.

Giant Freshwater Whipray (Himantura chaophraya)

The disc-shaped Giant Freshwater Whipray can grow to over 6.5 feet (2 m) in diameter and 660 pounds (300 kg) in weight, with some individuals reported to weigh as much as 1,325 pounds (600 kg). This makes it one of the largest rays in the world, and it may surpass the Mekong Giant Catfish as the largest Mekong-dwelling vertebrate. It was first formally described in 1990, although fishermen and regional scientists knew of it far earlier. Though described from the Chao Phraya River system in Thailand, it also occurs in the Mekong River in Vietnam, Cambodia, Laos, and Thailand and in other river systems in Indonesia, Australia, and possibly New Guinea. Limited surveying means that the ray's distribution is still poorly known.

Unlike most whiptail stingrays (seventy species in the Family Dasyatidae), which are marine, the Giant Freshwater Whipray is one of approximately eight rays restricted to freshwater ecosystems in the Indo-Malayan region. This whipray inhabits sandy river bottoms, where it feeds primarily on bottom-dwelling invertebrates, sucking prey up through the mouth located on its underside. It breathes by drawing in water through a hole behind each eye and expelling it through gill slits on the underside of the disc. The body is a thin disc, slightly longer than it is wide, brown to gray above and white with a distinctive broad black band around the outer margin below. The tail is thin, whiplike, and longer than the body. Like all members of this family, whiprays are live-bearers, and the young are about 12 inches (30 cm) in diameter at birth.

The Giant Freshwater Whipray is apparently taken both by directed fisheries and as by-catch; the flesh is marketed fresh, with large individuals cut into pieces. It is also threatened by habitat degradation (siltation and pollution) and dams, which isolate portions of the population from reproducing with each other. There is evidence that the Giant Freshwater Whipray populations from distinct regions, including Indochina, Indonesia, and New Guinea, may represent different species. This makes local conservation efforts along the Mekong River even more important.

Invertebrates

Lowland, tropical species dominate the invertebrates of the Mekong Delta, especially those that can adapt to the highly altered conditions of most of the landscape. And as is the case throughout Vietnam, this group remains poorly studied. This is despite the significant contributions that the delta's invertebrate diversity makes to Vietnam's domestic and export economies.

Economically important marine invertebrates—including crabs, shrimps, and mollusks—are harvested from the wild in coastal areas in southern Vietnam for consumption and sale. Only recently has the identification of two common mud crab species heavily harvested from wild mangrove ecosystems been confirmed (*Scylla olivacea* and *S. paramamosain*). Wild resources are now supplemented by rapidly expanding aquacultural shrimp production, almost exclusively for export. Both native and non-native species are used, the most important being the Black Tiger Shrimp (*Penaeus monodon*), whose natural distribution includes East Africa, the Philippines, and Australia. In 2002 Vietnam exported 45,000 tons of shrimp, valued at approximately $480 million, to the United States alone, and that rate almost doubled by the first half of 2003.

Invertebrate diversity is also relevant to the health of regional agriculture. Some of the best known of the delta's insects are the planthoppers (Family Delphcaidae) and leafhoppers (Family Cicadellidae). These sap-feeding groups are important rice pests worldwide, reducing crop yields by blocking the plants' circulation and transmitting diseases. An introduced invertebrate, the Golden Apple Snail (*Pomacea canaliculata*), is also an important rice pest. Research is also focusing on those invertebrates that are natural enemies of agricultural pests and can potentially play an important role in pest management.

Giant Clams (Genus Tridacna)

The nine species of giant clam in the Family Tridacnidae are the largest living bivalve mollusks, a group that also contains the oysters, mussels, and scallops, and they are a distinctive component of coral reef systems in the tropical Indo-Pacific region. The species *Tridacna gigas* can live for forty years and reach 4.5 feet (1.4 m) across and weights of 580 pounds (265 kg). The two species found on Vietnam's coral reefs, *T. squamosa* and *T. maxima,* are smaller, growing to a little over a foot (31 cm). Both have brightly colored mantles (the external folds of body tissue exposed when the clam is open), often mottled blue and green.

Like most of their mollusk relatives, giant clams feed largely on detritus and microscopic organisms filtered from the water. They are also host to symbiotic algae called zooxanthella that live in the clam's mantle. These algae are able to photosynthesize and are a source of food for the clams. In return, they are protected by living within the clam's hard shell. More than one species of zooxanthella can apparently live in a single giant clam at the same time, though they are likely in competition for space. This may allow the clam to adapt to different light levels, because different zooxanthellae have varying light preferences. Because photosynthesis requires sunlight, tridacnids are restricted to shallow water, often living at the top of coral reefs. Apparently, they can orientate the exposed lobes of their mantles to maximize the exposure to sunlight, much as a plant orients its leaves. Other giant clam residents include some shrimp species and a parasitic snail.

Tridacnids are hermaphroditic, meaning that they possess sexual organs of both sexes and release both sperm and eggs into the water. The fertilized eggs become larvae (an immature stage) that disperse freely through the water. After several days, these larvae begin to settle and become clam-like in appearance. After another week, they become sedentary and will develop over the course of years into giant clams.

The distribution of Vietnam's clams is poorly known though they can be found around Phu Quoc Island and the Con Dao Archipelago. Their global distributions are wide, stretching from the Red Sea and East Africa to the western Pacific Ocean.

Pacific cultures have long used these clams for food, but harvesting and other pressures on populations have recently increased. Their reef habitats are threatened with coral mining and destructive fishing techniques, and increased siltation caused by tree cutting and onshore development harms them by decreasing light for photosynthesis. The IUCN lists both *T. maxima* and *T. squamosa* as Low Risk–Conservation Dependent.

VIEWING WILDLIFE IN SOUTHERN VIETNAM

Southern Vietnam offers areas that harbor large waterbirds, diverse marine communities, and the possibility (though uncommon) of spotting one of the rarest land mammals in the world. Some of the protected areas described here are difficult to get to, but they are well worth the effort.

Cat Tien National Park
(Dong Nai, Lam Dong and Binh Phuoc Provinces)

In addition to being home to mainland Southeast Asia's last remaining population of Lesser One-horned Rhinoceros, Cat Tien National Park is also the most likely place to spot large mammals in the south. A night drive through the park's grasslands may uncover large herds of Sambar (*Cervus unicolor*), a large deer species, as well as the occasional muntjac. Daytime is most rewardingly devoted to birds, butterflies, and plants, though a walk to the Crocodile Lake should provide a glimpse of the reintroduced Critically Endangered Siamese Crocodiles. Although bamboo is the predominant vegetation in the park, there are also lowland evergreen and semi-evergreen forests and freshwater wetlands. The lakes, lagoons, and ponds scattered throughout the park are home to many aquatic birds, as well as the stunning Crested Serpent Eagle (*Spilornis cheela*). The park also boasts at least sixty-two orchid species and many medicinal herbs.

Tram Chim National Park (Dong Thap Province)

The Sarus Crane Reserve at Tram Chim National Park provides an opportunity to see not only these rare birds (and, if fortunate, their spectacular dances) but also more than 200 other species, including kingfishers, herons, and dippers, as well as warblers, wagtails, and shrikes. Eastern Sarus Cranes also visit the seasonally inundated grasslands of Kien Luong, in Kien Giang Province, during the dry season.

Can Gio Man and the Biosphere Reserve (Ho Chi Minh Municipality)

From My Tho, located on one of the Mekong's branches in Ben Tre Province, one can take a boat trip downstream into the coastal mangrove belt, which extends 220 miles (350 km) southward to the tip of Ca Mau Province. The Biosphere Reserve lies on the coast below Ho Chi Minh City. Its mangrove forests are home to a large number of egrets, storks, pelicans, and other aquatic birds, as well as to Long-tailed Macaques (*Macaca fascicularis*). The mudflats and sandbanks there are important habitats for migrating shorebirds.

U Minh Thuong National Park (Kien Giang Province)

The U Minh wetlands are located on the western side of Ca Mau Province, some 225 miles (365 km) southwest of Ho Chi Minh City. The region was an important base for resistance fighters during the wars with the French and the Americans. Remarkably, despite wartime disturbances and more recent fires, the U Minh region still harbors the most extensive, oldest, and most species-rich wetland forests in the Mekong Delta. Growing on the thickest peat in the delta (3–9 feet, 1–3 m), the swamp forests here provide important services to outlying regions, including filtration of groundwater; storage and slow release of fresh water during the dry season; and prevention of acidification of soil and water.

The extensive mangrove swamp in U Minh Thuong National Park flowers in June and November with a wealth of blossoms and attendant bees. The water, nearly black from the high peat content, teems with shrimp and crabs as well as the occasional turtle—all of which can be encountered, in somewhat changed circumstances, at the local markets. Of the 186 birds recorded at this site, many are widespread forest or woodland species. Mixed in with these are rarer and more threatened species, including a breeding population of Lesser Adjutants, as well as Oriental Darters, Black-headed Ibises, and Painted Storks. In addition to the rediscovered Hairy-nosed Otter, other mammals recently reported include the Asian Small-clawed Otter, Variable Squirrel (*Callosciurus finlaysoni*), Common Palm Civet (*Paradoxurus hermaphroditus*), Large Indian Civet (*Viverra zibetha*), Large-Spotted Civet (*V. megaspila*), and Sunda Pangolin (*Manis javanica*).

Threats to the biodiversity of the U Minh region include human-induced forest fires, clear-cutting or other conversion of land to agriculture, peat dry-out, hunting, and unsustainable tourism. Planned infrastructure development for tourism includes construction of a road leading to the center of the core area.

Con Dao and Phu Quoc National Parks
(Ba Ria–Vung Tau and Kien Giang Provinces)

The islands of Con Dao and Phu Quoc offer some of the most pristine marine environments in Vietnam. The Con Dao Archipelago, located 50 miles (80 km) southeast off the coast of Ba Ria–Vung Tau Province, is one of the most important sites in Vietnam for marine and coastal biodiversity conservation. For more than a century, until 1985, a series of governments (predominantly the French and South Vietnamese) operated an infamous penal colony housed in dismal facilities on Con Son, the largest island in the archipelago. The location is a national pilgrimage site because of the many famous political refugees who were imprisoned there.

In part because of Con Dao's previous usage, the terrestrial and marine natural areas are relatively intact compared with others in Vietnam. The archipelago's sixteen islands support a diverse range of natural ecosystems, including lowland evergreen forests, coastal swamps and marshes, inland

and coastal sand dunes, and seasonal freshwater streams and lakes. Mangrove forests are found off the western coast of Con Son Island and lining Ba Island. Forests blanket more than 80 percent of the land and many of the 882 recorded vascular plant species are endemic. Several bird species seen in the archipelago have not been found anywhere else in Vietnam, including the Nicobar Pigeon (*Caloenas nicobarica*), Red-billed Tropicbird (*Phaethon aethereus*), Pied Imperial Pigeon (*Ducula bicolor*), and Masked Booby (*Sula dactylatra*). Further inland, it is possible to catch sight of the rare Con Dao Black Giant Squirrel.

The Con Dao Archipelago lies at the juncture of warm, northerly flowing and cool, southerly flowing sea currents. Both bring larval species to the islands, creating a high diversity of marine groups. Con Dao's fringing and patch coral reefs harbor large grouper (Family Serranidae) and giant clam populations and the highest recorded density of coral reef fish of any coastal reef in Vietnam. Sea-grass beds serve as habitat for Dugongs and Green Turtles. The archipelago is important for marine turtle conservation. In 1998, five monitored beach sites yielded 500 turtle nests on Con Dao and an additional twelve to thirteen nesting beaches dot the archipelago.

Phu Quoc Island, located 25 miles (40 km) off the Cau Mau Peninsula's western coast in the Gulf of Thailand, is the largest island in its archipelago. Lowland evergreen forest, the predominant vegetation on Phu Quoc, still covers much of the island. Little is known about the fauna of Phu Quoc Island. A Dugong population of unknown size has been identified from these waters, though it is clearly under great hunting pressure; at least six individuals were killed in 2002 alone.

Leatherback Turtles, Loggerheads, Green Turtles, and Hawksbills have all been seen in this area. Green Turtles were formerly common, but populations are in decline owing to destruction of nest sites, collection of eggs, and overharvesting for food and shells. Phu Quoc is also known for the high quality of the *nuoc mam* (fermented fish sauce) produced here. Nearly half the island's population is economically dependent on its production. The coral reefs around the island, good places for diving and snorkeling, offer a chance to see beautiful tropical fish and other marine life.

NINE

Threats to Vietnam's Biodiversity

Paradoxically, as Vietnam's biodiversity is becoming better understood, many species as well as entire ecosystems face intense pressures that imperil their existence. A high proportion of Vietnam's plants and animals are threatened with extinction. In 2004, IUCN biologists listed roughly 16 percent of Vietnam's mammals, 9 percent of its reptiles (including all but four turtles), and 5 percent of its birds as globally threatened. Many plant species have also been listed, including 63 percent of the country's twenty-four cycad species. These figures are surely underestimates since little is known about most plant and animal abundances and distributions, much less the health of their populations.

Continuing the trends of past millennia, Vietnam's human population and consumption rates are increasing as the ability of the land and waters to support them declines. The country's population grew dramatically in the twentieth century, from 15.6 million people in 1921 to 54 million in 1982, to a total of almost 80 million in 2004; it may reach 150 million by 2050. Its population is also young, with 50 percent of the people younger than twenty-five. Population density averages around 620 people per square mile (240 people/km²), peaking in the regions of Hanoi and Ho Chi Minh City at about 7,500 and 6,200 people per square mile (2,900 and 2,400 people/km²), respectively. Despite urbanization trends, three-fourths of the population lives in rural areas. As the country's population increases, so, too, do demands on its natural resources. Unsustainable consumption of aquatic and terrestrial resources throughout the country, propelled by demand from local, regional, and international markets, constitutes a significant and direct threat to Vietnam's biodiversity. Other underlying threats include poverty and weak governance (inadequate legislation, lack of enforcement of existing regulations, and limited budgets and capacity).

Government programs and policies have often mediated and at times exacerbated the impact of threats to biodiversity. During the second half of the twentieth century, government-sponsored relocations shifted large numbers of people around the country, usually from high-density and largely agricultural lowlands to highland regions that were felt to be insufficiently productive. Unsustainable and large-scale conversions of forest to agriculture followed, as did the loss of biodiversity. Similarly, the Vietnamese government has for many decades encouraged farmers to grow valuable agricultural crops for export. These policies emphasize productivity without a commitment to sustainability and promote the conversion of natural forests to cash crops, such as coffee in the highlands or shrimp cultivation along the Red River and Mekong Deltas. Negative effects on the environment have been exacerbated by the government's Doi Moi policy initiated in the mid-1980s.

Inappropriate land tenure and allocation policies often contribute to the mismanagement of natural resources, threatening existing biodiversity in a region. Some are promulgated with little thought to their consequences for the natural environment, whereas others actually try to address conservation issues. One effort, the Land Law of 1993, sought to ease conflicts between logging enterprises and local people, stimulate local investment in forest management, and conserve remaining forested areas. The policy's essence was transfer of control over land and forests from the state to individual households.

Belief in the land allocation policy's potential for success in balancing human needs with forest conservation rested on the transfer of responsibility for forest management to the farmers who received land. Moreover, the policy gave local people, especially swidden cultivators, long-term rights over the land. The presumption was that the local population would manage the resources sustainably. Unfortunately, some difficulties have arisen. In some areas, state-legislated privatization and local property affairs are disconnected, leading to resentment or rejection of the policy because of potential weakening of existing village- or household-level control over land. In other areas, privatization of land has led to accentuated socio-economic differences within communities, with some households acquiring large land holdings and others none at all. Also, the fallow lands maintained under traditional systems of swidden agriculture now appeared vacant and available for redistribution. Loss of fallow plots handicapped the swidden system, forcing farmers to cultivate smaller plots of land more intensively by lengthening the time their fields are in crop and shortening the fallow period. This leads to environmental degradation such as decreased soil fertility and may force farmers to clear new lands.

In addition to these underlying threats to Vietnam's biodiversity, several direct threats have a more obvious impact. The two most important and immediate threats to Vietnam's biodiversity are the overharvesting of natural resources and habitat degradation and loss. The relative importance of their impacts depends on the species or habitat in question. A less well understood threat stems from invasive species (native or exotic, introduced deliberately or unwittingly), whose rapidly expanding populations outcompete other species and have the potential to endanger whole ecosystems. Pollution is also potentially important, but little information exists regarding its direct effects on biodiversity in Vietnam. Similarly, the effects of global climate change are little understood but will likely have strong, long-term effects, given the country's extensive coastlines and low-lying deltas. Although a single threat might not be sufficient to cause the extinction of a wildlife population or species or to destroy an ecosystem, multiple threats in combination are a different matter.

OVEREXPLOITATION OF WILDLIFE AND PLANTS IN VIETNAM

The overexploitation of natural resources in Vietnam involves a variety of activities that include nonsustainable hunting, fishing, logging, and collection of plants and animals. Overexploitation has become a serious threat to Vietnam's biodiversity and involves an ever-expanding catalog that already contains hundreds of wildlife and plant species. Hunting and collecting serve an almost equally wide variety of needs and economic sectors, from local subsistence through the (largely illegal) trade in national and international markets. The last of these is huge, both in scope and in the degree of its threat to global biodiversity. Current estimates place the value of Asia's wildlife trade between $5 and $10 billion annually, an illicit international market that trails only those in drugs and guns.

The demand that drives wildlife exploitation has deep cultural roots formed over the past two millennia. Traditional Asian values regarding wildlife consumption are based on an intricate combination of nutrition and medicine. Eating wildlife is thought to have a tonic effect, providing restorative and stimulative benefits as the consumer draws into him- or herself the particular energy that formerly flowed through the animal. Strong or unusual-looking species such as pangolins (genus *Manis*) apparently offer greater energy flow. Individuals also believe that specific characteristics and strengths associated with animals can be transferred to them through consumption, correcting internal imbalances thought to be responsible for affliction or disease. For example, the natural attributes of snakes — their flexibility and periodic shedding of skin — are tapped for the treatment of arthritis and skin disease.

Exploitation of and Trade in Plants

Vietnam's flora is exploited throughout the country. Fruit, flowers, barks, roots, resins, wood, and entire plants are collected for a range of purposes, from food and medicine to fine crafts, textile and furniture manufacturing, and the horticultural trade in live plants. Two of Vietnam's most threatened plant groups, cycads and orchids, are, not coincidentally, strongly represented in the live plant trade.

Rattans, roughly 600 species of vinelike climbing palms in the Subfamily Calamoidea distributed across the Old World tropics, form a botanical group with a long history of exploitation for the international market, either in the form of finished furniture or as the raw materials to construct it. Valued and highly preferred for their combination of strength and flexibility, almost all rattan stems (canes) continue to be harvested from the wild throughout their range. Vietnam is home to (at minimum) twenty-one species, of which five are classified as globally threatened. Little to nothing specific is known about the status of the wild populations other than their state of near exhaustion as a source of canes. Instead, Vietnam's domestic demand and export trade is supplied by illegal importation from Laos (and probably Cambodia), and rattan collection remains a significant threat to well-forested national parks in the northern (Pu Mat and Vu Quang) and central (Kon Ka Kinh and Chu Mom Ray) Truong Son Range. In addition, cultivation by small landholders began more than a century ago, and many people depend on forest products to generate cash.

Many threatened plant species experience high rates of exploitation to supply the medicinal trade. Vietnamese Ginseng (*Panax vietnamensis*) is a rare member of a genus also containing the American (*P. quinquefolius*) and Asian (*P. ginseng*) Ginsengs. These ginsengs are used for treatments and tonics in the East and West. Discovered by scientists in 1973 on Mount Ngoc Linh in Kon Tum Province, Vietnamese Ginseng had long been used by the local Xo-dang ethnic group to treat a variety of illnesses and bolster physical strength. Finally described as a new botanical species in 1985, it is known from evergreen forests between elevations of 5,600 and 6,600 feet (1,700–2,000 m) in two provinces in the Central Truong Son Range. Pharmacological benefits attributed to Vietnamese Ginseng include a general stimulation of the body and mind, anesthetic properties, and the ability to combat local inflammation and bacterial and fungal infections. Because of continuing traditional demand, its increasing presence in Vietnam's domestic medicinal plant trade, and the lack of alternative cultivated sources, it is seriously threatened by illegal overexploitation. Vietnamese Ginseng is now one of 250 rare, threatened, or endangered species included in the *Red Data Book of Plants for Vietnam.*

One of the most valuable nontimber forest products harvested in Southeast Asia is agarwood, also known as aloeswood, eaglewood, and *gaharu*. Agarwood is the highly resinated heartwood that develops within some trees in the genus *Aquilaria*, probably as a response to wounding, fungal infection, or both. It is harvested by felling the entire tree and cutting out the resin-containing woods. However, not all *Aquilaria* trees contain agarwood; estimates in a given population range from zero to 10 percent. Because its presence cannot be reliably predicted, many trees are cut down without yielding any profit, since the wood itself is too soft for construction or other use. In Vietnam, the agarwood-producing tree is *A. crassna,* a species that is found in the Mekong Delta and below elevations of 2,600 feet (800 m) northward along the coasts and in extreme northeastern Vietnam. Agarwood is used for a variety of treatments in Ayurvedic, Tibetan, and traditional East Asian medicine, valued for its perfume in the Middle East, and burned as incense by Muslims, Hindus, and Buddhists. Grade-one agarwood sells in Vietnam for $1,590 per pound ($3,500 per kg), and medicinal agarwood (*ky nam*) derived from resinous roots can fetch as much as $6,800 per pound ($15,000 per kg). It is difficult to know how much agarwood is exported annually from Vietnam; known annual exports have fallen to 10 tons from a high of 50 tons in the mid-1980s, though the actual trade is probably much higher. How much of this agarwood originates in Laos and Cambodia is unknown. The IUCN lists *A. crassna* as Critically Endangered because of rapid population losses exceeding 90 percent over the past decade.

The extraction of high-value timber species for local use, domestic trade, and export puts great pressure on a subset of Vietnam's trees. Two northern Vietnamese conifers are under pressure from local use: Taiwania (*Taiwania cryptomerioides*), a cypress known from only two other highly disjunct Asian populations (Taiwan and the Chinese-Myanmar border), and the endemic Golden Vietnamese Cypress (*Xanthocyparis vietnamensis*), described in 2002. Both persist in minute populations and are threatened by habitat degradation and direct exploitation of their resinous, fragrant timbers for construction, coffin-making, and fine crafts (the Golden Vietnamese Cypress may also be harvested for incense and smoke sticks). The IUCN classifies these trees as Critically Endangered. Loggers also extract rosewood species in the genus *Dalbergia* at an extremely high and unsustainable rate. The heartwood is deep red- to purple-brown in color and streaked with black resinous layers. Though hard to work, the resinous wood takes a high polish and is used for musical instruments, cabinet-making, and other woodworking. IUCN specialists list seven of Vietnam's rosewood species as Vulnerable or Endangered owing to overexploitation for their timber.

Wildlife Hunting and Collecting

Direct exploitation is an acute problem for many of Vietnam's vertebrates. Although rare and striking invertebrates are collected for sale to tourists at such well-known sites as Tam Dao National Park, most noncommercial species are far more threatened by habitat degradation and loss than by overharvesting. For vertebrates, the demands that drive hunting and live animal collection range from subsistence-level requirements for food and medicine through an ever-widening circle of local and domestic markets to the booming international trade. This demand is met by an almost equally wide variety of methods and trading ingenuity. Hunting with guns has diminished subsequent to a government ban on and confiscation of private guns beginning in the early 1990s. Unfortunately, other hunting techniques such as snare lines, mist nets, catapults, and sometimes elaborate pitfall traps, are at best only weakly selective and inadvertently capture many nontarget species. Pitfall traps for mammals typically involve a fence built across a popular game trail that directs animals toward a large pit camouflaged with vegetation. At the bottom of the pit lie sharpened sticks to impale the falling animal. Nondiscriminating traps are particularly problematic for large and terrestrial forest-dwelling birds such as Vietnam's restricted-range pheasants, Edwards's Pheasant (*Lophura edwardsi*), Germain's Peacock Pheasant (*Polyplectron germaini*), and Crested Argus (*Rheinardia ocellata*). Both the intensity and reach of wildlife exploitation are glimpsed on those occasions when markets provide the first evidence of species presence in the country (Vietnam White-headed Munia, *Lonchura maja vietnamensis*) or the world (Annamite Striped Rabbit, *Nesolagus timminsi*).

Animals harvested for local consumption cover a range of both sizes and taxonomic groups and may account for a significant amount of the protein consumed by a community when other food sources are scarce. Species consumed include: large frogs such as those in the genera *Paa* and *Rana,* even though some ranids require special handling owing to noxious skin secretions; rodents, including the Black Giant Squirrel (*Ratufa bicolor*), which can weigh up to 6.6 pounds (3 kg), and the East Asian (*Hystrix brachyura*) and Asian Brush-tailed (*Atherurus macrourus*) Porcupines; venomous and nonvenomous snakes; a range of birds, especially larger species, such as partridges and pheasants (Family Phasianidae), large waterbirds such as herons and egrets (Family Ardeidae), pigeons and doves (Family Columbidae), magpies and crows (Subfamily Corvinae), and all medium-sized passerines such as thrushes (Subfamily Turdinae), bulbuls (Family Pycnonotidae), and laughingthrushes (Subfamily Garrulacinae); Water Monitors (*Varanus salvator*), semi-aquatic reptiles weighing 2.2–15.4 pounds (1–7 kg); mid-sized terrestrial animals including the Hog Badger (*Arctonyx collaris*) and Chinese (*Manis pentadactyla*) and Sunda (*M. javanica*) Pangolins; Vietnam's many civet (Family Viverridae) and primate (Order Primates) species; and all larger mammals such as the artiodactyls Red Muntjac (*Muntiacus muntjak*), Sambar (*Cervus unicolor*), Southern Serow (*Naemorhedus sumatraensis*), Eurasian Wild Pig (*Sus scrofa*), and the Asian Black (*Ursus thibetanus*) and Sun (*U. malayanus*) Bears. Subsistence consumption of rare or highly valuable species such as Vietnam's turtles is probably much lower than it once was because of their high cash value in a well-established trade network. Only about 10 percent of turtles in Vietnam's wildlife markets are consumed domestically; the remaining 90 percent or so are destined for China and Hong Kong.

As the value of wildlife in markets escalates with increasing demand and decreasing supply, hunting purely for trade is eclipsing hunting primarily for food. This trend affects not only Vietnam but also adjacent Laos and Cambodia, which, with their smaller populations and more extensive natural forests, have deeper natural reservoirs to tap. Most major cities and towns in Vietnam have wildlife markets that tender an enormous breadth of live animals representing every major vertebrate group, from geckoes, turtles, and frogs to pangolins, deer, and primates. Specialty restaurants routinely serve wildlife, sometimes advertising dishes with price lists next to posters originally produced for conservation education. Prospective diners can regularly view caged live animals (including globally threatened species) such as civets and snakes. Alongside wild organisms and meat destined for consumption, vendors market an increasingly wide variety of live birds, with the largest markets in Hanoi and Ho Chi Minh

City. People value live songbirds as pets for their beautiful plumage and songs and because the display of such exquisite birds advertises wealth and status in the community. The most frequently traded songsters include parakeets (genus *Psittacula*), pigeons and doves, starlings and mynas (Family Sturnidae), laughingthrushes and other babblers (Family Timallidae), and white-eyes (genus *Zosterops*). Tamed birds that have been taught to sing through exposure to wild birds or tapes are more valuable. Hill Mynas (*Gracula religiosa*), which can be taught to talk, can be sold for $200 or more apiece.

Live birds are also purchased for ceremonial release by Buddhists who believe that such compassion will garner them good fortune and a long life. Lowland flock-forming species that can be captured in bulk are common, including munias (genus *Lonchura*), weavers (genus *Ploceus*), finches (Family Fringillidae), and sparrows (Family Passeridae). Captured in rural areas and transported to cities or exported, surviving birds are often in poor shape when they are released. A final group of live birds for sale includes larger species, such as hornbills (Family Bucerotidae) and raptors (Families Accipitridae and Falconidae), bought for pets or zoo displays.

Wildlife parts and products are also well represented in Vietnam's marketplaces. Consumed primarily for pharmacological and restorative benefits, these secondary items include: tiger bones and the balm made from them; bear bile and whole gall bladders; a variety of deer antlers, especially immature ones covered in velvet; pangolin scales; musk glands from deer and civets; dried meat and bones of primates used in medicinal balms and other preparations; rhinoceros horn; and wines made by steeping organisms (usually wild-caught venomous snakes but occasionally primates) in rice alcohol. Rarer animals such as Saola (*Pseudoryx nghetinhensis*) and Tiger (*Panthera tigris*) are almost never traded live but instead appear on the market as skins, bones, and horns or already processed into balms. Wildlife is also processed for the tourist trade, both domestic and international. Widely available products include boxes and chopsticks made from rare tropical hardwoods, seahorses (Family Syngnathidae) and starfish (Family Stelleroidae), Hawksbill (*Eretmochelys imbricata*) tortoiseshell products such as fans, combs, and cigarette holders, snake wine, and wildlife trophies (fig. 62). Not all wildlife parts and preparations are authentic, especially rarer and more valuable items such as tiger bone, rhinoceros horn, and elephant ivory. Even snake wine often contains embalmed snakes that are venomous in appearance only, such as the Green Trinket Snake (*Elaphe prasina*), whose coloration strongly resembles that of venomous green tree vipers in the genus *Trimeresurus*.

Vietnam's wildlife supports extensive markets beyond its borders. Important trading partners include Thailand, Singapore, South Korea, China, and other countries with populations maintaining traditional uses of wild plants and animals. As Asians emigrate to other countries, they take traditional culinary and medicinal practices with them. Strong, culturally rooted food preferences are among the last traditions abandoned during acculturation. Adding to the pressure of exploitation for health purposes is the desire to serve rare, exotic, and expensive species at celebrations and as evidence of wealth. Many of these traditions live on in expatriate Asian communities after they have fallen out of fashion in their country of origin.

Over the past twenty years, China has become an increasingly significant consumer of wildlife originating from Vietnam and elsewhere in the region. As their economy flourishes, more and more Chinese are able to afford the wild plants, animals, and products they value as important cultural ties and with which they can signify their success and prosperity through conspicuous consumption. Slowly warming relations between China and Vietnam led to the reopening of the border in 1989. Coupled with increasing convertibility of the Chinese yuan, the open border has led to a dramatic increase in illegal wildlife flowing into China to meet the swelling demand.

It is extremely challenging to estimate either the volume of wildlife that flows illicitly across Vietnam's borders into China or the value of this trade. The one certainty is that all measures are underestimates. An intensive 1993–1996 survey of the flow of wildlife from Vietnam into China's adjacent Guangxi Province remains one of the few thorough attempts to document the trade's content, volume, and consumption dynamics. Because of Guangxi's better transportation facilities, 95 percent of Sino-Vietnamese trade in wildlife occurs across this border; the volume of trade crossing Yunnan's border with Vietnam is far smaller and primarily supplies local

Figure 62. Stuffed muntjacs (genus *Muntiacus*), civets (Family Viverridae), and other wild-caught mammals for sale at a roadside stand in north-central Vietnam (Photograph by Cal Snyder)

consumption. Daily wildlife imports from Vietnam through three Chinese ports (two inland, one marine) ranged from 2.3 to 29.3 tons, of which turtles made up 61 percent of the volume by weight and snakes (13 percent) and lizards (11 percent) the majority of the rest. Almost all of these live imports were consumed as food, with a far smaller portion used for traditional medicines. Surveys in four of Guangxi's cities (including the capital, Nanning, famous for its relatively inexpensive wildlife meals) found that the majority (63 percent) of high-quality restaurants served wildlife, either on the menu or by request. These dishes are always the most expensive, costing two to twenty times more than common food and consumed by the wealthy, including tourists drawn specifically by its availability. Although this study identified a minimum of fifty-five species during four days of market observations, others have recorded 190 vertebrates in the Sino-Vietnamese trade.

A subsequent survey (January–June 2002) of the illegal trade in wildlife and wildlife meat within Vietnam estimated an annual volume of 3,050 tons, roughly half of which is consumed domestically. Valued at $66.5 million, this illegal trade generates $21 million in profits annually, a value more than three times the total budget for the Forest Protection Department staff, the Vietnamese government's chief wildlife enforcement body. Again, much of the wildlife passing across Vietnam's borders no longer originates in the country and is instead sourced from Laos, Cambodia, and Myanmar (fig. 63). Vietnam acts as a critical regional trade corridor whose well-established networks are capable of handling orders from Chinese traders along its northern border that can largely be filled in a matter of days to a week from hunters in Indochina and beyond. What does originate in Vietnam flows primarily from protected areas in the Truong Son with freshwater reptiles also caught in the Mekong Delta.

Illegal traders use multiple routes and means to traffic wildlife across international borders, especially the Sino-Vietnamese one. This border remains porous on both sides, with many alternative crossings next to official ones. Contraband is smuggled on foot, by boat, in private vehicles, and via public transportation; it may be hidden among legal livestock, inaccurately labeled (freshwater turtle shipments identified as seafood), or passed off with fake permits; and almost always it travels under the additional protec-

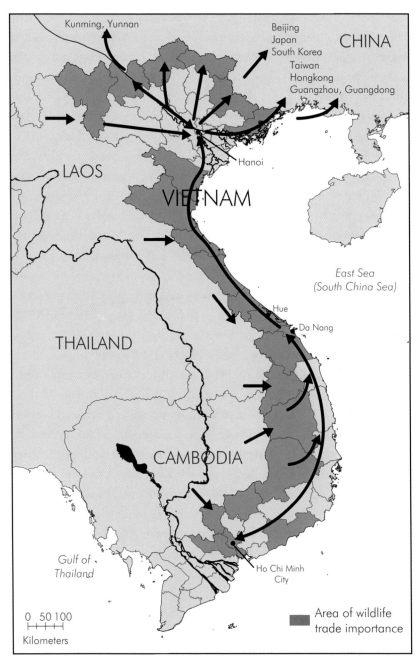

Figure 63. The flow of wildlife trade through Vietnam
(After Compton and Le Hai Quang 1998)

tion of well-cultivated relationships between a few dominant players and their official counterparts, cooperative officials and border guards. Further hampering enforcement efforts is an explosion of cell phone use in Vietnam, enabling smugglers to call ahead and avoid areas with increased inspection activity.

This trade in wildlife products can be extremely profitable, particularly for the rarer and more valuable species. Even for the hunter, who is likely the least well-compensated member of the trading network, the capture of a single, highly valuable animal such as a gibbon can provide the equivalent of many months' or even a year's income. Wildlife has long been an important food in remote areas where there are no stock animals to supply meat, and highland peoples have depended on forest products for cash income to purchase needed goods, including rice. It is not unusual for isolated upland communities in northern and central Vietnam to suffer four months or more of food shortages per year. As species become increasingly scarce, hunters switch from preferred species that are no longer available to secondary, previously less-acceptable options. This in turn transfers collection pressure from species that may be depleted to the point of near-extinction to new ones that will almost surely decline in turn as intense exploitation follows the demands of the marketplace.

As of June 2001, the export of all wild animals and rare and precious plants is prohibited, but not all wildlife trade is illegal. Vietnam permits the export of live wildlife and wildlife products that are farmed. Legal exports include Burmese (*Python molurus*) and Reticulated Pythons (*P. reticulatus*), crocodiles (Siamese Crocodiles, *Crocodylus siamensis;* Saltwater Crocodiles, *C. porosus;* Cuban Crocodiles, *C. rhombifer;* and their hybrids), and Long-tailed Macaques (*Macaca fascicularis*), the last primarily to Japan, the United States, and England for medical research. However, farmed animals are a nonviable replacement source of wildlife for many reasons. Often poorly managed, unsanitary, and overcrowded, these farms frequently rely on wild populations to provide breeding and replacement animals, and in some cases they merely launder wild-caught specimens. By increasing the availability of wildlife in the marketplace, captive breeding in some cases actually increases consumer demand for meat and other products. It is also an incomplete substitute, since consumers often prefer wild-caught animals, a desire expressed in continuing price differentials between the wild and farmed options. Wild-caught venomous snakes are known to fetch twice the price of farm-raised counterparts, and the price of bile taken from wild bears is much higher than that milked in bear farms. These preferences reflect a belief in the greater potency, and hence presumed health benefits, of food and medicine derived from wild-caught animals.

The direct exploitation of Vietnam's wildlife, whatever its final use and wherever its final destination, is the primary threat to a suite of Vietnam's vertebrate species, especially mammals, a subset of birds, and turtles. The main threat to Vietnam's crested gibbons (genus *Hylobates [Nomascus]*) and leaf monkeys (genera *Trachypithecus* and *Pygathrix*) is hunting for the commercial wildlife trade. Researchers have been able to quantify minimum countrywide hunting losses between 1990 and 2000 for two Vietnamese endemics, the Cat Ba Leaf Monkey (*T. poliocephalus poliocephalus*) and Delacour's Leaf Monkey (*T. delacouri*). Total numbers of both species were reduced by half over the decade, with a minimum of 100 and 316 individuals, respectively, lost to hunting. Wildlife hunters removed an additional thirty Cat Ba Leaf Monkeys between 2000 and 2002, and the world population in 2004 hovered around fifty to sixty. An estimated 270–302 Delacour's Leaf Monkeys remain.

Commercial trade is the primary threat to most of Vietnam's other larges mammals, including Tiger, Gaur (*Bos gaurus*), and Banteng (*B. javanicus*) populations. A 1998 status review of the three suggested Vietnamese populations were already severely depressed at 100, 500, and 170–195 individuals, respectively. The result of continued market-based pressure on the species will be either extremely small, relict populations, such as the heavily exploited Lesser One-horned Rhinoceros (*Rhinoceros sondaicus annamiticus*), or countrywide extinction, as in the case of the Kouprey (*B. sauveli*). Despite the wide collection of bird species for consumption, display, and release, commercial trade remains a lesser threat to these taxa than habitat loss and degradation. For both mynas and parakeets, especially the Red-Breasted Parakeet (*Psittacula alexandri fasciata*), however, collection for the commercial pet trade is the likely primary cause of population declines.

Wild populations of all of Asia's turtles have shrunk rapidly in the past decade. Trade to supply the region's food markets, particularly those in southern China, is the principle driver of these declines and is considered by far the group's most serious threat. Scientists believe that if exploitation pressure is sustained at its current high rate, many of Southeast Asia's species will become extinct in the wild in the near future. Virtually all turtles shipped to China are wild-caught, regardless of their country of origin, and with the exception of a few highly valuable species, the trade is unselective. For this reason, many turtles that are encountered either incidentally or by professional hunters, are collected and ultimately traded regardless of species or size. The remaining parts support medical preparations such as turtle jelly, produced by boiling down shells. An exception to the lack of consumer preferences is the Chinese Three-striped Box Turtle (*Cuora trifasciata*) of Laos, Vietnam, and southern China. Believed to provide a cure for cancer, wild-caught individuals have been sold at prices exceeding $450 per pound ($1,000/kg) in 2000.

This demand places enormous pressure on all of Vietnam's (and Southeast Asia's) turtle populations and complicates conservation efforts, since prioritization of either species or habitat is difficult. Vietnam is currently ranked second, behind only China, as a priority country for conserving Asia's turtle diversity, and new species continue to be described (three in the past decade). Of the country's thirty-four known species of freshwater and marine turtles, the IUCN lists over 80 percent (twenty-eight) as Vulnerable, Endangered, or Critically Endangered. It is not unreasonable to fear that Vietnam's turtle populations will collapse under the weight of international trade, burying with them as yet unrecorded diversity.

There are additional threats to Vietnam's wildlife beyond direct exploitation. Some animals are hunted because of wildlife-human conflict, as is the case with the Purple Swamphen (*Porphyrio porphyrio*). This medium-sized ground bird is hunted in the Mekong Delta, where it is considered a pest because it feeds on rice crops. Egg collecting for food also threatens birds, especially ground nesters and colonial breeders, and is a major cause for the decline of three species of sea turtles: Green (*Chelonia mydas*), Olive Ridley (*Lepidochelys olivacea*), and Leatherback (*Dermochelys coriacea*) Turtles.

Overfishing

Overexploitation also takes place in Vietnam's aquatic environments. Sea horses, lobsters (Class Decapoda), abalone (genus Haliotis), sharks (Class Chondrichthyes), sea cucumbers (Class Holothuroidae), sea turtles (Family Cheloniidae), and tuna (Family Scombridae) all fetch high prices in export markets and are thus vulnerable to overharvesting. Each year thousands of sea turtles are captured and sold as various products, including stuffed specimens. These activities have driven sea turtle populations nationwide into a serious decline. As a result, to supply the trade, fishermen are forced to purchase Hawksbill Turtles from foreign countries, such as Indonesia. As fishermen have adopted more efficient catch methods and the number of fishing boats has risen, marine fish harvests have greatly increased. Importantly, however, the same effort now yields a lower total catch, pointing to the likelihood that the seas cannot long sustain this level of fishing. Overharvesting and other threats have led to local extirpation of several species of lobster, sea cucumber, and grouper (Family Serranidae), and these species face complete extinction in Vietnamese waters. The bycatch of Dugongs (*Dugong dugon*) from fixed fishing nets in shallow sea-grass beds is a serious threat to Vietnam's precarious populations. Furthermore, destructive fishing methods that depend on explosives, electrical devices, and poisons to catch fish are highly nonselective in their lethal effects and imperil a broad range of species as well as entire ecological communities.

Confiscated Animals

An unfortunate by-product of the illegal trade in wildlife is the disposal of confiscated live animals and plants. Because of limited personnel and resources to manage confiscated animals, park rangers usually release wildlife into the wild immediately after confiscation. Vietnam's wide-reaching wildlife trafficking network means that the release often occurs far from where animals were collected (which may not have even been in Vietnam). Tam Dao National Park in northern Vietnam is a favored site for these releases, which may explain the presence there of both lowland and southern snake species that inflate the region's diversity.

Current unplanned and unsupervised release practices are a poor solution to the problem posed by confiscated animals. Many do not remain free for long; rangers report that local people often recapture the animals for sale soon after release. Survival rates are extremely poor to nil for most released animals because they are unable to respond effectively to novel weather, predators, and resources. Furthermore, released animals may transfer diseases to native species. And the few that do survive have the potential to invade their new ecosystem, flourishing in an environment where they face reduced predation rates, an increase in available resources, or both. A number of primate introductions by way of confiscated wildlife release have already occurred. Long-tailed Macaques released in the 1990s in Pu Mat National Park (north of their natural range) have successfully bred and now number several troops. They pose a threat to the stability of the native Rhesus Macaque (*Macaca mulatta*) population with whom they are known to interbreed. This has likely already occurred to the south in Cat Tien National Park, where, in an inverse of the Pu Mat introduction, Rhesus Macaques were released into a native Long-tailed Macaque population and there is now good evidence of mixed breeding.

LOSS AND DEGRADATION OF NATURAL HABITATS

Habitat degradation and loss are the most important threats to biodiversity globally. Outright conversion of natural areas to human-dominated landscapes via agricultural encroachment, mining, urbanization, industrial expansion, dam building, road construction, or other development activities leads to habitat loss and a concurrent loss of species. As development and agricultural footprints cover more of the landscape, the resulting fragmentation of formerly contiguous areas isolates plant and animal populations in smaller and smaller patches of natural habitat. Isolation threatens the long-term survival of populations and species as it becomes increasingly difficult to find resources (including mates) sufficient for survival. Smaller populations often depend on immigration from other fragments to maintain their numbers and are inherently more likely to go extinct. Small numbers and reduced or nonexistent immigration frequently leads to inbreeding, an increase in reproduction between closely related individuals. Inbred offspring are often less viable because their reduced genetic diversity makes them more vulnerable to harmful genes that normally remain unexpressed and may increase susceptibility to disease.

Forest Habitats

Most of the information available on habitat loss in Vietnam focuses on its forests. It is notoriously difficult to estimate forest loss accurately in countries with a long history of human exploitation and where few reliable records of forest cover and loss exist. Even estimates from the past decade are regularly hampered by nonsystematic and unreliable surveying methods that have generated incomplete or flawed data. Despite differences in estimates of forest loss, there is a consensus that deforestation and habitat alteration are major problems throughout the country (fig. 64). In addition, because of the long history of resource use in the country, no habitats in Vietnam remain unaltered, and few natural forests in Vietnam remain even close to intact.

The direct harvesting of timber (both legal and illegal) affects most of Vietnam's forests. At the end of the Vietnam-American War the government's forest policy focused on production. Quotas were set based on export markets and national needs (including industrial uses such as paper production) rather than on the ability of the forests to sustain such production. Much of the wood was extracted from state-run forests enterprises, which logged 42 million cubic feet (1.2 million m^3) of timber in 1992. Logging itself in many cases may not lead directly to deforestation, but is often followed by migration along logging roads into previously wild areas. Settlement introduces agriculture and hunting as well as fuelwood collection, the latter an important cause of deforestation in Vietnam.

During the 1990s, Vietnam ranked second only to Thailand in wood exports from mainland Southeast Asia to European Union and Japanese markets, though some of this trade represented the reexportation of timber obtained illegally from Laos and Cambodia. It was during this period

Figure 64. Deforestation in Tra My District, Quang Nam Province
(Photograph by Kevin Koy)

that Vietnam's timber extraction rates peaked and subsequently declined.
The reasons were twofold: a decline in economically extractable timber in
the forest enterprises and a realization by government agencies overseeing
forestry policy that usage must change or there would be no long-term sustainability of the forests. The Land Law of 1993 and the Forest Protection
Law of 1999 reduced logging quotas and encouraged forestry enterprises to
enhance harvesting efficiency. One proposed change was a move away from
intensive logging toward community-based forestry management (though
this has had unanticipated consequences, such as when communities prefer to convert forested land to agriculture).

The direct conversion of forests and other natural habitats to agriculture and plantations has severe repercussions for species diversity and the
welfare of people dwelling in or near the area. Vietnam's extensive postinde-
pendence relocations moved almost 5 million people into targeted migration areas known as New Economic Zones. In part the government wished

to relieve pressure on the densely populated lowlands; in part it desired the reclamation of land in Vietnam's biodiversity-rich uplands through clearance for agricultural use. Following the in-movement of translocated Viet people, extensive areas were logged for timber and subsequently cleared for growing food and cash crops such as coffee and cashews for export, and for pasturage. Begun in the highlands surrounding the Red River Delta and reaching as far south as Lam Dong Province in the central Truong Son, this migration accelerated upland forest loss. The prevailing philosophy behind the New Economic Zones was that settlers and capital were the main ingredients needed for successful development. What the strategists overlooked was the inability of these natural environments to support higher human populations. Characteristics of these upland areas, such as low soil productivity and susceptibility to erosion once natural vegetation is removed, make them unsustainable for such large agricultural populations. Resettlements have led to logging and deforestation, erosion and soil impoverishment, and the loss of biodiversity.

The Mekong Delta's floodplain forest habitat and the quality of the supporting soils (largely peat) have declined swiftly during the 1980s and early 1990s because of increased agriculture. These peat swamp forests harbor a characteristically high abundance of Cajeput (*Melaleuca cajuputi*), a fast-growing tree that flourishes in naturally acidic soils. Although the Vietnam-American War affected these wetlands, post-1975 declines are due directly to agricultural activities, primarily the drainage of large areas for rice cultivation. These cultivation attempts have largely failed. Once trees are felled, the soils dry out, become increasingly acidic, and severely reduce rice yields. Drier, more acidic soils suppress the reestablishment of Cajeput and other natural vegetation, and the residents lose a major source of fuelwood and construction materials. Loss of habitat reduces the biodiversity of an ecosystem harboring many species of plants, mammals, turtles, and large waterbirds, including the Lesser Adjutant (*Leptoptilos javanicus*) and Spot-billed Pelican (*Pelecanus philippensis*), both classified as Vulnerable by the IUCN.

Grassland Habitats

The loss of natural habitat in grassland ecosystems may be of greater concern than in forested ones because so little remains. This is particularly evident in the Mekong Delta, where people have converted almost all of its formerly grass- and sedge-covered floodplains to agriculture. The Mekong Delta encompasses 34 percent of Vietnam's farmland and provides 40 percent of its agricultural output. Sugar cane, pineapples, sweet potatoes, cassava, yams, watermelons, soybeans, and pumpkins are all grown, and there is interest in such commercial crops as mung beans, corn, and cotton. The delta is Vietnam's main rice producer and in 1999 supplied over 50 percent of the country's rice production and 4 million of the 4.5 million tons of rice exported.

These crops all depend on annual flooding cycles that bring water and millions of tons of sediment into the Mekong Delta. The floods enrich the soils and, with irrigation, allow some areas to produce two or three rice crops per year. The central delta's nonacidic soils support the region's best agriculture, while acidic wetland areas are the least productive, particularly for rice. Production in the delta is declining despite intensive application of chemical fertilizers; the reasons for this remain unclear. Local communities now attempt to grow food crops in areas that are marginal for agriculture but important for conservation, such as the U Minh wetlands.

Agricultural activities can so drastically modify a landscape by reducing soil fertility or changing water-flow patterns that restoration and recovery efforts are difficult if not impossible. The last two somewhat extensive grasslands remaining in Vietnam are the Mekong Delta's Ha Tien Plain in Kien Giang Province and Tram Chim National Park in Dong Thap Province. These irreplaceable, seasonally inundated grasslands support bird species found nowhere else in the country, including the eastern Sarus Crane (*Grus antigone sharpii*) and the Bengal Florican (*Houbaropsis bengalensis*). According to Vietnam's Land Law of 1993, the grasslands in Ha Tien Plain are regarded as unused and therefore open to development and resettlement. As a result, people have converted almost all the plain to agriculture, tree plantations, and shrimp aquaculture. The channel dredging necessary for this conversion alters drainage patterns so that soils are more likely to be exposed during the dry season. In acidic soil regions, increased oxidation produces high acid and aluminum levels in runoff waters. As with converted peat swamp forests in the floodplain, the resulting high acid content limits agricultural productivity and the ability of the natural vegetation to recover.

Coastal and Marine Ecosystems

Like their purely terrestrial counterparts, Vietnam's marine and coastal ecosystems face substantial habitat loss, yet even less is known about them. Their health is endangered directly by exploitation as well as indirectly by industrialization, agriculture, and other land-based activities.

Poorly planned land use has many negative consequences for Vietnam's coasts and offshore areas. Agricultural activities and development produce coastal sedimentation via soil erosion, sewage, and fertilizer run-off, leading to excess nutrients, explosive algae growth that reduces oxygen levels, and marine pollution. These threaten the continued presence of the communities and their associated biodiversity. Vietnam lost 40 to 50 percent of its sea-grass beds in the 1980s and 1990s owing to sedimentation from adjacent coasts. Undisturbed mudflats are threatened by monoculture mangrove plantations established to reclaim lands and protect shorelines from erosion. This has made them unsuitable for many bird species, including the globally threatened Black-faced Spoonbill (*Platalea minor;* Endangered).

Coral reefs growing atop the shallow seabeds in both northern and southern Vietnam are in extremely poor shape: human activities threaten almost all these formations (85 to 95 percent), and only a quarter are covered 50 percent or more by live, growing corals. Along with terrestrial activities, these reefs are directly threatened by coral mining for limestone and the use of cyanide to catch reef fish, a method that unintentionally kills corals. These habitats have also suffered from substantial coral bleaching and have been slow to recover. Bleaching occurs when corals expel the symbiotic microscopic plants living within them, exposing their white skeletons. Although still poorly understood, bleaching is likely caused by changes in environmental conditions, including water temperature. Vietnam's bleaching

BOX 15

Impacts of Climate Change

Evidence is mounting that the Earth's climate is growing warmer due mainly to human activities, primarily the burning of fossil fuels. This has serious implications for global biodiversity. Although the Earth has always experienced climactic cycles, the current change is occurring more rapidly and in a world transformed by humans. Organisms that might previously have shifted their ranges in response to climate change find their way blocked by human habitations, agricultural lands, and other barriers. Our almost complete elimination of escape routes magnifies the significance of even small changes in temperature and other aspects of climate.

The biodiversity of Vietnam is particularly at risk. Although Vietnam harbors a significant portion of the Earth's biodiversity, the country also has limited technical and financial resources to address the challenges that climate change poses. Forest and wetland areas are being rapidly reduced and many plant and animal species are threatened. Vietnamese ecosystems are in some cases fragile and may easily deteriorate with irregular climate fluctuations.

A rise in sea level will have substantial consequences for coastal wetland biodiversity. Large areas of Vietnam are within 3 feet (1 m) of mean sea level. A rise would inundate wetlands and lowlands, erode shorelines, exacerbate coastal flooding, increase the salinity of estuaries and aquifers and otherwise impair water quality, alter tidal ranges in rivers and bays, and change the locations where rivers deposit sediment.

Intertidal zones may be modified radically, and ecosystems such as mangroves could disappear along with all that live in or rely on these ecosystems if they do not adapt quickly enough to the changes. The physical characteristics of shallow waters might change considerably, impairing the functioning of ecological systems. Significant losses of resources such as bird life, fish spawning and nursery grounds, and shellfish production are possible. Climate change and sea level rise will also threaten existing lagoons and nesting places of sea turtles. Coral reefs are susceptible to the effects of global warming; a rise in sea temperatures can cause bleaching, and coral systems are sensitive to changes in water depth.

Like many other developing nations, Vietnam relies extensively on its natural resources. Losses in biodiversity caused by climate change will pose many difficulties for future socioeconomic development, particularly with fisheries. The Vietnamese government's Hydrometeorological Service is forming a national action plan for climate and climate-change issues that will strive to balance development demands and environmental protection.

Nguyen Huu Ninh, Center for Environmental Research, Education and Development, Hanoi

event of 1998 coincided with an El Niño warming that produced sea surface temperatures up to 5.5°F (3°C) above normal highs. Human activities continue to create environmental threats to Vietnam's corals, including climate change (box 15).

Shrimp Farms

Observant visitors to Vietnam's coastline will notice symmetrical diked ponds cut into the fringing mangrove forests. These ponds, most cleared since 1990, are used primarily to raise shrimp for export to Japan, the United States, and the European Union. Along with many other countries in South and Southeast Asia and South America, Vietnam has entered the global sea-food market, and production shrimp has rapidly become one of the economy's mainstays and a large earner of foreign exchange. In 2003, the United States imported $595 million worth of shrimp from Vietnam, accounting for roughly 50 percent of the country's exports.

This booming export trade has not come without a price, one paid by both the coastal environment and the peoples who depend on it for their livelihood. Vietnam's shrimp farming was practiced at first in an extensive manner, with low levels of effort and little capital expended. Only a small proportion of mangroves were cleared for the ponds, and farmers depended on a natural supply of shrimp seed to stock them. Beginning in the late 1980s, practices intensified and people accelerated conversion of land to shrimp farms. Between 1988 and 1992, 296,500 acres (120,000 ha) were cleared in Bac Lieu and Ca Mau, Vietnam's southernmost provinces. Ponds were seeded with hatchery-produced, postlarval shrimp, predominantly the native Black Tiger Shrimp (*Penaeus monodon*), and fed fish of no commercial value. The annual yield from these southern farms reached 400 pounds per acre (450 kg/ha), almost twice the 220 pounds per acre (250 kg/ha) under earlier practices. Such intensification of shrimp cultivation practices has occurred throughout Vietnam.

This rosy picture has not lasted. Beginning in 1992 and 1993, productivity decreased while environmental damage increased. To create a pond for shrimp farming, farmers clear mangroves, excavate the area to be enclosed to about 3 feet (1 m) in depth, and use the dredged soils to construct a dike, preventing almost all water flow. Because of sedimentation within the pond and erosion and shrinkage of the dike, farmers continue to remove soils from the pond and deposit them above ground on the dike or in adjacent mangrove forests. The acid sulfate soils oxidize when in contact with air, making the water in the ponds more acidic, causing poor growth rates and death of the growing shrimp. The acidified waters also leach metals, such as iron and aluminum, out of the soils, and concentrations can reach levels that endanger many aquatic organisms.

In addition to lowering water quality, the loss of mangrove forests removes nursing grounds for many native species, including those of wild shrimp. Combined with acidification and overexploitation, this habitat loss has reduced natural stock of shrimp seed to the point where low-intensity cultivation, at least in the south's Ca Mau Province, is unsustainable. Supplementing or replacing natural seed with postlarval shrimp from a hatchery is not feasible because of viral disease outbreaks that began in 1993 and affect the entire industry. One of the more deadly viruses, white spot disease, can cause mortality rates up to 100 percent and is now persistent in many species native to Vietnam's coastal waters.

Many coastal dwellers, seeking to increase their low incomes, borrow the capital necessary to clear, construct, stock, and maintain aquaculture ponds. Because of acidification, pollution, and disease, the ponds quickly become unproductive and are often abandoned after only a handful of years, leading to cycles of financial debt and habitat loss along the coasts. A final problem facing shrimp aquaculture is the stability of the export market. In the first six months of 2002, Vietnam's shrimp exports rose 10.7 percent in volume but only 4.4 percent in dollar value because of lower prices. It is probable that global oversupply will cause prices to continue to drop in the volatile seafood export markets, leaving only the most efficient producers standing. In July 2004, the United States applied steep antidumping tariffs to the country's shrimp imports; this may also destabilize the industry.

Infrastructure Development

In the last decade of the twentieth century, Southeast Asia's growing demand for electricity, coupled with the need to control flooding, spurred plans for hydroelectric power projects throughout the region, including Vietnam. Construction of the necessary dams and reservoirs modifies both terrestrial and aquatic habitats and often has profound effects on local human populations. Developments vary widely in size from small structures providing electricity for a handful of homes to enormous projects funded largely by foreign investment that have international environmental consequences. Their extent depends on the location and reach of the affected areas. China's 1,000-foot-high (300 m) Xiaowan Dam, located on the Mekong River and scheduled for completion in 2012, is expected to affect the entire lower Mekong region.

Freshwater habitats are drastically altered by hydroelectric power developments. Transforming flowing riverine environments (even sluggish ones) into lakes and reservoirs can cause local extinctions of river-adapted species that cannot survive in their new lake habitats. Proposed large-scale river basin development schemes can also devastate a river's hydrological regimes and endanger the species dependent on the flood-drought cycle throughout the watershed. Many organisms and even whole communities have evolved with natural cycles of inundation, depending on flooding for increased nutrient input and transportation to and from spawning grounds. In the Lower Mekong watershed, over 90 percent of the fish species spawn not in the rivers but in the seasonal lakes and surrounding, annually flooded forests and fields. Many fish do not even begin their annual breeding migration until water flow reaches a critical threshold. Under artificially regulated flow regimes, species such as these may not reproduce. Migrating fish are also physically blocked by dams and may be killed in the turbines.

Human populations suffer both directly and indirectly from dam construction. Because altered flow regimes disrupt fish biology, they have an effect on fishing in Vietnam, both for subsistence and as part of Vietnam's rapidly growing commercial fishing industry. About half of Vietnam's fish production depends on the Mekong Delta during some life stage. Of the Mekong Delta's known fish species, more than three-quarters contribute to commercial fisheries, though this is probably an overestimate as many fish remain to be discovered in the delta. The displacement of human communities is another negative consequence of damming. The construction of the Hoa Binh Dam in northern Vietnam in 1998 flooded some 75 square miles (200 km^2) of land, affecting the terrestrial biodiversity and forcing tens of thousands of people to move. Having few alternatives, these displaced people relocated to steep slopes at locations above their now-flooded homes. Agricultural plots on the 60-degree slopes accelerated soil erosion, dumping silt into the dam bed and shortening the estimated working life of the dam from 300 to about fifty years. Siltation threatens the productivity of other hydroelectric projects in Vietnam: the forty-year-old Da Nhim Reser-

Figure 65. Road constructed to a dam site, Que Son District,
Quang Nam Province (Photograph by Kevin Koy)

voir in Ninh Thuan Province already cannot generate electricity during the
dry season because of siltation, and the Thac Ba Reservoir in Yen Bai Province is inundated with some 5.35 million tons of silt annually.

Other consequences of dam construction for biodiversity and human
livelihoods are less easily foreseen, such as the influx of construction workers required to build the dam. The reduction of flow along river courses
can concentrate pollutants downstream. Changes in flood cycles may also
lead to the wider distribution of potentially harmful species such as the tri-
culine snail *Neotricula aperta,* a natural intermediate host for the human
parasitic disease schistosomiasis (*Schistosoma mekongensis*). Last, although
dams are perceived as helping to control floods, they are in fact built and
run to produce electricity and may paradoxically contribute to disastrous
flooding when improperly managed.

A second major threat to Vietnam's biodiversity posed by infrastructure development is road building at all scales (fig. 65). Until the turn of the

twenty-first century, the country's major north-south highway ran along the coast, where it was subject to severe floods in the rainy season, especially in areas near heavily deforested uplands. To improve transportation and communication, the government is building the 1,050-mile-long (1,690 km) Ho Chi Minh Highway both inland and upland from the existing route. As planned, the highway will pass through or near ten protected areas, including Cuc Phuong and Phong Nha–Ke Bang National Parks. Both during construction and after its completion, this major artery will disturb Vietnam's plants and animals via habitat fragmentation, heavy siltation of upland streams, hunting by construction workers, and permanent damage to fragile and unique cave systems from explosives used to cut through limestone areas. The Ho Chi Minh Highway will accelerate existing problems of illegal poaching and logging, increase accessibility of rural areas to wildlife trade networks and agricultural expansion, and disrupt the lives of the many ethnic minority populations living nearby.

Invasive Species

Invasive species, when placed in a novel or highly disturbed environment, can increase dramatically and outcompete, displace, or even extirpate local species. This threatens not only individual species but also the structure and function of ecosystems. Invasive species can be either exotics or native to the region. Exotics can be particularly problematic because traditional checks on population growth, such as predators and competitors for food and shelter, may be absent. Little is known about invasive plants and animals in Vietnam, and undoubtedly many of the most damaging species have neither been identified nor included in plans that would limit their effects.

Exotic species have entered Vietnam through myriad paths. Some, such as weeds, have been carried in by accident on boats or in trade goods. Siam Weed (*Chromolaena odorata*), a perennial from tropical America, was introduced to Asia in the 1800s, possibly in the ballast waters of cargo boats from the West Indies. It is not known when Siam Weed was introduced to Vietnam, but it was probably accidental and the weed is now widespread throughout the country. It lives mainly in disturbed areas, where it is tenacious, spreading rapidly and dominating other vegetation via chemicals it releases to suppress germination and growth of adjacent plants. Other invasive species, including a number of fish and snail species, were deliberately introduced for their potential economic benefits.

One example is the Golden Apple Snail (*Pomacea canaliculata*). Native to South America, it was introduced to Vietnam around 1988 to be cultivated for both local markets and export, an effort that failed owing to their lack of palatability to the Vietnamese. The snail soon escaped the culture ponds and within ten years had affected fifty-seven of sixty-one Vietnamese provinces. It is now a serious rice pest and may threaten native snail populations, as has happened in Malaysia, where scientists think that its introduction has caused the decline of the country's native Apple Snail (*Pila scutata*).

Invasive plant species have been a particular threat to Vietnam's wetlands and aquatic environments. The introduction of the Giant Mimosa (*Mimosa pigra*), native to Mexico and Central and South America, is a serious threat to wetland ecosystems throughout Vietnam. This species, which flourishes in sunny areas and is common along riverbanks and canals, has invaded many sites in the Mekong Delta. The grassland area in Tram Chim National Park has shrunk enormously because of the invasion of the Giant Mimosa. Fortunately, eradication methods that include cutting the stems during flood season, burning stems and seeds, and chemical treatment appear to be successful in some areas. In May 2000, the weed was eliminated from U Minh Thuong Nature Reserve. In Tram Chim, by contrast, the area covered by this weed appears to be expanding, increasing from 1,210 to 4,940 acres (490–2000 ha) between 2000 and 2002. The Water Hyacinth (*Eichhornia crassipes*), an aquatic plant native to the Amazon Basin, now lives in Vietnam's waterways. Scientists believe that this species decreases aquatic biodiversity by blocking sunlight from the lower levels of waterways and shading out phytoplankton and algae. As the plants decay, oxygen levels fall, reducing populations of zooplankton and the other prey aquatic species depend on.

A special category of invasive species, emerging infectious diseases such as avian influenza and severe acute respiratory syndrome (SARS), has led to major public health problems and devastated Vietnam's tourism and poultry industries. These diseases also have implications for wildlife, because control efforts have included nonsystematic killing of wild birds and suspected vectors for SARS such as civets.

Pollution

There is growing concern over the impacts of pollution on the environment in Vietnam, especially in light of increasing economic development. After opening up to the global market much of the country's resources have gone toward building new industrial plants and developing agriculture. Mining and other resource extraction activities have also increased. All these activities have become major sources of pollution in Vietnam. However, little is known about the effects of pollution on the country's flora and fauna because most studies were not designed to elucidate the connection between pollution levels and the responses of living, nonhuman organisms.

Vietnam has about 7,000 large plants and factories, many of which still use old technologies and release untreated waste directly into the environment. Oil refineries, along with metal, textile, paper, food, and chemical factories, are of special concern because their discharge contains such toxic metals as arsenic, copper, mercury, and lead. Vietnam has some 560 mines, mostly coal mines concentrated in Quang Ninh and Bac Thai Provinces, but also operations for metals (including gold) and gems. Mining companies have left barren hills and reduced forested areas, and their operations have led to increased soil erosion, sedimentation, and contamination with heavy metals in nearby water bodies.

The East Sea has recently become an active area for oil exploration and exploitation. Marine areas that have the potential for oil exploitation include the Bac Bo Gulf, the Gulf of Thailand, and the Truong Sa Archipelago (internationally known as the Spratly Islands). Routine marine shipping activities as well as oil exploitation and transportation are the major causes of oil pollution in the ocean. Each year, about 200 million tons of oil are transported off Vietnam's coastline. Leaks and spills can occur during exploitation and processing at offshore oil platforms and can cause severe ecological damages and economic losses.

Not all pollution comes from industrial sources or extractive activities. Farmers frequently use pesticides and fertilizers on agricultural lands, which cover over 20 percent of the country. Many pesticides contain a high residual toxicity with serious ecological consequences. In addition, within a market-driven system, there is an increasing tendency toward the use of less expensive, more hazardous pesticides; some banned in the United States, including DDT and arsenic, remain in regular use.

TEN

Conservation

The Future of Vietnam's Living World

Many Vietnamese individuals and government agencies recognize an array of human activities that threaten Vietnam's species, habitats, and ecosystems and the need for rapid conservation efforts to counter them. As a result, individuals and organizations, both national and international, are undertaking a wide range of conservation efforts that include improved legislation regarding wildlife protection, development of a protected area system, species-level conservation efforts, and economic incentives to conserve biodiversity. Vietnam, along with neighboring countries, ranks as a high priority for conservation action by the major international conservation organizations. These organizations, limited by scarce resources, employ a variety of strategies to set global priorities to focus and guide investment of their efforts. Such strategies generally combine estimates of species richness, presence of endemic species, severity of threats, and the likelihood of achieving specific goals, to rank regions for conservation action.

Approaches are varied, as are the scales at which they are applied. The World Wildlife Fund developed the Global 200 Ecoregions initiative to identify target areas for conservation worldwide. Scientists classified natural areas by habitat type and then chose outstanding locations around the world that are high in species richness and endemism and represent extraordinary ecological or evolutionary events, such as the large hoofed-mammal migrations on the Serengeti plains, or rapid species diversification, as exemplified by the Galapagos finches. Of the areas selected, five lie partly within Vietnam.

Conservational International's priority-setting strategy identifies relatively large global regions based on two criteria: each must contain at least 1,500 endemic plant species, and 70 percent of the region's original habitat (at minimum) must be gone. This approach attempts to conserve as many species in as small an area as possible; the thirty-four hotspots identified to date cover 2.3 percent of the world's total area. All of Vietnam is included in the Indo-Burma Hotspot, which encompasses mainland Southeast Asia and southern China.

BirdLife International focuses one of its priority-setting strategies on one group, birds, and one characteristic, the number of endemic species in an area. The ranges of birds whose global distributions can be contained in areas of less than 20,000 square miles (50,000 km^2) are mapped and designated as restricted-range species. Areas containing two or more restricted-range species are designated Endemic Bird Areas and become the focus of conservation efforts. Four such areas lie within Vietnam, all associated with the Truong Son Range.

National and local-level conservation efforts have a long history in Vietnam, and some of these movements have strong cultural and spiritual roots. Formal efforts by the Vietnamese government began soon after independence. In 1960, Ho Chi Minh, then president of North Vietnam, launched a tree-planting campaign called the Tet Tree-Planting Festival. Its multiple aims included producing timber, fruit, and fuelwood; mitigating erosion; reforesting; and improving the country's landscape and environment. In 1962, he stepped away from the Vietnam-American War long enough to set aside North Vietnam's first national park, Cuc Phuong National Park, a far-sighted initiative, given the political climate (fig. 66). Less than a year later, at a meeting with officials from the uplands of northern and central Vietnam, he said: "The current destruction of our forests will lead to serious effects on climate, productivity, and life. The forest is gold. If we know how to conserve and manage it well, it will be very valuable" (Vo Quy et al. 1992, 76).

Figure 66. Cuc Phuong National Park in northern Vietnam
(Photograph by Peter J. Ersts)

NATIONAL AND INTERNATIONAL CONSERVATION POLICY AND LEGISLATION

The Vietnamese government initiated an ongoing series of national conservation efforts in 1981 when it introduced legislation to protect rural environments. In 1985, the Committee for the Rational Utilization of Natural Resources and Environmental Protection, an autonomous body of specialists drawn from diverse disciplines, collaborated with the World Conservation Union (then called the International Union for Conservation of Nature and Natural Resources; the acronym IUCN remains) to draft a National Conservation Strategy for Vietnam. This document detailed the major threats to Vietnam's biodiversity and proposed actions that both conserved the natural environment and met human needs.

In 1986, the government passed regulations establishing a national protected area system, a network of parks and reserves dedicated to conserving biodiversity. In the same year, recognizing that the distribution of biodiversity rarely conforms to political boundaries, Vietnam signed several international agreements with the governments of Cambodia and Laos to collaborate across borders on wildlife conservation. The government developed a National Plan for Environment and Sustainable Development in 1991, and in the same year the Ministry of Forestry (now the Ministry of Agriculture and Rural Development) completed the Tropical Forestry Action Programme, which provided guidelines for forestry management. In 1994, the Law on Environmental Protection, an outgrowth of the National Plan, created a legal mandate for the government to carry out environmental assessment, pollution control, and environmental planning.

In 1994, the government ratified two important international conventions: the Convention on Biological Diversity, which focuses on sustainable use and may be the most important existing global treaty concerning biodiversity conservation, and the Convention on International Trade in Endangered Species of Wild Flora and Fauna, or CITES, the international treaty regulating trade in endangered species (box 16). Vietnam is among the few Southeast Asian countries to have ratified all four significant global conventions pertaining to biodiversity conservation.

The surprising number of new species discoveries that were reported

BOX 16

Convention on the International Trade in Endangered Species of Wild Flora and Fauna

The Convention on International Trade in Endangered Species of Wild Flora and Fauna (CITES) is the principal means through which the international trade in plants and animals is controlled. Administered by the United Nations Development Programme, CITES was introduced in 1975 and is now one of the best known of all conservation treaties, with 167 member countries in 2005. It is organized around a set of three appendixes listing species and groups with varying levels of threat and associated trade restrictions. Species listed in appendix 1 are threatened with extinction and for all intents and purposes cannot be legally traded. As of 2004, sixty-three animals (including six primates, seventeen birds, and six turtles) and fifteen plants (all in the slipper orchid genus, *Paphiopedilum*) from Vietnam had been placed on this list.

In spite of these efforts, a thriving illegal wildlife trade continues. This is due to the lack of trained enforcement staff, political and social commitment, and resources; insufficient national legislation; and the vast sums of money involved. In response, TRAFFIC, the wildlife trade-monitoring program of World Wildlife Fund and the World Conservation Union, and Vietnam's Forest Protection Department under the Ministry of Agriculture and Rural Development, developed a conceptual framework in early 2001 aimed at controlling Vietnam's wildlife trade. Upwards of sixteen activities were identified and grouped under four main objectives: (1) strengthening government capacity to implement and enforce CITES and relevant national laws; (2) reducing the demand for endangered and threatened species, primarily through education and pub-

lic awareness; (3) improving wildlife trade-monitoring knowledge; and (4) developing economic incentives or alternatives
to illegal and unsustainable wildlife trade. Concerted national
and international efforts will be required to attain the ultimate
goal: protecting Vietnam's biodiversity from overexploitation
through the wildlife trade.

Le Dien Duc, Vietnam National University, Hanoi

beginning in the early 1990s increased awareness of Vietnam's biodiversity
both nationally and internationally. Surveys were being carried out in remote and previously little-explored regions, and the areas of species discovery became prime candidates for the creation of new protected areas and
expansion of established ones. Following the discovery of the Saola (*Pseudoryx nghetinhensis*) in Vu Quang Nature Reserve and the Large-antlered
Muntjac (*Muntiacus vuquangensis*) across the border in Laos, local authorities responded by more than tripling the reserve's size and banning logging.
During the 1990s, Vietnamese scientists began compiling information on
threatened and endangered species for Vietnam's Red Data Books, published for animals in 1992 (revised in 2000) and for plants in 1996. Both the
World Wildlife Fund and BirdLife International established offices in Vietnam during the early 1990s and began supporting national conservation
efforts.

In 1995, Vietnam's government approved a Biodiversity Action Plan
for the country that, together with the National Plan of 1991, served as the
basis for environmental policy during the 1990s (box 17). After reviewing
progress on the Biodiversity Action Plan, the government completed the
National Strategy for Environmental Protection 2001–2010 and established
a five-year action plan that started in 2000.

Each of these efforts paved the way for future policy and legislation.
Over the final two decades of the twentieth century, the Vietnamese gov-

BOX 17
Biodiversity Action Plan

In 1993, government officials, Communist Party members, veterans, teachers, and other community leaders throughout Vietnam met to collect ideas and input for Vietnam's first Biodiversity Action Plan. The preparation of this document was a key obligation of the Convention on Biological Diversity, which Vietnam had signed that year. These provincial-level consultations gave ordinary citizens across the country an opportunity to set targets and goals for conserving Vietnam's natural heritage. Because of this early effort, Vietnam was among the first countries in the world to prepare a Biodiversity Action Plan.

Although environmental planning had been done within individual governmental sectors such as forestry, this action plan was the first comprehensive environmental planning document prepared for Vietnam. It included sections on forestry, wildlife, wetlands and freshwater systems, marine concerns, agricultural diversity, pollution, and information on the distribution and richness of Vietnam's species that had not been gathered in one document before. Monthly meetings of experts assembled under the leadership of Dr. Nguyen Ngoc Sinh of the State Committee for Sciences (now the Ministry of Science, Technology, and Environment) brought together representatives from Vietnamese ministries, universities, the United Nations Development Programme, and such international conservation organizations as BirdLife International and the World Wildlife Fund. The results of the provincial-level consultations were reviewed and synthesized into a portfolio of chapters that would become the framework for the published plan. The final product, printed in both Vietnamese and English, outlined a series of time-bound goals that would create the foundation for future biodiversity conservation actions.

The Biodiversity Action Plan still serves as an important point of reference for conservation planning in Vietnam. A review of the original project list reveals that of the fifty-six projects proposed in 1993, more than forty-five are already implemented or being considered for funding. This illustrates the crucial role the plan has played in setting the environmental and biodiversity conservation agenda for Vietnam well beyond its original five-year mandate. An important document, the Biodiversity Action Plan was prepared at a pivotal time in Vietnam's changing relationship with the international community.

David Hulse, MacArthur Foundation, Chicago

ernment promulgated more than thirty legal instruments related to biodiversity conservation, including the establishment of national parks and nature reserves, a ban on elephant hunting, gun control to limit hunting, the protection of endemic plants and animals, and a complete ban on logging in natural forests (table 5).

TRANSBOUNDARY ISSUES: MANAGING THE MEKONG RIVER

Natural areas do not generally respect political boundaries, and Vietnam is no exception, sharing many resources with neighboring countries. The Mekong River abuts five countries in addition to Vietnam: China, Laos, Myanmar, Thailand, and Cambodia. Consequently, effective and equitable conservation necessitates regional action. In the early twentieth century, as human populations expanded along the Mekong and demand for water increased, largely for irrigation, all six countries experienced the ripple effect

Table 5. Key national legislation and international agreements addressing
biodiversity conservation

Year signed by Vietnam	International agreement/ conservation legislation	Subject of regulation
1985	National Conservation Strategy (NCS)	Threats to biodiversity (national)
1986	Creation of national protected area system	Protected areas (national)
1987	World Heritage Convention	Natural and cultural sites (global)
1989	Convention on Wetlands of International Importance (Ramsar Convention)	Wetlands (global)
1991	National Plan for Environment and Sustainable Development (NPESD)	Biodiversity protection (national)
1991	Tropical Forestry Action Programme	Management of forests (national)
1994	Convention on Biological Diversity	Biodiversity (global)
1993	Law on Environmental Protection	Environmental assessment and planning, pollution (national)
1994	Convention on International Trade in Endangered Species (CITES)	Trade in endangered species (global)
1995	Biodiversity Action Plan (BAP)	Biodiversity status (national)
2001	National Strategy for Environmental Protection 2001–2010	Natural resource management and protection (national)

of development activities at a single site, such as dams, both up and down
the river's course. In the 1950s, the problem of equitable access to the resources of the Mekong River became a major issue for these nations and
the international development community. In 1957, the United Nations'
Economic Committee for Asia and the Far East responded by forming the
Committee for the Coordination of Investigations in the Lower Mekong
Basin, known more commonly at that time as the Mekong Committee. The

committee's members drew from Cambodia, Laos, Thailand, and what was then the Republic of Vietnam (South Vietnam). China's exclusion from the committee was a product of the Cold War and attempts (largely by the United States) to limit communist access to resources. The U.S. government, though not a member of the committee, was represented by an American who served as the committee's administrative head.

The Mekong Committee was initially charged with capturing the river's potential and steering the region toward economic development. Early efforts focused on hydrological studies to determine appropriate dam sites and irrigation schemes. During Indochina's armed conflicts from the 1960s through the 1980s, the committee tabled much of its work. Toward the end of this dormant period, the international financial community began to take greater interest in moving the three Indochinese countries toward more open and market-friendly economies. The concomitant influx of financial resources reinvigorated interest in development along the Mekong. In 1995, the organizing body became the Mekong River Commission.

Simultaneously, concerns were coalescing globally over the human and environmental impact of development projects such as those being planned for the Mekong region. As a response, the commission expanded its mandate beyond siting dam projects to include environmental impact and cultural issues and ramifications. Unfortunately, because it cannot act apart from the will of individual governments on the commission, its effectiveness in these matters is limited. To the best of its ability, the commission encourages the wise management and conservation of water and related resources of the Mekong River basin and promotes their equitable use. Focusing on sustainable management, it supports water-quality monitoring, fisheries management, agricultural development, flood mitigation, and hydropower planning. Major problems include the fact that China and Myanmar, now by their own choice, are still not represented on the commission. All bordering countries must be involved in far-reaching decisions, such as the size and placement of dams, that have implications well beyond a single nation's boundaries.

PROTECTING AREAS FOR CONSERVATION

In developing a system of parks and reserves dedicated to the conservation of species and habitat diversity, Vietnam has employed both national and international approaches to inform the size, location, and structure of individual protected areas. A number of international classifications developed to protect globally important regions have included Vietnam in their analyses. Biosphere Reserves, coordinated by the United Nations Education, Scientific, and Cultural Organization (UNESCO) are established in globally important ecosystems, recognizing biodiversity conservation and sustainable use as joint goals. Most are set up as a series of concentric circles, each with a specific function: an inner core area focused on long-term protection of biological resources; a surrounding buffer zone, where a limited amount of low-impact activities such as collecting forest products can take place; and an outer transition zone, where more intensive yet sustainable practices can be developed. At many of these sites, local communities participate in research, monitoring, and protection activities. Vietnam has four designated Biosphere Reserves: Can Gio Forest Park, Cat Tien National Park, Cat Ba Island, and the Red River Delta.

UNESCO also establishes World Heritage Sites, which conserve cultural as well as natural features. Under the Convention Concerning the Protection of the World Cultural and Natural Heritage (Paris, 1972), which Vietnam adopted in 1987, signees pledge to conserve the listed sites that fall within their boundaries. As of 2004, five World Heritage Sites were recognized in Vietnam: Hoi An Ancient Town, My Son Sanctuary, the Complex of Hue Monuments, Ha Long Bay, and Phong Nha-Ke Bang National Park, the last two for their scenic beauty and biological diversity as well as their cultural significance.

The Convention on Wetlands has designated one site in Vietnam as a Wetland of International Importance: Xuan Thuy National Park in the Red River Delta. Also known as the Ramsar Convention after the location where the treaty was developed and signed, the convention provides a framework for conserving wetlands and promoting their wise use through national action and international cooperation.

Since the 1960s, Vietnam's government has been working to develop a protected area system. Protected area designations vary depending on the types of extractive activities allowed within their borders and whether they are administered at a national, provincial, or local level. Vietnam's National Parks must have strictly protected core areas, harbor either a few endemic species or more than ten threatened ones, and include predominantly natural habitat with little agricultural or residential usage.

By 1999, Vietnam's system of parks and reserves grew to eighty-seven sites, covering 3.2 million acres (1.3 million ha), equivalent to about 4 percent of the country's land area. Without well-developed conservation priorities, sites were added somewhat haphazardly as the system developed. Criteria used to select sites included their potential to protect endemic species and preserve species and habitats that are rare or under the greatest threat. Decisions were not always made based on protecting biodiversity, however, and several areas extremely important for conservation, including most of Vietnam's four Endemic Bird Areas, remain outside the system. Many areas within the reserve system are far from pristine, threatened by agricultural expansion, logging, and wildlife trade, or too small for conserving biodiversity.

Accordingly, in the late 1990s, the Ministry of Agriculture and Rural Development decided to expand the protected area system with an eye to including all of Vietnam's natural forest types, conserving globally threatened species, and increasing the system's effectiveness. The ministry's goal is to almost double the size of the protected area system to 5 million acres (2 million ha) by 2010. One of its divisions, the Forest Inventory and Planning Institute, worked with BirdLife International to identify areas within the system that were no longer forested and to locate unprotected natural forest areas that should be included. Remote-sensing technology, one tool they used to examine forest type, health, and distribution, played a key role in making these decisions (box 18).

In the early twenty-first century, Vietnam's government began to look beyond terrestrial regions to the country's marine and coastal ecosystems. Worldwide experience shows that marine protected areas can increase the abundance, diversity, and size of marine organisms and that reserves, sanctuaries, and other no-fishing or no-take zones increase the productivity of

BOX 18

Remote Sensing Analysis for Biodiversity and Conservation

Remote sensing, the science and art of obtaining and interpreting satellite imagery and aerial photography, can give scientists a bird's-eye view of the Earth's landscapes. Because it can provide visually powerful maps and images, which decision-makers can use to identify and help solve conservation problems, this technology is increasingly important for biodiversity conservation.

Much of Vietnam was photographed from airborne cameras in the 1950s, particularly by French institutions. These photographs still exist and provide a fascinating view of the pre–Vietnam-American War landscape. From 1958 until 1972, the U.S. military collected images of Vietnam through the CORONA satellite program, which provided the world's first satellite imagery of the Earth's surface (fig. 67). The program was highly classified and existed principally to monitor Soviet missile activity. It is now widely recognized that the high-resolution imagery obtained from the CORONA missions, more than 800,000 photographs, has many uses beyond military surveillance, and the images are now declassified. In combination with more recent data, these early images enable scientists to study how Vietnam's landscape has changed over time.

Scientists have made tremendous advances in remote sensing since the inception of CORONA. Several satellites now relay digital images of the Earth's surface every day. New advanced satellites, such as the Landsat Enhanced Thematic Mapper Plus, record images containing information undetectable by the human eye. These images allow scientists to map a variety of landscape features, including natural areas, agriculture, and

Figure 67. Planes equipped with nets recovering photographic film ejected from
CORONA satellites over the Pacific Ocean. To prevent interception of the classified
photographs, these capsules were equipped with salt plugs designed to dissolve
within two days, causing them to sink. (Photograph from Jensen 2000)

human habitation. They also provide insights into forest health
and other important conservation planning factors, such as
changes in the relative proportions of different land-use types
over time. Remotely sensed data can provide powerful graphics
and statistics to illustrate models that predict future change in
natural areas in Vietnam. Decision-makers planning the expansion of the protected area system can use these predictions to
understand changes in the land over time. When combined with
other data, this information helps to determine areas of high
conservation value.

Kevin Koy, Center for Biodiversity and Conservation,
American Museum of Natural History, New York

adjacent fisheries. In 2001 Vietnam's first Marine Protected Area was established at Hon Mun in Nha Trang. Integrating the local community into the reserve's design and management was critical because a majority of residents make their livelihood in either the tourist or fishing trades. In 2004 a second Marine Protected Area was designated at Cu Lao Cham in Quang Nam Province, and an additional thirteen national-level Marine Protected Areas are planned.

Additional challenges confront Vietnam in its goal of developing an effective network of protected areas in important habitats that remain unprotected, most critically the country's wetlands and grasslands. Wetlands have been receiving greater national attention in Vietnam, though both threats and a lack of official recognition as a land-use category pose continuing challenges (box 19). Grasslands remain largely unprotected, particularly in southern Vietnam, where these habitats harbor important species such as the Endangered Bengal Florican (*Houbaropsis bengalensis*). In general, the government classifies land as either agricultural, forestry, rural, urban, special use, or not in use. Grasslands fall under land not in use and are therefore extremely vulnerable to exploitation. What remains of Vietnam's natural terrestrial areas are small and fragmented, requiring additional strategies to ensure their conservation. These include the creation of corridors to connect isolated patches and further conservation initiatives that transcend political boundaries, both between administrative districts within Vietnam and between Vietnam and its neighbors. Adequate enforcement of boundaries and regulations is critical to terrestrial and marine systems. Vietnam's forest rangers deserve considerable credit for their efforts (box 20).

RESTORING DEGRADED AREAS

In 2002 scientists mapped the impact of human activity across the globe using information on population density, land transformation, access, and power infrastructure. Inspecting this human footprint, they estimated that 83 percent of the land's surface is directly affected by human beings. For this reason ecological restoration — aiding damaged, degraded, or even destroyed ecosystems toward recovery — is a growing field. Across Vietnam's

BOX 19

Wetland Restoration and Conservation

Many conservation experts consider wetland ecosystems to be among the Earth's most threatened habitats: both the physical extent and the quality of wetlands declined steadily in the twentieth century. The sustainable use of wetlands in the Red River and Mekong Deltas is critical to the long-term economic and social welfare of the Vietnamese. The two deltas harbor the highest densities of people in Vietnam and generate a significant percentage of food and raw materials for domestic and export markets. To maximize food production, people have converted much of the land to use for rice cultivation, for aquaculture to produce fish, shrimp, and edible aquatic plants, and for human settlement.

In 1989 the Vietnamese government signed the Ramsar Convention on Wetlands of International Importance. The first Ramsar site (Xuan Thuy National Park) lies in the Red River Delta, and the government plans to add other sites, including the Mekong Delta's Tram Chim National Park in Dong Thap Province. In 2000, UNESCO listed Can Gio mangrove forest along Ho Chi Minh City's coastal zone as Vietnam's first Biosphere Reserve. Since then the government has identified sixty-eight wetlands as having biodiversity and environmental importance, several of which are protected as special-use forests.

In spite of these efforts, wetlands have yet to gain official recognition in Vietnam as a distinct land-use and conservation management category. Their management is scattered across different government departments and ministries. Conflicting goals, for instance mangrove reforestation versus shrimp farming versus coastal zone protection, result in conflicting actions on the ground. Because wetland management is institutionally not clarified and wetland functions and values are poorly under-stood, especially at the community levels, wetland ecosystems are being seriously degraded or lost at alarming rates.

Even though wetlands are under severe threat in Vietnam, there is a slow but steady increase in initiatives aimed at revers-ing these negative trends, including the preparation of a na-tional strategy for wetland conservation, collaborative projects aimed at raising awareness for policy makers and the public, and a call for a national wetlands program. The challenges are enormous. Wetland ecosystems cover a huge area of Vietnam, are relatively unknown and unappreciated, and exist in an in-stitutional and legal void. A long-term, concerted effort is nec-essary to build the knowledge base and the institutional and legal framework, to increase public and political appreciation, and to enhance the capacity at community levels for sound wet-land management. Although such an effort may start as a rela-tively small program, it will need to grow into a comprehensive National Wetland Sector partnership in order to generate the critical mass needed to arrive at sound wetland management to benefit the Vietnamese people and the environment.

Le Dien Duc, Vietnam National University, Hanoi

landscapes, heavily dominated by human activities, restoration efforts are taking place in both aquatic and terrestrial systems.

Restoration of Dong Thap Muoi, or the Plain of Reeds

Dong Thap Muoi, also known as the Plain of Reeds, is located in the Me-kong Delta's northwestern sector. The plain is a large, flat inland region, with an average elevation of a only few feet (1 m) above sea level. It typically floods to 6–10 feet (2–3 m) during the wet season. Once this section of the

BOX 20

Forest Rangers of Vietnam

The position of forest ranger was established by the government of Vietnam in 1972 and is now part of the Forest Protection Department within the Ministry of Agriculture and Rural Development. The country's small corps of 1,600 forest rangers faces a daunting set of responsibilities: forest rangers draft forest protection programs and plans; patrol protected areas; control exploitation and enforce relevant laws; promote community involvement in forest protection and development; guide forest owners in planning and implementing forest protection programs; and help to forecast and prevent forest fires.

Forest rangers encounter many obstacles in their work. People's awareness of how biodiversity loss affects their livelihood, especially in inaccessible areas with much of Vietnam's remaining biodiversity, remains poor. This leads to misunderstandings and violations of the law. Many Asian countries, including Vietnam, have a long tradition of using wildlife to produce medicines, making it harder to control illegal trade in wildlife. Legal documents relating to forest and nature conservation are still incomplete, and enforcement is often not effective. As a developing nation, Vietnam faces budget difficulties in meeting the real cost for forest protection and biodiversity conservation in general.

It is crucial that Vietnam develop a professional forest ranger staff that can effectively enforce the law and strengthen people's awareness of conservation issues. In addition, to counter the tremendous profits inherent in wildlife and timber smuggling, forest rangers and other government sectors, such as law enforcement and the judicial system, must increase their collaboration. Additional resources for training programs

to help officials identify endangered or CITES species are also
critical. In the long term, it is important to complete and review all legislation concerning conservation of Vietnam's biodiversity and promote development activities that will enhance
people's livelihoods while conserving, and even expanding, the
forest and its precious natural resources.

Nguyen Ba Thu, Forest Protection Department, Hanoi

delta was covered with seasonally flooded natural grasslands and marshes
mixed with Cajeput (*Melaleuca cajeputa*) paperbark forest, and it harbored
a large, species-rich community of breeding waterbirds. Most of the land
in the plains has now been converted to agriculture.

Drainage canals built to enhance agriculture in the late 1950s and early
1960s severely changed the hydrological regime, reducing the regional water
table in the dry season and decreasing the number of months the area was
flooded from seven to five. This drainage dried out the vegetation, facilitating the spread of wildfires that in turn dessicated and exposed the underlying soils. After the Vietnam-American War, displaced people migrated
into the area by the thousands, and local leaders established dikes to capture water and manage the wetland areas for agricultural production and
natural resources. Marsh sedges yielded fodder for water buffalo, wetland
animals such as fish, shrimp, crabs, and turtles were a source of protein,
and extensive rice paddies provided grain.

In the short term, the dikes trapped enough water to foster the return of
many native species of flora and fauna. Sightings of the eastern Sarus Crane
(*Grus antigone sharpii*) in particular led Vietnamese scientists to petition
local authorities to establish the Tram Chim Nature Reserve (fig. 68). A mosaic of grasslands, paperbark forest, and permanently inundated marsh-
land, the area was declared a national park in 1998.

Unfortunately, the same dikes that allowed for wetter conditions and
the influx of native species in the short term also isolated water within the

Figure 68. The eastern Sarus Crane (*Grus antigone sharpii*)
(Photograph by Eleanor Briggs)

reserve. This prevented the inflow of nutrients from the Mekong flood-waters and trapped decomposition by-products within the reserve. In the long term, the resulting stagnant, standing waters inhibited regeneration of both floral and faunal communities. Recent efforts by the International Crane Foundation and Vietnamese colleagues suggest that restoration of the natural hydrological processes of the region may be critical to maintaining this biodiversity.

Terrestrial Reforestation Efforts

Reforestation of degraded lands remains one of the most frequently used conservation tools, mainly because it appears to be so straightforward. Done correctly, reforestation transforms barren or degraded lands, which can contribute to such conservation problems as erosion and siltation of waterways, into vegetated areas that hold soils and perhaps even regenerate their fertility. Wood harvested from plantations also has the potential to release pressure on natural forests for fuelwood, timber, and other wood products. However, reforestation efforts often provide suboptimal habitat for native plants and animals, and an emphasis on reforestation can distract from efforts to conserve existing natural forests.

President Ho Chi Minh's encouragement of intensive tree-planting programs in the 1960s eventually led to the replanting of 3.5 million acres (1.4 million ha). In 1992, the government initiated the 327 Program to promote community involvement in forest restoration and establishment activities. This program initially supported a broad range of activities, but in 1995 the government honed its priorities to focus on protection and rational use. Building on this and other reforestation programs, the government developed the 5-Million-Hectare (12.5 million acres) Program in the late 1990s. Between 1998 and 2010, it aims to establish 7.5 million acres (3 million ha) of production forest — 5 million acres (2 million ha) to produce raw materials for pulp and paper mills as well as timber and nontimber forest crops and 2.5 million acres (1 million ha) for fruit trees and other crops. The program also calls for rehabilitation or establishment of 5 million acres (2 million ha) of forests, half to protect watersheds and coastal areas and the other half to protect biodiversity in general. Together with existing forest protected through the system of parks and reserves, this program would bring the amount of forested area in the country to 43 percent.

Reforestation efforts have met with mixed success overall in Vietnam. The trees planted are often all the same species, lowering overall species diversity in an area. Also, people frequently plant fast-growing, exotic species such as eucalyptus (genus *Eucalyptus*) and acacia (genus *Acacia*) that maximize short-term economic benefits but drain the water table. Low-quality seeds and seedlings as well as improper planting techniques result in poor establishment, low growth rates, and high disease rates. Plantings are often too dense, resulting in slender-stemmed trees that are vulnerable to high winds from the frequent tropical storms. Projects also often take place along coastlines, where erosion is not a critical problem and natural mangrove colonization might otherwise have occurred. Reforestation efforts often have significant implications for biodiversity conservation, and their potential to help or harm depends on their design and implementation.

SPECIES-LEVEL CONSERVATION ACTIONS

Direct exploitation of wild animals and plants forms the basis for Vietnam's profitable illegal wildlife trade and constitutes one of the most important threats to its biodiversity. Vietnam's government is making concerted efforts to reduce international wildlife trade, yet these attempts to curtail it are hampered by insufficient resources, inadequate knowledge to identify illegal activities and threatened species, and limited awareness of how serious the problem is. In an effort to control the continuing threat of cross-border wildlife trade with China, Chinese and Vietnamese authorities are developing strategies that include increasing the monitoring of illicit trade, sharing information regarding these illegal activities, increasing cooperation to stop the trade, expanding education activities, and improving awareness of the legal status of specific species.

Many organizations in Vietnam are working on the conservation of heavily exploited species and species groups with especially high extinction risks by researching their biology and designing programs tailored for their conservation needs. Two major species-level conservation initiatives are captive breeding, particularly of animals taken from the wildlife trade, and reintroduction of individuals to areas where population sizes are either low or extirpated (box 21).

The Endangered Primate Research Center, located on a 12.5-acre (5 ha) plot in Cuc Phuong National Park, was created to rescue, rehabilitate, breed, study, and conserve confiscated primates. Forest protection authorities have seized these animals from hunters and wildlife markets or from people keeping them illegally as pets. Another major effort of the center is educating the public about the importance of Vietnam's endangered primates, their ecology, behavior, and natural habitat, and the urgency of conservation action. The center's staff collaborates closely with forest protection authorities to enforce wildlife protection laws. In 2004, the rescue center housed more than 110 leaf monkeys, gibbons, and lorises representing fourteen species and subspecies. Six of these primate species are not kept in captivity anywhere else in the world, and almost all are extremely difficult to see in the wild.

The Cuc Phuong Turtle Conservation Center (TCC), occupying 8.5

acres (3.5 ha) in Cuc Phuong, was started in 1998 to protect Vietnam's turtles, almost all of which are globally threatened. As with the Endangered Primate Research Center, the Turtle Conservation Center has multiple goals, including fostering healthy populations of native species, raising public awareness, training wildlife protection authorities, and research. The facility's turtles were confiscated from the illegal wildlife trade and are released back to their native range when possible; in 2004 they held approximately 450 turtles of fourteen species. In 2001, some 366 Elongated Tortoises (*Indotestudo elongata*), a species listed as Endangered by the IUCN, were reintroduced to Cat Tien National Park. The Turtle Conservation Center is also involved in enhancing wildlife trade monitoring and enforcement, with particular focus on developing national expertise on turtles and their conservation. Cuc Phuong is also home to the Owston's Civet (*Chrotogale owstoni*) Conservation Program, which rescues, breeds, and studies the basic biology of this Vulnerable carnivore endemic to Indochina. As of the end of 2004, there were twenty-eight civets in the program, twenty of which were born in captivity. Six pairs have been sent to the United Kingdom to establish a breeding population, and there are plans for another six pairs to be sent to the United States.

ECONOMIC INCENTIVES

Economic incentives for biodiversity conservation, such as ecotourism, have grown in recent years in Vietnam. Ecotourism has many definitions, but most emphasize a low impact on local environments and people, accrual of direct financial benefits to conservation efforts and neighboring communities, respect for local cultures and needs, and an increase in environmental awareness among all participants. Vietnam is one of the fastest-growing tourism markets in the world, and the government is expressly interested in attracting more tourists. Ecotourism ventures are in their infancy, however, and tourists would do well to question the operators regarding their policies on ecotourism, including what percentage of their profits directly supports biodiversity conservation and local communities, how they accomplish this, the educational opportunities included on the trips, and how the trips minimize their impact on the environment.

BOX 21
Crocodile Farms

Crocodile farms and zoos in Thailand, Cambodia, and Vietnam simultaneously pose the best chance for and the greatest danger to crocodile reintroduction programs. They represent an important source for reintroduction because they make up the largest pool by far of Critically Endangered Siamese Crocodile (*Crocodylus siamensis*) individuals in the world. However, crocodile farmers actively hybridize the Siamese Crocodile with the Saltwater Crocodile (*C. porosus*) and the Cuban Crocodile (*C. rhombifer*) to increase skin yields (Saltwater and Cuban Crocodiles are much larger than the Siamese species). In captivity, hybrids have a more aggressive demeanor than the purebreds, but otherwise little else is known about them. They represent a loss of genetic diversity, and their release into the wild is essentially the introduction of an exotic species.

Because the Siamese Crocodile is extinct in the wild in Vietnam, any introductions will become the only wild source of genetic diversity in the country, and it is imperative that only purebreds are released. Fortunately, scientists have successfully isolated genetically pure individuals of the Siamese Crocodile from wild sources as well as from Vietnamese zoos and crocodile farms. Through these efforts, Siamese Crocodile individuals were reintroduced to Cat Tien National Park beginning in 2001. Whether these individuals can be protected from the poachers who extirpated the species remains to be seen.

Raoul Bain, Center for Biodiversity and Conservation,
American Museum of Natural History, New York

Other economic incentives include sustainable harvesting of wildlife. One of the best examples of this practice comes from central Vietnam, where people harvest the nests of cliff-dwelling swiftlets for use in soup (box 22).

Conservation efforts in Vietnam face several imposing problems. The growing human population places considerable pressure on natural resources. In addition, as elsewhere in the world, conflicting agendas across ministries hinder conservation efforts. Most sectors of the government emphasize maximizing short-term production over the sustainable-use or long-term management of natural resources. Although the government is developing an institutional and legislative framework for conservation efforts, law enforcement is minimal; the roles and responsibilities of various ministries involved in conservation are not yet clear; and there is an evolving but still small cadre of trained individuals to carry out conservation at both the policy and implementation levels. Vietnam's biodiversity is of great importance nationally and globally. Clearly, much work remains and many people will need to be involved, acting at the individual, community, government, and institutional level to ensure that the spectacular biodiversity of Vietnam survives well into the twenty-first century.

BOX 22
Edible Birds' Nests

Some of the world's most valuable birds live in rocky cliffs and caves along Vietnam's coast. Their value derives not from their feathers or flesh but solely from the quality of the nests they construct with their saliva, which may sell for nearly $2,000 per pound ($4,400 per kg). This value, greater by weight than pure silver, has led to the uncontrolled and unsustainable harvesting of their nests throughout their range.

Although many swifts and all of the diminutive swiftlets use under-the-tongue salivary glands to secrete a viscous nest-

Figure 69. Male and female Germain's Swiftlets (*Collocalia germani*)
in flight and spittle nest (facing page)

building material, only the edible-nest swiftlets (generally identified in Vietnam as Germain's Swiftlet, *Collocalia germani;* fig.
69) construct nests made entirely of saliva, without supporting
grasses, twigs, or feathers. For hundreds of years, these hard
white nests have been the necessary ingredient in bird's nest
soup, valued for treating numerous ills, including respiratory
ailments, stomach ulcers, and AIDS. Scientific research initially
failed to identify medically significant ingredients in the nests,

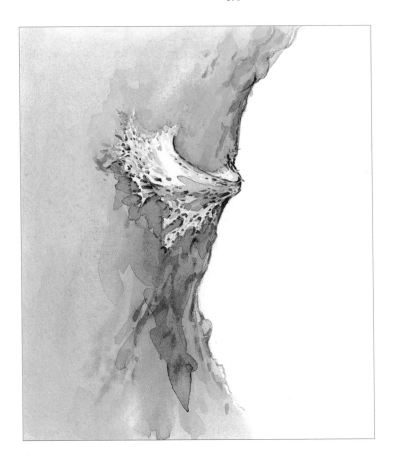

but a study in 1987 discovered the presence of a protein that
stimulates cells to grow and divide. Scientists have yet to prove
the health benefit of nest consumption.

This lack of scientific support has done nothing to diminish consumer demand. The world market for edible nests, centered on Hong Kong, trades as many as 20 million nests each
year. Their value increased fiftyfold over the last two decades of
the twentieth century. Vietnam's edible-nest swiftlets produce
high-quality nests, commanding the highest average prices of
any nation in the Hong Kong market.

More than half of the Vietnamese nest harvest comes from a state-owned company in Khanh Hoa Province. The company's science department, under the direction of Dr. Nguyen Quang Phach, has conducted years of research into how the swiftlets feed, build nests, breed, and raise their young. Indeed, for a relatively small player in this unique international market (2.5 percent of the global market), Vietnam is a world leader in swiftlet research and in the adoption of guidelines for sustainable nest harvests.

When nests are removed from cave and cliff walls, the birds rebuild, usually in the same location, up to four times during the nesting season, from December to June. But how many times a year can the nests be taken before the swiftlet population declines? Nguyen and his assistants discovered that Vietnamese swiftlets cannot generate nest-building saliva after June. This pattern, they reasoned, stemmed from the birds' preference to rear young when the monsoon climate fostered the maximum availability of insects, their exclusive diet. Nguyen also found that each rebuilt nest was smaller than the previous one and that each successive nesting effort yielded a smaller average production of eggs and of successful fledglings. These studies provided scientific principles for optimal nest harvesting.

As a result, nests in Khanh Hoa are harvested twice a year: once when 10–15 percent of the swiftlets' first nests have eggs, and again when all fledglings raised in the second breeding have left the nest. This pattern permits virtually all swiftlet pairs to rear one brood of chicks, and no birds are required to construct more than two nests annually. The new harvesting practices have led to an increase both in the quantity of nests collected and in the numbers of breeding swiftlets. Instead of the declining bird numbers and threatened populations reported from other parts of the world, the swiftlets of Khanh Hoa Province now total nearly 500,000 and are approaching the capacity of the caves in which they breed.

Some regions have not implemented such rigorous practices, and even in Khanh Hoa nest theft is a continuing problem. Nest theft is often accompanied by cliff defacing to hide the thievery, which leads to lower renesting rates. As Dr. Nguyen Quang Phac is the first to concede, a few years of success is no guarantee of long-term sustainability. Still, the preservation and study of the edible-nest swiftlet in central Vietnam appears at this stage to be an exemplary merger of conservation and economic needs.

Walt Bachman, Center for Biodiversity and Conservation, American Museum of Natural History, New York

Appendix 1. Ethnic groups and their distribution in Vietnam

Official name	Approximate population size	Geographical distribution	Language group	Map key
Ba Na	137,000	Central	Mon Khmer	42
Bo Y	1,450	North	Tay-Thai	4
Brau	250	Central	Mon Khmer	37
Bru-Van Kieu	40,000	Central	Mon Khmer	31
Cham	99,000	Central, some South	Malayo-Polynesian	43
Cho-ro	15,000	South	Mon Khmer	51
Chu-ru	11,000	Central	Malayo-Polynesian	50
Chut	2,400	Central	Viet-Muong	32
Co	23,000	Central	Mon Khmer	38
Co Lao	1,500	North	Co Lao	5
Co-ho	92,000	Central	Mon Khmer	46
Cong	1,300	North	Tibeto-Burman	11
Co-tu	37,000	Central	Mon Khmer	33
Dao	474,000	North	Hmong-Dao	15
E-de	195,000	Central	Malayo-Polynesian	44
Gia-rai	242,000	Central	Malayo-Polynesian	41
Giay	38,000	North	Tay-Thai	13
Gie-Trieng	27,000	Central	Mon Khmer	35
Ha Nhi	12,500	North	Tibeto-Burman	10
Hmong	558,000	North, some Central	Hmong-Dao	3
Hoa	900,000	South, some North	Han	52
Hre	94,000	Central	Mon Khmer	39
Khang	4,000	North	Mon Khmer	19
Khmer	895,000	South	Mon Khmer	53
Kho-mu	43,000	North, some Central	Mon Khmer	23
La Chi	8,000	North	Co Lao	6
La Ha	1,400	North	Co Lao	22
La Hu	5,400	North	Tibeto-Burman	9
Lao	10,000	North	Tay-Thai	21
Lo Lo	3,200	North	Tibeto-Burman	1
Lu	3,700	North	Tay-Thai	7
Ma	25,000	Central	Mon Khmer	47
Mang	2,300	North	Mon Khmer	8
Mnong	67,000	Central	Mon Khmer	45

Appendix 1. *Continued*

Official name	Approximate population size	Geographical distribution	Language group	Map key
Muong	914,000	North, some Central	Viet-Muong	25
Ngai	1,200	North, Ho Chi Minh City	Han	28
Nung	705,000	North, some Central, Ho Chi Minh City	Tay-Thai	17
O-du	100	North, some Central	Mon Khmer	30
Pa Then	3,700	North	Hmong-Dao	14
Phu La	6,500	North	Tibeto-Burman	18
Pu Peo	400	North	Co Lao	2
Ra-glai	72,000	Central	Malayo-Polynesian	49
Ro-mam	250	Central	Mon Khmer	40
San Chay	114,000	North	Tay-Thai	26
San Diu	94,630	North	Han	27
Si La	600	North	Tibeto-Burman	12
Ta-oi	26,000	Central	Mon Khmer	34
Tay	1,190,000	North	Tay-Thai	16
Thai	1,040,000	North, some Central	Tay-Thai	20
Tho	51,000	Central	Viet-Muong	29
Viet (Kinh)	55,900,000	North, Central, South	Viet-Muong	
Xinh-mun	11,000	North	Mon Khmer	24
Xo-dang	97,000	Central	Mon Khmer	36
Xtieng	50,000	Central	Mon Khmer	48

Appendix 2. Endemic and restricted-range mammals and birds in Vietnam

English common name	Scientific name	Distribution in Vietnam	Endemic region	Threat status	Range notes
Mammals					
Northern Smooth-tailed Treeshrew	*Dendrogale murina*	C, S	2		Reported SE Thailand
Vietnam Leaf-nosed Bat	*Paracoelops megalotis*	C	1	CR	Known only from description (1947)
Owston's Civet	*Chrotogale owstoni*	N, C	2	VU	
Lowe's Otter Civet	*Cynogale lowei*	N	1	EN	Reported S Yunnan
Pygmy Loris	*Nycticebus pygmaeus*	N, C, S	3	VU	
Con Son Long-tailed Macaque	*Macaca fascicularis condorensis*	S	1		
Red-shanked Douc	*Pygathrix nemaeus nemaeus*	C	2	EN	
Gray-shanked Douc	*P. nemaeus cinerea*	C	1	EN	
Black-shanked Douc	*P. nigripes*	C	2	EN	
Tonkin Snub-nosed Monkey	*Rhinopithecus avunculus*	N	1	CR	
Delacour's Leaf Monkey	*Trachypithecus delacouri*	N	1	CR	
François's Leaf Monkey	*T. francoisi francoisi*	N	3	VU	
Black Leaf Monkey	*T. francoisi ebenus*	C	2	VU	
Annamese Leaf Monkey	*T. francoisi hatinhensis*	C	2	VU	
Cat Ba Leaf Monkey	*T. poliocephalus poliocephalus*	N	1	CR	

Appendix 2. Continued

English common name	Scientific name	Distribution in Vietnam	Endemic region	Threat status	Range notes
Black-cheeked Crested Gibbon	Hylobates (Nomascus) concolor concolor	N	3	EN	
Eastern Black-cheeked Crested Gibbon	H. (N.) sp.cf. nasutus nasutus	N	1	CR	
Eastern Black-cheeked Crested Gibbon population	H. (N.) sp.cf. nasutus population	N	1	CR	
Northern White-cheeked Crested Gibbon	H. (N.) leucogenys leucogenys	N	3	DD	
Southern White-cheeked Crested Gibbon	H. (N.) leucogenys siki	C	2	DD	
Yellow-cheeked Crested Gibbon	H. (N.) gabriellae	C, S	2	VU	
Heude's Pig	Sus bucculentus	C	2	DD	
Large-antlered Muntjac	Muntiacus vuquangensis	C	2	DD	
Annamite Muntjac	M. truongsonensis	C	2	DD	
Roosevelts' Muntjac	M. rooseveltorum	C	2	DD	
Kouprey	Bos sauveli	S	2	CR	SE Thailand
Saola	Pseudoryx nghetinhensis	C	2	EN	
Red-throated Squirrel	Dremomys gularis	N	3		
Osgood's Rat	Rattus osgoodi	C	1		
Fat-nosed Spiny Rat	Maxomys moi	C, S	2		
Chapa Pygmy Dormouse	Typhlomys chapensis	N	1	CR	Known only from description (1932)
Annamite Striped Rabbit	Nesolagus timminsi	C	2	DD	

Birds

Orange-necked Partridge	*Arborophila davidi*	S	1	EN	
Annam Partridge	*Arborophila merlini*	C	1	DD	
Imperial Pheasant	*Lophura imperialis*	C	1	EN	
Edwards's Pheasant	*Lophura edwardsi*	C	1	EN	
Vietnamese Pheasant	*Lophura hatinhensis*	C	1	EN	
Germain's Peacock Pheasant	*Polyplectron germaini*	C, S	2	VU	
Crested Argus	*Rheinardia ocellata*	C	RR	VU	Peninsular Malaysia, C, S Laos
Red-collared Woodpecker	*Picus rabieri*	N, C	3	NT	
Red-vented Barbet	*Megalaima lagrandieri*	N, C, S	2		
Ward's Trogon	*Harpactes wardi*	N	RR	NT	Bhutan, NE India, W Yunnan, N Myanmar
Coral-billed Ground Cuckoo	*Carpococcyx renauldi*	N, C	2		
White-eared Night Heron	*Gorsachius magnificus*	N	3	EN	
Giant Ibis	*Pseudibis gigantea*	S	2		Formerly Thailand
White-winged Magpie	*Urocissa whiteheadi*	N, C	3		
Yellow-billed Nuthatch	*Sitta solangiae*	N, C	3	NT	
Chestnut Bulbul	*Hemixos castanonotus*	N	3		
Broad-billed Warbler	*Tickellia hodgsoni*	N	RR		E Nepal, Bhutan, NE India, SW China, N Myanmar

Appendix 2. *Continued*

English common name	Scientific name	Distribution in Vietnam	Endemic region	Threat status	Range notes
Black-hooded Laughingthrush	*Garrulax milleti*	C	2	NT	
Grey Laughingthrush	*Garrulax maesi*	N	3		
White-cheeked Laughingthrush	*Garrulax vassali*	C	2		
Chestnut-eared Laughingthrush	*Garrulax konkakinhensis*	C	1	VU	
Orange-breasted Laughingthrush	*Garrulax annamensis*	C	1		
Golden-winged Laughingthrush	*Garrulax ngoclinhensis*	C	1	VU	
Collared Laughingthrush	*Garrulax yersini*	C	1	EN	
Red-winged Laughingthrush	*Garrulax formosus*	N	3		
Short-tailed Scimitar Babbler	*Jabouilleia danjoui*	N,C	2	NT	
Sooty Babbler	*Stachyris herberti*	C	2	NT	
Grey-faced Tit Babbler	*Macronous kelleyi*	C, S	2		
Black-crowned Barwing	*Actinodura sodangorum*	C	2	VU	
Streaked Barwing	*Actinodura souliei*	N	3		
Spectacled Fulvetta	*Alcippe danisi*	C	2		
Grey-crowned Crocias	*Crocias langbianis*	C	1	EN	
Mekong Wagtail	*Motacilla samveasnae*	C	2	NT	
Vietnamese Greenfinch	*Carduelis monguilloti*	C	1	NT	

Endemic Status: 1: Vietnam 2: Indochina 3: Indochina and Southern China RR: Restricted-range species outside criteria 1–3

Threat Status: CR: Critically Endangered EN: Endangered VU: Vulnerable NT: Near Threatened DD: Data Deficient

Appendix 3. New terrestrial vertebrates described from Vietnam, 1992–2004

English common name	Scientific name	Distribution in Vietnam	Publication
Mammals			
Cao Van Sung's Mountain Shrew	*Chodsigoa caovansunga*	N	2003
Annamite Mouse-eared Bat	*Myotis annamiticus*	C	2001
Grey-shanked Douc	*Pygathrix nemaeus cinerea*	C	1997
Silver-backed Chevrotain	*Tragulus versicolor*	C	2004
Large-antlered Muntjac	*Muntiacus vuquangensis*	C	1996
Truongson Muntjac	*Muntiacus truongsonenesis*	C	1998
Saola	*Pseudoryx nghetinhensis*	C	1993
Annamite Striped Rabbit	*Nesolagus timminsi*	C	1999
Birds			
Chestnut-eared Laughingthrush	*Garrulax konkakinhensis*	C	2001
Golden-winged Laughingthrush	*Garrulax ngoclinhensis*	C	1999
Black-crowned Barwing	*Actinodura sodangorum*	C	1999
Turtles			
Striped Asian Leaf Turtle	*Cyclemys pulchristriata*	N	1997
Bourret's Indochinese Box Turtle	*Cuora bourreti*	C	2004
Painted Indochinese Box Turtle	*Cuora picturata*	Unknown	2004
Lizards			
Phong Nha–Ke Bang Bow-fingered Gecko	*Cyrtodactylus phongnhakebangensis*	C	2002
Deharveng's Blind Skink	*Dibamus deharvengi*	S	1999
Greer's Blind Skink	*Dibamus greeri*	C	1992
Con Dao Blind Skink	*Dibamus kondaoensis*	S	1992
Vietnamese Leaf-toed Gecko	*Dixonius vietnamensis*	C	2004
Baden's Pacific Gecko	*Gekko badenii*	C	1994
Ulikovski's Pacific Gecko	*Gekko ulikovskii*	C	1994
Gracile Chinese Eyelid Gecko	*Goniurosaurus araneus*	N	1999

Appendix 3. *Continued*

English common name	Scientific name	Distribution in Vietnam	Publication
Obscure Gecko	*Gonydactylus paradoxus*	S	1997
Peters's Butterfly Lizard	*Leiolepis guentherpetersi*	C	1993
Keeled Writhing Skink	*Lygosoma carinatum*	C	1996
Rare Tree Skink	*Paralipinia rara*	C	1997
Southeast Asian Green Glass Lizard	*Takydromus hani*	C	2001
Murphy's Keeled Skink	*Tropidophorus murphyi*	N	2002
Wrinkled Skink	*Vietnascincus rugosus*	C	1994
Snakes			
Bourret's Cat Snake	*Boiga bourreti*	C	2004
Slowinski's Krait	*Bungarus slowinski*	N	2004
Dao Van Tien's Keelback Snake	*Opisthotropis daovantieni*	C	1998
Siever's Three Horn-scaled Pitviper	*Triceratolepidophis sieversorum*	C	2000
Amphibians			
Ba Na Spadefoot Toad	*Leptobrachium banae*	C	1998
Yellow-spotted Spadefoot Toad	*Leptobrachium xanthospilium*	C	1998
Na Hang Asian Toad	*Leptolalax nahangensis*	N	1998
Rainy Asian Toad	*Leptolalax pluvialis*	N	2000
Sung's Asian Toad	*Leptolalax sungi*	N	1998
Warty Asian Toad	*Leptolalax tuberosus*	C	1999
Gerti Mountain Toad	*Ophryophryne gerti*	C	2003
Hansi Mountain Toad	*Ophryophryne hansi*	C	2003
Spiny Asian Toad	*Vibrissaphora echinata*	N	1998
Ruddy Rice Frog	*Microhyla erythropoda*	C	1994
Marbled Rice Frog	*Microhyla marmorata*	C	2004
Small-thumbed Rice Frog	*Microhyla nanapollexa*	C	2004
Speckled Rice Frog	*Microhyla pulverata*	C	2004
Spinyback Torrent Frog	*Amolops spinapectoralis*	C	1999
Near Cascade Frog	*Rana attigua*	C	1999
Bac Bo Cascade Frog	*Rana bacboensis*	N	2003
Ba Na Cascade Frog	*Rana banaorum*	C	2003

Appendix 3. *Continued*

English common name	Scientific name	Distribution in Vietnam	Publication
Dao Cascade Frog	*Rana daorum*	N	2003
Hmong Cascade Frog	*Rana hmongorum*	N	2003
Iridescent Cascade Frog	*Rana iriodes*	N	2004
Large-eared Cascade Frog	*Rana megatympanum*	N,C	2003
Morafka's Cascade Frog	*Rana morafkai*	C	2003
Tobacco-colored Cascade Frog	*Rana tabaca*	N	2004
Tran Kien's Cascade Frog	*Rana trankieni*	N	2003
Spotted-leg Bubble-nest Frog	*Philautus abditus*	C	1999
Large-horned Bubble-nest Frog	*Philautus supercornutus*	C	2004
Spotted-belly Flying Frog	*Rhacophorus baliogaster*	C	1999
Dubois's Flying frog	*Rhacophorus duboisi*	N	2000
Spinybottom Tree Frog	*Rhacophorus exechopygus*	C	1999
Hoang Lien Flying Frog	*Rhacophorus hoanglienensis*	N	2001
Orlov's Flying Frog	*Rhacophorus orlovi*	C	2001

Appendix 4. New plant genera described from Vietnam, 1992–2004

Genus	Family	Publication
Zeuxinella Aver.	Orchids (Orchidaceae)	2003
Vietorchis Aver. and Averyanova	Orchids (Orchidaceae)	2003
Caobangia A.R. Sm. and X. C. Zhang	Ferns (Polypodiaceae)	2002
Xanthocyparis A. Farjon and Nguyen Tien Hiep	Cypresses (Cupressaceae)	2002
Metapanax J. Wen and D. G. Frodin	Ginsengs (Araliaceae)	2001
Rubovietnamia D. D. Tirvengadum	Madders (Rubiaceae)	1998
Vidalasia D. D. Tirvengadum	Madders (Rubiaceae)	1998
Fosbergia D. D. Tirvengadum and C. Sastre	Madders (Rubiaceae)	1997
Distichochlamys M. F. Newman	Gingers (Zingiberaceae)	1995
Grushvitzkya N. T. Skvortsova and L. V. Averyanov	Ginsengs (Araliaceae)	1994
Vietnamia P. T. Li	Milkweeds (Asclepiadaceae)	1994
Vietnamochloa J. F. Veldkamp and R. Nowack	Grasses (Poaceae)	1994
Christensonia J. R. Haager	Orchids (Orchidaceae)	1993
Deinostigma W. T. Wang and Z.Y. Li	Gesneriads (Gesneriaceae)	1992

BIBLIOGRAPHY

Abegg, C., and B. Thierry. 2002. Macaque evolution and dispersal in insular south-east Asia. *Biological Journal of the Linnean Society* 75:555–576.

Adger, N. W., P. M. Kelly, Nguyen Huu Ninh, and Ngo Cam Thanh. 2001. Property rights, institutions and resource management: Coastal resources under *doi moi*. In *Living with environmental change: Social vulnerability, adaptation and resilience in Vietnam,* ed. N. Adger, P. M. Kelly, and Nguyen Huu Ninh, 79–92. London: Routledge.

Aitchison, J. C., A. M. Davis, Badengzhu, and H. Luo. 2002. New constraints on the India-Asia collision: The Lower Miocene Gangrinboche conglomerates, Yarlung Tsangpo suture zone, SE Tibet. *Journal of Asian Earth Sciences* 21:251–263.

Akira, Y. 2003. Inundation due to fresh water and saline intrusion at coastal area. The Mekong Delta in Vietnam: http://cantho.cool.ne.jp/.

Alerstam, T. 1990. *Bird migration.* Cambridge: Cambridge University Press.

Ali, J. R., and R. Hall. 1995. Evolution of the boundary between the Philippine Sea Plate and Australia: Palaeomagnetic evidence from eastern Indonesia. *Tectonophysics* 251 (1–4):251–275.

Amato, G., M. G. Egan, and G. B. Schaller. 2000. Mitochondrial DNA variation in muntjac: Evidence for discovery, rediscovery, and phylogenetic relationships. In *Antelopes, deer, and relatives: Fossil record, behavioral ecology, systematics, and conservation,* ed. E. S. Vrba and G. B. Schaller, 285–295. New Haven and London: Yale University Press.

Amato, G., M. G. Egan, G. B. Schaller, R. H. Baker, H. C. Rosenbaum, W. G. Robichaud, and R. DeSalle. 1999. Rediscovery of Roosevelts' Barking Deer (*Muntiacus rooseveltorum*). *Journal of Mammalogy* 80 (2):639–643.

An, Z. 2000. The history and variability of the East Asian paleomonsoon climate. *Quaternary Science Reviews* 19:171–187.

Andersen, M., and C. C. Kinze. 2000. Review and new records of the marine mammals and sea turtles of the Indochinese waters. *Natural History Bulletin of the Siam Society* 48:177–184.

Andriesse, J. P. 1988. Nature and management of tropical peat soils. Rome: Food and Agriculture Organization of the United Nations.

Ashton, P. S. 1995. Towards a regional forest classification for the humid tropics of Asia. In *Vegetation science in forestry: Global perspectives based on forest eco-*

systems of East and Southeast Asia, ed. E. O. Box, R. K. Peet, T. Masuzawa, I. Yamada, K. Fujiwara, and P. F. Maycock, 453–464. Dordrecht, Netherlands: Kluwer Academic.

Attwood, S. W., and D. A. Johnston. 2001. Nucleotide sequence differences reveal genetic variation in *Neotricula aperta* (Gastropoda: Pomatiopsidae), the snail host of schistosomiasis in the Lower Mekong Basin. *Biological Journal of the Linnean Society* 73:23–41.

Aubreville, A., N. L. Tardieu-Blot, and J. E. Vidal, eds. 1960–1996. *Flora du Cambodge, du Laos et du Vietnam* [Flora of Cambodia, Laos, and Vietnam]. 28 vols. Paris: Museum National d'Histoire Naturelle.

Averianov, A. O., A. V. Abramov, and A. N. Tikhonov. 2000. A new species of *Nesolagus* (Lagomorpha, Leporidae) from Vietnam with osteological description. *Contributions from the Zoological Institute, St. Petersburg* 3:1–22.

Averyanov, L. V., and A. L. Averyanov. 2003. *Updated checklist of the orchids of Vietnam.* Hanoi: Vietnam National University Publishing House.

Averyanov, L., P. Cribb, Phan Ke Loc, and Nguyen Tien Hiep. 2003. *Slipper orchids of Vietnam with an introduction to the flora of Vietnam.* Portland, OR: Timber Press.

Averyanov, L. V., Phan Ke Loc, Nguyen Tien Hiep, and D. K. Harder. 2003. Phytogeographic review of Vietnam and adjacent areas of eastern Indochina. *Komarovia* 3:1–83.

Bain, R. H., A. Lathrop, R. W. Murphy, N. L. Orlov, and Ho Thu Cuc. 2003. Cryptic species of a cascade frog from Southeast Asia: Taxonomic revisions and descriptions of six new species. *American Museum Novitates* 3417:1–60.

Bain, R. H., and Nguyen Quang Truong. 2004. Herpetofaunal diversity of Ha Giang Province in northeastern Vietnam, with descriptions of two new species. *American Museum Novitates* 3453:1–42.

Bangs, O. 1932. Birds of western China obtained by the Kelley-Roosevelts expedition. *Field Museum of Natural History, Zoological Series* 18 (11):343–379.

Bangs, O., and J. van Tyne. 1931. Birds of the Kelley-Roosevelts expedition to French Indo-China. *Field Museum of Natural History, Zoological Series* 18 (3):33–119.

Baltzer, M. C., Nguyen Thi Dao, and R. G. Shore, eds. 2001. Towards a vision for biodiversity conservation in the forests of the Lower Mekong Ecoregion complex. Hanoi: World Wide Fund for Nature Indochina Programme.

Barden, A., N. A. Anak, and T. Mulliken. 2000. Heart of the matter: Agarwood use and trade and CITES implementation for *Aquilaria malaccensis.* Cambridge: TRAFFIC International.

Bates, P. J. J., and D. L. Harrison. 1997. *Bats of the Indian subcontinent.* Kent, UK: Harrison Zoological Museum.

Beilfuss, R. D., and J. A. Barzen. 1994. Hydrological wetland restoration in the Mekong Delta, Vietnam. In *Global wetlands: Old World and New,* ed. J. W. Mitsch. Amsterdam: Elsevier.

Bennett, K. D. 1997. *Evolution and ecology: The pace of life.* Cambridge: Cambridge University Press.

Beresford, M. 1988. *Vietnam: Politics, economics and society.* London: Pinter.

BirdLife International. 2001. *Red data book: Threatened birds of Asia.* CD-ROM. Cambridge: BirdLife International.

BirdLife International in Indochina. 2004. *Sourcebook of existing and proposed protected areas in Vietnam.* 2nd ed. Hanoi: BirdLife International in Indochina / Ministry of Agriculture and Rural Development.

Boisserie, J.-R., F. Lihoreau, and M. Brunet. 2005. The position of the Hippopotamidae within the Cetartiodactyla. *Proceedings of the National Academy of Sciences* 102:1537–1541.

Bourret, R. 1936a. *Les serpents de l'Indochine.* Vol. 1: *Étude sur la faune* [The snakes of Indochina. Vol. 1: Survey of the fauna]. Toulouse: Henri Basuyau.

Bourret, R. 1936b. *Les serpents de l'Indochine.* Vol. 2: *Catalogue systématique descriptif* [The snakes of Indochina. Vol. 2: Descriptive systematic catalogue]. Tolouse: Henri Basuyau.

Bourret, R. 1941. *Les tortues de l'Indochine* [The turtles of Indochina]. Hanoi: G. Taupin.

Bourret, R. 1942. *Les batraciens de l'Indochine* [Batrachia of Indochina]. Hanoi: Gouvernement genéral de l'Indochine.

Brandon-Jones, D. 1996. The Asian Colobinae (Mammalia: Cercopithecidae) as indicators of Quaternary climatic change. *Biological Journal of the Linnean Society* 59:327–350.

Brandon-Jones, D., A. A. Eudey, T. Geissmann, C. P. Groves, D. J. Melnick, J. C. Morales, M. Shekelle, and C.-B. Stewart. 2004. Asian primate classification. *International Journal of Primatology* 25 (1):97–164.

Brandt, J. H., M. Dioli, A. Hassanin, R. A. Melville, L. E. Olson, A. Seveau, and R. M. Timm. 2001. Debate on the authenticity of *Pseudonovibos spiralis* as a new species of wild bovid from Vietnam and Cambodia. *Journal of Zoology, London* 255:437–444.

Briggs, J. C. 2003. The biogeographic and tectonic history of India. *Journal of Biogeography* 30:381–388.

Brocheux, P. 1995. *The Mekong Delta: Ecology, economy and revolution, 1860–1960.* Madison: Center of Southeast Asia Studies, University of Wisconsin–Madison.

Brookfield, M. E. 1998. The evolution of the great river systems of southern Asia during the Cenozoic India-Asia collision: Rivers draining southward. *Geomorphology* 22:285–312.

Buckton, S. T., Nguyen Cu, Ha Quy Quynh, and Nguyen Duc Tu. 1999. Conservation of key wetland sites in the Mekong Delta. Hanoi: Birdlife International Vietnam Programme.

Campden-Main, S. M. 1970. *A field guide to the snakes of South Vietnam.* Washington, DC: Smithsonian Institution Press.

Cao Van Sung. 1989. On the problem of zoogeographical division of the rodent fauna of Vietnam (Mammalia, Rodentia). *Vertebrata Hungarica* 23:57–66.

Cao Van Sung, ed. 1998. *Environment and bioresources of Vietnam: Present situation and solutions.* Hanoi: Gioi Publishers.

Casellini, N., K. Foster, and Bui Thi Thu Hien. 1999. The "white gold" of the sea: A case study of sustainable harvesting of swiftlet nests in coastal Vietnam. Hanoi: World Conservation Union (IUCN).

Chanratchakool, P., and M. J. Phillips. 2002. Social and economic impacts and management of shrimp disease among small-scale farmers in Thailand and Vietnam. In *Primary aquatic animal health care in rural, small-scale, aquaculture development*, ed. J. R. Arthur, 177–189. Rome: Food and Agriculture Organization of the United Nations.

Cibois, A., M. V. Kalyakin, H. Lian-Xian, and E. Pasquet. 2002. Molecular phylogenetics of babblers (Timaliidae): Revaluation of the genera *Yuhina* and *Stachyris*. *Journal of Avian Biology* 33:380–390.

Cima, R. J., ed. 1989. *Vietnam: A country study*. Washington, DC: Federal Research Division, Library of Congress.

Ciochon, R. R., and J. W. Olsen. 1986. Paleoanthropological and archaeological research in the Socialist Republic of Vietnam. *Journal of Human Evolution* 15: 623–633.

Compton, J., and Le Hai Quang. 1998. Borderline: An assessment of wildlife trade in Vietnam. [Hanoi]: World Wide Fund for Nature Indochina Programme.

Coolidge, H. J., Jr. 1940. The Indo-Chinese Ox or Kouprey. *Memoirs of the Museum of Comparative Zoology at Harvard* 54 (6):421–531.

Corbet, G. B., and J. E. Hill. 1992. *The mammals of the Indomalayan region: A systematic review*. Oxford: Oxford University Press.

Cracraft, J., K. F. Barker, and A. Cibois. 2003. Avian higher-level phylogenetics and the Howard and Moore checklist of birds. In *The Howard and Moore complete checklist of the birds of the world*, ed. E. C. Dickinson, 16–21. Princeton, NJ: Princeton University Press.

Craik, R. 1998. Bird trade in Vietnam. *Oriental Bird Club Bulletin* 28:22–23.

Dang Hung Vo, ed. 1996. *Vietnam national atlas*. Hanoi: Ministry of Science, Technology and Environment.

Dang Huy Huynh. 1998. Ecology, biology and conservation status of prosimian species in Vietnam. *Folia Primatologica* 69:S101–108.

Dang Nghiem Van, Chu Thai Son, and Luu Hung. 2000. *Ethnic minorities in Vietnam*. Hanoi: Gioi Publishers.

Dang Ngoc Can, A. V. Abramov, A. N. Tikhonov, and A. O. Averianov. 2001. Annamite Striped Rabbit *Nesolagus timminsi* in Vietnam. *Acta Theriologica* 46 (4):437–440.

Darevsky, I. S. 1999. The herpetofauna of some offshore islands of Vietnam, as related to that of the adjacent mainland. In *Tropical island herpetofauna: Origin, current diversity, and conservation*, ed. H. Ota, 27–42. Amsterdam: Elsevier.

de Graaf, G. J., and T. T. Xuan. 1998. Extensive shrimp farming, mangrove clearance and marine fisheries in the southern provinces of Vietnam. *Mangroves and Salt Marshes* 2:159–166.

de Koninck, R. 1999. *Deforestation in Vietnam*. Ottawa: International Development Research Centre.

Delacour, J. 1977. *The Pheasants of the World.* 2nd ed. Hindhead, UK: Spur Publications / World Pheasant Association.

Delacour, J., and P. Jabouille. 1931. *Les oiseaux de l'Indochine française* [The birds of French Indochina]. 4 vols. Aurillac, France: Impr. du Cantal Républicain.

Dickinson, E. C. 1970. Birds of the Legendre Indochina Expedition, 1931–1932. *American Museum Novitates* 2423:1–17.

Dao Van Tien. 1978. An experience of zoogeographical regionalization of Vietnam. [In Russian.] *Zoologicheskii Zhurnal* 57 (4):582–586.

Do Dinh Sam. 1998. The forest policy of Vietnam and the role of people's participation in forest protection and development. Tokyo: Institute of Global Environmental Strategies' interim report.

Donovan, D. G. 2001. Cultural underpinnings of the wildlife trade in Southeast Asia. In *Wildlife trade in Asia: Cultural perspectives,* ed. J. Knight, 88–111. London: Routledge Curzon.

Dransfield, J., F. O. Tesoro, and N. Manokaran, eds. 2002. Rattan: Current research issues and prospects for conservation and sustainable development. Rome: Food and Agricultural Organization of the United Nations.

Duckworth, J. W. 1998. A survey of large mammals in the central Annamite mountains of Laos. *Zeitschrift für Säugetierkunde* 63:239–250.

Duckworth, J. W., P. Alström, P. Davidson, T. D. Evans, C. M. Poole, T. Setha, and R. J. Timmins. 2001. A new species of wagtail from the Lower Mekong Basin. *Bulletin of the British Ornithologists' Club* 121 (3):152–182.

Duckworth, J. W., G. Q. A. Anderson, A. A. Desai, and R. Steinmetz. 1998. A clarification of the status of the Asiatic Jackal *Canis aureus* in Indochina. *Mammalia* 62 (4):549–556.

Duckworth, J. W., and S. Hedges. 1998. Tracking tigers: A review of the status of Tiger, Asian Elephant, Guar and Banteng in Vietnam, Lao, Cambodia and Yunnan Province (China), with recommendations for future conservation action. Hanoi: Worldwide Fund for Nature Indochina Programme.

Duckworth, J. W., and R. H. Pine. 2003. English names for a world list of mammals, exemplified by species of Indochina. *Mammal Review* 33 (2):151–173.

Duckworth, J. W., R. E. Salter, and K. Khounboline. 1999. *Wildlife in Lao PDR: 1999 status report.* Vientiane, Lao PDR: Wildlife Conservation Society.

Dudgeon, D. 1995. The ecology of rivers and streams in tropical Asia. In *River and stream ecosystems,* ed. C. E. Cushing, K. W. Cummins, and G. W. Minshall, 615–657. Amsterdam: Elsevier.

Dudgeon, D. 2000. Large-scale hydrological changes in tropical Asia: Prospects for riverine biodiversity. *BioScience* 50 (9):793–806.

Duong Van Ni, R. Safford, and E. Maltby. 2001. Environmental change, ecosystem degradation and the value of wetland rehabilitation in the Mekong Delta. In *Living with environmental change: Social vulnerability, adaptation and resilience in Vietnam,* ed. W. N. Adger, P. M. Kelly, and Nguyen Huu Ninh. London: Routledge.

Eames, J. C. 2001. On the trail of Vietnam's endemic babblers. *Oriental Bird Club Bulletin* 33:20–27.

Eames, J. C., and C. Eames. 2001. A new species of Laughingthrush (Passeriformes: Garrulacinae) from the Central Highlands of Vietnam. *Bulletin of the British Ornithologists' Club* 121 (1):10–23.

Eames, J. C., F. R. Lambert, and Nguyen Cu. 1995. Rediscovery of the Sooty Babbler *Stachyris herberti* in central Vietnam. *Bird Conservation International* 5:129–135.

Eames, J. C., Le Trong Trai, and Nguyen Cu. 1995. Rediscovery of the Grey-crowned Crocias *Crocias langbianis*. *Bird Conservation International* 5:525–535.

Eames, J. C., Le Trong Trai, and Nguyen Cu. 1999. A new species of Laughingthrush (Passeriformes: Garrulacinae) from the western highlands of Vietnam. *Bulletin of the British Ornithologists' Club* 119 (1):4–15.

Eames, J. C., Le Trong Trai, Nguyen Cu, and R. Eve. 1999. New species of Barwing *Actinodura* (Passeriformes: Sylviinae: Timaliini) from the western highlands of Vietnam. *Ibis* 141:1–10.

Eudey, A. A. 1987. *Action plan for Asian primate conservation: 1987–1991.* Riverside, CA: World Conservation Union (IUCN).

Eve, R. 1996/1997. The rediscovery of Edwards's Pheasant. *Annual Review of the World Pheasant Association* [1996/1997]:40–42.

Farjon, A., Nguyen Tien Hiep, D. K. Harder, Phan Ke Loc, and L. Averyanov. 2002. A new genus and species in Cupressaceae (Coniferales) from northern Vietnam, *Xanthocyparis vietnamensis. Novon* 12:179–189.

Farjon, A., P. Thomas, and Nguyen Duc To Luu. 2004. Conifer conservation in Vietnam: Three potential flagship species. *Oryx* 38 (3):257–265.

Findlay, R. H. 1999. Review of the Indochina–South China plate boundary problem; structure of the Song Ma–Song Da Zone. In *Gondwana dispersion and Asian accretion: IGCP 321 final results volume,* ed. I. Metcalfe, R. Jishun, J. Charvet, and S. Hada, 341–361. Rotterdam: A. A. Balkema.

Fitzsimmons, N. N., J. C. Buchan, Phan Viet Lam, G. Polet, Ton That Hung, Nguyen Quoc Thang, and J. Gratten. 2002. Identification of purebred *Crocodylus siamensis* for reintroduction in Vietnam. *Journal of Experimental Biology* 294:373–381.

Fjeldså, J., E. Lambin, and B. Mertens. 1999. Correlation between endemism and local ecoclimatic stability documented by comparing Andean bird distributions and remotely sensed land surface data. *Ecography* 22:63–78.

Flux, J. E. C. 1990. The Sumatran Rabbit *Nesolagus netscheri.* In *Rabbits, hares and pikas: Status survey and conservation action plan,* ed. J. A. Chapman and J. E. C. Flux, 137–139. Gland, Switzerland: World Conservation Union (IUCN).

Fontaine, H. 2002. Permian of Southeast Asia: an overview. *Journal of Asian Earth Sciences* 20:567–588.

Fontaine, H., and D. R. Workman. 1978. Review of the geology and mineral resources of Kampuchea, Laos and Vietnam. In *Proceedings of the Third Regional*

Conference on Geology and Mineral Resources of Southeast Asia, Bangkok, November 14–18, 1978, ed. P. Nutalaya, 541–603. Bangkok: Asian Institute of Technology.

Fooden, J. 1996. Zoogeography of Vietnamese primates. *International Journal of Primatology* 17 (5):845–899.

Forest Inventory and Planning Institute of Vietnam. 1996. *Vietnam forest trees.* Hanoi: Agricultural Publishing House.

Foster, S. 2001. Vietnamese ginseng: A rare species of *Panax. HerbalGram* 52:50–54.

Freyhof, J., and D. V. Serov. 2000. Review of the genus *Sewellia* with descriptions of two new species from Vietnam (Cypriniformes: Balitoridae). *Ichthyological Exploration of Freshwaters* 11 (3):217–240.

Freyhof, J., D. V. Serov, and Nguyen Thi Nga. 2000. A preliminary checklist of the freshwater fishes of the River Dong Nai, South Vietnam. *Bonner Zoologische Beitrage* 49 (1–4):93–99.

Frost, D. R. 2004. *Amphibian species of the world: An online reference.* Version 3.0 (22 August 2004). New York: American Museum of Natural History. Available at http://research.amnh.org/herpetology/amphibia/.

Galbreath, G. J., and R. A. Melville. 2003. *Pseudonovibos spiralis*: Epitaph. *Journal of Zoology, London* 259:169–170.

Garnier, F., and J.-P. Gomane. 1985. *Voyage d'exploration en Indochine* [Voyage of discovery in Vietnam]. Paris: La Découverte.

Garson, P. 2001. Pheasant taxonomy: A cunning way to remove species from the Red List! *Oriental Bird Club Bulletin* 33:52.

Gatinsky, Y. G., C. S. Hutchinson, N. N. Minh, and T. V. Tri. 1984. Tectonic evolution of Southeast Asia. Paper read at 27th International Geological Congress: Tectonics of Asia, Moscow, 4–14 August 1984.

Gaubert, P., and G. Veron. 2003. Exhaustive sample set among Viverridae reveals the sister-group of felids: The linsangs as a case of extreme morphological convergence within the Feliformia. *Proceedings of the Royal Society of London, Series B, Biological Sciences* 270:2523–2530.

Geissmann, T., Nguyen Xuan Dang, N. Lormee, and F. Momberg. 2000. Vietnam primate conservation status review 2000; Part 1: Gibbons. Hanoi: Fauna and Flora International.

Glover, I. C., and C. F. W. Higham. 1996. New evidence for early rice cultivation in South, Southeast, and East Asia. In *The origins and spread of agriculture and pastoralism in Eurasia,* ed. D. R. Harris, 413–441. Washington, DC: Smithsonian Institution Press.

Gomiero, T., D. Pettenella, Giang Phan Trieu, and M. G. Paolett. 2000. Vietnamese uplands: Environmental and socio-economic perspective of forest land allocation and deforestation process. *Environment, Development and Sustainability* 2(2): 119–142.

Greene, H. 1997. *Snakes: The evolution of mystery in nature.* Berkeley: University of California Press.

Gower, D. J., A. Kupfer, O. V. Oommen, H. Werner, R. A. Nussbaum, S. P. Loader, B. Presswell, H. Müller, S. B. Krishna, R. Boistel, and M. Wilkinson. 2002. A molecular phylogeny of ichthyophiid caecilians (Amphibia: Gymnophiona: Ichthyophiidae): Out of India or out of South East Asia? *Proceedings of the Royal Society of London, Series B, Biological Sciences* 269:1563–1569.

Gregory, J. W. 1925. The evolution of the river system of South-eastern Asia. *Scottish Geographical Magazine* 41:129–141.

Groves, C. 1981. Ancestors for the pigs: Taxonomy and phylogeny of the genus *Sus*. Canberra: Department of Prehistory, Research School of Pacific Studies, Australian National University.

Groves, C. 2001. *Primate taxonomy*. Washington, DC: Smithsonian Institution Press.

Groves, C. P., G. B. Schaller, G. Amato, and Khamkhoun Khounboline. 1997. Rediscovery of the wild pig *Sus bucculentus*. *Nature* 386:335.

Groves, C. P., and G. B. Schaller. 2000. The phylogeny and biogeography of the newly discovered Annamite artiodactyls. In *Antelopes, deer, and relatives: Fossil record, behavioral ecology, systematics, and conservation,* ed. E. S. Vrba and G. B. Schaller. New Haven and London: Yale University Press.

Gubry, P. 2001. The population of Vietnam: Its evolution and related issues. *CEPED News* 9:1–3.

Ha Van Tan. 1985. The late Pleistocene climate in Southeast Asia: New data from Vietnam. *Modern Quaternary Research in Southeast Asia* 9:81–86.

Hall, D. G. E. 1981. *A history of South-East Asia*. 4th ed. New York: St. Martin's Press.

Hall, R. 1998. The plate tectonics of Cenozoic SE Asia and the distribution of land and sea. In *Biogeography and geological evolution of SE Asia,* ed. R. Hall and J. D. Holloway, 99–131. Leiden, Netherlands: Backhuys.

Hall, R. 2001. Cenozoic reconstruction of SE Asia and the SW Pacific: Changing patterns of land and sea. In *Faunal and floral migrations and evolution in SE Asia–Australasia,* ed. I. Metcalfe, J. M. B. Smith, M. Morwood, and I. Davidson, 35–56. Lisse, Netherlands: A. A. Balkema.

Heaney, L. R. 1991. A synopsis of climatic and vegetational change in Southeast Asia. *Climatic Change* 19:53–61.

Heffernan, P. J., and Trinh Viet Cuong. 2004. A review of the conservation status of the Asian elephant in Vietnam. Cambridge: Indochina Asian Elephant Programme, Fauna and Flora International.

Hendrie, D. B. 2000. Status and conservation of tortoises and freshwater turtles in Vietnam. *Chelonian Research Monographs* 2:63–73.

Heude, Pierre Marie. 1888–1898. Étude sur les Suilliens [A study of the Suilliens]. *Memoires Concernant l'Histoire Naturelle de l'Empire Chinois* 2:52–64, 1888; 2:85–111, 1892; 2:212–222, 1892; 3:189–194, 1896; 3:113–133, 1898.

Hewitt, G. 2000. The genetic legacy of the Quaternary ice ages. *Nature* 405:907–913.

Hijman, R. J., S. Cameron, and J. Parra. 2004. *WorldClim*. Version 1.2. Available at http://biogeo.berkeley.edu/.

Hill, M. J., and A. L. Monastyrskii. 1999. Butterfly fauna of protected areas in north and central Vietnam: Collections, 1994–1997; (Lepidoptera, Rhopalocera). *Atalanta* 29 (1/4):185–208.

Hoang Van Thang, G. Hodgson, E. Hresko, C. Ovel, and Nguyen Thi Dao. 1998. *Coastal biodiversity priorities in Vietnam.* Hanoi: World Wide Fund for Nature Indochina Programme / Hong Kong University of Science and Technology.

Hogan, Z., N. Pengbun, and N. van Zalinge. 2001. Status and conservation of two endangered fish species, the Mekong Giant Catfish *Pangasianodon gigas* and the Giant Carp *Catlocarpio siamensis,* in Cambodia's Tonle Sap River. *Natural History Bulletin of the Siam Society* 49:269–282.

Hsü, J. 1983. Late Cretaceous and Cenozoic vegetation in China, emphasizing their connections with North America. *Annals of the Missouri Botanical Garden* 70:490–508.

Hua Chien Thang. 1998. Marine pollution and biodiversity. In *Coastal biodiversity priorities in Vietnam,* ed. Hoang Van Thang, G. Hodgson, E. Hresko, and C. Ovel, 51–57. Hanoi: Hong Kong University of Science and Technology, Forest Protection Department, World Wide Fund for Nature.

Hutchinson, C. S. 1989. *Geological evolution of South-East Asia.* Oxford: Clarendon Press.

Inger, R. F. 1999. Distribution of amphibians in Southern Asia and adjacent islands. In *Patterns of distribution of amphibians: A global perspective,* ed. W. E. Duellman, 445–482. Baltimore: Johns Hopkins University Press.

Inger, R. F., N. Orlov, and I. Darevsky. 1999. Frogs of Vietnam: A report on new collections. *Fieldiana: Zoology,* n.s., 92:1–46.

Inskipp, T., N. Lindsey, and W. Duckworth. 1996. *An annotated checklist of the birds of the Oriental Region.* Sandy, UK: Oriental Bird Club.

Irvin, G. 1995. Vietnam: Assessing the achievements of Doi Moi. *Journal of Development Studies* 31:725–750.

Iverson, J. B. 1992. *A revised checklist with distribution maps of the turtles of the world.* Richmond, IN: John B. Iverson.

Jablonski, N. G. 1993. Quaternary environments and the evolution of primates in East Asia, with notes on two new specimens of fossil Cercopithecidae from China. *Folia Primatologica* 60:118–132.

Jablonski, N. G., ed. 1998. *The natural history of the Doucs and snub-nosed monkeys.* Singapore: World Scientific Publishing.

Jablonski, N. G., M. J. Whitford, N. Roberts-Smith, and X. Qinqi. 2000. The influence of life history and diet on the distribution of catarrhine primates during the Pleistocene in eastern Asia. *Journal of Human Evolution* 39:131–157.

Jablonski, N. G., and P. Yan-Zhang. 1993. The phylogenetic relationships and classification of the Doucs and snub-nosed langurs of China and Vietnam. *Folia Primatologica* 60:36–55.

Jamieson, N. 1993. *Understanding Vietnam.* Berkeley: University of California Press.

Kelly, P. M., Tran Viet Lien, Hoang Minh Hien, Nguyen Huu Ninh, and W. N. Adger.

2001. Managing environmental change in Vietnam. In *Living with environmental change: Social vulnerability, adaptation and resilience in Vietnam,* ed. W. N. Adger, P. M. Kelly and Nguyen Huu Ninh, 35–58. London: Routledge.

Kershaw, A. P., D. Penny, S. van der Kaars, G. Anshari, and A. Thamotherampillai. 2001. Vegetation and climate in lowland Southeast Asia at the Last Glacial Maximum. In *Faunal and floral migrations and evolution in SE Asia–Australasia,* ed. I. Metcalfe, J. M. B. Smith, M. Morwood, and I. Davidson, 227–236. Lisse, Netherlands: A. A. Balkema.

Khong Dien. 2002. *Population and ethno-demography in Vietnam.* Chiang Mai, Thailand: Silkworm.

Kirkpatrick, R. C. 1995. The natural history and conservation of the snub-nosed monkeys (genus *Rhinopithecus*). *Biological Conservation* 72:363–369.

Kottelat, M. 1989. Zoogeography of the fishes from Indochinese inland waters with an annotated checklist. *Bulletin Zoölogisch Museum Universiteit van Amsterdam* 12 (1):1–54.

Kottelat, M. 2001. Freshwater fishes of northern Vietnam: A preliminary check-list of the fishes known or expected to occur in northern Vietnam with comments on systematics and nomenclature. Washington, DC: World Bank.

Kuznetsov, A. 2000. The forests of Vu Quang Nature Reserve: A description of habitats and plant communities. Hanoi: World Wide Fund for Nature.

Kuznetsov, G. 2000. Mammals of coastal islands of Vietnam: Zoogeographical and ecological aspects. *Bonner Zoologische Monographien* 46:357–366.

Lang, C. R. 2001. Deforestation in Vietnam, Laos, and Cambodia. In *Deforestation, environment, and sustainable development: A comparative analysis,* ed. D. K. Vajpeyi. Westport, CT: Praeger.

Le Ba Thao. 1997. *Vietnam: The country and its geographical regions.* Hanoi: Gioi Publishers.

Le Cong Kiet. 1994. Native freshwater vegetation communities in the Mekong Delta. *International Journal of Ecology and Environmental Sciences* 20:55–71.

Le Dien Duc. 1993a. Rehabilitation of the Melaleuca floodplain forests in the Mekong Delta, Vietnam. In *Towards the wise use of wetlands,* ed. T. J. Davies. Gland, Switzerland: Ramsar Convention Bureau. Available at http://www .ramsar/org/lib/lib_wise.htm.

Le Dien Duc. 1993b. *Wetland reserves in Vietnam.* Hanoi: Center for Natural Resources Management and Environmental Studies.

Le Khac Quyet and T. Ziegler. 2003. First record of the Chinese Crocodile Lizard from outside of China: Report on a population of *Shinisaurus crocodilurus* Ahl, 1903 from north-eastern Vietnam. *Hamadryad* 27 (2):193–199.

Le Trong Cuc. 2003a. Uplands of Vietnam. In *Landscapes of diversity: Indigenous knowledge, sustainable livelihoods and resource governance in montane mainland Southeast Asia,* ed. X. Jianchu and M. Stephen, 113–119. Kunming, China: Yunnan Science and Technology Press.

Le Trong Cuc. 2003b. Uplands of Vietnam. In *Landscapes of diversity: Indigenous knowledge, sustainable livelihoods and resource governance in montane main-*

land Southeast Asia, ed. X. Jianchu and M. Stephen, 113–119. Kunming, China: Yunnan Science and Technology Press.

Le Xuan Canh, Pham Trong Anh, J. W. Duckworth, Vu Ngoc Thanh, and L. Vuthy. 1997. *A survey of large mammals in Dak Lak Province.* Hanoi: World Wide Fund for Nature / The World Conservation Union (IUCN).

Lee, T.-Y., and L. A. Lawver. 1995. Cenozoic plate reconstruction of Southeast Asia. *Tectonophysics* 251 (1–4):85–138.

Leloup, P. H., R. Lacassin, P. Tapponnier, U. Schärer, Z. Dalai, L. Xiaohan, Z. Liang-shang, J. Shaocheng, and P. T. Trinh. 1995. The Ailao Shan–Red River shear zone (Yunnan, China), Tertiary transform boundary of Indochina. *Tectono-physics* 251 (1–4):3–84.

Linden, O. 1995. The state of the coastal and marine environment of Vietnam. *Ambio* 24(7–8):525–526.

Lundberg, J. G., M. Kottelat, G. R. Smith, M. L. J. Stiassny, and A. C. Gill. 2000. So many fishes, so little time: An overview of recent ichthyological discovery in continental waters. *Annals of the Missouri Botanical Garden* 87 (1):26–62.

Lunde, D. P., G. G. Musser, and Nguyen Truong Son. 2003. A survey of small mammals from Mt. Tay Con Linh II, Vietnam, with the description of a new species of *Chodsigoa* (Insectivora: Soricidae). *Mammal Study* 28:31–46.

MacDonald, A. A., and Lixin N. Yang. 1997. Chinese sources suggest early knowledge of the "unknown" ungulate (*Pseudonovibos spiralis*) from Vietnam and Cambodia. *Journal of Zoology, London* 241:523–526.

Macey, J. R., J. A. I. Schulte, A. Larson, Z. Fang, Y. Wang, B. S. Tuniyev, and T. J. Papenfuss. 1998. Phylogenetic relationships of toads in the *Bufo bufo* species group from the eastern escarpment of the Tibetan Plateau: A case of vicariance and dispersal. *Molecular Phylogenetics and Evolution* 9 (1):80–87.

Macey, J. R., J. A. Schulte, II, A. Larson, B. S. Tuniyev, N. Orlov, and T. J. Papenfuss. 1999. Molecular phylogenetics, tRNA evolution, and historical biogeography in anguid lizards and related taxonomic families. *Molecular Phylogenetics and Evolution* 12 (3):250–272.

MacKinnon, J., ed. 1997. *Protected areas systems review of the Indo-Malayan Realm.* Canterbury, UK: Asian Bureau for Conservation.

Maltby, E., P. Burbridge, and A. Fraser. 1996. Peat and sulphate soils: A case study from Vietnam. In *Tropical lowland peatlands of Southeast Asia,* ed. E. Maltby, P. Immirzi and R. J. Safford, 187–198. Gland, Switzerland: World Conservation Union (IUCN).

Matthysen, E. (1998). *The Nuthatches.* London, T and A D Poyser.

Meijaard, E., and C. P. Groves. 2004. A taxonomic revision of the *Tragulus* mouse-deer (Artiodactyla). *Zoological Journal of the Linnean Society* 140:63–102.

Metcalfe, I. 2001. Palaeozoic and Mesozoic tectonic evolution and biogeography of SE Asia–Australasia. In *Faunal and floral migrations and evolution in SE Asia-Australasia,* ed. I. Metcalfe, J. M. B. Smith, M. Morwood, and I. Davidson, 15–34. Lisse, Netherlands: A. A. Balkema.

Métivier, F., and Y. Gaudemer. 1999. Stability of output fluxes of large rivers in

South and East Asia during the last two million years: Implications on flood-plain processes. *Basin Research* 11:293–303.

Meylan, A. 1988. Spongivory in Hawksbill Turtles: A diet of glass. *Science* 239:393–395.

Meylan, P. A. 1987. The phylogenetic relationships of soft-shelled turtles (Family Trionychidae). *Bulletin of the American Museum of Natural History* 186:1–101.

Mitchell, M. 1998. The political economy of Mekong Basin development. In *The politics of environment in Southeast Asia: Resources and resistance,* ed. P. Hirsch and C. Warren, 71–89. London: Routledge.

Monastyrskii, A. L., and A. L. Devyatkin. 2000. New taxa and new records of butter-flies from Vietnam (Lepidoptera, Rhopalocera). *Atalanta* 31 (3/4):471–492.

Monastyrskii, A. L., and A. L. Devyatkin. 2002. *Common butterflies of Vietnam field guide.* Hanoi: Labour and Social Affairs Publishing House.

Morris, S. 2001. Bird trade in Hanoi. *Oriental Bird Club Bulletin* 33:34–36.

Nadler, T. 1997. A new subspecies of Douc Langur, *Pygathrix nemaeus cinereus* ssp. nov. *Der Zoologische Garten* 67 (4):165–176.

Nadler, T., and Ha Thang Long. 2000. The Cat Ba Langur: Past, present and future; the definitive report on *Trachypithecus poliocephalus,* the world's rarest pri-mate. Hanoi: Frankfurt Zoological Society.

Nadler, T., F. Momberg, Nguyen Xuan Dang, and N. Lormee. 2003. Vietnam pri-mate conservation status review 2002; Part 2: Leaf monkeys. Hanoi: Fauna and Flora International.

Narayan, G. 1990. General ecology and behaviour of the Bengal Florican. In *Status and ecology of the Lesser and Bengal Floricans with reports on Jerdon's Courser and Mountain Quail: final report,* 17–33. Bombay: Bombay Natural History So-ciety.

National Geographic Society, U.S. 1999. *Atlas of the world.* Washington, DC: Na-tional Geographic Society.

Naylor, R. 1996. Invasions in agriculture: Assessing the cost of the Golden Apple Snail in Asia. *Ambio* 25 (7):443–448.

Nguyen Anh Tuan. 1997. Energy and environmental issues in Vietnam. *Natural Re-sources Forum* 21 (3):201–207.

Nguyen Duc Tu, Nguyen Cu, and S. Buckton. 2001. Wetlands and waterbirds in the Mekong Delta. *Oriental Bird Club Bulletin* 33:30–33.

Nguyen Khac Vien. 1999. *Vietnam: A long history.* Hanoi: Gioi Publishers.

Nguyen Khanh Van, Nguyen Thi Hien, Phan Ke Loc, and Nguyen Tien Hiep, eds. 2000. *Bioclimatic diagrams of Vietnam.* Hanoi: Vietnam National University Publishing House.

Nguyen Nghia Thin and D. K. Harder. 1996. Diversity of the flora of Fan Si Pan, the highest mountain in Vietnam. *Annals of the Missouri Botanical Garden* 83:404–408.

Nguyen Tien Hiep. 1998. The gymnosperms of Vietnam. In *Floristic characteristics and diversity of East Asian plants: Proceedings of the First International Sympo-sium of Floristic Characteristics and Diversity of East Asian Plants,* ed. A. Zhang and S. Wu, 91–103. Beijing: China Higher Education Press; Berlin: Springer-Verlag.

Nguyen Tien Hiep and R. Kiew. 2000. *Wild plants of Ha Long Bay*. Hanoi: Thanh Nien Publishing House.

Nguyen Tien Hiep and Phan Ke Loc. 1999. The cycads of Vietnam. In *Biology and conservation of cycads: Proceedings of the Fourth International Conference on Cycad Biology, Panzhihua, Sichuan, China, May 1–5, 1996*, ed. C. J. Chen, 24–32. Beijing: International Academic Publishers.

Nguyen Van Huy and Laurel Kendall. 2003. *Vietnam: Journeys of body, mind, and spirit*. Berkeley: University of California Press.

Nguyen Van Song. 2003. Wildlife trading in Vietnam: Why it flourishes. Singapore: Economy and Environment Program for Southeast Asia.

Nguyen Xuan Dang, Pham Trong Anh, and Le Hing Tuyen. 2000. *Results of otter survey in U Minh Thuong Nature Reserve, Kien Giang Province, Vietnam, from 1 to 30 March, 2000*. Hanoi: Care International in Vietnam.

Nisbett, R. A., and R. L. Ciochon. 1993. Primates in northern Vietnam: A review of the ecology and conservation status of extant species, with notes on Pleistocene localities. *International Journal of Primatology* 14 (5):765–795.

Oliver, W. L. R., ed. 1993. *Pigs, peccaries, and hippos: Status survey and conservation action plan*. Gland, Switzerland: World Conservation Union (IUCN).

Orlov, N. L., R. W. Murphy, N. B. Ananjeva, S. A. Ryabov, and Ho Thu Cuc. 2002. Herpetofauna of Vietnam, a checklist; Part I: Amphibia. *Russian Journal of Herpetology* 10 (2):81–104.

Orlov, N. L., R. W. Murphy, and T. J. Papenfuss. 2000. List of snakes of Tam-Dao Mountain Ridge (Tonkin, Vietnam). *Russian Journal of Herpetology* 7 (1):69–80.

Osgood, W. H. 1932. Mammals of the Kelley-Roosevelts and Delacour Asiatic Expeditions. *Field Museum of Natural History, Zoological Series* 18 (10):193–339.

Page, S. E. 2000. Interdependence of peat and vegetation in a tropical peat swamp forest. In *Changes and disturbance in tropical rainforest in South-East Asia*, ed. D. M. Newbery, T. H. Clutton-Brock and G. T. Prance, 161–173. London: Imperial College Press.

Pantulu, V. R. 1986. Fish of the Lower Mekong Basin. In *The ecology of river systems*, ed. B. R. Davies and K. F. Walker, 721–741. Dordrecht, Netherlands: W. Junk.

Pedersen, A., S. S. Nielsen, Le Dien Thuy, and Le Trong Trai. 1998. The status and conservation of threatened and near-threatened species of birds in the Red River Delta. *Bird Conservation International* 8:31–51.

Pelley, Patricia M. 2002. *Postcolonial Vietnam: New histories of the national past*. Durham, NC: Duke University Press.

Pham Mong Giao, Do Tuoc, Vu Van Dung, E. D. Wikramanayake, G. Amato, P. Arctander, and J. R. MacKinnon. 1998. Description of *Muntiacus truongsonensis*, a new species of muntjac (Artiodactyla: Muntiacidae) from Central Vietnam, and implications for conservation. *Animal Conservation* 1:61–68.

Pham Nhat and Nguyen Xuan Dang. 2000. *Field guide to the key mammal species of Phong Nha-Ke Bang.* Hanoi: Fauna and Flora International Indochina Programme.

Pham Nhat and Nguyen Xuan Dang. 2000. *Field guide to the large mammal species of Pu Mat Nature Reserve (with an annotated list of bat species).* Hanoi: Fauna and Flora International Indochina Programme.

Pham Nhat, Nguyen Xuan Dang, and G. Polet. 2001. *Field guide to the key mammal species of Cat Tien National Park.* Hanoi: World Wide Fund for Nature Cat Tien National Park Conservation Project / Fauna and Flora International Indochina Programme.

Phan Ke Loc. 1998. On the systematic structure of the Vietnamese flora. In *Floristic characteristics and diversity of East Asian plants: Proceedings of the First International Symposium of Floristic Characteristics and Diversity of East Asian Plants,* ed. A. Zhang and S. Wu, 102–129. Beijing: China Higher Education Press; Berlin: Springer-Verlag.

Phan Nguyen Hong and Hoang Thi San. 1993. *Mangroves of Vietnam.* Bangkok: World Conservation Union (IUCN).

Pine, R. H. 1994. New mammals not so seldom. *Nature* 368:593.

Polet, G., Tran Van Mui, Nguyen Xuan Dang, Bui Huu Manh, and M. Baltzer. 1999. The Javan Rhinoceros, *Rhinoceros sondaicus annamiticus,* of Cat Tien National Park, Vietnam: Current status and management implications. *Pachyderm* 27: 34–48.

Polet, G., and S. Ling. 2004. Protecting mammal diversity: Opportunities and constraints for pragmatic conservation management in Cat Tien National Park, Vietnam. *Oryx* 38 (2):186–196.

Pritchard, P. C. H. 2001. Observations on body size, sympatry, and niche divergence in softshell turtles (Trionychidae). *Chelonian Conservation and Biology* 4 (1):5–27.

Rainboth, W. J. 1996. Fishes of the Cambodian Mekong. Rome: Food and Agricultural Organization of the United Nations.

Rambo, A. T. 1995. Defining highland development challenges in Vietnam: Some themes and issues emerging from the conference. In *The challenges of highland development in Vietnam,* ed. A. T. Rambo, R. R. Reed, Le Trong Cuc, and M. R. DiGregorio, xi–xxvii. Honolulu: East-West Center.

Rambo, A. T. 1997. Development trends in Vietnam's northern mountain region. In *Development trends in Vietnam's northern mountain region.* Vol. 1: *An overview and analysis,* ed. D. Donovan, A. T. Rambo, J. Fox, Le Trong Cuc, and Tran Duc Vien, 5–52. Hanoi: National Political Publishing House.

Reid, D., M. Jiang, Q. Teng, Z. Qin, and J. Hu. 1991. Ecology of the Asiatic Black Bear (*Ursus thibetanus*) in Sichuan, China. *Mammalia* 55 (2):221–237.

Roberts, T. R. 199. Mekong mainstream hydropower dams: Run-of-the-river or ruin-of-the-river? *Natural History Bulletin of the Siam Society* 43:9–19.

Robichaud, W. G. 1998. Physical and behavioral description of a captive Saola, *Pseudoryx nghetinhensis. Journal of Mammalogy* 79 (2):394–405.

Robson, C. 2000. *A Guide to the Birds of Southeast Asia: Thailand, Peninsular Malay-*

sia, Singapore, Myanmar, Laos, Vietnam, Cambodia. Princeton, NJ: Princeton University Press.

Rookmaaker, L. C. 1980. The distribution of the rhinoceros in Eastern India, Bangladesh, China, and the Indo-Chinese Region. *Zoologischer Anzeiger* 205 (3/4): 253–268.

Roos, C., and T. Nadler. 2001. Molecular evolution of the Douc Langurs. *Zoologische Garten* 71 (1):1–6.

Safford, R. J., Duong Van Ni, E. Maltby, and Vo-Tong Xuan, eds. 1997. *Towards sustainable management of Tram Chim National Reserve, Vietnam: Proceedings of a workshop on balancing economic development with environmental conservation.* London: Royal Holloway Institute for Environmental Research.

Safford, R. J., Tran Triet, E. Maltby, and Duong Van Ni. 1998. Status, biodiversity and management of the U Minh wetlands, Vietnam. *Tropical Biodiversity* 5 (3):217–244.

Sauvel, R. 1949. Distribution géographique du Kou-prey (*Bibos sauveli* Urb.) [Geographic distribution of the Kouprey (*Bibos sauveli* Urb.).] *Mammalia* 13:144–148.

Schaller, G. B., and E. S. Vrba. 1996. Description of the giant Muntjac (*Megamuntiacus vuquangensis*) in Laos. *Journal of Mammalogy* 77 (3):675–683.

Schlegel, H. 1880. On an anomalous species of hare discovered in the Isle of Sumatra: *Lepus netscheri. Notes from the Leyden Museum* 2:59–65.

Schmid, M. 1974. *Végétation du Viet-Nam: Le massif sud Annamitique et les régions limitrophes* [Vegetation of Vietnam: The south Annamese massif and adjacent areas]. Paris: ORSTOM.

Schmid, M. 1989. Vietnam, Kampuchea and Laos. In *Floristic inventory of tropical countries: The status of plant systematics, collections, and vegetation, plus recommendations for the future,* ed. D. G. Campbell and H. D. Hammond, 83–90. New York: New York Botanical Garden.

Scotese, C. R. 2001. *Atlas of earth history.* Vol. 1: *Paleogeography.* Arlington, TX, PALEOMAP Project.

Seidenfaden, G. 1992. The orchids of Indochina. *Opera Botanica* 114:1–502.

Sikor, T. 2001. The allocation of forestry land in Vietnam: Did it cause the expansion of forests in the northwest? *Forest Policy and Economics* 2:1–11.

Sikor, T. 1998. Forest policy reform: From state to household forestry. In *Stewards of Vietnam's upland forests,* ed. M. Poffenberger, 18–37. Berkeley, CA: Asia Forest Network.

Smith, B. D., T. A. Jefferson, S. Leatherwood, Dao Tan Ho, Chu Van Thuoc, and Le Hai Quang. 1997. Investigations of marine mammals in Vietnam. *Asian Marine Biology* 14:145–172.

Sneddon, C., and Nguyen Thanh Binh. 2001. Politics, ecology and water: The Mekong Delta and development of the Lower Mekong Basin. In *Living with environmental change: Social vulnerability, adaptation and resilience in Vietnam,* ed. W. N. Adger, P. M. Kelly and Nguyen Huu Ninh, 234–262. London: Routledge.

Spitzer, K., J. Jaros, J. Havelka, and J. Leps. 1997. Effect of small-scale disturbance on butterfly communities of an Indochinese montane rainforest. *Biological Conservation* 80:9–15.

Stott, P. 1984. The savanna forests of mainland Southeast Asia: An ecological survey. *Progress in Physical Geography* 8:315–335.

Stott, P. A., J. G. Goldammer, and W. L. Werner. 1990. The role of fire in the tropical lowland deciduous forests of Asia. In *Fire in the tropical biota: Ecosystem processes and global challenges,* ed. J. G. Goldammer, 32–44. Berlin: Springer-Verlag.

Stuart, B. L., P. P. van Dijk, and D. B. Hendrie. 2001. Photographic guide to the turtles of Thailand, Laos, Vietnam and Cambodia. Phnom Penh: Wildlife Conservation Society.

Stuart, B. L., and J. F. Parham. 2004. Molecular phylogeny of the critically endangered Indochinese Box Turtle (*Cuora galbinifrons*). *Molecular Phylogenetics and Evolution* 31 (1):164–177.

Stuart, B. L., and J. Thorbjarnarson. 2003. Biological prioritization of Asian countries for turtle conservation. *Chelonian Conservation and Biology* 4 (3):642–647.

Surridge, A. K., R. J. Timmins, G. M. Hewitt, and D. J. Bell. 1999. Striped rabbits in Southeast Asia. *Nature* 400:726.

Taylor, D., P. Saksena, P. G. Sanderson, and K. Kucera. 1999. Environmental change and rain forests on the Sunda shelf of Southeast Asia: Drought, fire and the biological cooling of biodiversity hotspots. *Biodiversity and Conservation* 8:1159–1177.

Taylor, K. W. 1983. *The birth of Vietnam.* Berkeley: University of California Press.

Thomas, H., A. Seveau, and A. Hassanin. 2001. The enigmatic new Indochinese bovid, *Pseudonovibos:* An extraordinary forgery. *Comptes Rendus de l'Académie des Sciences. Série III, Sciences de la Vie* 324:81–86.

Thomas, O. 1927. The Delacour exploration of French Indo-China — mammals. *Proceedings of the Zoological Society of London* [1927]:41–58.

Thomas, O. 1928a. The Delacour exploration of French Indo-China — mammals; II: On mammals collected during the winter of 1926–1927. *Proceedings of the Zoological Society of London* [1928]:139–150.

Thomas, O. 1928b. The Delacour exploration of French Indo-China — mammals; III: Mammals collected during the winter of 1927–1928. *Proceedings of the Zoological Society of London* [1928]:831–841.

Timmins, R. J., and J. W. Duckworth. 1999. Status and conservation of Douc Langurs (*Pygathrix nemaeus*) in Laos. *International Journal of Primatology* 20 (4):469–487.

Timmins, R. J., J. W. Duckworth, C. R. Robson, and J. L. Walston. 2003. Distribution, status and ecology of the Mainland Slender-tailed Treeshrew *Dendrogale murina. Mammal Review* 33 (3):272–283.

Timmins, R. J., and Trinh Viet Cuong. 2001. *An assessment of the conservation importance of the Huong Son (Annamite) Forest, Ha Tinh Province, Vietnam, based on the results of a field study for large mammals and birds.* New York: Center for Biodiversity and Conservation at the American Museum of Natural History.

Tordoff, A. W. 2002. *Directory of important bird areas in Vietnam: Important sites for conservation.* Hanoi: BirdLife International in Indochina.

Tordoff, A. W., R. J. Timmins, R. Smith, and Mai Ky Vinh. 2003. A biological assessment of the central Truong Son landscpe. Hanoi: World Wildlife Fund Indochina.

Tran Triet, R. J. Safford, Tran Duy Phat, Duong Van Ni, and E. Maltby. 2000. Wetland biodiversity overlooked and threatened in the Mekong Delta, Vietnam: Grassland ecosystems in the Ha Tien Plain. *Tropical Biodiversity* 7 (1):1–24.

Tran Viet Lien and Nguyen Huu Ninh. 1999. A preliminary study of the impacts of climate change and sea-level rise on the coastal zone of Vietnam. *Current Topics in Wetland Biogeochemistry* 3:161–174.

Uetz, P., R. Chenna, T. Etzold, and J. Hallermann. 2003. The EMBL reptile database (1 July 2004). Heidelberg: European Molecular Biology Lab. Available at http://www.reptile-database.org/.

van Dijk, P. P., and C. R. Shepherd. 2004. Shelled out? A snapshot of *bekko* trade in selected locations in South-east Asia. Petaling Jaya, Malaysia: TRAFFIC South-east Asia.

van Dijk, P. P., B. L. Stuart, and A. G. J. Rhodin. 2000. *Asian turtle trade: Proceedings of a workshop on conservation and trade of freshwater turtles and tortoises in Asia, Phnom Penh, Cambodia, December 1–4, 1999.* Lunenburg, MA: Chelonian Research Foundation.

van Peenen, P. F. D., P. F. Ryan, and R. H. Light. 1969. *Preliminary Identification Manual for Mammals of South Vietnam.* Washington, DC: Smithsonian Institution Press.

Vermeulen, J., and T. Whitten. 1999. *Biodiversity and cultural property in the management of limestone resources: Lessons from East Asia.* Washington, DC: World Bank.

Veron, G., S. H. Rosentahl, B. Long, and S. Roberton. 2004. The molecular systematics and conservation of an endangered carnivore, the Owston's palm civet *Chrotogale owstoni* (Thomas, 1912) (Carnivora, Viverridae, Hemigalinae). *Animal Conservation* 7:107–112.

Vidal, J. E. 1979. Outline of the ecology and vegetation on the Indochinese Peninsula. In *Tropical Botany,* ed. K. Larsen and L. B. Holm-Nielson, 109–124. London: Academic Press.

Vo Quy and Le Thac Can. 1994. Conservation of forest resources and the greater biodiversity of Vietnam. *Asian Journal of Environmental Management* 2 (2):55–59.

Vo Quy and Nguyen Cu. 1999. *Checklist of the birds of Vietnam.* Hanoi: Center for Natural Resources and Environmental Studies.

Vo Si Tuan, and G. Hodgson. 1997. Coral reefs of Vietnam: Recruitment limitation and physical forcing. In *Proceedings of the Eighth International Coral Reef Sym-*

posium, Panama. June 24–29, 1996, ed. H. A. Lessios and I. G. Macintyre, 477–482. Balboa, Panama: Smithsonian Tropical Research Institute.

Vogel, C. J., P. R. Sweet, L. M. Hung, and M. M. Hurley. 2003. Ornithological records from Ha Giang Province, north-east Vietnam, during March–June 2003. *Forktail* 19:21–30.

Voris, H. K. 2000. Maps of Pleistocene sea levels in Southeast Asia: Shorelines, river systems and time durations. *Journal of Biogeography* 27:1153–1167.

Vu Trung Tang. 2001. *The Eastern Sea: Resources and environment*. Hanoi: Gioi Publishers.

Vu Van Dung, Pham Mong Giao, Nguyen Ngoc Chinh, Do Tuoc, P. Arctander, and J. MacKinnon. 1993. A new species of living bovid from Vietnam. *Nature* 363:443–445.

Walston, J., and G. Veron. 2001. Questionable status of the "Taynguyen civet," *Viverra tainguensis* Sokolov, Rozhnov and Pham Trong Anh, 1997 (Mammalia: Carnivora: Viverridae). *Zeitschrift für Säugetierkunde* 66 (3):181–184.

Wassersug, R. J., K. J. Frogner, and R. F. Inger. 1981. Adaptations for life in tree holes by Rhacophorid tadpoles from Thailand. *Journal of Herpetology* 15 (1):41–52.

Wege, D. C., A. J. Long, Mai Ky Vinh, Vu Van Dung, and J. C. Eames. 1999. Expanding the protected areas network in Vietnam for the twenty-first century: An analysis of the current system with recommendations for equitable expansion. Hanoi: BirdLife International Vietnam Programme.

Wharton, C. H. 1957. *An ecological study of the Kouprey, Novibos sauveli (Urbain)*. Manila: Institute of Scence and Technology.

Workman, D. R. 1977. Geology of Laos, Cambodia, South Vietnam and the eastern part of Thailand. *Overseas Geology and Mineral Resources* 50:1–33.

Yap, S. Y. 2002. On the distributional patterns of Southeast–East Asian freshwater fish and their history. *Journal of Biogeography* 29:1187–1199.

Yiming, L., and L. Dianmo. 1998. The dynamics of trade in live wildlife across the Guangxi border between China and Vietnam during 1993–1996 and its control strategies. *Biodiversity and Conservation* 7:895–914.

INDEX

Page numbers in italics refer to illustrations